REPORT ON THE
MURDER
OF THE
GENERAL SECRETARY

REPORT ON THE
MURDER
OF THE
GENERAL SECRETARY

KAREL KAPLAN

Translated by

KAREL KOVANDA

OHIO STATE UNIVERSITY PRESS

Columbus

This book was published with the support of the Central and East European
Publishing Project.

Library of Congress Cataloging-in-Publication Data

Kaplan, Karel.
    Report on the murder of the General Secretary / Karel Kaplan :
translated by Karel Kovanda.
        p.   cm.
    Translated from Czech.
    Bibliography: p.
    Includes index.
    ISBN 0–8142–0477–5
    1. Slánský, Rudolf—Trials, litigation, etc.   2. Trials (Treason)—
Czechoslovakia—Prague. I. Title.
KJP41.S59K36   1990
345.437'120231—dc20
[344.371205231]   89–15983
                                                                       CIP

The paper in this book meets the guidelines for permanence and durability of
the Committee on Production Guidelines for Book Longevity of the Council on
Library Resources.

Printed in the U.S.A.

9 8 7 6 5 4 3 2 1

THE COURTS constitute an important tool in the struggle of the working class against its class enemies. The task of the people's democratic judiciary is to protect our Socialist construction and to contribute to the struggle for world peace. The vehicles for attaining these tasks include well-prepared public trials, properly used for propaganda purposes. These trials not only strike the class enemy hard, but they also serve as effective instruments in educating working people and in training them to heighten their vigilance. The system of State Courts has the particular task of highlighting the connections between in-country class enemies and foreign enemy agencies.

Many trials lack the necessary political polish and therefore yield less political capital than they could and should. This is a shortcoming. In many trials, judges and prosecutors have to rely exclusively on protocols supplied by the investigative authorities, and trial proceedings suffer from insufficient evidentiary material. This, too, is a shortcoming.

There is yet another error that follows from insufficient cooperation: artificially formulated questions in protocols, which defendants answer as drilled by security authorities. Such answers are not credible and leave the impression of a show rather than of court proceedings.

(From a report for the Organizational Secretariat of the Central Committee of the Communist Party of Czechoslovakia [CC KSČ] dated 5/14/1952, on "making full use of important trials in public educational campaigns.")

CONTENTS

CONTENTS

ILLUSTRATIONS

INTRODUCTION

WORLD WAR II fundamentally altered the political map of Europe. The United States and the Soviet Union, two great powers whose influence over Europe used to be rather limited, intervened ever more strongly in the continent's fate. One was a non-European power, the other didn't understand Europe.

The Soviet Union introduced many features in countries of its bloc that were typical for a Communist regime but foreign to Europe. They prominently included massive disregard for legality, culminating in illegal, fabricated political trials. These methods at first helped install Communist power in the Soviet sphere of influence; later they helped enforce Moscow's intentions, and also maintained and strengthened the totalitarian supremacy of local leaders. Political trials affected a variety of victims: genuine opposition, potential or illusory enemies of the Communist regime, people who refused to submit to the dictates of power as well as those who accepted the new regime with hope and sympathy. Prisons filled up with hundreds of thousands of politicians, military officers, intellectuals, clergy, farmers, artisans, and workers. Waves of unchecked license eventually swept up many of the creators and pillars of the regime themselves—high-level Communist officials.

Political trials of the first postwar decade fill a tragic page not only in the history of the Soviet bloc but of Western Europe as well. They had a negative effect on Europe's political left and on the unfolding of East-West relations. Inasmuch as political trials constitute the truest picture of a Communist regime's character, it is impossible to understand the system that generated them, or indeed to grasp the history of postwar Europe, without comprehending the trials themselves.

This book has one objective: to describe, on the basis of archival material, how a show trial was produced. It will trace the two main aspects of engineering these trials: the political motivation and intentions of their creators, as well as their "production techniques."

I selected the trial of "the leadership of the antistate conspiratorial center headed by Rudolf Slánský" for several reasons. First, it was postwar Europe's largest trial of Communist officials. Second, it clearly reflected Moscow's great-power interests and the direct role it played. Third, it affected members of the power elite, many of whom were familiar with, or indeed had helped to create, the machinery of political trials. Finally, this is the trial about which the greatest detail and the greatest number of documents were available to me: largely from the CC KSČ Archive in Prague.

The CC KSČ has two archives: the Archive of the Marxism-Leninism Institute, and the CC KSČ Archive. The first holds documents concerning the labor movement, particularly the KSČ history since 1948, but does not include its central bodies and the apparatus of the CC KSČ. These documents are in turn housed in the CC KSČ Archive. This archive also includes several personal collections, most importantly the Gottwald collection (100/24) and the confidential and unorganized Slánský collections, in addition to the Political Trials and the Šváb collections.

Access to the Archive of the Marxism-Leninism Institute is granted to scholars (mostly historians) including those who are not party members, by the Institute's director. Access to certain politically sensitive collections is restricted only to a small circle of Communist scholars.

Requests to study in the CC KSČ Archive have to be submitted by the institution where the applicant works. They have to include the exact list of the documents requested. The CC KSČ secretariat then decides whether to grant the request; if the applicant works for some institution of the party, a CC KSČ secretary can approve it. Employees of the CC KSČ apparatus are given access by their superior, that is, a CC KSČ department head. The applicant receives only the documents requested and approved. Photocopying them is not permitted. The scholar may take notes on numbered sheets of paper which bear a CC KSČ Archive stamp. These notes do not belong to the scholar and must be returned on demand. When I worked there, however, this rule was not enforced and scholars used to keep their notes.

Four commissions of the CC KSČ have at different times dealt with exonerating Communist officials who were sentenced during Czechoslovakia's political trials. These commissions gathered a vast amount of documentation, conducted a number of interviews, and prepared research papers and final analyses. All these resources are filed in the CC KSČ Archive, in the secret collection called "Political Trials."

The files pertain to the so-called [Rudolf] Barák Commission of 1955–57 (there were actually two commissions, A and C, referred to in endnotes as Commission I/I and Commission I/II); the [Drahomír] Kolder Commission of 1962–63 (Commission II); the [Jan] Piller Commission of 1968–69 (Commission III); and the Barnabitky Commission of 1963 (named after a Prague cloister where it met), which dealt with the trial of so-called Slovak bourgeois nationalists.

The Political Trials collection contains extensive interrogation records of the ministry of the interior (listed as MV + name). Many documents, dating particularly to 1948–50, are preserved in the so-called [Karel] Šváb Collection, which also is a part of the CC KSČ Archive. The Piller Commission report, which largely focuses on the history of piecemeal rehabilitation of the victims, was published in several languages (Pelikan, ed., 1971); the Kolder Commission report, which focuses in great detail on how the trials themselves were staged, has so far appeared only in German (Pelikan, ed., 1972).

I started studying Czechoslovakia's postwar history in the mid-fifties. I had the opportunity to do research in the archives of the CC KSČ, although access to documents was limited. This opportunity expanded considerably when, in 1960, I started work for the CC KSČ secretariat as a consultant. For five years I was able to study all the collections of the CC KSČ Archive, except those concerning political trials and top secret ones. The most important of the available collections pertained to the central organs of the party, particularly meetings of the CC KSČ presidium and of its politburo. I occasionally came across documents that directly or indirectly concerned the trials of the early fifties, particularly those with high-level Communists. However, I could actually focus on these issues only in 1963, and especially in 1968–69. In 1963, I headed one of the research groups for the Barnabitky Commission, which was reviewing charges of bourgeois nationalism meted out against several Slovak politicians. In 1968 I was a member and the secretary of the Piller Commission, appointed in April of that year, with the charge of completing party rehabilitations, that is, restoring Communist party membership, albeit posthumously, to show-trial victims.

Commission members approved my recommendation that both the political trials themselves and inconsistent rehabilitation of their victims be subject to a comprehensive analysis. I was in charge of drafting what would become the commission's final report. I gathered a team of several dozen historians, economists, and legal scholars who had access to archival documentation concerning the trials and the rehabilitation, that is, to all the collections mentioned above. I personally had access to all collections of the CC KSČ Archive, including classified personal ones.

Our team worked daily for almost a year; not even the Soviet invasion of August 1968 interrupted our work. We gathered a remarkable body of knowledge from studying files of the earlier commissions, previously unknown documents, and from interviews and written depositions of former leading officials. I studied the vast majority of these documents personally, and familiarized myself with others through reports of my colleagues. The team's work resulted in the commission's *Final Report* and in almost fifty research papers totaling some twelve hundred type-written pages.

During the fifteen years that I worked in various archives of the Communist party, labor unions, ministries, and other institutions, I gathered vast numbers of notes, excerpts, and copies of documents. In 1972, the State Security discovered a cache with a large part of my personal archive and confiscated it. However, I still managed to save a considerable portion, including the research papers written for the Piller and the Barnabitky commissions, and an array of other documents concerning political trials.

I have tried twice since 1963 to write a book that would illustrate the genesis and evolution of a political show trial. In 1968, after publishing a paper on this topic in *Nová mysl* (Kaplan, 1968), I prepared a manuscript about the Slánský trial. It reached the printers; however, after Gustáv Husák was installed as the KSČ leader in April 1969, the printing and the plates were destroyed. In 1970, soon after I was fired from the Institute of History and banned from working as a historian, I wrote several papers about the preparation of this trial. Some appeared in Czechoslovakia in unofficial, "samizdat" editions. I kept both my manuscripts and the samizdat editions. In the late '70s, after arriving in West Germany, I finally managed to fulfill my intentions. I wrote this book on the basis of archival documents and the mentioned manuscripts, all of which I managed to spirit out of Czechoslovakia. In another book, which was published in Munich in 1986 by the Collegium Carolinum, I discuss all political trials that took place in Czechoslovakia.

This book does not analyze the alleged crimes of the defendants, essentially for reasons of space. Quite unequivocally, all charges were either fabricated or they did not amount to punishable crimes: political errors were classified as criminal offenses. This has been quite evident since 1955 and 1956, at the latest, when interrogator Bohumil Doubek and prisoners Artur London, Leopold Hofman, and Josef Smrkovský made certain depositions, and when Josef Vondráček, Marie Švermová, Pavel Reiman, and others retracted their testimonies. Nevertheless, only in 1963 was the trial repudiated as a whole and were all of its victims fully judicially exonerated.

To conclude, an acknowledgment: This book could not have been written without the research done by my colleagues on the Piller Commission. I dedicate this book to them as an expression of gratitude and in memory of our cooperation.

1

THE WITCH HUNT

THE YUGOSLAV PROBLEM

SEPTEMBER 1947. A convoy of vehicles is making slow progress along a long-unused, almost impassable road leading to the Polish border. The crew of the lead vehicle, a military one, is removing road blocks. In two others, a Czechoslovak delegation is heading down the secret road to a secret meeting in the little Polish spa of Sklarska Poręba.

The delegation is headed by Rudolf Slánský, general secretary of the Communist Party of Czechoslovakia (KSČ). From September 22 to 26 he and his colleagues will confer with eight other groups—from Bulgaria, France, Italy, Poland, Hungary, Yugoslavia, Romania, and the Soviet Union—at the founding meeting of the Information Bureau of Communist Parties, or Cominform.

The Cominform was established at Moscow's insistence. It was to play an important role in its foreign-policy intentions: to help unify the international Communist movement and completely subordinate it to Moscow, to denounce the still-extant concept of a national, democratic path to socialism, and to help form the Soviet power bloc.

Yugoslav delegates at the Cominform meeting, Eduard Kardelj and Milovan Djilas, vociferously denounced naive illusions about "a parliamentary road toward socialism" and sharply attacked the policies of the French and the Italian Communist parties. The Yugoslavs outdid even the harsh condemnations of the Soviet delegation, expressed in the keynote speech of Andrei Zhdanov and in the presentation of Georgi Malenkov.

The Polish hosts discussed the mission and the rules of the germi-

1

nating organization. Władysław Gomułka, general secretary of the Polish party, emphasized that the Cominform "should serve only to exchange information and to coordinate activity after prior agreement of participating parties."[1]

July 28, 1948. Stalin informs the leadership of his party about Cominform's second meeting, which ended two days earlier in Bucharest. The agenda featured criticism of the Yugoslav Communist Party. However, its participants waited in vain for the Yugoslavs to arrive. Belgrade refused to take part in a staged trial at which it couldn't have defended itself and whose results were a foregone conclusion. The trial therefore took place without the defendants, and meted out the preordained sentence: the "Resolution on the Nationalist Errors of the Leadership of the Yugoslav CP."[2]

Only nine months separated the Yugoslav leadership's full involvement at Cominform's first meeting from its full condemnation at the second. This condemnation was foreshadowed by an exchange of letters between Moscow and Belgrade. Stalin criticized the Yugoslavs and voiced his suspicions about them, while Tito defended himself and rebutted slanderous, incorrect, and imprecise information. Their correspondence, of course, masked the more profound real cause of the conflict—Moscow's great-power interests and intentions.

In the fall of 1947, after the announcement of the Marshall Plan, Moscow decided to create its own power bloc in Europe, a single-minded organization under the centralized management of Moscow. Creating such a power bloc called for the total and unconditional subordination of all Communist leadership to Moscow, which arrogated the right to interfere in the internal affairs of other Communist parties and countries. Moscow revived practices of the Comintern, disbanded in 1943; practices which would now affect CP's and, more importantly, Soviet-bloc countries. Events in these countries would now be decided not by domestic leaders but by the Soviet ambassador and a group of Soviet advisors.

Yugoslavia resisted. Its leaders did not want to surrender their monopoly of power and refused to become Moscow's obedient puppets. Yugoslavia's foreign policy also posed an obstacle to Soviet great-power interests, although the Soviets approved of it as late as in the second half of 1947. Now they suddenly looked askance at the great authority Tito enjoyed in Central and Eastern Europe. Furthermore, they viewed his statements about the possibility of a Balkan federation and about a Yugoslav-Albanian union as a direct threat to their own efforts to organize their great-power bloc. This was the main cause for Stalin's measures against the Yugoslav leadership. When Molotov in 1955 defended the Soviet posture, he made it very clear:

> Well known, too, is comrade Tito's attempt to emphasize the idea of creating a Balkan federation centered in Belgrade. Yugoslav leaders intended to usurp the leadership of the federation. In early 1948 we opposed this plan which was aimed at disengaging Balkan countries from the Soviet Union.
>
> Let us not forget that the opposition of the Soviet CP and later of other CP's to the nationalism of Yugoslav leaders helped strengthen the worldwide ranks of CP's, especially in the people's democracies, for some nationalist vacillation had appeared in other parties as well.
>
> It was therefore absolutely imperative to denounce the nationalist opinions of Yugoslav leaders. Not by accident did these opinions turn into anti-Soviet hostility. This only proved that in essence they amounted to bourgeois, anti-Communist opinions.[3]

Early on in his correspondence with Tito, Stalin wanted to sound a warning, get Tito and his friends to agree that Soviet reproaches and criticism were justified, and force them into submission. The Yugoslav reaction, however, was not what the Kremlin was accustomed to: for a long time there had been no insubordination within its own Communist ranks. Moscow was surprised to receive a polemical response refuting the fabricated accusations instead of humble self-criticism. Further correspondence only confirmed that Belgrade had no intention of caving in. The Soviet leaders saw relatively insignificant disagreements turn into a major challenge. The original causes of the conflict retreated into the background; the danger now was Tito's insubordination in and of itself, and its possible contagious character.

The Kremlin therefore decided that as the next step, the conflict would be internationalized and turned into a conflict between the entire Communist movement and Yugoslavia, for openers, within the Cominform. In the spring of 1948, leaders of Cominform-member CP's received copies of the Stalin-Tito correspondence. They in turn sent their own letters to Belgrade, naturally backing the Soviets.

Internationalizing the conflict had two objectives: it increased the pressure on the Yugoslavs, but it also cowed into submission the leaders of other Soviet-bloc countries who saw the consequences of their own potential insubordination described as "nationalism." One of these objectives was largely attained: the leading Communists of the people's democracies became totally subordinated to Moscow. They obeyed the Soviet ambassadors and feared any conflicts with them. Klement Gottwald, the KSČ chairman and president of Czechoslovakia, privately complained about the intolerable behavior of Soviet Ambassador M. A. Silin. "And I can't say a thing," said Gottwald, "because they would immediately turn me into a Titoist—there [in Yugoslavia] it also started with the ambassador."[4]

The second objective—coordinated pressure on Belgrade—misfired. Chances dimmed that Yugoslavia would capitulate. Moscow therefore increasingly leaned toward its second alternative for settling conflicts: if one could not discipline insubordinate leaders, one had to oust them. This plan was going to be implemented in stages. The first two stages were described by Stalin on July 14, 1948, in his response to Gottwald's letter suggesting that Tito's leadership be removed:

> I feel from your report that you're counting on the defeat of Tito and his group at the Yugoslav CP Congress.
>
> I have to say that we Muscovites have not been and are not counting on so early a defeat of Tito's group. Our objective in the first stage was to isolate it in the eyes of other Communist parties, and to reveal its shady machinations. We have attained this objective. The second stage will be a matter of gradually detaching Communist-Marxist groups within the Yugoslav Communist Party from Tito and his group. This takes time and we have to be good at waiting. I see that you lack patience. But I advise you to arm yourself with patience, for there is no doubt that Marxism-Leninism will in time prevail in Yugoslavia.[5]

By "attaining the first objective" Stalin was referring to the results of the second Cominform meeting in June 1948 and to the response to it. All European Communist parties except the Yugoslav one agreed with its resolution denouncing the Yugoslav leadership and its nationalism as an anti-Soviet ideology. The meeting was in fact quite dramatic. Slánský informed his party leadership about the critical point:

> After the Cominform meeting was convened, we waited for two days for the Yugoslav leaders to arrive. We received the response that charges against the Yugoslav CP had been leveled on the basis of one-sided information, that they amount to slander, that the Yugoslav CP had been condemned in advance, and that they were in an unequal position. They therefore decided not to take part and didn't arrive.[6]

Participants of the meeting viewed this justified Yugoslav absence not only as the pinnacle of insubordination but also as treachery. Slánský continued:

> At the first meeting of the Cominform, when issues of the Italian and French CP's were discussed and criticized, Yugoslav representatives were the

Rudolf Slánský

most critical of all . . . It was clear that leaders of the Yugoslav CP don't want to discuss matters. The attitude of the Yugoslav CP was therefore qualified as betrayal of international solidarity, as abandonment of the unified Socialist front, as a transition to bourgeois nationalism.[7]

In June 1948, the Soviet-Yugoslav quarrel expanded into an open conflict between Europe's Communist movement and Yugoslavia. Moscow's concept of forming pro-Soviet groups among Yugoslav Communists, which would then overthrow Tito's leadership, soon proved unrealistic. On the contrary, the unity of Yugoslav leaders and the people further strengthened, on anti-Stalinist grounds. Instead of unseating Tito, the Communist parties unleashed a long "trench war." They employed all means of struggle: political and economic pressure, provocations, slander, and mud slinging. The "war" ended in 1955, two years after Stalin's death; Moscow lost.

The Yugoslav conflict was a direct consequence of Moscow's foreign-policy objective of forming a power bloc. It affected the entire Communist movement very strongly and had a particularly heavy and tragic impact on countries of the Soviet sphere. Moscow unfolded the anti-Yugoslav campaign in line with the Soviet great-power appetite and with the ideological heritage of the Comintern, according to which the greatest enemy is insubordination within one's own ranks. The European Communist movement escalated its attacks on Yugoslavia and expanded them into all spheres. Parties of the Soviet bloc severed all political and economic ties with Yugoslavia without regard to their own losses. They orchestrated extensive campaigns against their own nationalists, nationalisms, and Titoists. Under cover of these attacks, various groups of Communists settled old accounts among themselves and satiated their lust for power.

The role played by security services was exceptionally nefarious. Soviet security, controlled by Lavrenti Beria, did its best to help fan the flames of the conflict. Stalin and his circle decided on their course of action largely on the basis of intelligence reports that Beria had intentionally colored.[8] The Moscow security center fomented tensions in Soviet-Yugoslav relations and, from the fall of 1948 onward, helped shift the Yugoslav problem onto an entirely different plane. The security apparatus, feeling that it had to contribute its own ways and means to prove that the Cominform resolution on Yugoslavia had been correct, presented Yugoslavia's leaders as organizers of international plots directed against the Soviet Union and its allies. A new idea was developing: the idea of cooking up and "uncovering" a major international anti-Soviet conspiracy centered in Belgrade, and of staging an international show trial directed against Yugoslavia.

POLAND

Cominform party leaders started scurrying the moment they received Stalin's first letter to Tito. It is hard to tell why they displayed such initiative. Did these disciplined and experienced students of the Comintern want to earn Moscow's plaudits by discovering a nationalist or two all their own? Or did they grasp at the opportunity to eliminate their own adversaries under the cloak of struggling against nationalism? Maybe they were propelled by fear: they realized that someone had to fall victim to nationalism in their country, too. The power calculation was simple—I might be sacrificed if no one else is.

Romania led the pack. In March 1948 the Communist leadership stripped Justice Minister Lucrețiu Pătrășcanu of all his offices. A month later he was accused of nationalism and arrested. It took the Romanians six years to stage a trial that resulted in his political murder.

Poland followed. Here, the blow was aimed high, at Władysław Gomułka, general secretary of the Communist Party and deputy premier. He was the highest-placed Soviet-bloc official whose opinions occasionally diverged from Moscow's or the Cominform's, and who disagreed with other leaders of his own party. In addition, he was the only CP head in the Soviet sphere (apart from Albania) who had not spent World War II in exile in Moscow but had operated at home. He thus represented a suitable target for a campaign against nationalism on several counts.

Gomułka's political and personal fate between spring 1948 (when he was first criticized) and July 1951 (when he was arrested) went up and down in three big waves. The first wave started rising at the founding meeting of the Cominform. He discussed the Polish party's objectives, which completely clashed with the spirit of Cominform's later resolution on Yugoslavia:

> The low level of our agricultural production and of the production of industrial consumer goods necessarily requires, indeed makes desirable, under certain circumstances and within certain limits, the flourishing of wealthy farms in the countryside and of artisan and private firms in the cities.[9]

Gomułka also had certain reservations, later qualified as "vacillation," concerning the analysis of the international situation presented by

Andrei Zhdanov. In April and May of 1948, during the Stalin-Tito correspondence, his views of the conflict with Yugoslavia differed from Moscow's. Later, he was considered "soft" on the Yugoslavs.[10]

These "deviations" were criticized only subsequently, in August and September of 1948. The story was different at the June 3, 1948, session of the Polish party's central committee. Gomułka discussed ideological and organizational preparations for merging the Polish Socialist Party into the Communist Party. Following his presentation, central committee and politburo members criticized him for the first time for "ideological capitulation to the nationalist traditions of the Polish Socialist Party." Gomułka at first defended himself, but later accepted certain aspects of the criticism.

He soon recovered from these attacks, though. On June 15, 1948, he defended his presentation and actually criticized the politburo resolution concerning it, in a letter to his politburo colleagues.

However, politburo members, encouraged by Moscow's escalating attacks against "Yugoslav nationalism," didn't give up either. They counterattacked with even harsher criticism. Gomułka requested a day for reflection. He reversed himself, and at a politburo meeting admitted again that the criticism of his presentation had been justified. He retracted his letter of June 15, requested a vacation for health reasons, and considered resigning.[11]

After a month's hiatus, the second wave of the campaign surged. The differences and the power struggle within the leadership now acquired an ideological label—"nationalism." The immediate impulse for furthering the case was Gomułka's decision to hold on to the job of party chief after all, and his reservations to certain passages of the Cominform Yugoslav resolution concerning agriculture. At the August 12, 1948, meeting of the politburo, he stated that "differences of opinion between [himself] and the Cominform are purely of a technical nature," but as Molotov asserted later, even these were viewed in Moscow as serious vacillation.[12]

The Polish politburo met several times between August 18 and 28, 1948. It was preparing a central committee session—particularly a presentation and a resolution "On the Rightist and Nationalist Deviation in the Party, its Causes, and Ways to Overcome it." The draft resolution described Gomułka as the main representative of this deviation. The draft was submitted to the politburo without Gomułka's knowledge (behind the back of the party's own general secretary). Gomułka rejected the accusations, defended himself, attacked his critics, and officially announced that "it will be best for the party if [he] continue[s] as the highest official of the party." However, he met with staunch resistance. Politburo members were united against him. They relied on the wind from Moscow and became uncharacteristically courageous (for Communist officials) in struggling against the first man in the party. They were also relieved to have found someone to sacrifice as a nationalist and insisted that their victim admit his guilt. Under great pressure Gomułka backtracked and made a self-criticism at the CC session. He also gave his approval to the draft resolution, except for a passage which discussed his alleged mistakes and vacillation dating back to World War II.

The Central Committee met from August 31 to September 3, 1948. The presentation on the rightist and nationalist deviation in the party leadership was made by Bolesław Bierut.

The charges against Gomułka amounted to a transposition of Cominform's charges against Yugoslavia to the situation in Poland. They focused on his supposed effort to disrupt Polish-Soviet relations and the cooperation of the two CP's. Gomułka made a self-criticism admitting all the errors he was charged with, which was accepted by the politburo and the CC. The case of Gomułka's nationalism appeared closed. Its victim hoped so, too.:

> The crisis that developed in the party as a result of different ideological opinions between us and the leadership is today a matter of the past . . . My positions on fundamental political questions were false and anti-Marxist, and resulted in the danger of a rightist, nationalist deviation within the party. This danger to the party leadership has been averted and eliminated.

Gomułka was stripped of his offices as general secretary and politburo member; however, he kept his seat in the Central Committee and was confirmed in this position by the December 1948 party congress. On August 28, 1948, the politburo officially invited Bolesław Bierut, a seasoned official, to take over the top job in the party. Beirut had worked in the Soviet Union before and during World War II, among other things as an NKVD interrogator under the name of Orlov.

Gomułka's case had gone on for an entire year as a case of ideological deviation and political error, with a corresponding solution: self-criticism and dismissal from offices. However, a third wave of repression carried it up again in November 1949, with an added dimension. The impetus came from Budapest: from the trial of László Rajk, directed against the Yugoslav leadership who were considered to be organizers of an anti-

Soviet conspiracy. On November 11–13, 1949, the CC of the Polish party derived its own conclusions from the Rajk trial:

> Facts about the criminal subversion of imperialist agencies, revealed in the Rajk trial, have *a general international character.* For that very reason they cannot be underestimated. It is enough to analyze a little more penetratingly our specific Polish conditions to see that *the danger of espionage, sabotage, conspiracy, terrorism, and every other subversion* has a deeper objective and subjective basis in Poland than elsewhere.[13]

And Bierut got specific. He discussed alleged prewar agents of the Polish security who during the war had wormed their way into high offices in the CP and in the state administration. Some had been uncovered and imprisoned but no one knew how many were still running free. On top of that he traced a direct connection between the rightist, nationalist deviation of 1948 and what he deemed "criminal" personnel and political work of Gomułka, Zenon Kliszko, and Marian Spychalski.[14]

A political deviation was transformed into a punishable crime with hostile intent. Spychalski made a self-criticism. He listed, among his sins, confidence in Gomułka and, among his merits, his help in "isolating Gomułka and his group as much as possible" although Bierut included him in this group. Gomułka, however, resolutely rejected the charges of deliberately posting agents in various offices and of holding incorrect opinions during the war. Likewise, he denounced efforts to link him with Tito, stating, "My attitude and Tito's represented two different positions which have nothing in common as far as our relationship to the USSR and to the Soviet CP is concerned." He also revised his earlier opinion of the Yugoslav case: "I, too, see the Tito affair differently today." The Rajk trial had apparently stripped him of his last doubts. In much sharper light and "quite clearly I now see that nationalism is the breeding ground of imperialism."[15]

Yet, however sincere or fearful the self-criticisms, they couldn't forestall the tragic culmination of the case; it had acquired its own momentum. The self-critical admissions of fabricated errors only proved that the transformation of a political error into a crime occurred with the connivance of the victims themselves, who helped cultivate the soil which in turn would breed the question that Bierut tossed out to CC members:

> Can one be silent now that Belgrade has become the center for imperialist subversion of the anti-imperialist camp? Why, the rightist nationalist group attempted to rally to the aid of the Titoists! Why, the Titoists reciprocated by relying on this group in Poland.

Gomułka, Kliszko, and Spychalski were expelled from the CC and stripped of their right to stand for any party office. Spychalski was arrested the following year. On July 31, 1951, Gomułka met with the same fate. He was held in a "safe house" of Polish security. On December 31, 1951, the Polish Parliament surrendered Gomułka and Spychalski to the courts as suspects in antistate activity, subject to a political trial. However, although Polish security personnel sought evidence against Gomułka everywhere, including Czechoslovakia, the trial never took place. Gomułka was released on April 21, 1955, followed later by Kliszko and Spychalski.[16]

The question is, why the campaign against nationalism in Poland did not lead up to a show trial although evidence of its preparations goes back to November 1949. The main reason is timing. Gomułka's political errors were not qualified as punishable until after the Rajk trial was over. Preparing yet another spectacle would have taken at least another six months; but Moscow was, meanwhile, losing interest in anti-Yugoslav performances. Also, leading party bodies had not brought additional charges against Gomułka. Polish security and their Soviet advisors, therefore, lacked the incentive and the ability to create a show trial with political content commensurate with the stature of a secretary general. They hobbled along a dead-end trail until the Soviet bloc started rehabilitating victims of show trials, then they simply had to release Gomułka and his comrades from their four-year investigation custody.

ALBANIA

Immediate postwar relations between Albania and Yugoslavia were so close and multifaceted that every Yugoslav event of any importance was bound to affect the life of its tiny neighbor with just over one million people. On July 9, 1946, the two countries signed a Treaty of Cooperation and Mutual Aid, which was followed by economic agreements that introduced a customs union, regulated currency exchange and established joint companies, a common bank, and a mixed committee for economic cooperation. Yugoslavia extended a major loan to Albania. On the other hand, Belgrade was not happy about the extensive Soviet-Albanian economic agreement of 1947.[17]

Moscow lauded Albanian-Yugoslav cooperation as exemplary. In January 1948, *Izvestia,* the Soviet government paper, wrote:

Of key significance in strengthening the close comradely cooperation between Albania and Yugoslavia is the fact that both countries are nations of a
new type, that is, people's democratic republics. This has dramatically influenced the nature of their relations. Instead of old imperialistic relations . . .
they are developing new forms of cooperation based on full equality of sovereign nations and aimed, by way of altruistic mutual aid, at rapidly restoring
and elevating the working people's standard of living.[18]

Moscow changed this opinion a few days later. Georgi Dimitrov,
leader of Bulgarian Communists, publicly stated that it might be advis-
able to form a federation of Central and Southeastern European countries. In an official statement of January 28, 1948, the Soviet press agency
categorically denounced all federative projects and efforts. Moscow interpreted them as intentional resistance to forming its own power bloc.
Yet two months later, Yugoslavia tried to expand its influence in Albania
through military cooperation, offering to move in several divisions of its
forces as a response to heightened international tensions. The Soviets
strongly disapproved, and Stalin's mistrust of Tito grew. The Soviet
reaction is illustrated by the protocols of the July 1955 CC CPSU session:

N. S. Khrushchev: Consider the issue of nationalist errors of the Yugoslav
CP. As I've said, such errors and tendencies existed. It is enough to mention
Yugoslavia's intention to control Albania. Without clearing it with the Soviet
Union, Yugoslav leaders decided to send a division of theirs into Albania.
When they were informed that such a step would lead to international com-
plications, they were offended.
    N. A. Bulganin: At that time, information reached us from Albania that
Tito had decided to move in a division without having asked Stalin. That only
added fuel to the fire.[19]

Tirana also radically shifted its attitude to Albanian-Yugoslav cooperation. On January 1, 1948, Enver Hoxha told the nation:

Our friendship with the Soviet Union, that staunch defender of peace,
freedom, and democracy the world over, headed by the great Stalin, a genius,
the dearest and most beloved friend of our nation, has further strengthened
and deepened. We are joined in unbreakable brotherhood with the heroic
people of the new Yugoslavia of Marshal Tito—who educates our nation and
all other Balkan nations about freedom, independence, and sovereignty—
which provided our country with noble fraternal help both during the war and
now during our all-round reconstruction.[20]

But here is Hoxha again, immediately after Cominform's Yugoslav
resolution:

Tito's clique inaugurated its policy of colonizing Albania by providing an enslaving loan. Albania was to work for Yugoslavia under Belgrade's tutelage. Tito's group used economic pressure to force Albania to abolish its customs border and attempted to take over all of Albania's mines. When he was in Albania, Tito's agent Savo Zlatić went so far as to suggest that Albania and Yugoslavia develop mutual relations comparable to those of the Benelux countries.[21]

In his 1948 New Year's speech, Hoxha mentioned Albania's relationships with the Soviet Union and with Yugoslavia in the same breath. This wasn't accidental. The leadership of his party had been arguing for some time over which of the two should be given priority in economic issues, internal political influence, and foreign policy. The main advocate of the pro-Soviet orientation was Nako Spiru, and indirectly Enver Hoxha and Mehmet Shehu. The Yugoslav orientation was promoted by Koçi Xoxe, deputy premier and interior minister, and by Pandi Kristo. In late 1947, Xoxe defended "Yugoslav priorities"; and on December 7 he and Kristo attacked Spiru for only half-heartedly supporting cooperation with Yugoslavia. Albanian-Yugoslav relations were thereafter regularly featured on the agenda of politburo meetings in Tirana.

The conflict came to a head in February 1948, at the Eighth Plenum of the CC CP of Albania, where Xoxe and Kristo once again sharply attacked Spiru and denounced his political line. The majority of CC members supported their pro-Yugoslav policy and expelled Spiru and his friends from the party as "traitors and petit-bourgeois rebels."[22]

The cards turned three months later: the Stalin-Tito correspondence strengthened the pro-Soviet group led by Hoxha. Its members pounced on the pro-Yugoslav faction, which tried in vain to dilute the influence of the Soviet campaign against Belgrade. The June 1948 Cominform meeting encouraged Hoxha to launch the decisive battle: and in September 1948, the CC CP of Albania denounced the pro-Yugoslav "Trotskyite" faction headed by Xoxe and Kristo. They and some others were stripped of their offices in the party and, on October 31, in the government as well. Their political liquidation was completed by the November 1948 Congress of the Albanian CP. In an extensive review of how Xoxe's Trotskyite group was "uncovered," Enver Hoxha, the CC general secretary, declared that it was instigated from Belgrade, that its leader maintained direct contacts with Tito and Ranković and followed their instructions that would have disengaged Albania from the Soviet Union.[23]

The party Congress finished off the Xoxe-Kristo case but also invested it with a criminal dimension. The two leaders were arrested. On March 4, 1949, the parliament stripped them of parliamentary immunity "because they have been charged with cooperating with Yugoslav Trotskyites." On May 12, a trial opened in Tirana with former high officials of the Albanian CP: Koçi Xoxe, Pandi Kristo, and Kristo Themelko. They were charged with cooperation with Yugoslavia, with the objective of conspiring against the country, linking Albania with Yugoslavia, and disengaging it from the Soviet Union. According to the fragmentary information available about the trial, Xoxe apparently confessed to cooperating with leaders of the Yugoslav CP and admitted that "economic relations between the two countries were directed at exploiting Albania's economy."

Xoxe was sentenced to death on June 10 and executed the following day. Others were sentenced to long years of hard labor.[24]

The Albanian trial of the former general secretary was the first in the series of trials with high CP officials generated by the Soviet-Yugoslav conflict. Albanian leaders strongly emphasized this outside impulse and highlighted the role of the Soviet leadership. At the CP Congress in November 1948, Hoxha stated that "letters of the CC of the Bolshevik party saved our country from a catastrophe." In 1961, he reiterated:

> During this time [1948–49], our party had to wage a fierce life-and-death battle against the Titoist pack's interference and its vicious attacks against our party and our country, as well as against the Trotskyite and subversive activity of Tito's tool Koçi Xoxe and his friends . . . Our party was helped in this struggle by the CC of the Soviet CP and by J. V. Stalin who in their well-known letters about the situation in the Yugoslav CP unmasked in front of the entire world the true face of this band of renegades.[25]

There was also an internal power-struggle aspect to the Koçi Xoxe case. Hoxha and his followers used it to eliminate all who stood in their way and to enforce their own monopolistic position. This is the main reason why Albania is the only country that to this day has not rehabilitated Communist victims of its show trials of forty-odd years ago.

CZECHOSLOVAKIA

On September 13, 1948, Klement Gottwald left for his first trip to the Soviet Union since becoming the country's president. Just the day before, Arnošt Kolman had finished writing an article intended for *Tvorba*, a cultural-political weekly of the CC KSČ. It had a suggestive title: "For

Bolshevik Self-Criticism in the KSČ." It challenged party leaders to critically and self-critically examine the party's policies. Three days later, on September 15 and 16, all employees of the KSČ headquarters held a party meeting. Kolman expounded his views and expressed regret that he hadn't spoken earlier. He had apparently only recently realized that the party suffered not from isolated errors but from "a whole system of errors which all have the same direction and the same cause."[26]

Arnošt Kolman was the son of a small Czech bureaucrat but had lived in the Soviet Union since 1915, when he was twenty-three. In 1918 he joined the Bolshevik party. A mathematician and philosopher by training, he occupied important positions in the Soviet scientific establishment. After World War II, he requested repatriation to Czechoslovakia. The request was granted: the Czechoslovak Communist community in Moscow exile felt that Kolman would strengthen the party line in ideology. He soon became a familiar figure in Prague's scientific circles. He was appointed professor at Charles University and headed the party's propaganda department.

Having lived abroad, however, Kolman understood Czechoslovak circumstances only poorly and insisted on dogmatically transferring Soviet practices and Soviet Marxism onto Czechoslovakia. From early 1948, his opinions on some issues were very radical and at variance with the party leadership's line. This and other reasons led to his dismissal from the propaganda department. But there was more at stake: Kolman shared his critical views with the Soviet ambassador in Prague. As Ambassador Silin told Slánský in the spring of 1948, Kolman had described the KSČ as a "non-Marxist, non-Leninist and non-Bolshevik party." During the Stalin-Tito correspondence, Gottwald and Slánský considered Kolman's informing the Soviet ambassador as particularly dangerous.[27]

Why was Kolman so critical? The following exemplifies his views:

> The nationalist betrayal of Yugoslavia and the right-wing opportunism in Poland suggest conclusions that Czechoslovakia should draw as well. Party leaders should conduct self-criticism but they are reluctant to do so. In many respects, the KSČ isn't yet a true Marxist-Leninist party because its day-to-day leadership (Slánský, Švermová, Gustav Bareš) doesn't correctly implement Gottwald's political line. Deviations from revolutionary theory have had severe consequences for the practical policies of the KSČ. The party is being trained in a one-sided national rather than in a class spirit and its vigilance therefore hasn't been mobilized. Key enemies of the people's democracy have escaped to foreign imperialist countries, and domestic reactionaries are raising

their heads again. Quite a few destructive elements are burrowed in industry and in agriculture; some of our reforms have aided the kulaks instead of strengthening the village poor. In the field of culture, no differences are made among intellectuals, we pander to the petite-bourgeoisie, and have done little to train a qualified intelligentsia.

The KSČ is breeding anti-Semitism and moral decay. It is blending with the class enemy. All of this logically follows from its day-to-day leadership having abandoned the class revolutionary essence of the party and the Marxist-Leninist line.[28]

Kolman's position dovetailed with the criticism that had been meted out against other Communist leaders—Dimitrov, Tito, and Gomułka. Kolman figured that it was Czechoslovakia's turn and underscored this international connection. He believed that the "day-to-day leadership" of the party should conduct open self-criticism because its errors "have the same right-wing opportunist character as in Poland. This can be no accident. It is therefore imperative to speed up their self-criticism." He also figured that speaking out would advance his own power ambitions.

However, actual events developed very rapidly, in an entirely different direction. On September 16, Slánský convened a meeting of KSČ leaders Václav Kopecký, Jaromír Dolanský, Antonín Zápotocký, Gustav Bareš, and Marie Švermová, who were particularly disturbed by Kolman having spoken out directly after Gottwald's departure for the Soviet Union.

On September 17, Slánský dispatched the decisions of the meeting to Gottwald: "All comrades unanimously described [Kolman's] article and his presentation as incorrect and factional." A copy of the manuscript and a steno recording of Kolman's speech were attached. He also sent Gottwald a telegram with excerpts from the documents, in Russian. As for Kolman, Slánský told him:

> On behalf of the party presidium I inform you that we find the article you sent to *Tvorba* and your presentation at the meeting harmful to the party. We have therefore decided not to publish your article, and we forbid you to express the views it contains anywhere, within the party or outside it.[29]

On September 20, Soviet Foreign Minister Vyacheslav Molotov passed on Slánský's telegram to Stalin's secretary, Poskrebyshev, asking him to forward it to Gottwald. (The telegram went the diplomatic route, via the Soviet foreign minister. Gottwald was spending his time in the Crimea where Stalin was vacationing.)

On the evening of September 22, Gottwald was invited to one of his three meetings with Stalin. Gottwald knew that Stalin had received the Kolman information and felt very insecure. He couldn't dismiss the possibility that the affair had been instigated by Moscow, in which case he might not even be returning to Prague.

Gottwald was very disturbed on his way to Stalin but returned quite calm. Right away he described the meeting (which was also attended by Beria and Poskrebyshev) to his closest friends. Stalin apparently wanted to hear Gottwald's version, and then suggested: "He [Kolman] might be a Trotskyite." And Beria confirmed: "Yes, he is an old Trotskyite." Poskrebyshev was of the same opinion and reminded Stalin of Kolman's activity during the '30s.[30]

Based on Gottwald's report, Kopecký later described to the CC KSČ presidium how Soviet leaders immediately recalled Kolman's earlier activity in the Soviet CP, recommended that the strongest possible measures be taken against his "destructive" activity, and demanded that he return to the Soviet Union. "Comrade Gottwald," said Kopecký, "got confirmation during his visit to the Soviet Union that A. Kolman's hostile, Trotskyite, disruptive attack against our party is a continuation of his malicious activity in the USSR."[31]

On September 24, Slánský received a message from Gottwald instructing him to ban Kolman from disseminating "antiparty and factional agitation" and "to be very strict about it." On the same day, Slánský received a message from the Soviet embassy, addressed to the CC KSČ:

> Kolman waves the banner of self-criticism but he doesn't deserve your confidence. The Soviet government requests that Kolman be taken into preliminary custody and sent to the USSR. We have grounds for serious charges against him, which have to be appropriately investigated as soon as he is transported to the USSR.[32]

On September 25, Kolman was isolated in a Prague villa occupied by security personnel. His wife and daughter were held elsewhere.[33]

On September 26, Kolman sent the CC KSČ presidium an extensive self-criticism. In it he stated:

> I have reflected upon my errors and searched my conscience. I had the best intentions, but I injured rather than helped the party. I feel bad, comrades, like a dying man, seeing that you have lost confidence in me, that you forbid me to voice my condemned opinions even outside the party and that you have isolated me lest perhaps I obviate this ban.

On September 28, Kolman was put on a plane to Moscow. His wife and daughter followed.[34]

In Czechoslovakia, the Kolman case was closed after Gottwald returned from the Crimea. On October 4, the CC KSČ presidium decided to expel Kolman from the party. Justifying this, Kopecký fitted the case into the currently fashionable ideological framework and painted it in the darkest colors. Two thoughts from his presentation follow:

> Kolman speculated that Klement Gottwald left for the Soviet Union in order to hear out criticism of the KSČ's political line, just as the Yugoslav CP or W. Gomułka's concepts in Poland had been criticized. Kolman decided to come out fast so as to appear as a critic "from the left" early, even before Klement Gottwald's return, and thus to qualify as a pretender for the role of a leading official of some "new day-to-day party leadership."
>
> Kolman hypocritically pretended to agree with the KSČ line, but in reality he opposed it long before [the] February [1948 Communist takeover]. He apparently opposed the KSČ policy even earlier and harmonized as a "faction" with the Titoists [Milovan] Djilas, [Aleksandar] Ranković, [Boris] Kidrić, and similar "right-wing Marxists" whom he considered true blue revolutionaries.[35]

In the Soviet Union, the case turned into a tragedy. Kolman spent three-and-a-half years in jail without trial and was released only in February 1952, after the arrest of Slánský. Soviet security interrogated him about KSČ leaders, including Gottwald. His wife and daughter lived in difficult exile conditions in Ulyanovsk. His stepson spent five years in a concentration camp in the Far North. He was sentenced on the basis of a most brutally extracted confession to a fantastic "crime": he allegedly intended to murder the American ambassador and thereby to provoke World War III.[36]

Kolman's case suggests two important questions. One concerns his motivation. Was Kolman's stance a result just of his own reflection, his own calculation, and his desire for a high office, or was it backed by some Soviet institution or officials? The theory of Soviet backing lacks a detailed analysis of which group would have benefited. Our current knowledge, however, doesn't allow a definitive answer.

The second question concerns the position of the Soviet leadership, Stalin in particular. If he had been interested in instigating criticism or a campaign against Czechoslovak leaders, he could have used Kolman's activity to this end. Czechoslovak leaders were at least as guilty of "right-wing opportunism" as was Gomułka, measured by the yardstick of the times. However, Moscow's most important problem was Yugoslavia, and its attacks focused on those who vacillated or might vacillate on this point. In this respect, Moscow had complete trust in the Czechoslovak leadership. None of its members doubted for one second the correctness of the Soviet attitude toward the Yugoslav CP. Moscow also realized that the formerly professed Czechoslovak-Yugoslav friendship concealed a discordant trait: Czechoslovak politicians felt that the Yugoslavs held them in some disdain. "All we ever heard from them was criticism of our situation" (Slánský). Others complained that the Yugoslavs "systematically treated us with hostility and disloyalty" (Clementis). Moscow was also fully aware of Tito's critical, even condescending attitude toward Gottwald, whom he considered a sycophantic lackey of the Soviets, a politician without a will of his own. Gottwald's insistence, mentioned above, that Tito be expeditiously removed only strengthened Moscow's confidence that Prague unambiguously supported the Soviet side on the Yugoslav issue. And finally, Gottwald brought back from the Crimea Stalin's own interpretation of those parts of Cominform's Yugoslav resolution that Gomułka objected to, particularly dealing with the collectivization of agriculture.

NOEL FIELD

Cominform's first Yugoslav resolution of mid-1948 inspired the idea of staging a major Central European international political show trial with high Communist officials. Originally it was to have an anti-American orientation, but it soon acquired a strong anti-Yugoslav tinge as well. The American citizen Noel Field, or perhaps "the case of Noel Field," became the starting point—although not more than that—for constructing such a trial.

After graduating from Harvard, Noel H. Field became a left-leaning diplomat in the U.S. Foreign Service. In the early thirties he gravitated toward intellectuals with strong pro-Soviet sympathies, among whom the Soviet secret service sought collaborators. In 1933, Noel Field met the German anti-Nazis Paul and Hede Massing. They had arrived in the United States from Moscow, with the objective of building up a network of Soviet agents among influential left-wing personalities. Field was one of their recruits. In 1936, much to Moscow's dismay,[37] he left the foreign service for the League of Nations in Geneva, where he worked first in the disarmament section and later was in charge of members of the International Brigades in the Spanish Civil War.

Hede Massing set up Noel Field with Ignatz Reiss and General Walter G. Krivitsky, who were in charge of Soviet intelligence in Switzerland. Soon after that, however, Reiss spoke out against Stalin's terror, and Moscow ordered him liquidated for this "betrayal of the USSR." In August 1937 Krivitsky appointed a new controller for Field. However, after the elimination of Reiss, Krivitsky also defected. Reiss's and Krivitsky's "treason" raised questions in Moscow about Noel Field as well: he may have influenced them or even helped turn them around.

These doubts subsided when in 1938, Noel and his wife, Herta, appeared in Moscow. They fulfilled their old desire to see the "promised land." In addition, Noel wanted to restore the broken intelligence link, and to join the CP USA.

He met with the Massings who helped him reestablish contact: he was given a password which his new controller would use in approaching him. Intelligence agencies did not consider his membership in the CP USA appropriate and instead recommended membership in the German CP, which would be secret, known only to two or three officials, and registered in a secret roster of the Comintern.[38]

More than four years passed before Field's controller contacted him. After giving assurances that he was still interested in the work, Field was to review in detail his contacts with Reiss and Krivitsky, as well as his activities over the previous five years. Field complied but still didn't meet his controller face-to-face. He heard nothing more until after the war, and then in a manner which made him so suspicious and doubtful that he simply threw out the messenger. Moscow's misgivings mounted accordingly.

Since 1939, Field had been operating in France and Switzerland as the director of the Unitarian Service Committee (USC) for Europe. His job was to help victims of Nazism. In the process he met dozens of German, Czechoslovak, Polish, Hungarian, and other Communists whom he helped reach exile. He even operated as a courier among underground Communist groups. In Switzerland he contacted officials of anti-Nazi organizations, including Communists. All told, the services he rendered to the Communists and their resistance were very valuable.[39]

One of his duties was to report to the USC headquarters in the United States about the political and economic situation and about resistance movements in Nazi-occupied homes of the exiles. He also supplied this information to Allen Dulles, the Swiss-based head of the American secret service, the OSS. In exchange Dulles helped out leftist resistance groups financially, materially, and logistically. Such cooperation was considered natural at the time, serving a common goal—the defeat of Nazism.

Two years after the war ended, in the fall of 1947, Noel Field lost his job with the USC. He decided to stay in Europe and to work as a journalist specializing in countries of the Soviet sphere of influence, writing for the U.S. press. Two considerations motivated him: on the one hand, he knew a number of Communist officials whom he had helped during the war and who now occupied high positions in Poland, Czechoslovakia, East Germany, and Hungary; on the other hand there was his "history with intelligence." Additionally, he had no place to stay, and he wanted to get a residence permit in one of the Soviet-bloc countries.

In April 1948, Oskar Kosta and Evžen Klinger, Czechoslovak Communists working in Geneva, invited Field to Czechoslovakia. He intended to meet his wartime friends, collect material for a book on the people's democracies, and settle the residency issue. Suddenly, however, his name started appearing in reports of the Czechoslovak intelligence. Alice Kohnová-Glaserová, who after the war had been sent to recruit agents among American intellectuals, recommended Field. She had known him from wartime, but being ultracautious, she demanded that he be further investigated. The case was taken up by Josef Šindelář, deputy head of the Czechoslovak intelligence, who was in charge of U.S. recruiting.[40] He turned to Switzerland for information. Max Horngacker, an official of the Swiss Communist party, recommended Field, whom he knew very well. So did Artur London, a Czechoslovak Communist who with Field's help was receiving medical treatment in Switzerland. London also passed on to Šindelář a letter by Field dated April 13, 1945. It was the French original, addressed to Horngacker. It read as follows: "Dear Sir: Attached please find a copy of the letter for Mr. Dulles which I promised you this morning. Yours sincerely, Noel H. Field."[41]

In August 1948, the Fields left Prague to visit Poland. There they learned that Hede Massing and her husband had left the Communist movement and were testifying before the House Un-American Activities Committee in Washington, D.C. Field wondered whether his name might be mentioned and whether he'd be able to return to the United States. Right away he raised the issue with Jakub Berman, a high official of the Polish Communist Party, "who promised help in solving his problem."[42]

After returning to Prague in September, Field multiplied his efforts to get a long-term residence permit in Czechoslovakia. The matter became even more acute when on October 16, 1948, the *New York Herald Tribune* published a report on the extensive testimony that Whittaker

Chambers had given to the House Un-American Activities Committee. Two groups of Soviet agents had been active in the U.S. Foreign Service according to Chambers: Alger Hiss's and Noel Field's. For Field, the way back to the United States was closed. It was imperative that he get a residence permit in Eastern Europe. He knew that his influential friends would help, as would proofs of his Communist party membership and solving the misunderstanding with Soviet intelligence.

On September 15, Leo Bauer, an old friend and a leading Communist in West Germany, passed on to Field a message from a leader of the East German Communist party (the SED) who said he had no objections to resolving Field's party matter. In October, Czechoslovak officials including Vilém Nový, Rudolf Margolius, Karel Markus, Alice Kohnová, and Gisela Kischová recommended that Field be granted the residence permit he sought. They approached Bedřich Geminder, head of the international department of the CC KSČ secretariat. On November 13, Gisela Kischová delivered to the Czechoslovak party leadership a letter from the CC SED, in which Paul Merker and Franz Dahlem, two of its leading officials, requested that Field be allowed to stay in Czechoslovakia for the time being. Soon after that Field complained in a letter to Bauer that he had "used all levers to get a residence permit in Czechoslovakia . . . but in vain."[43]

All these measures did have one effect: they incited the interest of security authorities, particularly of party security. Karel Šváb headed the records department of the CC KSČ secretariat, which was in charge of party intelligence. He asked Antonín Jandus from the Office for Party Defense to put Field under surveillance. Jandus gave the job to Alice Kohnová and received detailed information about Field's contacts in Czechoslovakia. Šváb was suspicious of Field's efforts to get a Czechoslovak residence permit. He therefore asked the State Security (StB), the Czechoslovak secret service, to investigate the matter, to interrogate Field, and to follow Field's contacts. The interrogation took place on November 19, 1948, in Jandus's presence.[44]

On the same day, Věnceslav Wehle, the commander of Czechoslovak intelligence, signed a report "On Field's connection with J. F. (should read: Allen) Dulles." Wehle saw proof of this connection in a letter from Field to Dulles, containing data on the resistance strength and political conditions in Nazi-occupied territories. It must have originated from the same source as the earlier letter which Šindelář received from Artur London. Participants of the interrogation learned about Field's earlier work with the Soviet intelligence and heard out his request to be put in touch with the Moscow security center. The Czechs refused to mediate this but did approve his residence request because "having interrogated N. Field one can state that he is of the socialist persuasion." The residence permit was good until May 1949.

In December 1948, Field and his wife left for France and Switzerland to settle personal matters. Czechoslovak security meanwhile held up their mail, which was being forwarded to Kischová. In France, Field met with Artur London, who was getting ready to return to Prague, and asked him to arrange contact with Soviet intelligence in order to clarify past misunderstandings.[45]

Moscow, however, didn't want to deal with Field any longer. There certainly was a place for him in the great game but an entirely different one than he had wished for. In January 1949, Moscow was aware of his difficulties in the United States, knew about his difficulties with a residence permit, and had his correspondence with Allen Dulles—all the material for turning Field into a "case" and for developing it into a major trial.

On January 23, 1949, Colonel Szűcs of the Hungarian security suddenly appeared in Prague and requested the help of his Czechoslovak colleagues in arresting Field, "a collaborator of A. Dulles." According to the notes of one "Val." who dealt with Szűcs, Budapest wanted the Czechs to lure Field to Prague, arrest him there, and hand him over to the Hungarians.

The Hungarians based their charges against Field on two of his letters to Dulles. One was mentioned above; the other contained a request that Dulles give the messenger permission to organize a committee of Hungarian and German anti-Fascists. The messenger was Tibor Szőnyi, a Hungarian Communist in Swiss exile.

Ivo Milén, a leading official of Czechoslovak security and a liaison officer with its Hungarian counterpart, learned from Szűcs that the Field case was based exclusively ". . . on a wartime letter by Field to Allen Dulles which the Hungarian security had acquired. I know that our foreign intelligence had the same or a similar letter as well."[46] Suddenly several of Field's letters to Dulles appeared, all from the same source. The Soviet intelligence had known about them; when Prague didn't react to one letter, they surfaced another one in Budapest.

Following the Hungarian request, the Czechoslovak intelligence (Šindelář) developed a plan to lure Field from Switzerland back to Prague. As a pretext, they told him to expect an interview to clarify the Soviet matter. Artur London, by now back in Prague and a deputy foreign

minister, arranged the formalities, and Field called him on May 5 from
Carlsbad. But none of his friends wanted to meet with him. They had
all known since January that there was something fishy about Field; there
were rumors about his espionage against the Soviet bloc. Nobody believed them, but all kept their distance.

Czechoslovak security advised Budapest about Field's arrival. Szűcs
immediately went to Prague and requested that Field be arrested; however, Jindřich Veselý, StB Chief, refused for lack of grounds. On May 9,
Gottwald received a radiogram from the leader of Hungary: "To Comrade Gottwald. Please comply with our request and detain Field, who
has just arrived in Prague. [Mátyás] Rákosi." The Soviet General
Belkin, masterminding the Field case from behind the scenes, also insisted. Gottwald agreed and explained his acquiescence to Veselý: "If
even General Belkin has looked into this and supports it, let them have
their way." Field was arrested and handed over to Hungarian security
personnel on May 11.[47]

In early August, Field's wife, Herta, followed him from Switzerland
to Prague, and his brother Hermann arrived from Poland. There had
been no news about Noel for three months, and Herta thought he had
been kidnapped by the CIA in connection with the Massing and Hiss
case. She wrote to Artur London in July: "I'm sure my husband fell in
a trap set by agents of the American government, either on the 11th of
May or on the evening of the 12th."

Herta and Hermann Field were followed from the moment they
crossed the Czechoslovak border. Herta called on London and Markus
who, instructed by Šváb, arranged an appointment with her in her hotel.
Security bugged the room and told the two Czech participants which
way to steer the conversation. Herta repeated her belief that her husband
had been kidnapped and said that she had decided to request the assistance of Czechoslovak security in finding him. If her hunch proved correct, she and Hermann would launch a political campaign for his release.
Although London and Markus knew that Noel Field had been arrested,
they agreed that she should turn to Czechoslovak security for help.[48]

She was received by State Security. She explained the logic of her
hypothesis and described in detail Field's cooperation with Soviet intelligence. Her story dovetailed with her husband's depositions to Hungarian security which were available in Prague. StB personnel promised
help in looking for her husband and assured her that they'd inform her
whenever they learned anything.

On August 22, Hermann Field made a quick trip to Warsaw and

landed in the hands of Polish security. On August 25, Oldřich Papež, a CC KSČ official, submitted to Slánský a request to have Herta Field arrested. A similar request arrived from Budapest. On August 26, Gottwald agreed. On August 27, Czechoslovak security informed Herta Field through her two friends that they had received some information about her husband and promised to take her to meet with him.

On August 28, security personnel took her toward the Austrian border but in Bratislava she was handed over to the Hungarians who arrested her and took her to Budapest.[49]

No trial of the Fields ever materialized. Those in Moscow and Budapest who had them arrested were not interested in a trial. The Fields played a different role. Noel Field served as a starting point for a major Central-European show trial with Communist officials. He was suited for this in many respects. He knew and had helped many highly placed officials, including resistance fighters from the Western front and members of the Spanish International Brigades to whom Moscow was particularly allergic. He maintained contact with them even after the war. Some of them provided him with quite harmless information that, however, could be presented as intelligence. Moreover, Field had had wartime contact with Allen Dulles. This allowed the Communists to construct a scenario of uninterrupted cooperation with the American intelligence directed against the Soviet bloc. One could even argue that Field had turned his friends into a spy network penetrating Central Europe. Moscow could thus counter the uncovering of its own network in the United States with the "uncovering" of an extensive network of American spies, developed by that same Field who in his own country was charged with cooperating with Soviet intelligence. Finally, it allowed Moscow to settle some old accounts with Field who, after all, knew something about Reiss and Krivitsky.

All three Fields were released in October 1954.

HUNGARY

When he visited Prague in January 1949, Colonel Szűcs confidentially informed his Czechoslovak colleagues that Foreign Minister László Rajk, a member of the Hungarian politburo, was being secretly investigated. Reports from the Czechoslovak embassy in Budapest also suggested that something was afoot concerning Rajk.

On August 5, 1948, Rajk was reassigned from the interior to the foreign ministry, and the Czechoslovak ambassador made this comment:

Rajk is said to have left the interior ministry because he did not agree with every aspect of the harsh policies concerning kulaks that are to be implemented.

And his report covering October 1948:

> According to recent Budapest rumors, the current foreign minister, Rajk, belongs to the right wing of the party which shows a nationalist deviation from the Marxist-Leninist line . . . Rajk no longer plays the decisive role he used to and is no longer well informed about what's happening in the party. The orientation headed by Rákosi and backed by the Cominform has strengthened.[50]

Rajk's situation suddenly improved toward the end of January, 1949. On February 1, the founding congress of the Popular Front of Independence took place. Rákosi was elected chairman and Rajk its general secretary. On April 16, Rajk signed the Czechoslovak-Hungarian Friendship and Alliance Treaty. During May Day festivities, Rajk sat on Rákosi's right, "which was generally considered a sign that he had largely rehabilitated himself." He was reelected to the parliament on May 15. The ambassador commented on this turn of events in his report for May:

> It is worth noting that Foreign Minister Rajk, who was pretty much on the sidelines these past few months and who was expected to leave the government soon, has in the last three months clearly taken a front seat again. After an almost six-month absence he again made some public appearances. It seems that reservations about him (he had been criticized for alleged nationalist deviations) have been overcome. One can therefore once again count him in as having a future in Hungary's political life.[51]

We don't know the real reason for this sudden but short-lived improvement, but can make some assumptions. The impulse for the first campaign against Rajk followed Cominform's Yugoslav resolution, with which Rajk didn't completely agree, as he later admitted to a prison cellmate:

> It is not true that I'm a spy. It's not true that I conspired. The truth is that I have a different opinion than Rákosi on some issues, for example concerning Yugoslavia. I never concealed that. I never believed that Tito was a traitor. I always believed that this accusation would cause fateful disunity of the socialist camp.[52]

Thus the timing of the campaign against Rajk and its ideology of combating nationalism dovetailed with that against Gomułka in Poland. It had a similar power-struggle aspect as well: namely, strengthening the

"Moscow" group in the Hungarian party leadership (Rákosi, Ernő Gerő) against the "Western" group which included Rajk, a member of the Spanish International Brigades. It resulted in Rajk switching government portfolios. Toward the end of 1948, the campaign against nationalism was still only a political one: people were accused, but could defend themselves.

The Moscow security center must have realized that fabricating a major show trial on this basis would be difficult and, therefore, changed its tack. The change in attitude toward Rajk occurred just as Field's case started moving along, generating the desired concept of a show trial.

Noel Field was arrested on May 11. On May 18, Tibor Szőnyi, head of the personnel department of the Hungarian CC, was arrested. Others followed. The Czechoslovak ambassador reported to Prague on June 8:

> Late last week the news spread around Budapest that the political police uncovered nationalist cells in the Hungarian Labor Party (HLP) [official name of Hungary's CP]. Early in the week some of its members had been arrested. Apparently a hundred or so people from various ministries and offices have been arrested so far. . . .
>
> The threads of this affair lead to Foreign Minister Rajk, formerly minister of the interior. Various nationalist elements of the Hungarian Labor Party have apparently clustered around him, the kernel of which allegedly consists of former fighters of the Spanish International Brigades. Rajk himself had been a commander of the Rákosi Brigade in Spain.[53]

The ambassador evidently hadn't yet learned that Rajk himself had been arrested on May 30. On June 8, the inaugural session of the parliament took place. Rajk's absence was explained by his being "out of town." On June 9, international press agencies suggested that Rajk had been arrested but Hungarian authorities announced that "the minister is currently on a mission." On June 10, a new government lineup was introduced, without Rajk.

On June 11, Rákosi delivered a major speech to the politburo about the Rajk case. On June 12, the HLP daily published an extensive article about the Rajk case, entitled "Trotskyism and Nationalism as Means of Imperialist Infiltration." It suggested that Trotskyism, Fascism, Zionism, and anti-Semitism constituted the "family circle and ideological basis" which had nourished László Rajk, Tibor Szőnyi, Pál Justus, and other "traitors." On June 14, the CC HLP gathered to review documentation about the "case of Rajk and others" and expelled all the arrested "spies of imperialist powers" from the party.

Only on June 18 did the interior ministry publish an official report about the arrests. A month-long organized campaign followed, with assemblies of workers passing resolutions demanding the strictest possible punishment for the traitors of the labor movement. The arrests continued and affected two personalities important for the trial under preparation: Milan Ogyenovics, secretary of the Union of South Slavs in Hungary, and Lazar Brankov, councilor of the Yugoslav Embassy in Budapest.[54]

In August, the campaign suddenly ended. Resolutions demanding harsh punishment disappeared from the press. A new campaign followed, directed against Yugoslavia. It was exceptionally harsh: the Hungarian press "carried daily sharp attacks against Yugoslav leaders. The campaign culminated by publishing Soviet protest notes to Yugoslavia," as the ambassador reported to Prague.[55]

In early September, Hungarian government officials informed diplomatic missions of the Soviet bloc that Hungary's "leading comrades" had expressed the wish that the forthcoming trial of Rajk get as broad a coverage as possible in their respective countries.[56] On September 11, 1949, the Hungarian press published the indictment of Rajk.

Five days later, the trial opened. The defendants included László Rajk, György Pálffy, Lazar Brankov, Tibor Szőnyi, András Szalai, Milan Ogyenovics, Béla Korondy, and Pál Justus. On September 24, Rajk, Szőnyi, and Szalai were sentenced to death; on October 16, they were executed. Brankov and Justus got life, Ogyenovics got nine years. Pálffy and Korondy were handed over to a military tribunal that on October 21 sentenced them, as well as Lieutenant Colonels D. Németh and Otto Horváth, to death; they were executed four days later.[57]

When the show trials were over, seven people had lost their lives. Their staging and production didn't differ from similar trials, except that Rajk's arrest was not preceded by his "ideological unmasking," by criticism, and self-criticism. Otherwise, everything worked according to the rules established by Soviet advisors in the security apparatus, headed by General Belkin and two veterans, Makarov and Likhachev, who staged the whole affair. The machinery for molding public opinion operated flawlessly. It churned out angry resolutions agreeing with the sentences. The "people's wrath" against imperialism and its agents was suitably rousing as were thanksgivings to Rákosi for having saved the country. Nevertheless, there were doubts and misgivings. In his report of October 5, 1949, the Czechoslovak ambassador qualified misgivings as "creations of the reactionaries":

> Reactionaries reacted to the trial in two ways. Some were surprised that it would have been possible to betray a workers' party in such specific ways

and so dangerously for the current regime. Others, particularly those influenced by Western radio broadcasts, were not ready to accept any of the facts that transpired during the trial. They would repeat that the defendants had lost their free will and that they said in court what they had been told to.

One can say that the reactionaries' general attitude to the trial outcome is one of disbelief, if only because everything the trial demonstrated was too good to be true.[58]

Particularly noteworthy is the evolution of the trial's political focus. As late as June 1949, ideological grounds for "treason" included various major deviations frequently encountered in the Communist movement, but Titoism and pro-Yugoslav sentiments were not among them. One could, however, observe a note of anti-Zionism and anti-Semitism. The official Hungarian attitude toward Jews, particularly toward efforts to emigrate to Israel, had dramatically changed in the course of 1949. Emigration passports were no longer granted as liberally as before, and later were no longer granted at all. February negotiations of Israel's envoy in Prague with leading Hungarian authorities were fruitless in this regard. On March 24, the interior ministry disbanded the Hungarian Zionist Union (with perhaps a hundred thousand members), stating that it had been organized by a foreign power. Those who assisted people in getting abroad illegally, via Czechoslovakia, were prosecuted.

The trial's ideological flavor eventually contained something of everything: participation in Trotskyite organizations, anti-Soviet nationalism, Zionism (Szőnyi, for example, was interrogated about secret Zionist organizations) and, on the part of the producers, anti-Semitism. The judge intentionally emphasized the original Jewish names of four of the accused. When he pointed out that Rajk's grandfather's name was Reich, Rajk declared that he was "an Aryan, and a pure one, because I'm a Saxon on one side of my family."

The political concept was most prominently anti-American and anti-Yugoslav. Its main tenet was that with the aid of the Yugoslav leadership, the defendants wanted to overthrow Hungary's people's democratic system, detach the country from the Soviet bloc, turn it into a Yugoslav dependency, and thereby subjugate it to American imperialism.

The trial concept featured an anti-American orientation from the start. It was represented (although not exclusively) by Noel Field, who was introduced as Dulles's deputy in building up a network of American secret agents in Hungary, Poland, Czechoslovakia, and East Germany. The masterminds of the trial later deemphasized it a little, in favor of the anti-Yugoslav line which completely dominated by August 1949. The

Moscow designers of the trial's political concept attempted not only to reaffirm the correctness of Cominform's Yugoslav resolution, but also to push the Yugoslav case further and to present that country's leaders as criminals and spies.

All this followed from the failure of Stalin's anti-Yugoslav campaign. He never did manage to subjugate Tito's leadership, and there was no sign of the promised anti-Tito opposition that would fell him. Economic sanctions were hard to bear but didn't lead to popular disturbances and didn't force Belgrade to give in. On the contrary, Tito's authority strengthened.

The international dimension of the trial was particularly prominent. Its producers construed it as a vast conspiracy of American imperialism in Central European Soviet-bloc countries, and a Yugoslav conspiracy against the entire bloc. Rajk and the others recited statements cooked up by Hungarian security and their Soviet advisors about "Tito's plan," "Tito's special plan" or merely about "the master plan," according to which Yugoslavia was getting ready to overthrow the people's democratic regime of Soviet-bloc countries and to link them all in one or two federations, which under Belgrade's leadership and with U.S. support would constitute an anti-Soviet military alliance. With this objective in mind, Tito's leadership was supposedly building up its networks of agents and cells within the leaderships of all these countries. Lazar Brankov even discussed how "Tito's people" operated in some of them. The authors of this construct assumed that "Field's and Tito's agents" would feature in every show trial in every people's democracy. The plan didn't work out: trials in Romania, Poland, and Czechoslovakia took a different turn; only Bulgaria followed Hungary in this respect.

The political fallout of Rajk's trial was Cominform's second resolution on Yugoslavia, of November 1949, with the suggestive title, "The Yugoslav Communist Party in the Hands of Murderers and Spies." The trial and this resolution resulted in intensified persecution of "enemies" within Communist parties, and in escalating Soviet-bloc attacks against Yugoslavia. In 1955, when victims of the trials were being rehabilitated, Nikita Khrushchev admitted:

> [During the split with Yugoslavia], enemies of the people Beria, Abaku-
> mov, and their assistants staged the well-known Rajk case in Hungary. The
> trial and fabricated confessions of the defendants were used in a propaganda
> campaign against Yugoslav leaders.[59]

BULGARIA

Bulgaria, like Albania, also had very close political and economic ties with Yugoslavia. Leaders of the two countries even discussed a possible federation. From Moscow's point of view, the blow against Belgrade naturally had to hit Sofia as well. But there was more: Traicho Kostov, the overlord of Bulgaria's economy, wanted to cooperate with the Soviet Union, but only as an equal and sovereign partner; thus he implemented in economics the equality principle that the Yugoslavs followed in international politics. The Sofia trial was, therefore, initially built around economic issues. Additionally, it included a strong power-struggle element: Georgi Dimitrov, leader of the CPB and of the country, fell gravely ill, and a struggle for succession ensued.

In mid–1948, Bulgarian leaders disagreed about the Yugoslav conflict. The Czechoslovak embassy in Sofia reported:

> The Yugoslav situation casts a shadow on Bulgaria's domestic politics as well. Only hints and suggestions appear in public, but one senses certain differences exist within the government concerning both the attitude toward Yugoslavia and the collectivization of agriculture. . . .
>
> There is allegedly some disharmony in the government between former Bulgarian exiles in Moscow, headed by Georgi Dimitrov and his brother-in-law Vulko Chervenkov, and Communist ministers who don't have the Moscow schooling. These ministers also oppose precipitous collectivization of agriculture.[60]

These differences did not, however, trigger the trial. In December 1948 Dimitrov harshly condemned the Yugoslav leadership but also felt it necessary to highlight the unity of his own ranks.

The actual trigger point was the issue of Traicho Kostov, fifty-one, a veteran party official who had worked in the party apparatus since 1924 and had been a politburo member since 1937. In Bulgaria, he had operated constantly undercover; and when the September 1944 uprising liberated him from prison, he became a CC secretary. Two years later he occupied the country's highest economic post, and as a politburo member and deputy premier he was generally considered Dimitrov's second-in-command and heir apparent.

In the second half of 1948, Kostov spent two months in the Soviet Union. Nothing was made public about that trip, but Czechoslovakia's ambassador reported from Sofia:

After returning [from the Soviet Union] he was kept under house arrest while investigations continued. Several people in economic positions around Kostov have been arrested.[61]

CPB's politburo first discussed Kostov's "errors and shortcomings" in January 1949, criticizing his "incorrect" attitude toward the Soviet Union. The sharpest discussion took place on January 18. The most damning charge was that Kostov had Bulgaria's Official Secrets Act, which was directed primarily against "Anglo-American spies," enforced also with respect to Soviet officials, "whereby he clearly demonstrated his mistrust of the Soviet Union." After a long debate, Kostov finally made a self-criticism and admitted some of his alleged errors and short-comings—although admitting no anti-Soviet intentions. However, after a few weeks, he retracted this self-criticism in a personal letter to po-litburo members.

This provoked a new, even stronger attack, which culminated at a politburo meeting of March 7. Under great pressure, Kostov retracted the letter, apologized for having written it when he was "disturbed and under an attack of pathological depression," and performed another, even more sweeping self-criticism. This time, though, the leadership decided to push the case to its limits, present it to the central committee, and eliminate Kostov politically, his contrition notwithstanding.[62]

Power ambitions also inspired Kostov's enemies. Dimitrov's health was rapidly deteriorating, his imminent death was probable, and a suc-cessor had to be picked as soon as possible. A Czechoslovak diplomat relayed the following information about Dimitrov's health, which he had received from the Soviet ambassador to Sofia:

Dimitrov fell ill in early February [1949]. By mid-March his health had deteriorated so much that his old Moscow physicians flew him to Moscow half-dead. He is being treated in the Kremlin hospital. His situation has since improved, and he will soon be transferred to an official health resort south of Moscow or to the seaside. Dimitrov has a direct line to Sofia and is kept informed daily about important matters.[63]

"Grave political and party errors of Traicho Kostov" were the main topic on the agenda of the CC CPB session of March 26–27. Details of the session were not made public, but the Czechoslovak ambassador was kept informed officially by Bulgaria's deputy foreign minister. The polit-buro grouped Kostov's "errors" into four categories:

1. Kostov allegedly harbored strong nationalist tendencies: during economic negotiations he did not demonstrate sufficient sincerity and

friendship toward the Soviet Union, and supported anti-Soviet tendencies in the state apparatus. The ambassador wrote:

> Kostov refused to furnish the Soviet Union with Bulgarian economic data, which he wanted to keep in his own hands. Nor did he want to provide the USSR with the latest information about Bulgaria's trade with the West. A few months ago he gave Stalin an evasive answer to this question, which really amounted to a refusal. . . . The party considers Kostov's naive views about the significance and importance of Bulgaria, which disregard Soviet and Stalin's help, as a strong manifestation of great-Bulgarian nationalism and of Bulgarian Titoism.

2. Kostov deliberately failed to coordinate party and government work, in order to strengthen his own leadership position. From the ambassador's report:

> He decided even the most important economic matters to come before the Economic Council by himself. He didn't consult Dimitrov, the government or the politburo, and he often didn't even keep them informed. He surrounded himself—especially in the Economic Council—with a clique. He made decisions alone, in a dictatorial, non-Communist fashion.

3. He employed various maneuvers and intrigues to provoke disagreements within the party and to sow mistrust between the Bulgarian and the Soviet CP's. From the ambassador's report:

> During Dimitrov's prolonged illness and absence, Kostov deputized for him in the party and in the government. He exploited this position, abused Dimitrov's confidence, and plotted against him in an effort to build up his own position as a future dictator.

4. His self-criticism was shown to have been insincere, because he changed it according to the needs of the moment. The ambassador:

> Originally Kostov partially admitted his error. However, he used this partial self-criticism as a springboard for criticizing and attacking the erroneous policy of one group in the party leadership.[64]

The politburo particularly emphasized two of Kostov's alleged errors: nationalist anti-Soviet tendencies akin to "Titoism," and his power aspirations. In this phase of the attack, the latter actually dominated. At the CC session Kostov made a self-criticism, but the politburo found it unsatisfactory and ambiguous since he attempted to "discredit the politburo, split the CC membership and even sow mistrust between the CPB and the Soviet CP." In other words, Kostov explained many of the charges, he defended himself, and pointed a critical finger at the polit-buro and at some of its members individually. The CC therefore rejected his self-criticism and stripped him of all government posts and of polit-buro membership.[65]

After the CC CPB session, the Kostov case went public. An internal party campaign was followed by a public one, which the ambassador reported to Prague as follows:

> After several weeks, discussions of this matter in all party organizations have resulted in complete agreement with measures of the central committee, although one may have expected expressions of sympathy, considering the political position T. Kostov held until recently. Almost the very opposite has occurred. . . . Several basic and district conferences [of the party], headed by the local organization in Sofia, recommended that Kostov be given the most severe punishment, as a deterrent.[66]

Dimitrov, writing on May 10 from a Soviet health resort, also rec-ommended taking the next step:

> We do not yet consider the case of Traicho Kostov and of like-minded party members closed. After studying the minutes of the plenary session and especially Traicho Kostov's own long speech, I am fully convinced that we are dealing not merely with an intellectual individualist and a ruthless careerist but indeed with a crafty person, devious to the marrow of his bone, for whom there is no place in a true Bolshevik party.[67]

The intraparty discussion and Dimitrov's voice from the Soviet Union encouraged the politburo. Vasil Kolarov deputized for the sick Dimitrov, and in June he again presented Kostov's case to the central committee on behalf of the politburo. Kolarov expanded the March list of charges by including political errors that Kostov allegedly committed prior to World War II, including especially his newly "discovered" participation in the Trotskyite underground party leadership in 1929–1934 and in his mistrust of the Soviets mentioned earlier. All CC members approved the politburo recommendation that Kostov be expelled from the party, and Czechoslovakia's ambassador reported to Prague:

> This unanimity notwithstanding, I get the impression from some reports that certain members of the CC sympathized with Kostov and considered his expulsion from the party as too harsh a punishment. . . . However, in today's situation, disrupting the relationship with the USSR and the Soviet CP and harming the unity of the party is a grave and dangerous transgression, espe-cially considering how exposed Bulgaria is. It had to be punished with ex-emplary severity.[68]

The June session of the central committee finished off the Kostov case politically. Momentum drove it further, into the realm of criminal activity. Kostov was arrested. (Meanwhile, on July 2, Dimitrov died in the Soviet Union of a kidney ailment and diabetes, according to the official report.) On July 20, the parliament stripped Kostov of his parliamentary mandate and arrests of his colleagues followed. An extensive investigation launched preparations for a show trial influenced by the course and result of Rajk's trial in Budapest, which had a sharply anti-Yugoslav tenor. Engineers of the Sofia trial clarified its political concept, which Vulko Chervenkov, a politburo member and Dimitrov's second deputy, explained on November 11:

> Managed by the enemy, Traicho Kostov and his group advocated disengaging Bulgaria from the Soviet Union and attaching it to Yugoslavia and imperialist countries of the West. Our party succeeded in unmasking and purging these enemy agents. We shall hand them over to the arm of the law. . . . What is Kostovism? Traicho-Kostovism amounts to nothing other than Bulgarian-grown Titoism.[69]

The trial of Traicho Kostov and nine other high party and government officials opened a month later, on December 9, 1949. The defendants were charged as a group with an "antistate conspiracy to overthrow legal and constitutional state power," espionage, and treason. The indictment described Kostov as "a sectarian and a factionmonger, an agent-provocateur of Bulgaria's Monarchist-Fascist police, an active agent of the British secret service, and a close collaborator of the traitor Tito."

All the crimes he was charged with, including the intention of liquidating Dimitrov, were eventually featured in every show trial that Soviet advisors were preparing. The trial's anti-Yugoslav orientation had to be accentuated above all, particularly through Kostov and company's alleged efforts to turn Bulgaria into Yugoslavia's seventh constituent republic.[70]

The trial, as every other show of this type, followed a script. Its organizers expected the defendants to obediently recite their prescribed answers and confess to the most heinous crimes; however, it didn't quite work out that way. Kostov, the first to take the stand, confessed obediently until the judge asked him to discuss his treason during World War II: a fabricated charge that he had saved his own life during a trial of Bulgarian Communists by agreeing to cooperate with the Bulgarian police. Kostov's response shocked all the producers of the show trial, including the politburo members. He said:

> "I do not feel guilty of capitulating to the Fascist police, of having been recruited by the British secret service, or of conspiring with Tito and his clique." The judge then inquired: "Do you confirm your statements from the preliminary investigation?" Kostov: "These statements I do not confirm."

Panic prevailed in the courtroom, among the politburo members and the investigators. According to the Czechoslovak ambassador's report:

> Traicho Kostov rejected the statements and depositions he had signed earlier. Suddenly panic gripped the judges. They didn't know what to do, and Kostov started managing the trial himself. They eventually solved the situation by not letting him speak. Instead they read his written depositions made to security. Kostov was allowed only a final presentation in which he tried to prove that he was a friend of the Soviet Union. On orders of the judge, the militia sat him down and the court didn't allow him to speak. I have a report that Kolarov, Chervenkov, and other politburo members who were listening to a transmission of the court proceedings at the Council of Ministers, were livid about the embarrassing and politically ignorant conduct of Traicho Kostov's questioning. Soviet Ambassador Bodrov characterized the course of the trial as "political illiteracy."[71]

On December 14, 1949, the court announced the verdicts: Traicho Kostov, death; Ivan Stefanov, Nikola Pavlov, Nikola Nachev, Ivan Slavov, and Ivan Tutev, life; Boris Antonov, Tsonyu Gonchev, and Blagoi Ivanov, fifteen years; Vasil Atanasov, twelve years; Ilya Balaitsaliyev, eight years of hard-regime prison. Two days later the presidium of the parliament turned down a request for clemency and Kostov was executed.

On August 21–26, 1950, the first so-called follow-up trial took place, with twelve of Kostov's alleged collaborators, leading officials in the country's economy. A second trial with other economic specialists, members of "the conspiratorial gang of Traicho Kostov," followed on April 26–30, 1951. At the same time a third trial was taking place with two members of the CC CPB. Officers of the army and security were tried in several secret trials.[72] They were all rehabilitated in 1956.

If we set aside the power struggle for Dimitrov's mantle, the trial of Kostov and others played multiple roles in Moscow's foreign-policy designs. First, it was supposed to demonstrate alleged anti-Soviet tendencies in the economy. After the trial of Rajk, this economic emphasis became less significant; nevertheless, leaders of Bulgaria's economy figured prominently among the victims. Second, the trial was to represent a sort of "Balkan wing" of anti-Yugoslav trials, whereas the one held in Budapest was conceived of as the first, the model show trial for Central Europe. Finally, the trial was to unmask the anti-Soviet intentions and objectives of the Yugoslav leadership, in connection with the anticipated Balkan federation.

2

IN SEARCH OF
CZECHOSLOVAKIA'S RAJK

THE HUNGARIAN INITIATIVE

PRAGUE OFFICIALS thought that as far as they were concerned, arresting Field brought that matter to an end. Slánský assured Gottwald that top security officials were "scrupulously following your wishes that our authorities don't get involved with the Field case under any circumstances." Gottwald was afraid of Soviet security, and didn't really know what was going on. Czechoslovak authorities actually were already involved because that's what Budapest and the Soviet center in the background wanted. Gottwald had the courage to oppose Budapest, but he never went against Moscow.

The Ninth KSČ Congress was held from May 24 to 29, 1949. At the last moment, Colonel Fedor Belkin joined the Soviet delegation. The Hungarian one was headed by Mihály Farkas, Rákosi's right-hand man in preparing the Rajk trial. Karel Šváb, head of the CC KSČ records department, noted that a day before the congress ended, "comrade Szűcs again unexpectedly arrived in Czechoslovakia and recommended the arrest of [Gejza] Pavlík." Szűcs based his request on depositions made by Rajk and Szőnyi, according to which Pavlík, although a Slovak, was a member of a Hungarian Trotskyite group. Šváb and StB Chief Jindřich Veselý eventually agreed to have Pavlík and his wife arrested and transferred to Budapest.[1] However, before they left they were interrogated by Ivo Milén, an StB commander, and Oldřich Papež, a records department official in charge of Trotskyites. Šváb reported that the "first informational questioning," which lasted several hours, "didn't reveal anything substantive, though we did find that Pavlík has a broad circle of acquaintances."[2]

Slánský delivering his speech at Ninth Congress of the KSČ, May 25, 1949

Ladislav Kopřiva, head of the party headquarters' personnel department at the time, and Karel Šváb ordered the arrests to be kept top secret. The relevant instructions stated:

> It is imperative that State Security keep all those intervening on Pavlík's behalf [including those who requested that his disappearance be investigated] in the belief that he probably escaped abroad. Names of these parties should continue to be recorded.[3]

Security fulfilled these instructions so thoroughly and enthusiastically that on January 3, 1951, six full months after the Pavlíks had been secretly tried and sentenced (on June 29, 1950), the Public Security District Command for Prague 2 issued a criminal complaint against the couple for "suspicion of having illegally crossed the border": their whereabouts were unknown. The complaint stated:

> The Pavlíks lived in luxury and corresponded with acquaintances in the United States. According to the report of the house concierge, Pavlík had owned a villa in Ružomberok, [Slovakia,] which he sold and gradually remitted the proceeds overseas . . . It was established that Pavlík and his wife had been preparing to cross the border illegally. Both are of non-Aryan origin . . . The working class knew them as people from better circles.[4]

Who was Dr. Gejza Pavlík, fifty-five, and why did he attract the attention of Prague, Budapest, and even perhaps of Soviet security? He was a Slovak intellectual with leftist, pro-Communist leanings since his youth. After World War I he fought in the Red Army and was a member of the Soviet CP. Then he was sent to the battlefields of the short-lived Hungarian Soviet Republic. After its defeat, he settled in Slovakia as a lawyer and worked closely with the Communist party. In 1939 he left with his wife Charlotta for Switzerland, where he met Noel Field who provided some support, and Tibor Szőnyi of Hungary. These acquaintances became fateful.

Field appointed him head of the Unitarian Service Committee's Czechoslovak chapter. This charitable organization provided assistance but in return expected information about the social and economic situation in the receiving area. Pavlík informed three leading KSČ officials (Viliam Široký, Jaromír Dolanský and Anežka Hodinová) about this assistance, and they approved of it. During his short employment with the USC—the job ended in mid-1946—Pavlík sent the USC four reports. Later he worked as secretary of the Parliamentary Club of the Communist Party of Slovakia (KSS), and in October 1948 was appointed director of Čedok, the state travel agency.[5]

After the war, Pavlík met Szőnyi three times. Political discussions played no role in these meetings. During an interrogation on October 3, 1949 (after his sentencing), Szőnyi characterized Pavlík "as a person who can hardly be described as a politician . . . Whether we spoke in Hungary or in Prague, he was never informed about the specific situation in the party any better than anyone else who reads the papers and listens to the radio."[6]

One other point should be mentioned—Pavlík's ties with security. Documents of the CC KSČ Archive (contained in Collection MV 37 2, subvolumes IV, 1.123, 1.169, and V, 1.85) indicate that as director of the Čedok travel agency and as chairman of the foreign committee of the Red Cross Center, Pavlík cooperated with security authorities. He helped the StB plant its own people in the travel agency. An internal report of the officer in charge mentions that "Dr. Pavlík has already discussed this matter with Valchař from BA/d." Pavlík's notebook, confiscated during the house search, contained the code B/A with the address. During interrogation, Pavlík explained that this was an interior ministry code which he used to send important letters to the ministry. The significance of this relationship with security shouldn't be overrated. In those days such ties were routine for most leading Communist officials, who considered them a party duty.[7]

Arresting Pavlík further strengthened the cooperation between Czechoslovakia's and Hungary's state security organizations. Even before Rajk's arrest, Mihály Farkas had arranged to exchange information with Veselý and Šváb. After Field's arrest, Budapest promised to pass on to Prague his interrogation protocols. Hungarian security reported on May 31, 1949, that Pavlík had confessed to passing on important information to Field. Milén and Papež immediately flew to Budapest and attended Pavlík's interrogation of June 2, during which Pavlík reiterated his confession concerning Field. "Thus I became an agent of Field and of the Americans. I also confess that I held Trotskyite opinions when I lived in Switzerland."

Pavlík's information gathering amounted to his four reports for the USC. On June 16 Pavlík stated: "From the beginning of my intelligence activity until my arrest I always immediately burned all copies of the reports sent to Field, as well as Field's written instructions." This is interesting because when interrogated in Czechoslovakia, Pavlík noted that he actually kept copies of the reports in his safe. As indeed he did: security lifted them from there, and they ended up in the archive collection MV 373A–Va. They were never submitted to the court, despite the requests of Pavlík and his lawyer.[8]

This interrogation session of June 16 was particularly important. The interrogators extracted a confession concerning the hostile activity directed against Czechoslovakia. The long protocol stated:

> In March or April 1945 Field convened a meeting in Geneva attended by himself, [Rudolf] Feigl, [I.] Földi, Demeterová, and me. Field told us where to focus our espionage after we return [to Czechoslovakia].
>
> In addition to specific tasks, we considered it our topmost priority—as agreed in meetings with Field—to penetrate the KSČ and to attain positions which would allow us to implement the Trotskyite position. [A list of instances follows.][9]

Several interrogations in Budapest were conducted in the presence of StB officers Šváb, Papež, Milén, Josef Čech, or Vladimír Kohoutek, all of whom either directly witnessed or heard from Pavlík about the brutal investigation methods of the Hungarians. Pavlík for example had a strong salt solution poured down his throat; he was beaten with fists and weapons and, on the soles of his feet, with rubber hoses; he was deprived of sleep; he was threatened with "suicide" or an "escape attempt" during which he would be shot. After he first visited Budapest on June 2, Milén informed Veselý, Šváb and Osvald Závodský of the StB about these interrogation methods, but to no avail. On June 3, Milén and Papež presented the same report to Slánský, who wasn't interested either and commented, "Different country, different customs."[10]

Pavlík's Budapest depositions were replete not only with forced confessions of "enemy activity" but also with names of Czechs and Slovaks whom he had known. The Hungarian interrogators automatically labeled many of them as Trotskyites, enemies, and spies; others were classified as people whom the "Trotskyites" wanted to use for their own ends. The names included Vilém Nový, editor-in-chief of Rudé právo, the KSČ daily, and member of the CC KSČ presidium; Ludvík Frejka and Štefan Rais from the office of the president; Deputy Foreign Trade Minister Evžen Löbl; Laco Holdoš, a leading official of the Slovak Communist Party; Josef Goldmann, a leading economist; Jaromír Dolanský, a top KSČ leader; and many others. Entire groups were mentioned: for example, "[Gustáv] Husák and his group maintain a nationalist position." Field, too, in his deposition of June 17 stated that he had received information for his proposed book on Czechoslovakia from Pavlík, Kohnová, Dora Kleinerová, Rais, Nový, Löbl, Frejka, Feigl, and Kosta.[11]

Gottwald at the outset dismissed information from the Budapest interrogations. He did not believe that all the people mentioned could be American spies. Yet every new Hungarian report expanded the list of names and invited the key question: What is all this about? Gottwald decided it was imperative to get Pavlík back to Prague as fast as possible. He grew impatient as Pavlík's return was being delayed. Slánský was even more anxious because he felt that the Hungarians were nabbing all their enemies "while they let ours run rampant." But the appeals of the Prague interior ministry had no effect on Budapest, and Gottwald had to deal directly with Rákosi.

Rákosi visited Prague from June 21 to 24, to sign a treaty of alliance. His entourage included Péter Gábor, commander of the Hungarian state security. In a face-to-face discussion, Rákosi and Gottwald reviewed the continuing investigation of the Rajk case and its implications for Czechoslovakia. Rákosi submitted to Gottwald a list of some sixty high officials whose names had surfaced, "some of whom are even involved in the espionage we unmasked."

The list included ministers Václav Nosek and Vlado Clementis, deputy ministers Josef Goldmann, Vavro Hajdů, and Artur London from the foreign ministry and Evžen Löbl from the ministry of foreign trade, diplomats Eduard Goldstücker, Bohumil Laštovička, Richard Slánský, and Evžen Klinger, KSČ secretaries Otto Šling, Koloman Moškovič, Bedřich Hájek, Vítězslav Fuchs, and Ervin Polák, deputy speakers of the parliament Jozef Való and Anežka Hodinová, leading Slovak politicians Gustáv Husák, Eduard Friš, Ivan Horváth, Michal Falťan, Laco Holdoš, František Zupka, and Július Bránik, Nový, Frejka, and Rais mentioned earlier, and others. Rákosi emphasized that the common denominator of all the people on the list was wartime exile in the West or—for the Slovaks—homefront resistance. The list, and Rákosi's inferences based on the views of his Soviet advisors, really scared Gottwald.[12]

As for Pavlík, Rákosi promised to speed up his return. However, after he got back to Budapest on June 25, he asked to keep Pavlík for three more days. Prague was finally informed on June 29 that the Pavlíks would return the following day.[13] The Hungarians brought them back, with a final evaluation: "Pavlík wasn't the only one to feed intelligence to Field. It was his task to connect Field with others whom Field could then use for his espionage purposes. Pavlík is a dyed-in-the-wool Trotskyite, a conscious enemy. No doubt he hasn't yet revealed everything he knows."[14]

Pavlík's return somewhat calmed down Czechoslovakia's leaders. They believed that Pavlík would help them "track down" Czechoslovakia's Rajk, as Slánský put it on several occasions.

THE FUTILE CHASE

Pavlík was still languishing in a Hungarian jail when Gottwald, Slánský, Kopřiva, Šváb, and Czechoslovak security commanders decided to uncover the enemy in their midst by themselves. They never doubted the enemy's existence. They were also under pressure from the Hungarians, who felt that their Czechoslovak comrades were dragging their feet considering the speed with which they had prepared the Rajk trial. The Czechoslovaks were still inexperienced, though. They did their best but had nothing to latch onto. The impulse for action came only from Budapest, from the interrogation protocols of Pavlík, Field, and others.

The proliferation of Czech and Slovak names in the Hungarian protocols led Gottwald and Slánský to create a joint party-security commission charged with reviewing the accuracy of the charges. An earlier commission for the Pavlík and Field cases (headed by Kopřiva, Šváb and Závodský) was expanded and relabeled the T Commission. It was staffed with several people from party headquarters and from security.

On June 17, 1949, the commission ordered that Field's and Pavlík's close acquaintances be investigated along party and security lines; the effort was fruitless. On June 24, the last day of Rákosi's visit, Rudolf Feigl and his wife, Vlasta Veselá, were arrested only on the strength of Pavlík's and Field's depositions.[15]

The commission was at an even greater loss once the Pavlíks returned. On July 2, Šváb wrote to Gottwald: "I have been told that they are both broken, they feel guilty and realize their crimes."[16] But two short days later Pavlík recanted his Hungarian confessions. He thought Czechoslovak security would be genuinely interested in the truth. His first experiences actually justified this view. He discussed the brutal interrogation methods in Budapest, refused to qualify his contacts with Field as espionage, and resolutely denied ever belonging to any Trotskyite group. On July 6 he retracted all forced statements implicating Czechoslovak officials:

> Under extreme duress, indicated by the fact that its perpetrators themselves were amazed at my resistance and said I was an abnormal fanatic, with my last breath, I mentioned personalities whose honesty and political purity are so far beyond reproach that everyone at home was bound immediately to recognize that these statements could not have been voluntary and that their origin should be examined further.
>
> One interrogator told me: "There is an international espionage organization in Prague. We had to uncover it and lock you up . . ."
>
> I was questioned several times about leading party and government officials: whom do I know and whom had I been in touch with. Their main interest was in Clementis and Geminder, and they couldn't believe I don't know Clementis better.[17]

Pavlík's retractions had a calamitous effect on Gottwald, Slánský, and members of the T Commission. What little they had to go on—his earlier testimony—collapsed. They ordered that Pavlík be forced to reaffirm his Hungarian confessions, but in vain. Pavlík resisted. He soon realized that Czechoslovakia wasn't interested in the truth either and that he would be tried and sentenced; but he never ceased to believe in his eventual vindication. He revealed his hopes for the future even in his hopelessness, in a message to be smuggled to his wife. Security used Pavlík's cellmate to induce him to write her: they hoped to gather important leads for further investigation. The spirit of the message, however, was the very opposite:

> They want to force me to admit that I consciously decided to spy for the Americans . . .
>
> In Budapest I confessed to it, in order to save our lives, but I've retracted it all here. Now they are trying to force me to reaffirm my confessions.
>
> One has to count on being sentenced. I'm strong, so long as I know you're OK. I'm with you all the time, day and night. When they make me suffer, I feel your caresses and it doesn't hurt. Stay strong. Believe in me, and believe that we will yet be happy, though it may take a very long time before we're reunited. My dear good angel, I want to share some more happiness with you. That gives me strength to endure these trials. You know what I have and have not done and you know I am innocent. Yours until death.[18]

The situation was no better with others arrested in Pavlík's case. For example, the interrogators of Vlasta Veselá helplessly reported to their superiors:

> Dr. V. Veselá has political and theoretical knowledge. We were supposed to prove that she was guilty of Trotskyism or to demonstrate her Trotskyite opinions, but we had no evidence of Trotskyite activity to go on. We therefore tried to check her opinions on certain theoretical matters such as the issue of revolutionary theory, of strategy and tactics under the dictatorship of the proletariat and people's democracy, of the forms of class struggle, etc.[19]

The interrogators themselves started to show doubts. Their superiors told them that they were dealing with enemies and Trotskyites, but they didn't have a shred of evidence to go on. On top of that, the "enemies" emphasized their loyalty to the Communist party and their many years of service.

In this tricky situation, Gottwald and Slánský criticized the insufficient and fruitless activity of the T Commission. The commission discussed their remarks on July 20, 1949, agreed with them, and adopted several measures, in particular ordering security to interrogate Pavlík more harshly.[20] (Pavlík discussed these interrogation methods, the like of which he had experienced in Hungary, in January 1956.) Even that didn't help, though. On August 3, after a particularly brutal session, Pavlík still refused to reaffirm his Hungarian confessions.[21] Only after three more months of suffering, during which he was interrogated and beaten by Soviet advisors as well, only after begging his tormentors on his knees to believe in his innocence, only then did he break and make certain "confessions."

Meanwhile, on July 25, the T Commission decided to send Šváb to Budapest to interview Field. He returned empty-handed. He reported on August 5 that he had attended several interrogations of Field but could only confirm what Szűcs had told him: Field "doesn't admit anything."[22]

These setbacks didn't discourage the T Commission, though. On the contrary, they spurred its members into even greater activity. They visited jails, attended interrogations, speculated about what caused people to resist in the Pavlík case, and searched for enemy activity that they were sure existed. Kopřiva kept Gottwald and Slánský informed on the progress of the investigation, and instructed the interrogators. On July 28, he made some notes about his victims, which reflect the views of the T Commission as a whole:

> *Pavlík*—in my opinion, his testimony in Prague agrees with the main points of his testimony in Hungary. Of course, his Prague testimony is formulated very craftily, deliberately, so as to make the affair look innocent . . . His excuse that in Hungary he confessed under duress is irrelevant.
>
> *Pavlíková* [Mrs. Pavlík] tries to impress the investigating personnel with her sham sincerity and love for the party, but that shouldn't deceive them. They should view her as a very active collaborator of Field and of the Hungarian Trotskyite group which received systematic and planned guidance and which aided our class enemies.
>
> *Feigl* is guilty not only in the Field affair but also of other things we don't know about yet. He was probably in charge of the other half of Field's tasks, that is, contacts with Austria and Germany. In our opinion, he's a rogue of higher caliber.
>
> *Kohnová* (arrested on July 7) is Field's most able spy. She's exceptionally forward in her work for American espionage, though now she eats humble pie.
>
> *Veselá* seems all mixed up but in reality is crafty. She hopes that her poor health will help her out of trouble. [On June 14, 1950, Veselá committed suicide in prison.][23]

While the T Commission was treading water, having extracted not one substantial confession, Budapest intervened. The Hungarian and Soviet masterminds of the Rajk trial were dissatisfied with Prague. They had conceived of the Rajk trial as the beginning of a vast international conspiracy, but its Czechoslovak component was slow in materializing. And names of Czechoslovak officials couldn't be used in the Rajk trial because they were all running free. On September 3, 1949, Rákosi wrote Gottwald an insistent letter about this. Two days later it was delivered by his special emissary, Zoltán Biró.

Two motives inspired Rákosi, and the letter had two aspects: a Czechoslovak and a Hungarian one. As for the first, the letter amounted to criticism, suggesting that investigations should be accelerated and that they should be directed at higher levels. So far Prague's efforts had focused on individuals with no power and of no political consequence. Rákosi by contrast emphasized the number of highly placed spies in Czechoslovakia and the danger they represented.

> You have the names of people who, according to those arrested here, are either Czechoslovak spies serving Western imperialism or at least supply these intelligence services with information. The list indicates that the conspiracy in your country is as broad as in our country, except that in your people's democracy there are more returnees from wartime Western exile. They also occupy higher positions. We are very disturbed by the fact that these people, who can with good reason be suspected of serving American imperialists, . . . occupy such high positions in Czechoslovakia.

Rákosi expressed his mistrust of ministers Nosek and Clementis, and listed Frejka, Goldmann, and Nový as being under suspicion.

The Hungarian aspect of the letter pointed out that because Czechoslovakia and Gottwald were dragging their feet, it might not be possible to play up Rajk's espionage during the show trial to the fullest extent; and Rákosi reminded his Prague colleagues that Budapest considered the mentioned Czechoslovak officials as enemies:

> In two weeks the session with the first group of defendants in the Rajk trial will open. We will publish the indictment in a week. We're having difficulties with it. If we include in this group the spies who were sent from England to Hungary, dozens of Czechoslovak names you are familiar with will be mentioned as well. All these people, without exception, are running around scot free. This part of the session would come as a total surprise to the Czechoslovak public. One has to anticipate that most of the people in question will sharply protest statements at the trial that would implicate them with Titoists, who of course will spare no efforts in undermining the credibility of the charges we shall bring against them.[24]

Gottwald and Slánský were frightened. They were sure that Rákosi was echoing his Soviet advisors and hence the Moscow security center.

However, they did not know the position of the Soviet political leaders. The matter was all the more serious because as long as various government and party leaders were being accused, "not unmasking" them might cast a shadow of suspicion on Gottwald and Slánský themselves. They sent Šváb to Budapest again, to gather specifics and evidence about the espionage charges against Czechoslovak officials. As soon as he arrived, on September 7, Šváb talked with Rákosi and then with the masterminds of the trial, Hungarian security officers and the Soviet General Belkin. He returned to Prague on September 8, informed Slánský the following day, and wrote an extensive report for Gottwald. His message was even stronger and more straightforward than Rákosi's letter of September 3:

> In the course of our conversation, comrade Rákosi repeatedly expressed his fear that we are underestimating the whole matter. He even hinted that our interior ministry employs people who are purposefully sidetracking and downplaying this investigation while in charge of it. He mentioned that during his visit to Prague he elaborated on a number of serious phenomena which make him believe that some of Czechoslovakia's highest government offices . . . are occupied by decision-makers who work for the enemy.

Rákosi continued to view Pavlík as the "leading personality in this affair." He based his opinion on mere surmises, on doubtful and unconfirmed information and on depositions extracted under duress from people in detention. Rákosi's argument that an extensive network of spies existed among Czechoslovak Communist officials went as follows: "Considering how broad an attack they launched against relatively small and insignificant Hungary, one has to assume that international imperialists are even more interested in the greater and more important Czechoslovakia." And again he pointed his finger at the "London group" (party officials who had spent the war in Great Britain) and at veterans of the Spanish International Brigades. Šváb related Gottwald's question about the rationale behind Rákosi's suspicions of Clementis. Rákosi's answer was typical of his mysterious information. He said: "We intercepted a report of the French embassy in Budapest according to which Malenkov apparently personally intervened in the Czechoslovak foreign ministry. This report could only have originated from Clementis." Šváb added, "When I later requested more specific information from a leading official of the State Security, he told me he had heard nothing about the report mentioned by Rákosi."

Similar inconsistencies between Rákosi's statements and the actual situation transpired in Šváb's interview with Szűcs. When Šváb requested clarification or written documentation concerning the accusations against the "London group" (especially officials of Czechoslovakia's foreign and interior ministries), he did not receive any; in fact, Szűcs actually stated that while names of the "London group" did come up in the course of interrogations, such references proved nothing. Szűcs repeatedly emphasized that "he is responsible only for his own reports and activities, not for reports and activities of others." He meant Rákosi, who, according to Szűcs, frequently intervened in the interrogations and whose "otherwise valuable" advice "often takes deductions and suggestions for facts."

General Belkin told Šváb that he agreed with Rákosi's views concerning the enemy activity of Noel and Herta Field, the London group, International Brigades members and now, too, the "Yugoslav agency" in Czechoslovakia. As an experienced fighter "against enemies in the party," Belkin advised Prague: "Start with a broad review of all actual and potential suspects. Intensively gather all material, arrange for systematic observation and surveillance of their work via a special agency, make an arrest here and there."[25]

Three days after Šváb's return from Budapest and the day after the charges against Rajk and company were made public, StB Chief Jindřich Veselý appeared in Warsaw. The reason for his trip is not entirely clear. After receiving the crushing yet contradictory report from Hungary, the cautious and frightened Gottwald may have sought some reassurance from Poland's leader Bolesław Bierut, who, he thought, must have been under similar pressure.

If this was the case, his effort misfired. Veselý met with Bierut, Berman, Roman Zambrowski, Public Security Minister Stanisław Radkiewicz and with Jozef Rożański and Jozef Światło, officers in charge of the Field case. They all emphasized the gravity of the case uncovered in Hungary. Indeed, it had already resulted in the arrest of some fifty party officials in Poland. The Poles agreed with the Hungarians that Prague was seriously underestimating the situation and emphasized even more strongly the interest imperialists have in Czechoslovakia where the very center of the international conspiracy was supposed to be located. They repeatedly challenged Prague to take decisive steps. Veselý reported to Gottwald, "[Bierut and Berman] stated that in their opinion, the class enemy's chances in the Polish and Czechoslovak parties are quite good, and emphasized that necessary attention has to be paid to the case."

Bierut suggested that enemies would be found in the following groups: people planted in the party by the (prewar) police, Trotskyites, International Brigades members, and people who spent the war in the West. He had Veselý deliver to Gottwald a personal message in which he stated that he had "greater fears of the danger highlighted by the Hungarian case with respect to Czechoslovakia than Poland." Veselý's record of his interview with Radkiewicz stated:

> Many threads lead to this new group [that had been discovered in Poland] from or through Czechoslovakia. Comrade Radkiewicz therefore feels that the center or the head of this so-called Hungarian case has to be in Czechoslovakia. [Radkiewicz therefore recommended] that we hurry up and find the controlling organ for Czechoslovakia, or perhaps for the entire Hungarian case. He observed that we seem too afraid to falsely accuse people. He feels this is unwarranted because these people have a background that is foreign to the working class, both in Poland and in Czechoslovakia. He stated that there is no time for agency work and drawn-out efforts, that we have to reach the goal by arrests, interrogations, and, if necessary, by confrontations.[26]

The pressure from Budapest and Warsaw had a strong effect on Prague. It was augmented by the trial of Rajk, which opened on September 16. Gottwald and Slánský came to realize that not only Hungary and Poland, but also Moscow was waiting to see how they would react lest their continuing hesitation and caution be interpreted as covering up for or aiding and abetting the spies.

Pressures for a grand Central European show trial had been so far exerted via Budapest and Warsaw. They received the seal of approval from Soviet political authorities in the course of the Rajk trial and the subsequent Cominform resolution. Gottwald faced a decision the importance of which he hadn't even realized: either to continue investigating cautiously (on the basis of credible evidence of guilt and with grounds for suspicion) or to open up the party and his own closest political colleagues, in whose innocence he believed, to the worst kind of license. The first alternative risked a conflict with Moscow; the second risked jeopardizing his closest comrades and even himself. It would change him from a disinterested observer into a show-trial producer. Whenever Gottwald faced such a choice, he always decided in favor of the second alternative.

From mid-September 1949 on, the activity of the T Commission flourished. It ordered the arrests of Oskar Kosta (September 21), Karel Markus (September 24), and Evžen Klinger (September 29). The commission put under surveillance Arnošt Ungár, an alleged Trotskyite who was later arrested, and the "salon" of Gisela Kischová.[27] It made a series of fateful decisions on September 30, instructing that interrogations be escalated and furnishing State Security and party authorities with a number of new names to be investigated.

At its next meeting, on October 3, the T Commission decided "to initiate the investigation of certain former Spanish volunteers who either provoke suspicion or who have been unmasked as Trotskyites or as police informers, either in Spain or later, in French concentration camps." The list of names did not yet contain any high party officials. State Security was instructed to initiate round-the-clock surveillance, including checks on their mail and telephone, of Vilém Nový and of André Simone, prominent Communist journalists. Deputy Defense Minister Bedřich Reicin, formerly commander of defense intelligence, was given the task of "developing" the "Hungarian case" within the army. He was to prepare "a list of Communist officers who have any blot on their resumé and highlight their party contacts and connections."[28]

According to extant documents, the T Commission met for the last time sometime between October 7 and 10, 1949. It dealt primarily with Spanish veterans. It decided that more Communists, this time highly placed ones, should be questioned. Some were put under surveillance. The State Security chief was told to have "comrade Jarin Hošek initiate a review of former Spanish volunteers."[29]

Though the T Commission revived toward the end of its tenure, its output did not meet expectations. Party and security investigation of people who were at liberty did not uncover any "spies," however strenuous the efforts. Still, its work was not in vain. Every questioned person was marked by a shadow of suspicion, either because of the widespread mistrust or from fear that something more serious might be uncovered in the future. The wrap-up reports about the investigations include notes such as these:

> *Ludvík Frejka*: "There is no specific evidence of his contacts with enemy elements. Nevertheless, the matter has to be pursued further, especially to learn about his contacts and trips abroad."
>
> *Josef Goldmann* gave the impression of sincerity and loyalty to the party. "Nevertheless, his unusual wealth of foreign contacts make him a suspect." He was to be dismissed from his job.
>
> *Vojtěch Jančík*: "Despite all its efforts, the investigation team found no evidence of activity that could be described as hostile to the party . . . In our opinion, Jančík is not a spy. Nor is he a conscious enemy of the party and of

socialist construction. He is, however, not strong enough to be doing good personnel work because he lacks good people instincts."

Artur London: His investigation "was negative from the state-security standpoint but party measures are necessary!"[30]

All the pressures and all the effort notwithstanding, the Field case bore no fruit in Czechoslovakia. There was no major trial in the offing. StB commanders who were directly involved with the case wanted to fulfill their party instructions and engineer a trial of the Czechoslovak wing of Field's conspiracy, the existence of which they didn't doubt. They worked out the matter on paper to the point of developing "an organization chart of the conspiracy" with a number of names. This was their fantastic construction:

> The base was N. Field. In Czechoslovakia, four groups were linked to him: (1) Pavlík, Kohnová, the Kisch couple, and Veselá; (2) the Trotskyite group of A[rnošt] Ungár; (3) V. Nový, in the CC KSČ presidium; (4) [returnees from] abroad: the Vinklers, [Bedřich] Biheller, et al. Security believed that the first two groups had developed a network of collaborators in central authorities as well as in Slovakia.[31]

The Czechoslovak wing of Field's conspiracy got nowhere. Preparing the trial would have taken a long time because almost all those listed were still at liberty. Also, compared with the level of victims of the Rajk trial, these were third-rate officials. And finally, Soviet advisors, followed by Czechoslovak and Polish authorities, were nudging the Field case in a different direction. Their interest had decidedly concentrated on the London exile and on Spanish volunteers. Pavlík and people imprisoned with him, and the arrested officers of the former Polish Democratic Center in Switzerland, did not belong to these groups. They had known Field only in Switzerland and, at most, represented what one might call the "Swiss track." For all these reasons the Field-Pavlík case withered and did not turn into a major trial. On October 26, Šváb reported to Gottwald on "the group of Pavlík and accomplices. All those in jail are being intensively interrogated. It has become clear that these people will not be much help in uncovering more serious wreckers."

Two months later, on December 28, after Ungár had resolutely denied all accusations, Šváb reported that "It's hard to take this whole thing seriously because ever since his arrest, Ungár has been behaving like a notorious liar, refusing to confirm even inconsequential facts we have uncovered."[32]

In a deposition in 1951, Šváb stated that Soviet advisors soon "lost interest in this [Pavlík] case." It ended in a tragedy, though not in loss of life: On June 29, 1950, Pavlík was sentenced to fifteen years, his wife to ten, Feigl to thirteen and Markus to three years in prison, all for espionage.

SOVIET ADVISORS

Pressures from Budapest and the futile search for enemies in the party resulted in inviting Soviet advisors to help the State Security. Šváb visited Hungary on September 7 and 8, 1949, and Rákosi recommended that Prague enlist some of these veterans who had been so useful to Budapest. Szűcs also appreciated their help; and General Belkin, too, remarked that when Hungarian comrades requested help, the Soviet interior ministry supplied fifteen security officers. He suggested that Prague do the same "because Czechoslovakia is dealing with people with twenty or thirty years of espionage experience, whereas your people who are countering them have four years of experience at most. We [Soviets] have thirty years of experience and know how to go about these problems quite differently."[33]

The day the Rajk trial opened, Slánský submitted a telegram addressed to the Soviet party leadership to Gottwald for his signature.

> When Rajk's traitorous clique was uncovered in Hungary, some of its contacts led to Czechoslovakia. We request that the CC of the Soviet party dispatch a few specialists familiar with the results of the Hungarian legal investigations to assist us in investigating this matter.

Moscow responded a week later, on September 23:

> In response to your request, the ministry of state security has been instructed to select and send to Prague the necessary specialists.[34]

The 1949 arrival of Soviet advisors had a short overture. In 1946, the Soviet embassy in Prague had two intelligence officers, Tikhonov and Khazianov, who managed a fairly widespread Soviet network in Czechoslovakia. Štěpán Plaček, commander of Czechoslovak internal intelligence, maintained very close contacts with them. After the February 1948 Communist takeover, Plaček championed their idea that Soviet advisors should be invited to assist Czechoslovak security forces. Plaček submitted this recommendation as his own via Šváb to Slánský who, however, turned it down. Tikhonov and Khazianov were very upset about this. They continued to work with Plaček even after his dismissal in the fall of 1948, until they left for Moscow in November 1949. At a good-bye get-together, Khazianov told Plaček that one of the main reasons for their departure was Moscow's criticism: the Rajk investigation had generated a lot of talk about Czechoslovak officials, "and we don't know a thing."[35]

Gottwald requested help with one specific case rather than permanent assistance. Two advisors arrived in Prague in early October: N. T. Likhachev and Makarov. They turned the Czechoslovak search for enemies in the party in a new direction, put it on a new scale, and gave it new content. They started out by critically reviewing existing security operations. Several leading security officers later stated, "Their general impression was that our security was too soft and irresolute, that it got pushed about and didn't champion its opinions and requirements energetically enough. It handled the class enemy with kid gloves."[36]

The first advisors and their followers maintained the traditional Soviet view that enemies in the party can never be uncovered by the party itself but only by security. They took it for granted that nobody would admit to anything while at liberty, but that everybody softens up in custody. Jarmila Taussigová, a leading official of the Party Control Commission (KSK) from 1949 to 1951, later mentioned a discussion she had had on this topic with Šváb and the advisor Vladimir Boyarski:

> Karel Šváb told me that Beria's advisors sharply criticized our party investigations which, they said, could never uncover the enemy. Their description of Soviet experiences is etched in my mind: they said that people speak the truth only on security's turf, not on party turf. It is etched in my mind because I later questioned Boyarski about this. He confirmed Šváb's words and stated that my [different] opinions were wrong.[37]

According to the advisors, the main task of security (specifically: of State Security, the StB) was to seek out enemies and produce political trials. This, too, is how they saw their mission in Czechoslovakia. Likhachev on one occasion demanded that Teodor Baláž, a Slovak security commander, furnish information about enemy activity of Slovak high officials. He was particularly interested in Koloman Moškovič, secretary of the Communist Party of Slovakia (KSS), who had spent World War II in Britain. Baláž refused to help because the material simply didn't exist, because he believed Moškovič, and because the information at hand had been carefully verified. Likhachev yelled at Baláž, "Stalin sent me here to prepare a trial, and I have no time to waste. I didn't come here for discussions. I came to Czechoslovakia to see heads roll. I'll rather wring a hundred and fifty other necks than lose my own. I don't care where you get [the information] and I don't care how true it is. I'll believe it, and you leave the rest to me. What do you care about some Jewish shit, anyway?"

The frightened Baláž objected, saying that since the matter dealt with a KSS secretary he'd have to discuss it with KSS chairman Viliam Široký.

"No need," said Likhachev.

"And what about Široký, then?" asked Baláž.

"We'll kick his ass as well," said Likhachev.[38]

Soviet advisors played a great role in changes within the StB. The service, in chaos and out of control, was heading for a full-blown crisis. By the end of summer, Slánský had practically taken over the StB, without ever informing Václav Nosek, the titular interior minister. This step, taken with Gottwald's acquiescence, was motivated by Rákosi's suspicions of Nosek as a member of the "London group." Investigation teams were actually forbidden to keep the minister informed. Nosek didn't know where he stood. Toward the end of 1949 he told his deputy Josef Pavel that "the situation at the ministry is intolerable and that he will no longer assume responsibility for it. He [Nosek] asked me [Pavel] why I conceal the arrests of certain people from him."[39]

Even before their arrival, the advisors recommended forming a special StB unit for uncovering enemies in the party. Soon after, Slánský told Nosek, Veselý, and Pavel that the party leadership had decided to create such a unit, and outlined its charter:

> It has been decided to establish a special investigative sector for Communist party and political offenses . . . it will be headed by Šváb who, nevertheless, will continue to be employed by the party and will not answer to the interior ministry in anything. The party will provide Šváb with staff and the interior ministry will provide him with office space, vehicles and everything else he'll need to do his job. Šváb will be listed formally as a State Security deputy chief.[40]

At special briefings on October 4 and 5, StB's commander corps was informed about the rationale for this new unit: "The enemy has infiltrated the Communist party and it is necessary to focus on uncovering them." On October 10, Kopřiva, Šváb and Široký decided to form a similar unit in Slovakia, headed by Teodor Baláž.[41]

Šváb brought in several people from the party apparatus. They included Heda Synková, in charge of a team which evaluated investigation protocols of people in custody, and Bohumil Doubek, in charge of the interrogation team. But the anticipated rapid progress in uncovering enemies still didn't materialize. The unit was therefore considerably expanded in late 1949 and early 1950. It now included selected StB officers (Vladimír Kohoutek) and Communist officials—graduates of the party school (Karel Košťál and Jan Musil). The unit was turned into a regular StB section, designated IIa, and subdivided into departments responsible for investigations, "Trotskyites," "enemies within the party," Spanish veterans, "bourgeois nationalists," and "intelligence networks in the KSČ."

The anti-Trotskyite department was headed by Adolf Pimpara. It processed the depositions of the "Trotskyites" under arrest. The department for enemies within the party (headed by Heda Synková) processed the interrogation protocols of Pavlík, Nový, Löbl, and others.

The department for Spanish veterans (headed by Jarin Hošek) dealt with the past of International Brigades members. Slánský had suggested a meeting of these veterans because he felt that after the Rajk trial, it was necessary to evaluate the political and moral profile of every Spanish volunteer. The veterans were classified as "positive," "positive but needing some clarification," and "doubtful." Hošek's department had information at its disposal.

The department for bourgeois nationalists (headed by Oldřich Burian) gathered information about Slovak politicians.[42]

The department for intelligence networks within the KSČ consisted of the "Náchod Committee." This committee was created in the summer of 1948 on the initiative of Dr. Bohumil Smola, a judge from the town of Náchod, North Bohemia. Smola had suggested already in 1947 that all members of the Gestapo (the Nazi secret police) and of the prewar Czechoslovak police be gathered in one place and interrogated, so as to reconstruct their intelligence networks within the KSČ. Smola reiterated his idea to Veselý in the summer of 1948. Both Šváb and Veselý agreed with creating the committee in Náchod. For a long time it operated in secret, interrogating former Gestapo operatives. It gathered fantastic information behind the back of security organs, indeed against them. Only on September 30, 1949, did the T Commission decide that the StB chief should "confine the sentenced Gestapo personnel in the Hradec Králové prison and start their interrogation." This directive "legalized" the Náchod Committee which was charged with the special task of using Nazis to uncover enemies in the party. Toward the end of the year, Šváb consulted with his Soviet advisors and decided to abolish the committee altogether and reassign some of its members to an autonomous department of Section IIa, where they continued with the same task. Relations between Osvald Závodský, Šváb and Dr. Smola were soon bedeviled by mistrust for Smola's methods and results. His people presented unbelievably ridiculous accusations against anybody, including security commanders and the minister himself. Former Gestapo personnel were, for small favors, only too happy to fabricate such accusations on demand. By then, though, Smola was unassailable: his methods suited the Soviet advisors who backed him.[43]

The unit for seeking out enemies in the party was shaped in late 1949 and early 1950. It operated within the StB framework but never severed its ties with the Communist party apparatus. The two were actually interlinked, freely exchanging suggestions and results of interrogations and investigations.

Once it was in place, though, both this unit and the StB as a whole were hurled into a maelstrom of permanent change. The first series of changes ended in the summer of 1950; three of them were particularly significant.

One involved changes in Soviet personnel, which was rotated in the spring. The first batch of advisors failed to deliver the expected results. Six months had passed and there were still no signs of a show trial, whereas it had taken just a little longer to gear up completely for Rajk's and Kostov's trials. Additional advisors were therefore invited, with a different charter and a different position. They did not focus on any specific trial but were assigned to Czechoslovak security as permanent experts. This was more than Gottwald had originally bargained for.

The group, which eventually consisted of more than twenty people, was headed by chief advisor Vladimir Boyarski. Its better-known members included Galkin, Smirnov, and Yesikov. Boyarski advised not only the interior minister but also the party leadership. He emphasized this aspect of his work:

> I objected [Taussigová wrote later] that surely I couldn't discuss party matters with him [Boyarski], since he's an advisor to security. He pointed out that he had been sent to Czechoslovakia as a party official and that he's working with the politburo directly. As proof he showed me a printed list of direct lines to Gottwald, Slánský and other officials of the CC KSČ presidium."[44]

The second change was the replacement in March 1950 of StB Chief Jindřich Veselý, who had attempted suicide, by Osvald Závodský. In a letter of March 19, 1964, which preceded Veselý's second—and successful—suicide attempt, he wrote to party authorities:

> At that time I suffered a deep nervous depression. In January and February 1950 I was treated in the Jeseníky mountains but not cured. I felt a heavy burden on my chest, stemming from charges which the Soviet specialists Likhachev and Makarov had brought (albeit indirectly) against [Interior Minister] Nosek. At the time he was considered to be . . . a possible Czechoslovak Rajk or Kostov . . . I backed Nosek, but to no avail . . . I actually ended up being accused of lack of vigilance . . . Additionally, with my frayed nerves I imagined the role I might end up playing as [Nosek's] loyal friend . . . Then Plaček was arrested in the fall of 1949 for alleged espionage in favor of Yugoslavia. I was horrified to think that the interrogations, conducted by Šváb's department, might bring to light some of Plaček's "antics" of 1948 . . . in which I had taken part as well.[45]

The third change was the reorganization of the interior ministry. In May 1950, the party presidium decided to follow the Soviet example and to create a separate ministry of national security. Ladislav Kopřiva was appointed minister and Karel Šváb his deputy. Šváb continued to be in charge of the unit for seeking out enemies in the party.

Šváb came from an old Social-Democrat and, later, Communist family. He was a ruthless Communist fanatic who knew no bounds. In his voluntary deposition he stated: "I did whatever the leadership wanted and never stopped to think whether it was correct." Those who worked with him agreed that he absolutely mistrusted people, was rude to his subordinates, had no scruples in fulfilling party tasks, and was a willing tool of the advisors. This is what Petr Bechyně, an interpreter for the advisors, said about him: "His subordinates were literally scared of Šváb and approached him with fear. . . . Advisors regularly met with Šváb who monopolized contacts with them."

Šváb's statements were recorded by his co-workers:

> Everybody has as much authority as he can rip off.
> When you arrest a suspect, arrest also fifty people around him: they will tell you about the suspect's criminal activity.
> The agency [the network of one's own agents] is an insect that has to be used and then crushed.
> The whole party is our agency.[46]

By creating the unit for seeking out enemies in the party, the Communist leadership put the fate of high-level party officials, including their own, into the hands of security and Soviet advisors. One cannot tell whether Gottwald and his comrades actively effected this power shift, whether they only passively looked on, or how they may have felt about it. The fact is that Gottwald saw it as a safeguard against being accused himself of harboring enemies. Moscow could hold nothing against him, because everything was done by the advisors; Gottwald gave them a free rein and did not interfere with their work. He never resisted them and approved all their recommendations, all the proposed arrests.

Let us return to the first steps of Makarov and Likhachev in Czechoslovakia. In 1949 they lost interest in investigating the Pavlík case and focused on higher officials from among the Spanish veterans and from the London group. On December 31, 1949, Šváb received from Hošek the first extensive summary of investigations conducted by the Spanish-veterans department of Section IIa. The summary went not only to Gottwald, Slánský, and to the Soviet advisors, but also to Budapest. Colonel Szűcs in return furnished Hungarian findings about Spanish veterans. As for the London group, Makarov and Likhachev wanted to prepare a trial with the "British espionage line" which (as Rákosi wrote on September 3, 1949, to Gottwald) had to be excluded from the Rajk trial on account of Czechoslovakia. They focused their interest on Löbl, Nový, and Clementis.

In early November, 1949, Kopřiva (who at the time was in charge of personnel of the party headquarters) reported to Gottwald on the party and security profile of certain high-level officials. He wrote that Löbl, who had known Field, did not identify with the working class and was susceptible to foreign elements. Nový, who in 1939 helped Field organize the transfer of Communists from Poland to Britain, had allegedly lived a middle-class life in Britain and was arrogant. Löbl and Nový and their wives were arrested, on November 24 and 26, respectively. Also arrested was Milan Reiman, economic advisor to the prime minister; he committed suicide on December 7.

Löbl's arrest suggested that something more than just his acquaintance with Field was at stake and that Moscow was directly interested. A Czechoslovak diplomat recorded his conversation with his Soviet colleague Bodrov, who was also active in Prague:

> [Bodrov] stated that he was surprised at how long it took to remove Evžen Löbl and that he'd like to know how much damage Löbl had done to Czechoslovakia's economy. He said the Soviets had for a long time considered Löbl a die-hard enemy of the USSR who had always masked his negative attitude toward the Soviet Union behind his position of trade negotiator, defending the interests of Czechoslovakia.[47]

But, as Šváb reported, after a month-long investigation of Löbl and Nový, the advisors concluded that neither one would be fashioned into Czechoslovakia's Rajk. After he was detained himself, Šváb testified that "they [the advisors] lost interest in this case and focused fully on the investigation concerning Clementis and the group of Slovak nationalists."[48]

INTEREST IN CLEMENTIS

The Soviets had been keeping an eye on Clementis since he had shared with his friends his critical views of the August 1939 Soviet-German pact and of the 1940 Soviet-Finnish war. He was the only Communist parliamentary deputy and the only Slovak party leader who dared to doubt the correctness of Soviet foreign policy. At that time, he was in exile in France. He never wrote down his opinions; word of mouth alone spread them as far as Moscow, where members of the KSČ exile leadership had to step in. Three of them—Jan Šverma, Viliam Široký and Bruno Köhler (the ever-successful "hatchet man of politics")—drafted a report on Clementis, who was consequently expelled from the party. Moscow kept informed about Clementis's later activity in London through František Schwarz, formerly a right-wing, fiercely nationalistic member of the Czechoslovak parliament, who cooperated with the Soviet secret service.[49]

However, after the war Clementis made a self-criticism that allowed him to rejoin the party fold and to become a member of the government. His reunion with Gottwald was very cordial, and he was appointed state secretary in the foreign ministry.

The Soviets still kept an eye on him, though. Soviet advisors repeatedly asked Plaček about him. Yugoslav agents had doubts about him as well.

Additionally, Clementis was an old rival of Viliam Široký, chairman of the Communist Party of Slovakia, who felt that Clementis's popularity among Slovak Communists threatened his own position. Zdeněk Fierlinger was another KSČ leader who maintained very close connections with Moscow. He changed his attitude toward Clementis when on March 19, 1948, Clementis was promoted to foreign minister, to replace the deceased Jan Masaryk; Fierlinger took this as a personal insult because he was bent on getting the job himself.

Soviet mistrust was first actually voiced in the summer of 1948. Bohumil Laštovička, Czechoslovakia's ambassador to Moscow, was taken aback when Valerian Zorin, the Soviet deputy foreign minister and former ambassador to Prague, suggested that Clementis should leave the foreign ministry. In August 1948 and again in spring 1949, Soviet advisors asked Plaček to evaluate the internal political situation and to provide intelligence about KSČ leaders, including Clementis, who, they said, "is considered to be a traitor."

Karel Šváb, who maintained close contacts with Soviet intelligence, was busy along similar lines. On October 4, 1948, he copied Gottwald on notes that Hubert Ripka, a minister in Czechoslovakia's wartime exile government in London, had taken about an interview with Clementis. They had been found in Ripka's confiscated archive and concerned a routine discussion between two politicians. Šváb was obviously trying to raise Gottwald's suspicions about Clementis's "dubious contacts" in exile.[50]

In the course of 1949, these inconsequential remarks and reports turned into "the Clementis case." It developed according to all the rules of a show trial. The first impulse came from Budapest where Pavlík had been intensively questioned about Clementis. His name, however, was buried in a long list of other names, so the degree of interest in him was not obvious. However, Rákosi's letters and his message of September 1949 indicated unconcealed mistrust in Clementis.

Clementis at the time led the Czechoslovak delegation to the UN General Assembly in New York. His Prague job was in the interim taken over by Široký, who approved the arrest of several of the ministry's staff. Clementis learned about this not from Prague but from the Western press, which saw a similar fate in store for Clementis as well. Gottwald feared that his foreign minister might not return. Gustáv Husák later wrote about discussing this with Clementis:

> After returning from New York, Clementis told me quite bitterly that Široký never mentioned a word about the arrests at his ministry, though there was daily contact with our delegation in New York. Although Clementis was the minister, he learned about these measures from the U.S. press. This also inspired a rumor campaign in the Western reactionary press that Clementis would not return to Czechoslovakia and would remain in exile. Clementis was an honest man and a loyal party member. Of course he returned home.[51]

Gottwald and others who guaranteed Clementis's safety knew the real state of affairs, at least to a point. Clouds gathered in the fall of 1949. Almost all Communist officials in custody were being interrogated about him. The fabricated list of crimes was lengthening. In January

1950, Šváb summed up the results of the investigations in a report for leading officials, in which he assumed that Clementis was Czechoslovakia's Rajk.

After the Rajk trial, Cominform exhorted its member parties to heighten their vigilance and to uncover enemies in their own ranks. The Czechoslovak leadership took a number of measures, including an investigation of "dark spots" in the biographies of all high-level party officials. On December 8, 1949, Slánský gave the following instructions to regional KSČ secretaries:

> We cannot be satisfied with not having found our own Rajk or Kostov, for plenty of them have been planted here. We have to realize that we are far from uncovering and unveiling the complete network of agents in our midst. As the Cominform resolution states, our entire party has to heighten its revolutionary watchfulness and vigilance and systematically uncover agents . . . In this context it is imperative to conduct a far more vigilant personnel policy. Examine the past of every member, especially the dark spots in his history. There's a lesson to be learned from the case of Rajk and others. Clarify all such dark spots of every party member, examine his life, make sure he isn't double dealing.[52]

At the CC KSČ session of February 25, 1950, Kopřiva delivered a similar speech, which was then approved as a directive for party work.[53]

Kopřiva was at the time the CC KSČ secretary for personnel policy. On March 13, he reported to the CC KSČ presidium on the Clementis case. The report must have been oral because the minutes of the meeting record only its main points. He criticized Clementis for not purging his ministry thoroughly enough (this was a Moscow complaint), charged him with bourgeois nationalism, with harboring a hostile attitude toward the Soviet Union, and with an intellectual approach to the party. The presidium resolved:

> In the case of V. Clementis:
> 1a. Recall comrade Clementis from the office of foreign minister and give him the opportunity to work in some other sector so that he can prove through his labor that his intentions toward the party are good and honorable.
> 1b. Com. Clementis will submit to the CC KSČ presidium a written self-criticism about his activity in wartime exile, as well as about his activity as state secretary and foreign minister.
> 2. Acknowledge com. Clementis's statement, that is, his agreement with his dismissal from office.[54]

The presidium of the Slovak party was summoned to Prague for a sudden next-day meeting with representatives of the KSČ leadership, in order to discuss the Clementis case. Kopřiva repeated his presentation. He observed that Clementis disapproved of the German-Soviet pact and the Soviet occupation of a part of Poland in 1939, that before the war he had been a member of the Slovak literary circle DAV, that he showed insincerity toward the party and, above all, that "he hasn't yet performed a self-criticism of his anti-party and anti-Soviet position in exile, hasn't retracted, admitted, and eradicated his errors."

The Slovak participants were astounded but nevertheless agreed with the measures taken in the Clementis case. They even provided additional "arguments." Husák, particularly taken aback, single-handedly tried to excuse Clementis's errors, which he thought were caused by his (Clementis's) uncritical trust in people. In conclusion, Slánský summed up the rationale for taking steps against Clementis:

> Once we added up Clementis's entire past, his activity, his vacillation, his grave mistakes, his activity during the war and since 1945, we recognized that the connections are not accidental, that they cannot be ignored by the leadership and have to result in organizational consequences [i.e., dismissal from office].[55]

Slánský did not list the pressure from Moscow among his reasons. Nevertheless Gustav Bareš, one of the top party leaders, indirectly corroborated such pressure in a later deposition, stating that "something might have come from the Soviet Union about Clementis." Gottwald also reacted unusually. He sent the Moscow leadership a written report, something he did only when he was responding to some criticism or some pointer from Moscow: "We feel it necessary to inform you that on account of Clementis's history and the grave suspicions which have surfaced through interrogating several detainees, we have decided to recall Clementis from the post of foreign minister."[56]

Clementis then worked as an officer of the National Bank. He lived under constant security surveillance which he was aware of; he even made friends with his "protector." He remained isolated. None of his friends and comrades came to his defense. Leaders of the party, Gottwald, Slánský, and Zápotocký, finally had their Rajk. Široký was glad to be rid of some competition. Every leader heaved a sigh of relief that the role of Rajk hadn't fallen on him. Some even believed in the truth of the charges.

From March 1950 onward, the Clementis case appeared to be evolving into a major show trial. Lower-level party bodies were informed about the reasons for Clementis's recall. Most were not satisfied with the leadership's decision and demanded that Clementis be expelled from the party. He was often linked with Rajk and Trotsky; people didn't believe that he had changed and criticized the leniency of the party leaders. Some party officials described Clementis as a traitor and an enemy. Clementis wrote to Gottwald asking for satisfaction, but to no avail. He was told not to complain and to make, once and for all, an acceptable self-criticism.[57]

Clementis redrafted his self-criticism several times, but the party leadership never found it sincere enough or sufficient. In his first letter, he tried to refute false accusations, particularly those which were easy to check. It wasn't true, for example, that he never took a position concerning his 1939 views, for he had submitted a written self-criticism in 1945 when he was readmitted to the party. He was also being criticized for having been a member of the State Council in London without informing the party. Clementis pointed out that he was only a member of the Council's legal committee, as explicitly authorized by the party leadership. Another charge concerned his alleged membership in the Slovak Council in London which opposed a reunified Czechoslovakia. In fact, Clementis had been a member of the Slavic Council, a different organization altogether, also as directed by the party leadership.

Nobody in the KSČ leadership gave Clementis the time of day. Nosek, formerly a member of the London exile party leadership who obviously could have corroborated Clementis's rebuttals, kept his counsel. KSČ leaders wanted not the truth but a confession. On May 2, they resolved as follows: "The CC KSČ presidium rejects the letters of com. Clementis, finding them not self-critical but full of excuses." A commission consisting of Václav Kopecký, Gustav Bareš, and Bruno Köhler was charged with "drafting a brief but sharply worded response." The exceptionally harsh draft was approved on May 30:

> 1. . . . His entire attitude indicates that in the critical moment [1939], Clementis deserted to the enemy and agreed with the rabid attacks of Western imperialists on Soviet policies . . .
> 2. He has no right to request that the party shield him from the workers who consider such behavior treasonous. The party is therefore forced to solemnly ask com. Clementis to account for his actions in this respect as well.

Clementis wrote another self-criticism in which he in essence admitted the errors he had allegedly committed. He tried to explain them, though. The party leadership didn't like that either, described the letter as legalistic defense, and ordered him to rewrite it yet again. The self-criticisms he wrote for an April 6 and 7 meeting of the CC KSS and for the KSS's Ninth Congress (May 24–25, 1950) were received similarly. The calvary of self-criticism ended with Clementis on his knees. On June 27 he admitted everything, without any reservations. By that time, though, his case had moved so far that even this humiliation didn't suffice.[58]

Leading communists were satisfied that the Clementis case had moved in the direction of a show trial. They feared, however, that it might get sidetracked and that Moscow might suspect them of unwillingness to struggle against enemies to the end. On June 15, 1950, Slánský wrote to Kopřiva, "I have noticed that the interior ministry reported on December 6 that when Clementis looks at Prague from the Prague Castle, he apparently says he might be looking at it for the last time. Comrade Kopřiva, make sure Clementis does not fly the coop, if this is the mood he's in."[59] Was Clementis contemplating arrest or exile? The first seems more probable.

SLOVAK BOURGEOIS NATIONALISM

The official and public campaign was at first directed only against Clementis personally; but on April 3, 1950, it blossomed into a broader ideological campaign against Slovak bourgeois nationalism as a concept. This dimension developed unexpectedly, in a few leaps; yet behind-the-scenes efforts to get it rolling had been going on for several months.

The very first hint can be detected on June 28, 1948, when the KSČ leadership discussed Cominform's first Yugoslav resolution. Václav Kopecký attacked the bourgeois nationalism of the Yugoslav CP. He observed that "Similar tendencies have appeared in Slovakia as well. They have to be ruthlessly eradicated!" but his words met with no response.

A more serious effort occurred during Gottwald's September 1948 visit to the Soviet Union. Viliam Široký and his friends felt it was the Czechoslovak leadership's turn to be criticized, just as Yugoslav and Polish leaders had been. In anticipation, Široký convened a meeting of the CC KSS where he attacked bourgeois nationalism: "The influence of bourgeois nationalism on our party and thus on certain strata of our people is an important problem of our socialist development. We have to self-critically emphasize that even leading party organs have not been immune to this influence."[60] However, the anticipated criticism by Moscow never materialized, and the campaign against nationalism never had to be launched.

Relations among Slovak party leaders themselves, however, were poor if not hostile. They were particularly tense between two groups of officials. One included leaders like Gustáv Husák, Ladislav Novomeský, and Karol Šmidke who had headed the 1944 Slovak National Uprising against the Germans. They had been in charge of the KSS at home since 1943 and now occupied leading positions in Slovak national organs.

The other group included officials like Viliam Široký, Julius D'uriš, and Karol Bacílek, who at the time of the Uprising were either in prison or not in the leadership and who now represented Slovakia in the central Czechoslovak government. Both groups had their followers among Slovak officials.

The two groups had frequent differences starting in 1945. Široký and Husák, in particular, battled for power; a battle which further intensified after February 1948. Široký strengthened his position through patronage and didn't even need to resort to harsh methods against his adversaries. Although many Slovak officials did not agree with Široký and his followers and even complained about him, at the end of the day they all toed the line.

In the fall of 1949, however, the relationship between the two groups took a sudden turn for the worse. It began with preparations for the Rajk trial. Rákosi's notorious June 1949 list of sixty Czechoslovak officials included many Slovaks. During the trial itself, Brankov testified about his interview with Drudić, Yugoslavia's attaché in Prague, concerning the latter's spy network: "I asked him how he works in Czechoslovakia. He said that his greatest successes were in Slovakia, where he relied on Slovak nationalists and members of the Hlinka Guard [a pro-German organization of wartime Slovakia]."[61]

This mention of Slovak nationalists as the main support of Tito's alleged network in Czechoslovakia was not accidental. The producers of the trial used it to influence the direction of future investigations and attacks. In 1963, Husák stated that Široký himself had arranged this with Mihály Farkas, the Hungarian leader responsible for preparing the Rajk trial. They apparently knew each other well from before the war when Farkas worked as a Communist official in Slovakia. After the war, Farkas and Rákosi both criticized Czechoslovakia's national-minority policy, specifically efforts to expel ethnic Hungarians. Husák believed that "based on behind-the-scenes information, Rákosi and Farkas considered us [Husák, Novomeský, Clementis] to be the main culprits in this minority issue, which turned us into nationalists." Široký exploited this.[62]

In reality, though, the Rajk trial scared Široký at least as much as it did Husák. Široký could not be sure that Brankov's mention of Slovak Nationalists wasn't directed at him, the KSS chairman. Considering Likhachev's comment to Baláž about "kicking Široký's ass" and some Slovak Communists (Ernest Otto) having been interrogated mostly about him, Široký certainly did have grounds for fear. This very fear inspired him to be super-active in the political and security campaign against his adversaries. It was an act of self-preservation, following the principle he learned in the Comintern: point a finger at a bourgeois nationalist before one is pointed at you. And Široký made full use of his position in this campaign.

On February 5, 1949, KSS leaders were still resolutely denying rumors reported by State Security about disunity in their ranks and about the existence of two groups, an older generation around Široký and a younger one around Husák. Such rumors were described as "tricks of the class enemy" interested in eroding the unity of the party.[63]

But eight months later, Široký requested that material be gathered against the Uprising leaders and their friends. The Rajk trial had just ended and Soviet advisors had arrived in Czechoslovakia. Through Baláž, Široký was in charge of the Slovak security unit for seeking out enemies in the party. Another impulse came in November 1949. Cominform's second resolution about the Yugoslav CP called for an intensive struggle against bourgeois nationalism: "The Cominform believes that the most important tasks of Communist and Workers' parties include heightening their revolutionary watchfulness and vigilance in all possible ways, and uncovering and extirpating bourgeois-nationalist elements and agents of imperialism from their ranks."[64]

Karel Šváb's files on Clementis, Husák, Novomeský, Šmidke, and other Slovak politicians were growing. They contained the most varied information, often quite fantastic. It came from three sources. One was from the interrogations of detained Communists, including Ernest Otto, Rudolf Lančarič, Nový, Löbl, and Věra Hložková, and of condemned non-Communist politicians Ján Ursíny and Alexander Mach. The second was from "dark spots" picked out by officials of the CC KSS personnel department while investigating individuals fingered by Široký and Šváb. They also collected all manner of slander and fabrications and asked security to investigate these. The third source of information was security commander Teodor Baláž. Široký had him "work on the case of Husák,

Novomeský, and [General Anton] Rašla [a friend of Husák and chairman of the Slovak-Yugoslav Friendship Society]." Šváb too leaned on Baláž to write up everything about the "Husák case." When Baláž objected, Šváb pointedly informed him that this was an order from Široký, who himself repeatedly told Baláž to put Husák and others under surveillance. Široký also criticized Baláž for not being active enough and for attaining negligible results, since Baláž didn't even manage to uncover "illegal" meetings of Husák's friends.[65]

The feverish accumulation of material about Slovak politicians lacked any specific objective and a precise political concept. The circle of suspects was too broad: it included followers not only of the Uprising leaders but also of Široký who, himself, was interested primarily in Husák, Novomeský, and Šmidke. In addition, the then accepted ideological interpretation of bourgeois nationalism didn't quite fit Slovak politicians.

On January 27, 1950, the Slovak leadership discussed the danger of hostile activity within the party, but not of bourgeois nationalism. Široký simply observed that nobody had as yet been unmasked in Slovakia, which suggested that "we are still too soft." A month later, on February 25, Kopřiva's report to the CC KSČ about bourgeois nationalism paralleled the Cominform resolution: "Capitalist reaction employs an old trusted weapon in its struggle against [the people's] democracies and socialism—bourgeois nationalism. The bourgeoisie used to argue that our alliance with the Soviet Union is at the expense of our sovereignty and independence. We have to eradicate and uproot whatever remains of this bourgeois nationalism."[66]

In late May 1950, the Ninth KSS Congress was to meet. The first draft of the congress report, dated March 27, didn't even mention bourgeois nationalism. It contained only one general reference to "national prejudices." Nothing suggested that a frontal attack against Slovak party leaders was in the wings. And yet the first onslaught started only a week later.[67]

On January 11, 1950, Šváb and his Soviet advisors prepared a document called "Findings on KSS Leaders." The report listed a number of people as being suspect, but they were never investigated by the party or by security. The report resembled a pasteup job of diverse and not very credible data. It didn't make much of an impression on Gottwald, Slánský, Široký, and Zápotocký. This setback did not, however, deter the authors. They gathered information even more assiduously and tried to give the Slovak case a more precise shape and ideology; thus, Soviet advisors and Šváb coined the term "Slovak bourgeois nationalism."

According to investigator Bohumil Doubek, who was close to the authors, the phrase was generated by the following thought process: It was imperative to find a Czechoslovak Rajk; and since Slovakia is the part of the country closest to Hungary, closer contacts could be expected.[68] The meaning of the expression differed from the Cominform terminology. It amounted to an anti-Czechoslovak and anti-Czech posture; only secondarily was it anti-Soviet. This shift was tailored to Czechoslovak conditions, but it lacked a more precise concept and any serious theoretical and historical backing. The advisors and Šváb didn't have the ability to fill this gap. Evžen Löbl, then in custody, attempted to do this, with some success. He wrote up a "retrospective platform" of Slovak bourgeois nationalism and outlined its historical roots. He set its genesis in the prewar period, identifying it with the journals DAV and Šíp, led by Communist intellectuals. This narrowed down the circle of "suspects," focusing on Clementis, Husák, Novomeský, and Daniel Okáli.[69]

On March 8, Šváb and the advisors issued a second report on Slovak bourgeois nationalism. It was more specific than the first one, and politically and ideologically more credible. It contained "confidential material concerning the activity of individual officials of Slovakia." It opened by stating that "testimonies have indicated strong bourgeois-nationalist tendencies among leaders of the KSS, affecting particularly people from the former DAV group headed by V. Clementis and L. Novomeský. On the basis of these testimonies we have started collecting information about leading officials of the KSS and their activity before the [German] occupation, during the occupation, and since liberation."

The report then described "nationalist deviations" during these three periods and attempted to link the activity of so-called Slovak nationalists with the operations of a Yugoslav network in Czechoslovakia. It further discussed links with about 100 persons in various party and government positions. Apart from the familiar names, others cropped up as well, including Július Bránik, Široký's brother-in-law; and Ján Púll, a prominent Slovak Communist. The report ended with a look into the future: if the interrogation of one "V. H." was confirmed, "we'll be dealing with an extensive conspiracy against the republic and the Communist party."

V. H. was a woman journalist, a close friend of several high party officials. When the StB arrested her as an alleged spy, Karel Šváb and his people forced her to describe her liaisons in political and antistate terms. Šváb and the advisors at first valued her testimony very highly, believing that it would help them uncover a conspiracy. Husák, for example, quoted a remark of the interrogator Vladimir Kohoutek: "H. deserves a lot of credit. She was the first to unmask Slovak bourgeois nationalists, as early as in 1948."[70]

Clementis was recalled five days after Šváb issued this report. For three more weeks, Šváb worked on the Slovak-nationalist case behind the scenes with the advisors and some political leaders, particularly Široký and Slánský. They expanded the existing charges and further narrowed the circle of victims.

The first blow came on April 3; the timing was not accidental. The KSS Congress was to meet in six weeks, and the struggle against Slovak nationalism was to dominate the precongress campaign, culminating at the congress itself.

On April 3, Široký told the CC KSS presidium that the Clementis affair had to be viewed in a broader context. He said that several leaders of the party demonstrated nationalist deviations, with Husák and Novomeský the main culprits. These deviations were rooted in their past and their former opinions. He mentioned several instances of these "deviations," quoting from Šváb's report of March 8. Some of the participants later testified that they were taken aback by Široký's speech. Most of them had no idea what he was after and whom he was targeting. The outcome was unexpected: every one of those present took the criticism personally and confessed some bourgeois-nationalist misdemeanor or other. Široký had to intervene before the discussion focused on criticizing Husák and Novomeský. The following extracts were taken from the discussion:

> *Ladislav Novomeský*: "There is no time to prove where this criticism came from and it would be useless for the objective and purpose of com. Široký's speech. No need to go into that."
>
> *Gustav Husák* took exception to many statements by Široký, especially to his effort to blame him for all the postwar policy errors in Slovakia. Eventually he agreed that the discussion helped him clarify many points.
>
> *Ladislav Holdoš*: "Efforts like those we've seen in Yugoslavia would fall onto fertile soil if we didn't liquidate bourgeois nationalism."
>
> *Edo Friš* confirmed the existence of bourgeois nationalism in the party and took Husák to task for his incorrect attitude toward criticism, that is, for not being willing to accept it as justified.
>
> *František Zupka*: "All of us in the Slovak leadership have been under the influence of nationalism, some more, some less, Husák and Novomeský more than anybody."
>
> *Štefan Bašťovanský* reiterated the nationalist errors committed by Husák

and Novomeský and recalled their earlier efforts to stop Široký from combatting nationalism.

Viliam Široký in conclusion reviewed bourgeois-nationalist deviations since 1945.[71]

The entire CC KSS met unexpectedly three days later to deal with the issue. Široký slightly expanded his first speech from April 3. The situation repeated itself, especially on April 6, the first day of the session. Husák later wrote:

> Members of the CC KSS had no idea what was happening. One after the other they stood up with pathetic self-criticisms, saying essentially this: We're all guilty in some way, we all have our shortcomings at work, and the issue now is to cleanse ourselves of our errors and shortcomings and to improve the work of the party . . . This of course didn't suit Široký's objectives. In the evening he consulted with his faithful, and the next day the session took on an entirely different character. People from Široký's group stood up one after the other to harshly attack Husák and Novomeský, not mincing any words.[72]

Husák defended himself against two of the most egregious charges, which provoked Široký to an hysterical attack.

The CC KSS session was to launch a massive campaign against bourgeois nationalism. Lower-level party authorities were instructed to direct the precongress discussion in this direction and to take up the issue at regional KSS conferences, whose participants studied a CC KSS letter concerning Husák's and Novomeský's alleged nationalist deviation. The KSS leadership reported to Prague that the conferences took place "in an atmosphere of implacable struggle against bourgeois nationalism." They could not, however, conceal that the letter came as a surprise to everybody. The reality was even less favorable: some 200 delegates took the floor at the six regional conferences, but fewer than twenty so much as mentioned bourgeois nationalism.[73]

Meanwhile, criticism of bourgeois nationalism was "deepening." The issue was taken up at several meetings of the CC KSS presidium and, in late April, once again by the CC KSS as a whole. Široký further expanded the charges against Husák and Novomeský. With minor exceptions, they both agreed with Široký's points. On April 29, Husák, Novomeský, and Šmidke were stripped of their offices.

Attacks against bourgeois nationalism constituted the main focus of Široký's speech at the Ninth KSS Congress which met on May 24 and 25, 1950. He expanded somewhat his information and its implications, attempting to demonstrate the damage bourgeois nationalists had supposedly inflicted on every aspect of life.[74] As Doubek confirmed in his deposition of 1955, Široký's information was still based on Šváb's report of March 8. "This report formed the main basis for deliberations of the KSS Congress. I remember that when I read comrade Široký's speech, [I realized that] some of its sections had been lifted verbatim from the report turned in by Šváb."[75]

The campaign against bourgeois nationalism didn't have the expected impact on the delegates. Only eleven speakers mentioned it. They failed to see it as the "main problem of the party," as Široký had presented it. It was too alien and too complicated a matter for them. Not even self-critical speeches by Clementis, Novomeský, Šmidke, and Friš changed this.

Husák and Novomeský elaborated their self-criticism step by step, as Clementis had done earlier and as the engineers of the campaign demanded, and ended up agreeing with the most preposterous fabrications and lies. Twelve years later, Husák explained his behavior in something of a confession:

> I submitted as always to the authority of party leadership. Not knowing the causes and the background of the criticism, I submitted sincerely and with discipline. (December 20, 1962)
> Our defense against unfair criticism at presidium meetings and at the CC KSS session was smothered. In personal discussions with me and others, Široký and others made it quite clear that there are only two alternatives: either to submit unconditionally to the party and conduct a self-criticism, or to part ways with the party . . . We didn't want to part ways with the party, so we made the self-criticism.[76]

There was yet another aspect to submitting humiliating self-criticisms. Their authors hoped to save their party membership and to avoid arrest; but they themselves also buttressed the still shaky and incomplete accusations with more sophisticated political arguments.

In addition, they voluntarily requested that their self-criticism be published in the KSČ journal *Nová mysl*. In its June 1950 issue Husák wrote that he "accepted and agreed with the criticism to its full extent." He proceeded to list—in far more intelligent and credible a fashion than Široký could ever have mustered—a series of his own nationalist mistakes. He concluded his self-criticism with something of a confession which turned into a weighty prophecy: he stated that he realized the possible consequences of the policies he had admitted to:

If one abandons revolutionary ideology in some issue, one necessarily accepts bourgeois ideology, because there is no third one. And he who accepts—if only on a single issue—bourgeois ideology, finds himself drawn into bourgeois policies. This journey may lead into the enemy camp. When unconscious errors . . . turn into a conscious basis for policy, the journey becomes one of traitors to the working class and of agents of the bourgeoisie. Abandoning the principles of proletarian internationalism thus opens up the slippery path into the abyss of handservants of reaction and imperialism.[77]

Not much was really needed—just to describe unconscious errors as conscious ones.

Preparations for the campaign against bourgeois nationalists—conducted according to rules that had been in place since the Moscow show trials of the thirties—were coming to a head.

But suddenly the campaign came to a halt without developing any further. No arrests or trial followed.

This hiatus had two causes. First, the political framework was too localized: the issue was Slovak, anti-Czech nationalism, not an anti-Soviet conspiracy. A trial would not have had nearly the international impact that Rajk's trial did. Second, Soviet advisors rotated again. The new ones wanted to develop a show trial of truly national and international significance, with a group of party officials centered directly in the Prague leadership.

3

THE GREAT CONSPIRACY: THE FIRST CONCEPT

"ENEMIES" IN THE PARTY APPARATUS

STALIN FIRST expounded his bizarre theory—that class struggle continues and indeed escalates even after socialism is achieved—after Cominform's first Yugoslav resolution of June 1948. The theory immediately became the subject of a major propaganda campaign. Early in 1949 the campaign around it led to a frenetic search for enemies within Soviet-bloc Communist parties' own ranks. Following the Rajk trial and Cominform's second Yugoslav resolution (of November 1949), putative agents within these parties were considered the most dangerous enemies of them all. Searching for them turned into perhaps the greatest preoccupation of both party and security authorities. In 1949, Slánský exhorted regional KSČ secretaries to strive even harder along these lines every time he met with them:

> *March 11.* We must maintain the purity of the party. The most dangerous enemies are those hiding in our own ranks. Not even a party nonmember is quite as dangerous . . . We must realize that the purge has not cleansed our party thoroughly.
> *September 15.* We must scrutinize the background of every single party member, new and old . . . In Hungary, even some old party members turned out to be spies. We also have to pay attention to elements which have not completely integrated with the party. There are plenty of those. Our party has to be purged of such people.
> *December 8.* We have to realize that we are nowhere near uncovering and unveiling the complete network of agents in our midst and in the state and economic apparatus. As the Cominform resolutions state, it is our party's task

to heighten revolutionary vigilance and systematically to uncover agents. Of course there is a danger that comrades might start panicking as we discuss the existence of agents in our midst.[1]

This campaign created an unbearable atmosphere of fear both in the party and in society at large. Party members didn't believe each other, brothers mistrusted one another, neighbors were afraid to talk. "I wouldn't accept responsibility even for my brother because I know that even he might stumble," said a certain Communist deputy at a meeting. Unmasking too few enemies was considered a weakness; trusting one's colleagues, friends, and acquaintances was seen as a lack of class consciousness and revolutionary vigilance. Following instructions from above and adding their own bit, many party officials saw "the black hand of the class enemy" behind every social phenomenon and every political event that displeased them. "Agent-mania" struck the country and spread like a cancer on the body politic. It was only a matter of time before the search for enemies would expand to include its initiators and organizers (the party apparatus itself) and become the inspiration for fabricating a "great conspiracy."

It started with regional cases. Once Communism took hold of the country, leading Communist officials on all levels turned into dictators large and small. Disregarding the law, they persecuted innocent citizens, determined the fates of individuals and of entire families, intimidated people, interfered with their work and personal lives, and had people detained. Similar practices were rampant within the party itself as well.

In January 1949, Gottwald received an anonymous complaint about the dreadful behavior of Communist officials in two districts of the Carlsbad region, along Czechoslovakia's western borderland. Teams of the Party Control Commission (KSK) were dispatched to assess the situation. What they found went far beyond the scope of the original complaints. The teams identified several instances of Communists who had been detained for days just because they had criticized something. "There is quite some commotion in the party organizations because party members are being arrested and no one knows why." They learned about the practices of one district KSČ secretary "who went down the list and had all those opposed to him arrested." Not surprisingly, the official "had earned himself the reputation of a hangman" and Communists "called the regional KSČ headquarters a gangsters' den."

The people who verified the complaints concluded in their February 28, 1949, report to Gottwald that "It appears that certain comrades at the regional headquarters indeed do use the security apparatus to eliminate healthy and factual criticism. They first decide to expel someone [from the party] or to transfer him and then they use the security apparatus to collect evidence against him."[2]

Later reports, dated April 1949, focused on an "agent" and an "enemy" at the regional headquarters: "All this leads us to suggest that an actual member of the regional KSČ committee is a tool of a foreign intelligence service."

The KSK summarized these findings in a report which the CC KSČ organizational secretariat discussed on April 20. On this occasion, Jarmila Taussigová, chairman of the KSK, mentioned that "actual member" by name: Antonín Tannenbaum, the regional KSČ committee's secretary for security affairs; and she demanded that the entire regional leadership be speedily investigated.[3]

As a consequence, a five-member group including Šváb, Taussigová, Kopřiva, and two others arrived in Carlsbad on April 23 to launch what amounted to a dragnet. Early in the morning, the premises of the regional headquarters were locked up, and the telephones were disconnected. All its officials were locked in and interrogated. The offices and apartments of Tannenbaum and others were searched.[4]

On April 26, Kopřiva reported to the CC KSČ organizational secretariat that "We went to Carlsbad with the idea that an enemy is active in the regional leadership . . . but we didn't find anything, not even on the official in charge of security." The matter was therefore handled as a political issue. KSČ leaders treated it as a negative example and on May 2, 1949, passed a resolution criticizing party officials' dictatorial methods. Several officials in the Carlsbad region were immediately stripped of their party posts, and disciplinary measures were taken against more than 250 people.[5]

Taussigová interrogated Tannenbaum, on behalf of the KSK. On June 22 she telexed Slánský about Tannenbaum's admission that his activity had aided the class enemy. He had also lost some documents concerning protection of the state borders. She recommended that on these grounds he be expelled from the party and handed over to the law. She requested an immediate decision as to "what to do with this."

Šváb, who received the message, immediately passed it on to Slánský, with the new regional KSČ secretary's recommendation that Tannenbaum be prosecuted. Even though there was no direct evidence that he had any contact with the enemy, he argued, "the course we have taken to date has created a situation in which releasing Tannenbaum would only result in spreading slander about the party." Slánský wrote on the margin of Šváb's report: "Detain Tannenbaum . . ."[6] He was arrested by the StB. After the first round of questioning, from July 6 to 22, 1949, the investigator wrote to his superiors that "the interrogations did not reveal any antistate activity, certainly not in connection with any foreign power, and one can fully assume that the [suspect] is not an agent in the service of foreigners . . . I recommend that Tannenbaum be released and investigated at liberty."[7] However, he was not released. Two years later he was sentenced to nine years in prison, half of which he served. He was eventually rehabilitated.

The case of Josef Stavinoha, regional KSČ secretary in Olomouc, developed along similar lines. On January 5, 1949, Stavinoha copied Slánský on an agreement between the regional KSČ leadership and Jan Kučera, one of its members, who also headed the Regional Labor Union Council and the Olomouc National Committee (the city council). The agreement was to smooth out existing conflicts among leading officials in the region.[8]

This was a completely unusual phenomenon. It elicited the interest of the KSK, which had independently received complaints concerning the dictatorial behavior of some officials and about cases of corruption. The KSK investigated and on June 30, 1949, recommended that Stavinoha and two of his colleagues be dismissed because of dictatorial methods, bureaucratic working style, and differences with Kučera. The recommendation was rejected and Slánský even suggested that Stavinoha rebut the charges leveled by the KSK.[9]

Far from discouraging her, this setback provoked Taussigová to even greater activity. She had the regional security commander collect information about certain regional officials for her. The KSK thereby managed to gain access to criminal records, particularly from wartime. Their reliability was never tested, but it forced Slánský and his deputy to initiate a disciplinary investigation of two of Stavinoha's colleagues. This in turn uncovered further complaints against Stavinoha himself.[10]

In the first days of 1950, the case inescapably acquired a criminal dimension. Taussigová questioned Stavinoha, focusing on his activity during the war. He had spent two-and-a-half years in a Nazi concentration camp. Then he was released; but when after a short respite the Gestapo showed interest in him again, he joined the Ferdinand Harabiš underground resistance group. Fifteen years after the fact, Taussigová described her interrogation:

Stavinoha was interrogated and he confessed not only the bribes, not only his mercy plea to Hitler, that is, matters we had been aware of, but also things we hadn't known, such as that the Gestapo set him free because he signed on to cooperate with them, and in order for them to believe him, he snitched on a fellow prisoner who had sewn something in his coat. Since he freely mentioned these matters himself, we had no reason to disbelieve his statement that once he was released, he didn't do anything for the Gestapo.[11]

On January 9, 1950, based on the KSK's report, the CC KSČ presidium resolved "To strip Stavinoha, the political secretary of the Olomouc region, of his office, to expel him from the party, effective immediately, and to open criminal prosecution against him while at liberty."

However, before the meeting was over, Gottwald decided that Stavinoha should be detained after all, which happened that same night.[12] Three days later, the CC KSČ secretariat formed a team to draft a letter to lower-level party units concerning this "Olomouc case." While drafting it, Taussigová and the rest of the team argued over the nature of Stavinoha's misdeeds. Taussigová considered him a spoilt and egoistic working-class official who employed wrong working methods, whereas the team presented Stavinoha as an agent of the class enemy; Gustav Bareš even thought of him as an agent of the Vatican. The final text of the letter contained both views. Most damning was the paragraph concerning targets that class enemies would find most susceptible:

The investigation examined how Stavinoha, a former working-class official, could have sunken so deeply. It was established that he had allowed the Gestapo to break him, that fearing for his own life he betrayed his fellow prisoners, that he begged Hitler for mercy and ended up pledging cooperation with the Gestapo. Burdened by these crimes, which he kept a secret from the party, Stavinoha became a suitable target for the class enemy.[13]

As the party discussed this letter, the CC KSČ received some resolutions demanding the death penalty for Stavinoha. He was tried in March 1950 and sentenced to eighteen years in prison. Three years later his sentence was halved.[14]

THE ŠLING CASE

The two cases above had only a local impact. The Carlsbad and Olomouc regions were not very significant politically and economically, and it was impossible to link those involved to leading officials in Prague. Nevertheless, one fact remained: like most other operations of the KSK, the cases did result in political trials, whatever the original intentions. Clearly, the political work of the KSK offered one possible avenue for generating a major trial. These two cases may have lacked some of the necessary ingredients but taking a similar approach in an important region—say, Prague or Brno, with officials who were in contact with comrades at the center—offered exceptional potential.

The regional KSČ secretary for Brno was Otto Šling, a prewar Communist and a volunteer in Spain, who spent the war years in Britain. He had been in charge of this large regional party organization since liberation in 1945. He was considered the best regional secretary in the country and after 1948 was often praised as a model for other regions. He combined great energy with novel ideas. He went after his goals ruthlessly and strived to be the best in everything. His drive and his Communist fanaticism exceeded all expectations of the party. He invented and organized various activities which—although rather useless politically—won him praise at the center and made him popular. Šling's personality was marked by some negatives, nothing unusual for a party official of the time: dictatorial inclinations, persecution of critics, disregard for legality, and ruthlessness with ordinary citizens, including Communists.

Small wonder his methods found plenty of critics and opponents among party officials. Opposition to Šling reflected both policy disputes and power ambitions. In mid-1949, a party official assured top CC KSČ circles that "a case comparable to that of Karlovy Vary cannot be expected." Yet six months later the situation changed. The Stavinoha case inspired complaints about the situation in the neighboring Brno region. A comprehensive review was considered, but Taussigová turned down the idea, recommending that the Prague region should be reviewed instead of Brno. (She was concerned about critical voices emanating from Prague that were directed at the party center and about Antonín Novotný who "was advocating doubtful policies."[15]) In addition, the presidium of the Brno regional KSČ committee, augmented by Jaromír Dolanský and Bruno Köhler from the center, reviewed Šling's performance in March 1950, and gave him only high marks.

There were some reservations, though: the review referred to critical opinions of lower-level officials and to a noticeable increase in Šling's unpopularity. Still, Dolanský defended him:

> The policies of the regional committee and Šling's own role are by and large correct. Šling is implementing the party line, he knows how to make it

specific . . . he is imaginative and full of new ideas. This is to his credit. He is no copycat, he doesn't follow a routine. His imagination isn't aimless; it can be put into effect. His ideas are being implemented in all spheres. We have to say that the regional presidium, and Šling, are growing.

[Šling's unpopularity] is objectively caused by carryovers from the past, by remnants of capitalist elements. The class struggle, which is per force escalating, is one reason behind his unpopularity. It is manifest in voices of outright enemies and of workers who don't see things clearly enough. Subjective reasons include Šling's personality . . . comrade Šling's way of dealing [with people] shows grave shortcomings. He should be more patient. Šling has a feisty character. The battle is escalating but we cannot be overly sensitive.[16]

Šling was highly praised. In the spring of 1950 there was talk among officials of the CC KSČ secretariat that his abilities should be used in a more important position. They were preparing his promotion to the top job in the Prague region, politically the most important one in the country.

However, differences and conflicts between other regional secretaries and Šling were mounting. The center, too, was receiving more complaints. In the spring of 1950, the opposition to Šling included parliamentary deputy Marie Syrovátková-Palečková and Bohumil Ubr, chairman of the Brno Central National Committee (the city council). Both were concurrently presidium members of the Brno regional KSČ committee. Syrovátková-Palečková criticized the dictatorial conduct of party officials and the infusion of security-style methods into party work. Šling accused her of the "Yugoslav deviation," insisted on forming a special team to investigate her activity, and had security put her under surveillance. Under pressure from the center, he eventually backed off from further investigation. Ubr dispatched an extensive complaint about Šling to the KSK in early 1950. He awaited the KSK's investigation and meanwhile continued criticizing Šling. He relied on the backing of Communist workers from several Brno factories. The largest, Zbrojovka Brno (an arms works), opposed Šling openly. Šling, however, counterattacked, stating that "this is an organized campaign in which the class enemy is backing Zbrojovka's criticism."[17]

Such then was the local opposition against Šling in early April 1950, when suddenly the criticism broadened. Other regional committees and officials of the party criticized conditions at the Brno regional headquarters, including personnel policies and the party's interventions in economic matters.

On May 13, 1950, Taussigová informed Marie Švermová, a CC KSČ secretary, about the KSK's official critical stance concerning the situation in the Brno region, and recommended that certain matters be investigated. Both women agreed that the investigation would be conducted by a KSK representative joined by fifteen officials from local factories. The KSČ leadership in Brno received the news on May 23.

Šling immediately sensed the danger: he was haunted by the legal consequences of the Carlsbad and Olomouc cases. He tried to take countermeasures. When Švermová confidentially warned about the KSK's complaints, he demanded that Taussigová state them face to face. And indeed, on May 18, Švermová asked Taussigová to relate to Šling their earlier conversation, with Köhler, Geminder, and others present. Taussigová, not in the least intimidated by Šling, piled on some additional complaints. Thus, Šling's first effort to thwart the investigation by browbeating the KSK didn't work out. He then protested against the factory teams that were to conduct the investigation, seeing an uncanny resemblance with the Olomouc events. He managed to have KSK members substitute for most of the workers.

The investigation started on June 3. Local conflicts in Brno acquired a new shape. They turned into disagreements about implementing party policies; and additionally, they affected the party center in Prague. The conflict pitted Šling against the KSK, but also the KSK against the CC KSČ secretariat, most of whose leaders backed Šling.[18]

Šling's opponents in Brno and officials of the center pressed for a rapid completion of the investigation. The CC KSČ secretariat got the first report on June 20, in Slánský's absence. Taussigová reported that the investigation had spread to areas beyond the original charter. The CC KSČ secretariat requested a final report within three weeks.

Working teams of the KSK were gathering more and more information in districts of the Brno region. Two weeks later Taussigová and her colleagues realized that reviewing so many serious problems was beyond their capacity. They contacted Švermová and Köhler and requested that a team of the CC KSČ secretariat headed by Švermová finish the job. Both, however, turned her down and insisted that the report be submitted in three days. Extending the deadline was out of the question.[19]

The report, over a hundred pages long, discussed seventeen specific cases. The CC KSČ secretariat studied it and decided on July 12 to pass it on to Šling, without informing the KSK, and to convene a special meeting of officials from both Brno and the KSK.

The meeting started on July 15, again with Slánský absent. KSK's seventeen cases, not always fully verified and with no conclusions, were discussed one by one. Brno officials listed significant political circumstances about each one and pointed out instances of incorrect or one-sided information. Members of the CC KSČ secretariat backed Šling and pointed out the untrustworthiness of the report.

The meeting ended in KSK's defeat. Officials of the center used the opportunity to deal a blow to the KSK, whose activities were provoking fears and conflicts with heavy power and policy undertones. Švermová expressed these fears at the meeting: "If the KSK submits this to the CC KSČ presidium and if these documents are accepted, we will have to take disciplinary measures. People will have to be expelled from the party and criminally prosecuted."[20]

Taussigová later described the atmosphere at the meeting:

> The KSK sat in the dock and was attacked by everyone. Members of the CC KSČ secretariat would say things like: "We can't go on forever trying to persuade people. Party policies have got to be implemented. Party policies are unpopular because we want people to work. Šling is doing the right thing when he insists that objectives be met. Šling is unpopular because he forcefully implements party policies. The KSK information is a bunch of garbage." And Bruno Köhler topped it off in the evening when he tossed the files across the desk to Šling and said, "Here, you can have all this shit of theirs."[21]

Šling went home the victor and showed it. He boasted to members of his regional leadership: "The KSK got a beating and I will now settle accounts with everyone who turned to them."

His celebration was premature. No setback would deter Taussigová from continuing the battle. On the contrary, it spurred her on, particularly since she truly believed Šling was an enemy. She got the KSK leadership to complain, on July 18, to Gottwald and Slánský, who meanwhile had returned from medical treatment, about the way the KSK report had been treated and particularly about Švermová. According to the KSK, in tabling the report the CC KSČ secretariat had "expressed lack of confidence in the KSK." The KSK insisted that the situation in the Brno region was very serious.[22]

Slánský summoned Taussigová the very same day. He harshly reproached her for her actions during his absence, told her that all members of the CC KSČ secretariat were angry at her, and that she would be subjected to disciplinary proceedings. According to Taussigová, Slánský told her: "If what you stated were true, it would be disastrous" for Šling. Taussigová defended the results of the investigation and interpreted the ill will of the CC KSČ secretariat members as their unwill-ingness to admit that they didn't see the situation in the country's regions realistically. Slánský responded: "That would be mostly my responsibil-ity." On the same day he convened a meeting of the CC KSČ secretariat, at which a special team, headed by Anna Baramová, was charged with reviewing the KSK findings concerning the Brno region.[23]

Slánský hurried lest the conflict with the KSK escalate much further. He felt under dual pressure. If he didn't react, he could in the future be accused of abetting an enemy, for he realized that the KSK would not relent. On the other hand, the charges against Šling might affect him as well, as the head of the entire party apparatus. Thus, he decided to form the special team composed of three lesser officials, which sug-gested that he didn't consider the matter all that important.

A month later, on August 16, Baramová reported to the CC KSČ secretariat. With minor exceptions, her team corroborated the findings of the KSK. Secretariat members, however, still didn't favor radical mea-sures. Baramová was to get Šling's version of all the issues and to in-vestigate all the complaints in the KSK report. Josef Frank, a CC KSČ secretary, informed Šling about this on July 19 and pointed out that he hadn't completely rebutted all the KSK charges, that additional com-plaints had been arriving, and that he wasn't being self-critical enough.[24]

A day after this meeting of the CC KSČ secretariat, Slánský received an extensive complaint from Ubr, followed by complaints from leaders of several districts of the Brno region. On August 31, Slánský met with Ubr, who was angry. He saw no possibility of a compromise because Šling was taking revenge on people who had criticized him. Slánský asked him why he hadn't spoken up earlier, and Ubr said: "We used to believe Šling, but now we've grown some and don't believe him any more."[25]

Šling submitted his side of the story on September 9. He sounded defensive. He presented the facts about individual complaints and re-futed many of the charges. He categorically rejected suspicions of sab-otage, ill will, and of concealing matters from party authorities.[26] However, local dissatisfaction with Šling had by now spread further. Some even suspected that the CC KSČ secretariat was protecting him. Slánský sent Köhler and Baramová back to Brno to talk things over with regional KSČ officials and with the most outspoken districts.

In mid-September 1950 Köhler reported back. The CC KSČ secre-tariat resolved not to turn Brno into a big case, not to repeat a Carlsbad or an Olomouc. It tried to end the matter by passing a resolution that would highlight the successes of the regional party organization but also point out its shortcomings. Köhler drafted it and entitled it "About the Brno Regional Party Committee's Errors and Work Methods in Executing Personnel Policy." He did not anticipate any disciplinary measures and presented the negatives as shortcomings of the entire regional organization. Šling was criticized only in general terms. The draft recommended "involving more workers in the party apparatus to make it healthier, improving the political level of party work and fostering criticism and self-criticism."[27]

Following Slánský's instructions, Köhler asked the KSK leadership to comment on the draft resolution. They disagreed with it and clashed with its authors. Taussigová later commented: "The draft opened by stating: Despite the great successes achieved by the Brno regional organization under the leadership of com. Šling, [etc.] . . . All of us from the KSK objected to this tenor of the resolution. Köhler stated that he had reasons for formulating it in this way and that we would have to present any objections in writing, to the CC KSČ secretariat. We therefore submitted our objections and our reasons for them in writing."[28] The CC KSČ secretariat was to discuss this draft on October 8. It never happened. On October 6, Šling was arrested.

The impetus for the sudden arrest was a letter Šling had written to Emanuel Voska, dated April 17, 1939. During both world wars, Voska was an intelligence officer working for Czechoslovak resistance in the West. Between the wars he represented a U.S. corporation in Prague. He had been an official of the Social Democratic Party, and chairman of the Committee to Aid Democratic Spain. Šling first met him in 1937 when Voska helped him gather a group of medical workers for Spain. In 1939 he ran into Voska again and subsequently met him on a couple of other occasions, with the agreement of the London leadership of Czechoslovak Communists. The Communists used the Voska connection to expand their influence among Czechs involved with the British Trust Fund, a charitable organization.

Politicians and security suspected Šling of espionage ties with Voska. These suspicions were based first on the very existence of the letter, and later on these particular paragraphs:

> I have already started the work and am focusing on the following objectives: (1) agents in Czechoslovakia, names, descriptions; (2) [those] now in London; (3) a list of all possible elements. I will have a first summary ready by the end of this week and will send it to you immediately.
>
> On Friday I'll be able to give you many specific data. Tomorrow I plan to talk to the Major about the photograph.[29]

National Security Minister Ladislav Kopřiva received the letter from his deputy Karel Šváb. Both of them, as well as the Soviet advisor Boyarski, believed that the letter illustrated Šling's commitment to espionage and that it would serve as a starting point for uncovering an extensive enemy conspiracy in the Communist party. This was also what Kopřiva told Gottwald as he passed the letter on to him.

Gottwald decided to have Šling arrested. On Kopřiva's verbal order the arrest was made by Antonín Prchal, a high-ranking StB officer, who took care that the arrest remained secret. For four days the official line was that Šling and his family were spending a few days in Prague. The Brno regional KSČ leadership didn't learn about the arrest until October 10, and the CC KSČ presidium approved all the measures concerning the Šling case only on October 16.[30]

Two issues about the critical letter are noteworthy: its credibility and its discoverer. The letter was never proven to be genuine, and certain facts suggest it was fabricated. Bohumil Doubek and Karel Košťál, Šling's interrogators, stated that they had received a one-page letter, whereas the trial documents include a two-page one. The two interrogators, as well as Kopřiva and (in 1963) Marie Švermová, confirmed that the content of the letter in the trial dossier was different from the one they had seen in 1950, which contained mostly personal matters.

In another discrepancy, the letter was written on letterhead paper of the Strand Palace Hotel in London where Voska, rather than Šling, had been staying; indeed security had confiscated several blank sheets with this letterhead from Voska. And a third discrepancy: on April 14, 1939, Voska left by boat for the United States, and it is unlikely that Šling would have written him only three days later, knowing how long the passage would take. On the other hand, experts confirmed the handwriting as Šling's, while admitting that it would have been easy to forge it.

The question of who discovered the letter is even more complex. Solving it would clarify the political motives behind Šling's arrest. Voska himself was arrested on June 12, 1950, at which time his living quarters were searched and the letter allegedly found. However, it surfaced only four months later, just as the party investigation of Šling was winding down.

Second, Köhler told Gottwald that it was he who had found it; but in January 1954, Taussigová wrote from her prison cell to Antonín Zápotocký, Czechoslovakia's president after Gottwald's death, that "in this matter Gottwald was lied to," and stated that in fact, Kopřiva and she had discovered it. Nine years later she recalled a 1950 discussion with

Boyarski, who apparently said: "The person who discovered the Šling espionage letter had no idea about the KSK's investigations in Brno."

Thus there are three candidates: Köhler, Taussigová, and Boyarski's person. As for Köhler and Taussigová, one wonders how they could have gotten hold of the letter since they were not working in security. Nevertheless, they did have close ties with security personnel who could have drawn their attention to it. Then again, Taussigová declared later that "the KSK was never informed about the Šling espionage documents." Additionally, Köhler had drafted an essentially positive resolution on the situation in Brno; he was too experienced to do that if he had known about the "espionage document." That leaves Boyarski's person, in all likelihood Šváb, whom Kopřiva also later credited with finding it, or one of his underlings.[31]

Both Boyarski and Šváb expected that the Brno investigation of the KSK would put them on the track of a major conspiracy in the KSČ. Šváb had spent almost a year, and Boyarski more than six months, trying to uncover an enemy who would serve as the cornerstone for a show trial. They both pinned their hopes on Šling, a most promising candidate indeed: from a Jewish family, a Spanish volunteer, a wartime exile in London, with contacts at the highest KSČ levels, particularly with CC KSČ secretary Marie Švermová. The letter surfaced just as this great hope started fading; but StB personnel in Prague and in Brno had been ferreting out information against Šling even before then and interrogated Voska with the same objective.

Šling's arrest launched the case along two parallel but connected lines—the security and the party line. The first was aimed at having Šling confess hostile and espionage activity, gathering names of his collaborators, and splicing them into a show trial concept. The second helped develop the concept, particularly by furnishing the political and ideological rationale for it.

ŠLING IN JAIL

On *October 6, 1950,* when he was arrested, Šling was thirty-eight years old. He was taken to the Prague-Ruzyně prison. Bohumil Doubek, chief of the StB Interrogation Bureau, started questioning him that same day, focusing on his contacts with Emanuel Voska. Šling answered that since the Civil War in Spain, he had met Voska only on three insignificant occasions.

For the first four days, *October 8 to 12,* Šling's interrogators tried to uncover his supposed connections with Western intelligence agencies. They wanted him to volunteer information, but Šling said that he "had never been in contact with anyone involved with intelligence." Psychological and physical pressure mounted, starting on October 9, but to no avail. An interrogator's report of October 12 stated that Šling admitted only what there was evidence for, and even then he put up a struggle over every formulation. "He will not admit anything he is suspected of, even though he might figure that it has been proven."[32]

This was the situation for the next ten days. The report of *October 23* stated that Šling refused to qualify any aspect of his activity as sabotage and that he admitted only political mistakes (as opposed to punishable offenses). "Meanwhile he is under constant pressure as he's being told over and over that he's a saboteur and a spy." On *October 26,* three weeks after his arrest and after being publicly described as a wrecker, Šling stated, "As to whether I have ever talked or written to anyone about the I.S. (Intelligence Service) or whether anyone has written to me about it, I declare that except for the State Security commander in Brno I have never spoken or written about the I.S. to anyone and received no letters from anyone about it."

Kopřiva and Boyarski felt the investigation was leading nowhere. Gottwald and Slánský agreed. Kopřiva, Šváb, and Doubek therefore met on October 26 in Kopřiva's office to decide what to do next. They agreed on the following:

> On October 31, Šling will be interrogated by three officers simultaneously, to exhaustion. Keep him off balance as much as possible and give him no time for reflection. Interrogate him like this for several hours. Quote from resolutions addressed to the CC KSČ concerning his dismissal from office, in order to break him. At the right moment, when Šling will be cracking the most, ask that incriminating evidence be brought in. A folder will be brought in labeled: Šling—Incriminating Evidence. It will be passed around so that Šling can see this label.

If this trick didn't work, Šling was to be confronted with people who were arrested at the same time he was.

The meeting also decided that Šling should get a cellmate, a security officer. That happened the following day. On *October 28,* his "cellmate" reported:

> [Šling] says he was arrested wrongfully, that he's a Communist and that not even prison can change his Communist beliefs . . . that he's suspected of espionage and that probably someone sent a typewritten espionage report

abroad in his name, in order to compromise him. He expects to be in custody very long because he cannot confess what he's asked to. He says that if any evidence against him does exist, it must be forged and that the truth shall prevail. At first he apparently wanted to commit suicide, but he's gotten over that.

Šling was not very happy about his cellmate. He didn't appreciate the subversive talk with which the agent tried to win his confidence. Šling mentioned to his interrogator that he's "locked up with an out-and-out enemy of this regime and that he [Šling] is trying to make him see the light."

On *October 29* his interrogator hinted that pretty soon he would confront Šling with incriminating material about his espionage activity. For two days, *October 30 and 31,* Šling waited for it to be produced, "or else he won't talk." He was sure the information would turn out to be forged and was prepared "to say so, just as he did about all other material that has been submitted to him."

During these two days, Šling reflected constantly about his situation and his conduct. He didn't believe he could prove his innocence, although "he did have a trump card in hand which he won't use until last. He says he is privy to very confidential information which the West would be very interested in. He thinks that not having divulged it will prove that he didn't send other reports either." At the same time "he continues to explore possibilities for suicide in the cell and was wondering how people are executed." And in a letter to his wife, Marian, that he was allowed to write, but which she never received, he assured her about his innocence and asked her to tell deputy Karla Pfeifferová "that I never have been an enemy and that everything will be cleared up."

The incriminating material didn't arrive, and that strengthened Šling's resolve. On *October 31* "the interrogation tactic employed was that of getting him depressed, asking him to talk about his hostile activity, his crimes, etc. In none of these instances was it possible to prove any connection between Šling and wrecking activity. On the contrary, some of the explanations that Šling offered suggested that some of the reports have been insufficiently verified or developed."

His cellmate also picked up on Šling's change of mood: "Yesterday Šling appeared very self-satisfied in the cell, because, he says, he realized that we are groping in the dark and have nothing on him. He apparently figured this out because he's being interrogated about trifles. He thinks we're expecting him to give something away. He says it doesn't bother him to be described during interrogations as a criminal: he thinks about other things."

Šling's self-satisfaction was premature, though. On *November 1,* "he was interrogated so as to weaken his moral resolve," according to the interrogator, in preparation for implementing the procedure outlined at the meeting of October 26. "We painted his moral profile to him as one of a traitor, a bourgeois, a careerist . . ."

The planned attack started on *November 2.* Questioning went on nonstop for twenty-two hours. Doubek later stated that "during his entire interrogation career he had never seen a suspect treated as badly as Šling was in the early interrogation sessions."[33] Doubek himself instructed his subordinates "to turn the regional secretary into cow dung."[34]

After the first seven hours of this, Šling's letter to Voska, the immediate cause for his arrest, was produced. Šling at first tried to minimize its significance. "Then he thought better of it," the interrogator wrote, "but still denied having been involved in espionage after 1945." The interrogators turned the screws a notch. Šling was "interrupted in his sleep so that he didn't sleep all night. The next morning, *November 3,* he was brought back in and the intensive interrogation proceeded with no let up." Nevertheless, he insisted "that he had committed no crimes, had been involved in no espionage." This was the report from noon.

The interrogators kept up the pressure after lunch, and achieved their first result by the evening. Šling signed a protocol which stated, "Once I saw some of the incriminating evidence and reflected on the matter, I testified as to how I turned into a spy, how I tried to disrupt the KSČ and how in the services of imperialism I sabotaged the constructive efforts of the Czechoslovak people." Interrogators wanted names of his accomplices so Šling invented a nonexistent agent Benda and recalled Mrs. Mitchell, his wartime London landlady.

After he signed the protocol, Šling was dragged to his cell. His first "confession" affected him greatly. He was very quiet and tried to figure out how to backtrack on it. His cellmate asked him "why he was kept so long, and he [Šling] said that he had admitted some bullshit. Then he asked what would happen to a prisoner who would retract in court what he had confessed to the State Security."

The interrogators reported their result to their superiors and to the Soviet advisors. The interrogation protocol went all the way up to Kopřiva's desk, along with the interrogators' self-congratulatory and self-assured report of *November 4*: "It has so far been irrefutably proven that Šling made an espionage commitment. Šling owns up to the document that proves this [the critical letter to Voska]. On this basis he admitted that he consciously and systematically worked for the British service during and after the war, right up to the day he was uncovered and arrested."

Kopřiva called a meeting that same day. Its participants assumed that Šling had been broken and that he could now be forced to testify about specifics: to name names, admit to heading an antistate group of Communist officials and discuss its plan for overthrowing the regime. They decided to continue interrogating him as severely as possible, to show Šling a picture of his wife in prison and induce him to write her a letter in which "he'll tell her that he has admitted all about his espionage activity and will appeal to her to admit everything as well."

This ministerial plan looked good on paper but didn't count with the crisis that affects every political prisoner after his first false confession. The next day, *November 5* at 3 P.M., Šling retracted his statement. The interrogator immediately reported this, stating that Šling "is confusing real and imaginary events, truth and lies, and is intent on sidetracking from the root of the matter." That night he was shown the picture of his wife. "He was very depressed and stated that his wife was innocent. He was very concerned about the children." The interrogators, furious about his retraction, brutally demanded an explanation. Šling answered that "when he saw that we have his letter to Voska, he realized nobody would believe that he did nothing beyond writing it." Therefore, to get some peace, he made up the story about Mitchell and Benda. His interrogators didn't believe him, however, because according to them, "an innocent person would not make up something like that."

The next interrogation was exceptionally harsh: on *November 6 and 7*, Šling complained to his cellmate for the first time about its brutality. "He was put under great pressure during interrogation. He had to stand all the time. When he was exhausted, he confessed," and in order to get some respite he invented a connection with the British Intelligence Service via two other people. When he was asked about other accomplices, he retracted his confession once again. "If he named names, it would turn into a big trial. At this point he checked himself and said there's no one to name anyway, because he hadn't worked with anyone."

After these developments Šling again saw his case in the darkest colors and expected the worst. "He is afraid he'll be executed. He said it would be a miscarriage of justice and that eventually, facing the court, he would deny everything he said to the State Security," his cellmate reported.

Participants of Kopřiva's November 4 meeting were upset because Šling's resistance had frustrated their plans. They also realized that apart from the letter to Voska, there really was no evidence that would so much as hint at Šling's guilt. They decided to compile a list of acquaintances whom Šling had recommended for various posts. These people would furnish the "evidence." Most of all, though, they wanted Šling himself to talk and therefore ordered that severe interrogations continue.

Another exhausting all-night session followed on *November 8.* The next morning the prisoner, at the end of his tether, looked for a way to stop the escalating terror without endangering his friends. He started fantasizing and exaggerating. He invented a variety of spies in addition to the two British ones he had conjured up earlier. He mentioned one Hamson whom he was supposed to have been meeting at the British embassy in Prague. He dreamed up a connection with Margot Gale, with one Wernington and others. He also mentioned several Communists whom he had recommended to various offices.

Suddenly Šling got scared of his tactical game which so far seemed to have worked so well; he told his cellmate "that he had made up a bunch of fairy tales and is scared that when we find out, he'll be beaten to death." And Šling added sarcastically, "What a laugh the Brits would get when they read in the paper that that ugly old hag Mitchell had recruited him for the Intelligence Service. What an embarrassment it would be for Czechoslovak security!" As for the people he recommended for offices, "he listed those most devoted to the party and is delighted to be leading us on."

Every step of Šling's "confession" invited reflection about his own fate. Now "he takes the death sentence for granted and is considering suicide." After the night-long interrogation he said, "he will struggle with State Security, with the court and under the gallows till the very end." When his cellmate told him that he'd soon be moved to another prison from where messages could be smuggled out, Šling asked him to send this one to his friends: "Deputy Šling was tough."

On *November 9,* soon after the interrogation started, Šling retracted a major part of his confession. He later explained that the people and events he had made up obviously lacked credibility. As he told his cellmate, though, the true reason was that he planned to "retract his entire testimony to date and from now on to insist on his innocence. He'll combat the exhaustion that's getting the better of him."

The struggle was uneven. Šling faced the omnipotent security with its extensive apparatus and brutal methods all alone, with only two weapons: the courage not to confess to falsehoods and tactical moves. So far he had been partly successful with both. How long could he hold out, though?

Every time he used his "weapons," the interrogators escalated their brutality. On *November 10,* they forced their victim to admit all that he had retracted the day before and demanded an even more extensive statement. Šling argued that he had done nothing else and that "any other statements he'd have to invent." The interrogator qualified this as a tactical maneuver "to prove that when the heat is on, he makes things up hoping that we will then relax." But Šling still felt strong enough to struggle. He asked his cellmate to let his friends outside know that "Šling is standing firm and is innocent. He had no other messages for anyone, he wants no help from anyone and says he's strong enough to fight his battle alone."

The dissatisfied interrogators and advisors shifted from long inter-rogations to incessant ones, in order to completely exhaust Šling physi-cally and to break him morally. On *November 11 and 12,* they launched an interrogation session, which lasted over 30 hours, with the following schedule:

November 11	1 to 6 P.M.	Doubek, Košt'ál
	6 to 8 P.M.	Musil
	8 P.M. to 8 A.M.	Jistebnický, Majer
November 12	8 A.M. to 1 P.M.	Doubek, Košt'ál
	2 to 5:30 P.M.	Musil
	6 to 10 P.M.	Doubek, Košt'ál

Even after this session, the longest to date, an interrogator reported that Šling "still refuses to expand his statements." Extreme psychological pressure didn't help either: "He was asked to write a statement request-ing a name change for his children because he wouldn't want them to carry the name of a traitor and a spy." Šling wrote the statement. He was very disturbed. Ten minutes later he protested that he had thought it over and decided that after all, he did want his children to carry his name. Both interrogators were furious. They rejected his change of mind because "he too often retracts what he signs; and what he has signed today, we consider valid." (His children's names were not changed.)

In the morning of *November 12* he returned to his cell for breakfast.

He was exhausted but "his spirit was still strong. He was sure we have nothing else on him," his cellmate wrote, "because no new evidence is being presented." But the brutality of his treatment and the anticipation of repeated and ever longer interrogations overcame his determination and courage to resist. Late in the night *from November 12 to 13,* Šling did expand his confession. Again he exaggerated and invented things, hoping he'd draw attention to their implausibility. He mentioned the names of several officials in Brno and elaborated on consultations with the fictitious Benda about party matters including removing Gottwald. He mentioned Gottwald in order to elicit greater interest in his own case.

The tactical maneuvering had one key weakness: Šling confided in his cellmate, who kept the interrogators posted. On *November 14,* this cellmate reported:

> [Šling] is constantly afraid that he'll be severely punished once investigation reveals that he has been inventing fairy tales even during the last interrogation. [He told his cellmate that the tales were designed to sidetrack the investigation from the original charge.] Originally he made up a story on the spur of the moment but retracted it when he saw it wouldn't fly. He prepared the second story much better. He will retract everything at the trial where he will easily demonstrate that he had invented everything during the investigation. On top of everything else, that will embarrass the instigator of his arrest.

His latest confession helped Šling only up to a point, because its content didn't fit the concept of the show trial very well. Šling mentioned only insignificant provincial officials, and Benda and company (his British spies) couldn't be verified. Making up the stories, however, didn't dismay his interrogators one bit. They treated them all as facts, albeit incomplete ones.

On *November 15,* they threatened him with a punishment cell and persecution of his children. On *November 16,* "he talked [in his cell] only about his fear of the punishment cell and his anxiety about the fate of his children." From *November 17 to 21* his interrogators focused on expanding his testimony further. "Despite all efforts it has not been possible to have Šling [provide further details] about matters which he has already mentioned." On *November 22 and 23* the interrogators capitalized on Šling's fears and put him in the punishment cell.

This was a pitch-dark, filthy cellar with no heating, light, ventilation, water, or even a cot. Šling emerged from it unbroken. He told his cellmate (*November 24*) that "he doesn't know what will happen to him, that they want him to talk about things of which he knows nothing, which he cannot do," and later (*November 25*), that "he cannot tell them what they want to hear because he doesn't know anything. He insists he'll state that in court, too. . . . He's worried [*November 26*] that even harsher interrogations are in store for him."

The interrogators actually suggested what kind of people they were interested in: higher party officials. Šling wondered "whom to mention so that they leave him alone." On November 26 he decided to mention people so highly positioned that nobody could possibly doubt their loyalty to the party. Thus the protocol of *November 27* indicated that "Otto Šling had working contacts with Marie Švermová, Josef Frank, Jaromír Dolanský, Bedřich Geminder, Bruno Köhler [and] Rudolf Slánský." He certainly did pick out the party's best—members of the CC KSČ presidium and leading officials of its secretariat.

Šling wasn't sure, however, that his plan worked. These names weren't nearly as important to him as to his interrogators. He incidentally told his cellmate "that he had mentioned some names during the session but carefully picked people who cannot be arrested. He said nothing bad about anyone."

Again, as after every confession, he worried about his own case and his own fate. His resolve to retract the statements alternated with thoughts of suicide. Struggle alternated with resignation, hope with hopelessness. He said he would "retract everything he has signed so far. But also, to be at peace, he wants to exasperate the interrogators and force them to treat him so roughly that he will succumb physically."

Šling's latest testimony infuriated the interrogators and the advisors. They were not interested in officials in such high positions. They saw through Šling's intention of naming unassailable people (or rather, people so far unassailable). His statement would not help prepare a show trial. The regular meeting in Minister Kopřiva's office decided that next time Kopřiva himself should interrogate Šling. This seemed promising, for Kopřiva and Šling were old acquaintances.

Šling's questioning, which took place on *December 4* in Kopřiva's office (in the presence of Boyarski, Šváb, and Doubek), took a theatrical turn. Kopřiva lost his temper and yelled at Šling that the party had already condemned him and would force him to make the right statements; he pushed Šling about and threatened to crack his ribs; and he shouted that evidence existed about hostile activity of an organized group of high party officials, led by Šling, that wanted to gain control of the party and overthrow the regime. (Six years later Doubek stated

Slánský accompanying Marie Švermová, widow of the Czechoslovak World War II resistance fighter Jan Šverma and member of the Central Committee of the Communist Party of Czechoslovakia, as they leave Jan Šverma's grave in Mnichovo Hradište, Southern Moravia, Dec. 15, 1950

that Kopřiva also beat Šling on this occasion.)[35] It was all in vain. Šling said nothing new. The infuriated Kopřiva ordered him imprisoned in the building of the ministry and instructed that physical violence be used during interrogations.

Šling spent several of the cruellest days of his life in the punishment cell. He lived on bread and water, he couldn't sit or sleep, he was straightjacketed, and the interrogators beat him with fists and batons. The cell was unheated and while the interrogators, particularly Košt'ál, walked around in winter coats and hats, Šling was dressed in light prison garb with no shoes. Šváb often took part in the unending interrogations; he threatened Šling and repeated several times that he "will not get out of this, and not to think that he'll retract everything at the trial."

Following the advisors' instructions (which Kopřiva passed on to the interrogators as his own), the sessions focused on Šling's coconspirators and methods; however, even his terrible treatment on the ministry premises failed to yield the fast results anticipated. Šling continued to deny the existence of accomplices and didn't name anyone. Eventually he named a couple of comrades with whom he had been in routine working contact. Some he named merely in self-defense: such as Marie Švermová who, according to Šling, knew about all his party work. This piece of information was useful. It became the cornerstone of the enemy conspiracy concept. As will be discussed later, Švermová fell under suspicion.

Minister Kopřiva interrogated Šling again. Now, in *mid-December,* the composition of his attendants was changed slightly: Šváb, now himself under a cloud as Švermová's brother, was absent. Meanwhile Šling, trying to save his neck, contemplated an additional confession. He dreamed up an attempted change in the party leadership, with all the details. When Kopřiva started screaming, flailing his fists, threatening even harsher interrogations and appealing that he talk about the plot within the party, Šling produced his story: a national conference of shock workers, he said, was to pass a motion of nonconfidence in Slánský, who would then be dismissed from his post of general secretary of the party.

Both Kopřiva and the Soviet advisor were disappointed: they dismissed the fabrication out of hand, saying, "[T]his is not how conspiracies are hatched and no one would believe such amateurism." And they pressed Šling even harder to name his accomplices in the state administration, the economic apparatus, in the army, security, and the party.

The second ministerial interrogation made no progress in Šling's confession. Nevertheless, combined with eleven days in the punishment cell it wasn't entirely fruitless. Šling returned to his Ruzyně cell a changed man. He was experiencing a psychological crisis. He recognized that there was no way out and that no effective resistance was possible. He was broken. He realized, as he said to his cellmate, that on October 6, 1950, when he was arrested, "he died one way or the other; that is, either he'll be beaten to death or executed judicially" and "expressed his belief that one day, perhaps much later, after his death, it will all come to light and his name will be cleared." He compared his position with political trials in Soviet-bloc countries. He compared the State Security command and his interrogators to the practices of Genrikh Yagoda, the former Soviet interior minister. He compared the KSK leadership, which was gathering charges against him, to Nikolai Yezhov, the well-known Soviet hangman. He didn't believe in the truth of the Rajk trial "and even the Tito story is not the way the Cominform presents it."

In the second half of December, Šling took stock of his own psychological crisis and realized he lacked the strength for further resistance and tactical maneuvering. He also realized that his exaggerations and refusal to testify had been ineffective. His Communist ideals had completely collapsed: he was terrified by his mendacious and grotesque environment and horrified to realize what the party leaders were actually expecting of him. In this frame of mind he tried to bring the incessant cruelties to a halt and to weaken the pressure of the interrogators. That, however, could be achieved only by confessing everything they wanted.

Consequently, the names of Šling's co-workers started appearing in the protocols in January 1951. The interrogators were satisfied and moderated their handling of Šling. The endless brutal sessions ceased, and conditions in the cell improved. Šling even started debating with Doubek and cooperated in writing up the protocols.

Šling mentioned some of his friends, acquaintances, and officials of various institutions with whom he had had working relationships. For Šling, these were just people he had known. For the interrogators, though, this was the fabric of the conspiracy. And here they clashed again. Šling refused to jeopardize those he named. The moment his interrogators implicated them in the conspiracy and asked him to testify accordingly, he refused. These people didn't do anything, he said, "he cannot make the required statements because he doesn't know anything more." Later he argued that he had ticked them off for "wrecking activity" but hadn't actually involved them yet. His interrogators merely laughed at his reservations. They picked out whomever they needed for their conspiracy and even figured out its objective: to substitute Švermová for Slánský as general secretary of the party. The advisors and the interrogators finished developing this concept in February 1951. Šling rejected it more and more feebly and finally accepted it. He was powerless.

On *February 4, 1951*, an interrogator questioned Šling about his relationship with Rudolf Slánský. The protocol records this answer:

> *Šling*: Švermová and I had criticized Rudolf Slánský's positions and opinions even earlier, and the two of us led a campaign against him in this regard.
> *Interrogator*: Why did you want to remove Rudolf Slánský?
> *Šling*: Because Rudolf Slánský consistently defended the policy of alliance with the Soviet Union and with all people's democracies, and policies benefiting the working class. We opposed him especially because he was a serious obstacle in our struggle to overthrow the entire people's democratic policy of building socialism, inasmuch as he occupied the decisive party office. Since there was no way of influencing him, he had to be dismissed, that is, removed.

WIDESPREAD ARRESTS

Let us return from prison to political life. Officials of the Brno region learned about Šling's arrest on October 10, from Josef Frank (CC KSČ secretary) and Bruno Köhler. Meetings were then organized in factories, communities, and districts. The party welcomed Šling's arrest. A KSK representative reported to Prague that "The decision didn't surprise most people. In fact, it had been longingly and impatiently anticipated. The party is now reviving and the creative initiative of the masses is flourishing, as evidenced by pledges made in the factories."[36] This was typical of the information about the response.

The CC KSČ presidium wanted a resolution about the case, and Köhler drafted it by adapting his own earlier draft of a Šling resolution, which had been relatively complimentary. The tenor of the changes was clear from its new title: "On Uncovering an Enemy Agent in Brno and on Eliminating the Political Consequences of His Activity." While Köhler originally dealt with political errors, now he described the same events as activity of the enemy. Šling had, in his view, turned into "a spy of Western imperialists and a long-time collaborator of intelligence services of our republic's enemies." Gottwald and Slánský added some final touches on November 9, and Köhler's draft was approved and published. The Brno regional KSČ committee discussed it the next day, lower-level party authorities followed, and eventually the entire party reviewed and approved of the measures taken against the "spy and enemy."[37] The center was satisfied. Even so, the campaign unleashed certain dissonant voices as well. Officials in the Brno region were particularly insistent that certain members of the CC KSČ secretariat face the consequences, and demanded their self-criticism. Švermová, Dolanský, and others were mentioned by name.

Security measures unfolded in tandem with the political campaign. Many officials were dismissed and arrested. They included not only Šling's partisans but also additional "enemies" who could buttress the great conspiracy concept. The purge vacated many important positions, opening up career opportunities for lower-level personnel. In Brno alone hundreds were dismissed and dozens arrested.[38]

Thus on November 6 a special team was formed and charged with surveillance, interrogation, and unmasking of security officers who were in some way related to Šling. This "Operation B" was fruitful. Five weeks later, on December 14, the team provided background on a number of security personnel including commanders. All were later arrested.[39]

However, if the purge was to serve up suspects for the great conspiracy, it had to spread way beyond the Brno region and acquire a broader, national scope.

On November 13, the CC KSČ presidium ordered the CC KSČ secretariat to carefully investigate (along party rather than security lines) and "reexamine all officials whom Šling had placed in the party and state apparatus."[40] An "Extraordinary Commission for the Brno Case" was put in charge, headed by Köhler and Baramová. Bruno Köhler, who spearheaded and directed its activity, had actually kicked off its work already on November 8.

The seven working teams of the commission focused on searching out Šling's people (1) in the party, (2) in the economy, (3) in the state apparatus, (4) among Spanish veterans, (5) among former exiles in London, (6) in "illegal groups" in Brno, and (7) Trotskyites. As instructed by the CC KSČ secretariat, Baramová would immediately inform Minister Kopřiva about the most serious cases.[41] The commission finished its work by the end of 1950 and on January 3, 1951, reported its results to Gottwald: it had examined over 6,000 personnel files and uncovered a list of Šling's people in important positions eleven typewritten pages long.[42]

Leading political and security circles did not doubt that Šling's arrest had put them on the trail of the great conspiracy. Many, however, wondered whether it was headed by Šling or someone even higher up. Boyarski put this question to Taussigová; and both agreed that Šling was unlikely to have been its leader.

The focus shifted to Marie Švermová, who was a very popular personality in the party, both in her own right and as the widow of Jan Šverma, a Communist leader who lost his life during the Slovak National Uprising. She was a member of both the CC KSČ presidium and, as its secretary, of its secretariat.

After Šling's arrest, the Party Control Commission (KSK) pointed out that improper methods of work had been introduced into the party by the CC KSČ organization department, which had highly praised Šling and had even sent other regional KSČ secretaries to study Brno's experiences. Švermová headed this department. Other officials of the CC KSČ and in the regions also pointed to her close connections with Šling. Köhler said that certain regional KSČ secretaries "were forming a faction with Švermová." He was referring to a regular meeting of regional KSČ secretaries in Carlsbad that he had attended, too.[43] While the atmosphere was charged against Švermová, the actual impulse to take measures against her came from security: reports about Šling's interrogations (which were sent to Gottwald, Slánský, and Kopřiva) emphasized Šling's references to Švermová.

On December 14, the CC KSČ presidium discussed Gottwald's report on the Šling case and approved his motion that Švermová take a vacation and that she not perform her official duties or participate in party meetings until the next CC KSČ session.[44] Gottwald spoke with her several days before this meeting, and "spent an entire hour explaining how she should handle it," namely, to say everything she knew about Šling.[45]

Soon after the meeting, Švermová was subject to a party investigation. On January 22, the CC KSČ presidium appointed Václav Kopecký, Gustav Bareš, and Bruno Köhler to "investigate the political issues connected with the matter of M. Švermová" and to prepare a report with recommendations about the Šling case for the next CC KSČ session.[46]

Köhler took charge of the investigation even before the team actually met and conducted it in his typical manner, along both party and security lines. On the basis of Šling's forced statements, Köhler formulated a series of questions for Švermová and informed security about her answers. He also suggested additional questions for Šling. Since Köhler had known Švermová for some twenty years, his investigation had a rather informal, unofficial tone. But while the tone was informal, its substance was hard-hitting, as indicated by the questions for Šling:

Slánský (*right*) and one of the leading Czechoslovak resistance fighters, Jan Šverma
(*second from left*), in the Slovak mountains during the Slovak National Uprising, 1944

Were you, as a spy, interested in winning Máňa [Marie Švermová] for
yourself, in worming your way into the Šverma family and so to further
strengthen your criminal influence on the party?
Did Máňa see through you? Did you really want to have Máňa in your
grip, as she states?
Are you trying to say that Máňa is lying? What do you have to say about

what she has said? Máňa states that you used to manhandle comrades with jujitsu throws . . . Are you denying what she said? Is jujitsu a method of a Communist official or of an Intelligence Service agent?

Švermová was asked similarly phrased questions. However, Köhler and, later, members of his investigation team were not satisfied with her answers. He told her on November 28 that "her statements won't help us uncover Šling and Šlingism." Two weeks after the interrogation, she started believing in "Šling's hostile activity" and wrote Gottwald that she "sees ever more clearly the intrigues against the party and against the republic that this involved: all the heavier my blame." On January 9 she said to her interrogators: "I admit mistakes; but if you try to turn me into a criminal, I'll defend myself."

On January 26, she told Gottwald that she didn't have the slightest idea "about all these matters" and admitted certain political errors. The team, however, was not satisfied with errors: it wanted crimes.

On January 28, the CC KSČ presidium informed CC KSČ members that Švermová wasn't admitting anything and that she was shielding agents and traitors; she was to be detained. Two days later, Švermová wrote to Köhler's team: "The feeling that you don't believe me, comrades, weighs heavily on me. Comrade Kopecký has told me several times: 'So far you haven't said anything bad about Šling, you haven't even called him a villain or a scoundrel, and you haven't even said that you detest him.'" But Švermová stated that she denounced him for the damage he did to the party.[47]

Years later, Švermová wrote about this investigation:

> The team held me in isolation, under State Security guard, from January 29, 1951, until the CC KSČ session of February 21, 1951. Team members visited me twice and insisted that I confess. A day before the CC KSČ session they all sharply rebuked me for not wanting to confess even at that last minute. I asked them, in vain, what confession they are looking for. Kopecký finally stated that I had passed up my last chance but I still didn't know what he was talking about.[48]

Švermová's struggle, her effort to comprehend what was going on and to defend herself using reason and facts led nowhere. Security had by now completed their concept of "a conspiracy within the KSČ," in which they assigned her a leading role.

Šling's case supplied a useful pretext and impulse for a campaign against Spanish veterans and communists from London exile. Suspicions of Spanish veterans had mounted ever since the Rajk case. Karel Šváb had traded information about them with his Hungarian counterparts, and the StB had a special department focusing on them. After Šling's arrest, activity around them became even more feverish. Šling mentioned a number of his friends from Spain. Some had high positions, especially in the armed forces. Köhler was particularly active in uncovering Spanish veterans. He and Kopřiva decided to establish a so-called evaluation group which processed a large amount of material from the national-security ministry building, as well as statements of a number of Spanish veterans.

Köhler picked Bohumil Klícha, a parliamentary deputy and KSK member, to head the evaluation group. Other members included Pravoslav Janoušek, an NKVD officer who had once been retired from security services because of maltreatment of suspects, but now was a protégé of advisor Boyarski; Dr. Mudra, who had spent time in a forced-labor camp for his brutality during interrogations but who now found favor with the KSK; Dr. Bohumil Smola of the notorious Náchod group; and Alois Samec, who was recommended by Taussigová. The group's Soviet advisor was Smirnov, who targeted its activity particularly on Spanish veterans in high positions. The group had secret offices in a building in Melounova Street, provided by Defense Minister Alexej Čepička. The team studied files of the national-security ministry and of the KSK, which were hauled in, and depositions of Spanish veterans Jarin Hošek, Miloš Nekvasil, and their friend Andrej Keppert (who had collaborated with Soviet security since 1945). Particularly important were personnel evaluations prepared during and after the Spanish Civil War by special sections of the Comintern which focused on uncovering Trotskyites.[49]

The composition and the activity of the group corresponded to its charter: to uncover enemies, Trotskyites, and agents among the Spanish veterans, so that the engineers of the show trial could incorporate them into their concept. Members of the group were very active. Their reports amounted to collections of half-truths, slander, lies, and fabrications. It is hard to tell whether they themselves believed what they wrote. Their work was affected by two factors: One, almost all of them personally hated Spanish veterans in high security positions—who had demoted them or punished them in the past. This was why they had joined the group in the first place. Two, Smirnov was pleased with their reports because they contained what he needed: grounds for arrests. More than ten years after the fact, on January 26, 1963, Alois Samec spoke about the work of his group: "The reports which we prepared in Melounova

Street were for information only. Without proper verification they couldn't have served anyone, not even the stupidest security official, as grounds for arrest."[50] Which is of course exactly what they did serve.

Very important in this campaign against Spanish veterans was the attack against leading security officials: Deputy Minister Josef Pavel, State Security Chief Osvald Závodský and others. Šling's arrest transformed the complicated situation within the security apparatus—ridden with conflicts over power, turf, and authority—into a full-blown crisis. Deputy Minister Karel Šváb fell under suspicion that as Švermová's brother, he wasn't really interested in uncovering the "conspiracy." His lack of success in ferreting out enemies in the party was considered to be deliberate. Toward the end of 1950, he lost the confidence of the advisors and only marked time at the ministry.

The weakening of Šváb's position left the security field open for the KSK and Taussigová in particular. For quite some time she and her co-workers had been collecting information about leading security officers. They doubted the ability and willingness of some of them to bring the Šling case to a conclusion, as reflected in a KSK letter addressed to Slánský, of November 27, 1950:

> [Certain facts] raise serious doubts about [security commanders'] ability or willingness to conclude the Šling case thoroughly and systematically. State Security Chief O. Závodský, his deputy I. Milén, offensive commander O. Valeš, and a number of others represent an in-group which cooperated with Šling either in Spain or in England or after 1945 here, and they are all loyal to one another . . . This implies (a) that leading positions in security are occupied by people who knew about the wrecking activity of Šling and others, covered up for them, and sabotaged their interrogations after the party instructed that they be arrested, [and] (b) that the line of com. Šváb is in one direction identical with [that of] these people, in the sense that [they all want] State Security to control the party.

The letter called for an investigation of State Security "in which a foreign espionage agency has over the years built up a second position, dating back to the [Nazi] occupation."[51]

Taussigová and her colleagues were determined to have the security apparatus investigated. She later described where these efforts led:

> After discussing it in the KSK . . . we concluded that it is important to investigate the security apparatus along party lines. Inasmuch as Slánský was in charge of the CC KSČ security department, I approached him [in the letter of November 27, 1950] . . . We wanted to submit our recommendation to the

CC KSČ presidium. Slánský agreed and requested that I submit a written recommendation that same day at the presidium meeting . . . Soon after that Kopřiva summoned me and said that our recommendation had been approved and that Gottwald decided that the three of us—he, the Soviet advisor Boyarski, and I—figure out how to review the working methods of the security apparatus.[52]

In a letter of December 17, addressed to Kopřiva and Boyarski, Taussigová proposed two alternative methods for reviewing security's leading officers—no longer *only* its working methods. First, however, she answered Boyarski's question as to who headed the conspiracy. It wasn't Šling, she declared: "[The question] can only be answered with a hypothesis. Only the State Security can find the truth, so long as its top positions are in the hands of people who are unconditionally loyal to the party and to the working class and who work in closest cooperation with the party."

As for the review, she proposed a sharper and milder alternative:

[The sharper one:] Even though someone may be temporarily harmed, immediately dismiss comrades Šváb, Závodský, Valeš, Dr. [Karel] Černý, and others. After studying the materials . . . give all those who have family or friendly ties with those mentioned a leave of absence. Pending completion of the review, fill the vacancies with reliable party officials.

[The milder one:] Plant a KSK official who would pretend to be in training for a high job in security but who in fact will keep an eye on certain people and certain activities, report on what he finds and enlist informants to cooperate with the KSK.[53]

Boyarski was very impressed by Taussigová's letter. He took note of its author "who sees matters more clearly than the minister." The two of them and Kopřiva eventually decided to pursue the second alternative. All three firmly believed that the leadership of security was rife with enemies from among Spanish veterans. Taussigová later related the key moments of that meeting:

Boyarski had me explain why I suggested the review [of security]. And I told him everything I knew and how I felt . . . At that time, as is well known, all key positions in security were in the hands of former Spanish volunteers who, indeed, were responsible for the functioning of security. Cominform's Yugoslav resolution and the Rajk trial, the veracity of which I didn't doubt, taught me to heighten vigilance against these people . . . I also said, for example, that I feared that instead of the minister commanding security in the interests of the working class, some wild joker was trying to lead it astray, against these interests and against the party. Kopřiva nodded in agreement with this and other statements and Boyarski gave me full support, on the basis of Soviet experiences. I was elated at the confidence the party showed in me, and flattered that the leading Soviet advisor's views on security methods fully agreed with my own feelings and opinions. [The CC KSČ presidium had put Boyarski in control of security.] Thus it happened that I agreed without exception with all his recommendations as to how the review should be conducted . . . Boyarski in fact gathered all the critical voices, real or fabricated, which came either from Kopřiva's safe, or from the KSK, or from [Josef] Hora who had identified them during his review of branches of the security ministry and had them administratively processed by the KSK in personnel files. I was satisfied when Boyarski assured me in front of Kopřiva that he will have his own apparatus appropriately verify all the documentation. In short, I was happy to know that everything had reached the proper hands.[54]

Boyarski visited Taussigová several times on his own initiative by mid-February 1951. He was looking for help in uncovering the conspiracy within the KSČ.

I was surprised by the reason why Boyarski personally sought me out at the KSK. He said he feared for our party . . . He asked me whether I had ever considered that the KSČ might also be the target of a conspiracy similar to the Hungarian one . . . Boyarski pointed to the spies who had already been uncovered, including Reicin, Šling and others, and who were of course bound to have their center somewhere, and asked me where I thought this center might be. I said that for sure one center was in London and the other probably in Moscow. To this day I can see how Boyarski's expression suddenly changed. He asked sharply: "In Moscow? What do you mean?" I was thinking of the London center of the Intelligence Service and the agents that they or the Gestapo had recruited and sent to the USSR.[55]

Josef Hora, mentioned by Taussigová, was the KSK member sent to the national-security ministry to be "trained" in one department after another "for a high position." (In 1951 he would indeed become the StB chief for some ten months.) He passed on his findings about "enemy activity" to Taussigová, who forwarded them to Kopřiva and Boyarski. He also recruited informers, especially from the Náchod group. Their statements were processed by J. Hůla of the KSK, who made depositions about this work on September 30, 1955, and again on August 30, 1957:

Hora was to send informers from among State Security personnel over to the KSK where I was supposed to interview them . . . As far as I remember, I interviewed comrades [Bohumil] Smola, [Karel] Arasin, and [J.] Čermák who reported mostly about the enemy activity of Šváb. [I further interviewed] one comrade who charged Valeš with antistate activity, and [A.] Bouda, a former security officer from the Prague Command who had investigated the Schramm murder and who testified against [Štěpán] Plaček and [Bedřich] Pokorný.[56]

Given the turmoil in the StB command, the party leadership needed to create a separate force it really could trust. In early January 1951, Köhler gave Bohumil Klícha a new assignment: to establish and direct a special school for members of the people's militia, the armed units of the KSČ. Köhler handed Klícha the files on about a hundred members of the People's Militia, a paramilitary organization under exclusive KSČ control. Klícha was to handpick twenty or so, whom Köhler then invited to join the training. Each was told that he had been selected to fulfill an important top-secret task which the party could not entrust even to the security authorities.[57]

According to the deposition of Alois Samec, around January 20, 1951, advisor Smirnov told the group in Melounova Street "as a great secret that arrests [of top security personnel] are about to start and he gave us three days to wrap up all the cases we were working on."

A week later Kopřiva invited the branded security commanders to his office, supposedly to take part in a top-secret operation lasting several days. As they left his office, one by one, they got into cars where the militia from the secret school were waiting for them. They were driven out of Prague and handcuffed as they passed the building of the General Staff. The drivers opened an envelope with the destination: the Koloděje prison.

Arrests continued. Clementis was arrested the following day, as a result of a charade called "Operation Stones." He was kidnapped while taking a walk and driven off westward, until the car passed the stones marking Czechoslovakia's border. Clementis found himself at a West German police station. Officers in German and American uniforms welcomed him and inquired about the reasons for his defection. Clementis demanded to be taken back to Prague.

The border markers, the border patrol, and the American officers were all decoys. Clementis was driven to Koloděje, and a report for the country's top officials stated that he had been arrested while trying to escape abroad. Gottwald's personal secretary noted: "Gottwald chuckled that Clementis's arrest was arranged as he tried to drive across the border."[58]

A number of Spanish veterans serving in the army were arrested in the following days, as were Slovak politicians Gustáv Husák, Ladislav

Novomeský, Daniel Okáli, and Ladislav Holdoš. On February 6, three regional KSČ secretaries were invited to a meeting with Bruno Köhler. They were arrested on their way out. Bedřich Reicin, who had been responsible for the arrests of dozens of innocent people, was himself arrested two days later. As recently as February 1 he had plaintively and despairingly complained to Gottwald about being shadowed: "And now they take me for a criminal whose every step has to be watched . . . Instead I'm reeling in despair because although nobody questions me about anything and no one wants to know anything, I'm branded by the surveillance itself. I have one request: that my matter be discussed as soon as possible."[59]

The wave of arrests ended on February 16, with the detention of Šváb. It had, meanwhile, swept up some fifty high officials of the party and state administration. They included former minister Vladimír Clementis; deputy ministers Artur London, Josef Pavel, Karel Šváb, and Bedřich Reicin; deputies of the Slovak National Council Gustáv Husák, Ladislav Novomeský, and Ladislav Holdoš; security commanders Osvald Závodský, Ivo Milén, Oskar Valeš, and Karel Černý; regional KSČ secretaries Mikuláš Landa, Vítězslav Fuchs, Hanuš Lomský, and Ervin Polák; army officers Otakar Hromádko and Bedřich Kopold; and army generals Vladimír Drnec, Šimon Drgač, Zdeněk Novák, and Rudolf Bulander. They provided a wide enough selection of people to construct a grand conspiracy. The arrests were recommended by Ladislav Kopřiva and Vladimir Boyarski and approved by the country's four leading officials: Klement Gottwald, Rudolf Slánský, Antonín Zápotocký, and Alexej Čepička, sometimes by Jaromír Dolanský, and (as for the Slovaks) by Viliam Široký.[60]

The names of Bruno Köhler and Jarmila Taussigová come up very often in this story. Köhler successfully played the role of a gray eminence. He was an experienced Communist politician of German nationality, trained by the Comintern, a collaborator of Soviet security, a ruthless executor of Moscow's instructions, always extremely successful as a political hatchet man. He was universally feared, and after the war he was shunted aside as a German; nevertheless, his climb back to power was determined and unscrupulous. He demonstrated extraordinary energy in seeking out enemies while in charge of the CC KSČ personnel department.

Jarmila Taussigová, a prewar KSČ official, was equally fanatic about uncovering class enemies. She was continually recommending new reviews and checks of officials and of institutions, which invariably resulted in arrests and political trials.

Köhler and Taussigová were at war with each other, both striving for the laurels of seeking out enemies. Their battle over control of State Security was a part of it. After the wide-ranging arrests, their positions were about equal. Both profited from the removal of their former competitor Šváb and of the security commanders. Both kept in close contact with Boyarski and enjoyed his confidence. Minister Kopřiva feared them both; both of them had their own people in the security apparatus.

THE FIRST CONCEPT

All the officials arrested in January and February of 1951 were held in the Koloděje castle near Prague. Military and security personnel hastily transformed its cellars into prison cells and its rooms into interrogation offices. Soviet advisors and Kopřiva visited Koloděje two days before unleashing the wave of arrests and declared the adaptations to be satisfactory. The reality, however, was dreadful, the conditions gruesome: the cellars lacked elementary plumbing; there were no windows for light or ventilation; many prisoners suffered frostbite in the unheated cells. The conditions were exacerbated by insufficient and often execrable food.

Soviet advisors controlled the interrogations, but only seldom did they take an active part in them; they were actually conducted by two groups of interrogators. The first, headed by Bohumil Doubek, consisted mostly of members of the StB's Interrogation Bureau; the second group, headed by Pravoslav Janoušek, consisted of the so-called Náchod group and "returnees" (e.g., Dr. Mudra)—people previously dismissed from security service who had been recalled.

Both groups were augmented by students of the special People's Militia school, and by four so-called working-class prosecutors. None of the interrogators were really qualified to do their work. As a rule they lacked the necessary education and experience. Many worked as interrogators for the first time ever, or had only a few months behind them. They didn't know how to write protocols. They didn't know the laws (what was and wasn't legal). Then again, that didn't interest them: the party had given them instructions to follow.

In 1955 Doubek stated that as chief of interrogations he detained and released people "without the knowledge of the prosecutor's office, which I usually didn't inform about such matters because I felt it was good enough to get the OK of the minister or of his deputy. I didn't even know I was supposed to keep the prosecutor's office informed." And in 1963, Kopřiva stated to a KSČ commission: "Yes, the arrests were not made in accordance with the laws, but at that time those were ignored. Only later was it stipulated that laws had to be observed."[61]

The interrogator confronted the prisoner with only one guideline: here's an enemy, an agent, a Trotskyite, a traitor; and it's your party duty "to fix him up for it." The interrogator had no evidence to go on, other than the prisoner himself; "fixing him up for it" meant turning him into a source of "evidence." So much for the party duty. The interrogators did their best and competed in their achievements.

They started with biographies: the prisoner recited his life story, and the interrogator "uncovered" dark spots in it, which the prisoner had to clarify. This method was only partly successful because the interrogators were essentially illiterate in interpreting political events. Hence the second alternative: to beat a confession of fabricated charges out of a prisoner. Duress and psychological pressure were the main methods of interrogation. Prisoners were beaten and deprived of sleep; they had to march around their cells for days and nights on end; they were deprived of food and drink; and they were given no assistance when sick. Two members of the People's Militia seconded to Koloděje actually refused to use these methods. They felt that "the methods are too harsh even for class enemies." Since "they couldn't return to their original jobs for security reasons, they were put on kitchen patrol to peel potatoes."[62]

Duress, psychological pressure, and appeals to the prisoners that their party duty called for confessions eventually brought results. Boyarski's concept of a grand conspiracy within the KSČ was gradually fleshed out. It was "confirmed" by the accumulation of partial confessions to nonexistent crimes. Its authors kept refashioning the concept until it acquired its final form: a group of enemies headed by Švermová and Šling had been preparing a party coup aimed at removing Gottwald, Slánský, and Zápotocký. Clementis, Husák, and the other Slovaks had similar objectives.

This concept of an intraparty coup was politically approved at the highest KSČ levels. On January 28, the CC KSČ presidium postponed a planned CC KSČ session (to February 21–24) because Šling had not yet admitted preparing the coup and because Švermová, who admitted political errors in her January 26 letter to Gottwald, never admitted to any plotting either. The Kopecký-Köhler-Bareš commission was waiting for their confessions to finish its report. The pressure on Šling and others therefore escalated further. Švermová was detained. On February 20, the eve of the CC KSČ session, the CC KSČ presidium discussed the presentations that were to be delivered by Kopecký and Štefan Bašťovanský, and resolved: "(1) to approve the submitted reports but have comrades Kopecký and Bašťovanský incorporate remarks from the discussion; (2) to present the recommendations to the CC KSČ session on behalf of the presidium."[63]

Kopecký's report to the CC KSČ session contained truly fantastic charges augmented by the author's imagination and his theatrical delivery. His commission presented all the fabrications of the advisors and the forced confessions as proven truths and vividly outlined their political consequences. Thus the report declared that Šling "left for England in 1939, already an agent of the Anglo-American intelligence service." After February 1948, this service instructed him "to develop nefarious activities similar to Rajk's in Hungary and Kostov's in Bulgaria," and to "force a change in the party leadership."

> Acting in unison under the mantle of healthy interventions in the party, under the slogan of installing a new, youthful leadership, [Šling and his group] planned at a given moment to issue a call for an extraordinary KSČ conference. With the help of delegates secured by Šling-like regional KSČ secretaries, they would have then effected a coup in the party leadership, leading to a subsequent change in government. They already had a candidate in the wings to take over the position of the general secretary from R. Slánský [namely, Marie Švermová]. This candidate had to know Šling as a cynic, a thug, a criminal, and a murderer of his own mother . . . The party will [therefore] also treat M. Švermová without remorse as a criminal enemy.

Kopecký's speech was officially entitled "The Report of the CC KSČ Presidium's Investigation Commission on the Case of O. Šling, M. Švermová, and Other Criminal Malefactors and Conspirators." It was followed by Štefan Bašťovanský's report on "Uncovering the Espionage and Sabotage Activity of V. Clementis, and on the Factional Anti-Party Group of Bourgeois Nationalists in the Communist Party of Slovakia." Bašťovanský described the political errors of the "nationalists," pinpointed in 1950, as treason, espionage, and hostile activity.[64]

Švermová attended the meeting and later described her feelings:

> I left for the meeting after having been totally isolated for three weeks. I was accompanied by StB personnel and kept apart from other central committee members. I was prepared to refute the charges raised against me by

the members of the [Kopecký] commission and clarify what I did feel guilty of. During the entire interrogation it never dawned on me that I could be expelled from the party. Kopecký's report, which he presented on behalf of the investigation commission, shocked me all the more. I was being accused of conspiring to effect a party and government coup.[65]

In this unbearable atmosphere, ostracized by her own comrades, Švermová lost the courage to struggle. In the end she submitted to the party and talked in a different vein than she had originally intended:

This is the most difficult moment of my life . . . I have no excuse for my guilt. If someone doesn't recognize a criminal [Šling] even after five years, he has no right to be excused, no right for any appeals.

I accept any punishment, and I repeat: however great it is, it will not make up for my offenses against the party. Let my case serve as a warning to all party members and officials. I would like to add one thing here: I want you to believe that I had nothing to do with the vile and criminal plan to remove the party leadership. I may have been stripped of my party membership but believe me, I am sincere when I say: Long live our party and her son, K. Gottwald! Long live the Soviet Union and com. Stalin![66]

Not even this humiliation sufficed. Participants of the session weren't looking for an apology but for an unconditional confession of treason. Some of them ferociously attacked Švermová. The worst were her long-time co-workers:

Taussigová: Only a person who detests the party and the working class can behave as she does . . . Expelling her from the party will formally confirm her true loyalty: loyalty to the bourgeoisie, the archenemy of the party and our country.

Bareš: What she practiced and advocated, under Šling's influence, was in effect the political line and orientation that the Intelligence Service, the enemy agency, needed in Czechoslovakia.

Kopecký, in closing: For years I have had this feeling that Švermová is completely insincere. I thought of her as a devil with an angel's face. Today this angelic, hypocritical mask has been torn off and we see her real face: the face of a convicted malefactor and enemy of the party.[67]

The CC KSČ session ended on February 24, 1951. It approved the reports, that is, the concept of the great conspiracy, which thus became the binding political line for the producers of the show trial. The participants enthusiastically applauded Gottwald's repeated statement that Czechoslovakia would never be a second Yugoslavia. Švermová was arrested as she left the meeting hall and taken to Koloděje. The next day, a political campaign was unleashed. Party officials and members were acquainted with Kopecký's and Bašťovanský's reports. Invited by the central committee, party organizations expressed their opinions. Naturally they were all in agreement with the CC KSČ session, and demanded the strictest possible punishment for the traitors. The CC KSČ secretariat received hundreds of such resolutions from regional, district, and basic KSČ organizations. Some were published in the press. The interrogators included recitation of these resolutions as part of their interrogation plans and used them to pressure their victims psychologically.[68]

After a month in Koloděje, the investigation of the case shifted to the Ruzyně prison in Prague, but soon after the CC KSČ session it ran into difficulties. Advisors and interrogators were having trouble building up their concept of a great conspiracy. The interrogation progressed very slowly and then bogged down completely. Šling kept retracting and changing his statements. Švermová admitted political mistakes but rejected their classification as criminal acts. She was interrogated by one J. Roček who was supposed to extract admissions corresponding to Kopecký's report. Even he, however, didn't believe the charges against her and recommended that she be released. It proved equally impossible to get most of the Spanish veterans to "confess."

Thus the great conspiracy, which the party had already officially announced—complete with its political rationale—simply wasn't happening. This situation made both the advisors and the interrogators nervous, and resulted in the first major conflict among the interrogators.

The conflict had actually been smoldering from the very first days in Koloděje. It was based on a power struggle over who would control the interrogations between Doubek and his people, on the one hand, and Smola's Náchod group, on the other. Doubek had been appointed chief of the interrogation. Smola and his camp were not reconciled to this and waited for the first opportunity to counterattack. It came when the interrogation reached a dead end. They accused Doubek of being responsible for the failure, arguing that he couldn't investigate the case thoroughly because he himself was linked with Karel Šváb who had put him in charge of interrogating party officials. Smola and his people planted these views in other hotheads who, too, were dissatisfied with the lack of progress.

On March 8, 1951, seventeen working-class prosecutors and militia interrogators sent a delegation to Slánský. They complained that the interrogation was being sabotaged and that the advisors were being misinformed. They felt that someone even higher up than Šling was heading the conspiracy. They felt the investigation was unsuccessful because it was controlled by Doubek and Košťál (Šváb's people) and expressed their suspicion that several of the interrogators were actually involved in the case. They requested a check of all the interrogators, especially of Doubek and Košťál. Slánský asked them to write up their views, which then went to Gottwald.[69]

This complaint, addressed to the highest levels, fuelled quite open attacks by Smola's people on Doubek and Košťál. Kopřiva had to intervene; he backed Doubek. Later he explained his rationale to Zápotocký: "As for Doubek, we had to deflect the entire campaign [against him] which threatened to derail the interrogation. The working-class prosecutors were inadvertently influenced by people who, as we realize today, were stage-managed by Slánský and Taussigová. Mudra and Smola, who attempted to gain control of the investigation, used to visit Taussigová."[70]

Thus the victory in the first conflict over control of the investigation went to Doubek, thanks to the support of Minister Kopřiva and the advisors. In the quoted letter, Kopřiva pointed out another reason for the conflict: the role of Taussigová and the KSK. The conflict among interrogators in effect reflected the earlier conflict between Köhler and Taussigová, concerning positions in security. After the wave of arrests of January-February 1951, both Köhler's CC KSČ personnel department, and Taussigová's KSK cooperated with State Security even more closely. Security was, meanwhile, growing uncomfortable with the rapidly increasing role of the KSK in the "great conspiracy" investigation. Taussigová had such good sources in security that she kept herself informed about its progress and could indirectly even influence it.[71]

Whereas Taussigová supported the Náchod group, Köhler backed former party officials Doubek and Košťál. He was on the attack against the KSK, though from a different direction. He tried to curtail and even eliminate its control function, that is, its reviews and purges, and limit KSK's work to strictly disciplinary matters. In the spring of 1951 he didn't quite manage, but he scored his first success a few months later: he spread doubts about the reliability of the KSK's work among leading officials, including Gottwald.

For Doubek and Košťál, cooperation both with the CC KSČ personnel department and with the KSK was natural and useful. They made what use they could of both party organs. However, they wanted to have this relationship under their own control. They could not put up with Taussigová maintaining a network of informers in their group because she used their information to influence, via her access to the minister, the course of the interrogations. That, in turn, limited Doubek's and Košt'ál's own authority. They didn't have the power to actually eliminate the KSK informers but tried at least to weaken their position. Some of them were put under surveillance; and one J. Roček was, in fact, arrested just as he was on his way to the KSK building.[72]

These rivalries within the security apparatus, caused by the difficulties in uncovering the (nonexistent) "great conspiracy," were suppressed or papered over. Nevertheless, fleshing out the approved conspiracy concept still didn't get anywhere.

The advisors and the faction of disaffected interrogators were now, however, moving in a direction quite different from the publicly announced concept of the conspiracy.

4

THE NEW CONCEPT: HEADED BY THE GENERAL SECRETARY

THE HEAD OF THE CONSPIRACY

THE FEBRUARY 1951 session of the CC KSČ went very well for Czechoslovakia's leaders. They finally had a plot rivaling Rajk's or Kostov's, and they had survived it with their hides intact. Gottwald was also satisfied with the Soviet advisors who, in his view, conferred Moscow's blessing on the whole affair. The leaders felt they had paid their dues to the witch hunt and hoped the matter would now come to a close.

But just as they were placing their seal of approval on the political concept of an anti-party conspiracy of Šling, Švermová, and the Slovak nationalists, an entirely new concept was taking shape behind their backs. It differed from the original one at two points: the pivot of the conspiracy was not to be Šling and Švermová but rather Rudolf Slánský, CC KSČ's general secretary; and its ideological and political thrust was to focus on Zionism.

Moscow had been more interested in Slánský than in other leaders for some time. Soviet advisors and their Czechoslovak collaborators were aware of this. Slánský had had a black mark against him in Moscow since before the war: in January 1936, the Comintern had sharply criticized him and Jan Šverma for opportunism. Both were for a time excluded from KSČ's top leadership. Three years later, Slánský had problems getting a residence permit in Moscow, and it took Gottwald's personal intervention to resolve the issue. The animosity between Slánský and Kopecký (who was very close to Soviet security circles) burgeoned at this time into outright hostility, and the two were not on speaking terms for over a year. On the other hand, Slánský and Gottwald trusted each other more and more. Gottwald feared Kopecký as well, and unsuccessfully tried to mediate between the two antagonists. After the 1945 liberation of Czechoslovakia, Slánský returned to the country as the KSČ general secretary with a much stronger position in the party. After the KSČ assumed power in 1948, his influence expanded over the state administration as well. He controlled enormous sources of power: under his management, the KSČ apparatus routinely directed, controlled, and substituted for governmental administrative and economic offices. The KSČ frequently intervened without informing the appropriate ministers and other authorities.

Slánský's privileged position further strengthened his relationship with Gottwald, one of implicit mutual trust. Gottwald considered Slánský his right-hand man and left him in full control of party affairs, security, and for a time also the army. The two were very close on a personal level as well. Gottwald decided, for example, that his health bulletins be forwarded only to Slánský, although they actually should have been directed to the prime minister, Antonín Zápotocký. Slánský, in turn, monopolized the contact between the KSČ apparatus and Gottwald. In Gottwald's absence, he chaired meetings of KSČ bodies where he conveyed Gottwald's viewpoints. Slánský was Number Two in the country: a feared, capable man, a competent organizer, and political bureaucrat.

His position, his role as the country's second most powerful man, and Gottwald's confidence in him provoked animosity among others in the KSČ leadership, compounded by contemplations of a successor to Gottwald, whose poor health was general knowledge. Zápotocký battled the omnipotence of the KSČ apparatus and tried to win the Number Two slot for himself. Slánský was a dangerous rival in this struggle for Gottwald's mantle. Kopecký's earlier personal conflicts with Slánský flared up again in clashes over cultural policy between his ministry and the respective CC KSČ department, which he viewed as the long arm of the general secretary. Zdeněk Fierlinger considered Slánský "an evil spirit" in the leadership, because Slánský criticized him; he didn't realize that Slánský was merely voicing Gottwald's opinions. Alexej Čepička admitted in 1963 that his opinion of Slánský differed from and indeed contradicted that of Gottwald. Čepička saw Slánský as an obstacle to his own ambitions and actually managed to eliminate Slánský's influence over areas under his own control. In 1950, Josef Smrkovský discussed "R. Slánský and his relationship with him in Moscow with a representative of the CC CPSU secretariat." A number of other officials had conflicts with Slánský, including Antonín Novotný, regional KSČ secretary in Prague, and Husák in Bratislava.[1]

As mentioned above, Soviet intelligence officers Tikhonov and Khazianov had Štěpán Plaček recommend to Slánský already in mid-1948 that Soviet advisors be invited to help Czechoslovak security. When Slánský turned down the idea, the Soviet officers commented to Plaček that Slánský didn't want them "to poke about his pigsty." Their interest in him only mounted. Plaček was never to mention their discussions about Slánský, not even to Soviet advisors who eventually arrived in Prague.[2]

Slánský was meanwhile busy struggling with assorted villains, stage-managing political trials, and searching out enemies in the party. By 1950, however, he was trying to forestall searches that might lead into the KSČ apparatus or even into the CC KSČ secretariat itself, lest he— as the head of the apparatus—be endangered as well.

The early investigation of the Švermová-Šling case disturbed Slánský; but the concept of a "conspiracy" to remove, among others, him personally, dispelled his anxiety. However, one event in January 1951 shook him completely.

An important top-secret meeting of Soviet-bloc party chiefs and defense ministers was convened in Moscow. Stalin, Molotov, Malenkov, and several dozen marshals and generals represented the Soviet side. They listened to party chiefs of Soviet-bloc countries report on the situation to their armed forces. However, when Czechoslovakia's turn came, Molotov called up not Slánský but Defense Minister Alexej Čepička, who pointed out that Slánský actually had the report and spoke better Russian; but the Soviets insisted that Čepička deliver the report himself.

Nothing like this had ever happened to Slánský before. During his earlier visits, he had always been welcomed cordially. In January 1949 and in 1950 he even met with Stalin. Kopřiva related that after coming home, Slánský always used to report very enthusiastically about these meetings.[3] This time, however, he kept quiet. He mentioned only to his closest circle that not even his friends among Soviet officials, whom he brought presents for, had time to see him.

We don't know the reason for this sudden change in Moscow's attitude. It was no doubt influenced by Soviet criticism of "unreliable personnel" posted in Czechoslovakia's army, security, and in the state and party apparatus, for which Slánský was held responsible: the meeting took place just prior to the wave of major arrests in Czechoslovakia.

A month after this meeting, the CC KSČ approved the original concept of a "great conspiracy" directed, among other things, at removing Slánský; however, he—for the first time ever—didn't even speak at the CC KSČ session.

Two weeks later, Taussigová decided that at the next session of the CC KSČ she would criticize the work methods of the CC KSČ secretariat and sought Gottwald's approval to have these methods reviewed. Such a review would necessarily have been directed against Slánský as well. He tried to stall by delaying Taussigova's audience with Gottwald. She, anxious for this meeting, sought support of the zealous Čepička and of Boyarski—who, surprisingly, was cool to the idea. Taussigová later explained that KSK personnel were conducting reviews in Czechoslovakia's regions and felt that improper methods prevailed at the CC KSČ secretariat as well. Taussigová prepared a presentation for the next CC KSČ session, based on KSK's findings. "Since this criticism largely concerned work methods of the CC KSČ secretariat, I took it first to Köhler. He, however, refused to comment. Then I took it to Slánský who argued with many points but agreed with others, in particular with my intention of informing Gottwald before taking the floor."

Taussigová's criticism was directed particularly against the red tape that had become endemic in the CC KSČ apparatus. Slánský was mostly responsible for the bureaucratic procedures, whereas Köhler was largely responsible for poor personnel policies. She also gave Frank and Kopřiva advance notice of her speech and asked for an audience with Gottwald. His office didn't respond, and she therefore asked Čepička to tell Gottwald why she wanted to see him.

> I made this request to Čepička and he promised that he would inform Gottwald, so that he could find time for me. I read to Čepička the essence of our criticism of the working methods in the CC and its apparatus. As I came to the sentence, "Slánský shoulders the greatest responsibility for the bureaucratic methods of the CC KSČ secretariat," Čepička suddenly interrupted and said: "Slánský is not a bureaucrat but an enemy!" I don't remember exactly when this exchange took place. At the very latest it would have been before the end of May but it was probably earlier, in March or April of 1951. I strongly rebuked him for this statement. Čepička stuck to his opinion . . . Then he walked over to his safe and pulled out some document. He handed it to me, saying that I should see for myself about Slánský's enemy activity. The document was some chauffeur's statement that he had taken Slánský and Švermová to the British or American embassy.

A week or so later Taussigová was told that "he [Čepička] had spoken with Gottwald and informed him. He would apparently call me himself." After several weeks passed and Gottwald didn't call, she asked Boyarski for help.

> I told him I had requested an audience with Gottwald and asked Boyarski (who said he was in daily contact with Gottwald) to explain the urgency of the visit. I don't remember this discussion very clearly. I only know that I reviewed the essence of what I wanted to discuss with Gottwald: the necessity of thoroughly analyzing the working methods of the CC, and how surprised I was by Čepička's behavior and attitude [concerning Slánský]. [Boyarski acted] differently than before . . . he said that my assertions were contradictory, that I should think the matter over carefully, that this line of reasoning might unwittingly lead me to the platform of a class enemy. He refused to intervene with Gottwald on my behalf.[4]

Čepička's position was influenced by developments at the January meeting in Moscow and by fragmentary information from security about investigations of the conspiracy. Boyarski's position was based on his thorough familiarity with the interrogation protocols and particularly by the germinating new concept of the conspiracy. This must have been why he disapproved of Taussigová's efforts to review the CC KSČ secretariat, which would have complicated the intentions of his Moscow superiors.

Slánský's name cropped up more and more frequently in the interrogations. It had first appeared back in 1950, in depositions by Löbl and Nový: "in the matter of certain charges against them, these suspects said Slánský had known about them or had given instructions."[5] On Kopřiva's behest, Doubek forbade mentioning "prominent personalities" in the protocols. Interrogators therefore informed Doubek about these points verbally, and later in special reports. In the Koloděje prison, Slánský's name came up even more frequently. Since the ban on mentioning it in the protocols was still in effect, we have to rely on depositions that the interrogators made in 1955–1956.

Thus Hugo Čáp stated that Vítězslav Fuchs, formerly a regional KSČ secretary, spoke about Slánský in Koloděje. He defended some of his own alleged hostile actions by stating that Slánský agreed with them. In a protocol of February 6, 1951, Artur London listed people with whom he had been in touch while living abroad. He said that those who returned after the war to Czechoslovakia from France had been invited in a telegram from Slánský. Doubek stated that according to interrogator J. Kolínec, London had marked Slánský as an enemy already in Koloděje, but Kolínec was not allowed to pass on this information.[6]

Interrogators and advisors at first didn't pay much attention to these references to Slánský; they saw them merely as excuses or attempts of the suspects to defend themselves. They continued to conduct the interrogations according to the approved concept of the great conspiracy, which supposedly had fingered Slánský as its victim. However, the situation suddenly changed in late March 1951. The Moscow security center, which received detailed briefs about the interrogations, refocused and picked Slánský as the person responsible for posting "unreliable persons and enemies" in high-level positions, marking him as the possible leader of the conspiracy. Those interrogators who had close ties with the advisors encouraged their victims to speak about Slánský. At first they wrote special reports, which they passed on to the advisors secretly, behind Doubek's back. During this time, from March to May 1951, Doubek still kept the lid on recording depositions about prominent personalities.[7] Interrogator Karel Arasin later testified:

> Sometime in the spring of 1951, as I was doing a write-up on Zionism with [Josef] Vondráček, the conversation turned to the general secretary, com. Slánský. Vondráček told me that Slánský is an old collaborator of Geiringer-Grannville, a British or American journalist who during the First Republic [1918–1938] worked as a spy for the Zionists as well as for the British and American intelligence services. At the time I immediately informed [StB Chief,] comrade [Josef] Hora about this but all I got was a look of sympathy. I also informed com. Dr. Smola about this and he later interrogated Vondráček about the entire Slánský affair himself.[8]

Five years later, Josef Vondráček discussed his interrogation: "I had the feeling that this whole interrogation was staged so that I, a formal agent of the Intelligence Service, could confirm that Slánský had some contact with the I.S. Of course I could not do so."

On April 3, 1951, an StB agent wrote about her contacts with Vavro Hajdů and Artur London. London had told her about his work in Switzerland which he had done "on instructions from Slánský and [Bedřich] Geminder." Interrogators also extracted testimonies against Slánský from Osvald Závodský and Gen. Bedřich Kopold, who discussed Slánský's "destructive activity" in the army. According to interrogator Semínko, Šváb stated that Slánský had been aware of his (Šváb's) activity in a Nazi concentration camp and also used to instruct Šváb about work in security. Both activities were classified as criminal. According to interrogator Kohoutek, Evžen Löbl stated in late April or early May 1951 that neither his own activity nor that of others would have been possible if he hadn't enjoyed "Slánský's clear support." Kohoutek mentioned this to advisor Galkin who recommended that Löbl write the statement himself. Galkin checked it and later sent Kohoutek to show it to Kopřiva.[9] Interrogations at this time actually pursued two lines. The official line was followed by Doubek, Košťál, and others who stuck to the original concept of a conspiracy against the party, as approved in February 1951 by the KSČ leadership. The other line, as yet unofficial and secret, focused on Slánský. This line was pursued particularly by the Náchod group and its partisans—Smola, Karel Arasin, J. Holvek, Kohoutek, and others.

This was the situation until the end of June 1951. At that point the Moscow security center finished outlining a new concept of the Czechoslovak conspiracy—now headed by Slánský himself. In Prague, however, the official ban on questioning along these lines was still in force. Findings about Slánský were kept secret from Minister Kopřiva and from other leading politicians. They were shared only among a handful of interrogators, their advisors, and the Moscow center. Moscow must have started pressing for breaking out of these confines. The advisors realized the key importance of "legalizing" interrogations targeted on Slánský in order to develop the new conspiracy concept. They recruited particularly loyal interrogators to help break through the silence.

After extracting Löbl's testimony about Slánský, Kohoutek focused on London. Until then, London had been interrogated by Smola, who tested out particularly brutal methods of violence and torment. The switch to Kohoutek, who wasn't nearly as harsh, spelled a relief for London. Kohoutek used mostly psychological pressure. He counseled London, "You can save your life and get out of this hopeless situation if you follow my instructions. Otherwise we'll turn the thugs loose again." Under this pressure, London confessed his membership in a Trotskyite group directed against the party and the state, headed by someone else.

Interrogator Jaroslav Michálek, Kohoutek's subordinate, followed up with questioning as to who headed the Trotskyite conspiracy. After a while, Michálek later related, London actually did once mention Slánský. Michálek informed Kohoutek, who conferred with Doubek. Michálek himself was summoned to Doubek about an hour and a half later. At first, Doubek was angry; then he wanted to know whether Michálek hadn't intentionally led London on. In his advisor's presence, he eventually ordered that London write the statement himself.[10]

Doubek and his advisor immediately informed Minister Kopřiva about London's statement. At a subsequent meeting, Kopřiva, Doubek,

Slánský (*fourth from left*) and his wife, Josefa, attend the sports events in Prague on the occasion of Czechoslovak Army Day, July 10, 1951. Also in attendance is Viliam Široký (*left*), then Vice-Premier and Foreign Minister of Czechoslovakia

Košťál, Galkin, and Yesikov agreed on the following: (1) to forbid direct, leading, intentional interrogations targeted on Slánský but to allow anyone to say "whatever they want, whomever it may concern"; (2) to ask Šváb to write a deposition; (3) to have Kopřiva directly participate in London's interrogation so that he could see that "London is really volunteering information about Slánský," that he "is submitting specific facts," and that his testimony sounds credible.[11] This was the first step toward "legalizing" interrogations targeted for Slánský.

London finished writing his deposition on July 14. He stated: "After five months of silence I have decided to exculpate my crimes at least partially by fully confessing. The Trotskyite conspiracy in Czechoslovakia is headed by Rudolf Slánský, general secretary of the CC KSČ. [Bedřich] Geminder is his right-hand man, [Marie] Švermová his accomplice, and [Josef] Frank and [Štefan] Rais are loyal to them." The deposition also included other names of the so-called conspiracy group.[12]

Meanwhile, toward the end of June, the advisors, Doubek and Košťál were taking stock of the results to date. They reviewed the Švermová-Šling case but focused their attention on what they had on Slánský. The advisors, who convened the meeting, were after a well-defined objective: they had already tagged Slánský as a possible enemy and underlined the danger of Jewish bourgeois nationalism and Zionism.

In 1955, Doubek wrote about these discussions: "Advisors Yesikov and Galkin spoke to me and Košťál about Slánský as a possible enemy . . . particularly when it came to executing so-called Jewish-bourgeois-nationalist personnel policies."[13]

Participants at this meeting accepted the advisors' recommendation that authorities be informed about the danger of Zionism. They decided to sum up existing information about Slánský in a report which Doubek and Košťál wrote over the next two days. It was based mostly on statements from Löbl, London, Šváb, and others who had mentioned Slánský without necessarily describing him as an enemy; however, even innocuous statements could be interpreted in the light of London's and Löbl's depositions. The advisors read and revised the draft. Doubek submitted the final version to Minister Kopřiva, requesting that he decide whether to proceed with this line of questioning. Kopřiva passed the report on to Gottwald, whose decision he conveyed two days later: interrogate so as to "uncover all the facts about the hatching conspiracy."[14]

Even though interrogations directly targeting Slánský were still not permitted, the advisors considered this a success. Gottwald had been made aware of the new conspiracy concept, albeit only as a hypothesis, and the possibility of interrogating "in this direction" opened up.

The report was also translated into Russian and sent to Moscow. It was to serve as the basis for Slánský's arrest. This clearly was why the Moscow security center had it prepared in the first place and served up to Stalin and Gottwald, the only people who could decide to arrest Slánský.

But the case was not yet airtight. Filipov, the main Soviet advisor to Czechoslovak intelligence, presented Gottwald on July 21 with a letter from Stalin dated the previous day:

> We have received incriminating evidence about comrades Slánský and Geminder. We consider this evidence insufficient and believe there are no reasons for charging them. We believe that one cannot draw conclusions only from denunciations of known offenders; one needs facts which confirm these denunciations. This indicates an insufficiently serious approach to this work and we have therefore decided to recall Boyarski to Moscow.[15]

Gottwald felt easier. He had felt that the report on Slánský might have been backed by Moscow political circles; and fearing that he might be denounced for covering up enemies, he gave the instruction to "uncover all facts about the conspiracy." Now he was only too happy to agree with Stalin. He replied the very same day, July 21, 1951:

> We have received your code of July 20, 1951. I fully agree with you that based on materials from the investigation one cannot bring charges against the comrades in question, let alone draw any conclusions. This is all the more true since the depositions were made by proven criminals. This has been my opinion from the very first moment when I learned about this matter. Kopřiva, Gottwald, and up to a point Čepička, who was informed by Gottwald, are the only leading Czechoslovak comrades who are aware of the statements in question.

Gottwald also requested that Boyarski continue working in Prague because "he offers very valuable assistance to the ministry of national security . . . and recalling him would make our work in this sector far more difficult."

Stalin immediately invited Gottwald to Moscow to discuss the matter in detail. Gottwald excused himself on health grounds and sent Čepička instead.[16]

STALIN'S FIRST INTERVENTION: SLÁNSKÝ'S DISMISSAL

Čepička's trip to Moscow was top secret. The only one outside Gottwald to know about it was Foreign Minister Viliam Široký, who overnight had to arrange personally for travel documents with an assumed name and record the trip in the registry. But not even he was aware of the purpose of Čepička's sudden departure.

Čepička arrived in Moscow on July 23 and met that same day with Stalin and several other members of the Soviet politburo. He later related these discussions in a ten-page report, located today in the CC KSČ Archive in Prague.[17] All we know about his meeting with Stalin comes from this report and from Stalin's letter to Gottwald that Čepička delivered.

Stalin, Molotov, Malenkov, and other Soviet politburo members participated in the meeting, as did Vulko Chervenkov, the Bulgarian leader. The agenda included the work of Soviet security advisors. Chervenkov spoke first, discussing the reasons for arresting minister Georgi Tsankov. He emphasized that investigations indicated that certain members of the CC CPB were involved in activity hostile to the party and the state. Stalin was particularly interested in the work of Filatov, the chief Soviet advisor to Bulgaria's security. Chervenkov praised him; but Stalin disagreed and sharply reprimanded the Bulgarian leader for lack of control and oversight of the work of Filatov and the other Soviet advisors. He disapproved in the strongest of terms with applying security measures against ministers and CC members.

Then it was Čepička's turn. Gottwald had briefed him about his own view of the report about Slánský and Geminder, which Čepička presented. (Čepička was later accused of having injected an anti-Slánský bias in his report, and thereby sharing the responsibility for Slánský's later fate. However, Čepička would not have dared to intentionally color or bias anything, once he realized how well Stalin was informed about the investigation.)

The discussion focused on detailing and elaborating on some of the statements by London, Löbl, Šváb, and others. Stalin took the lead. He emphasized, for the second time, the importance of evaluating the statements of "such witnesses—criminals" very carefully because they might be an enemy provocation. In this context he mentioned several instances from the Soviet Union where traitors falsely accused honest party members. "The work of the investigating authorities could turn to the enemy's advantage," said Stalin, "if we didn't constantly control their activity and if we'd allow general mistrust in the highest offices to spread."

The discussion turned into a Stalin monologue. He repeatedly criticized Soviet advisors and the political leadership in Sofia and Prague: for irresponsible work in the one case and insufficient control in the other. He then expounded on the need to control leading party and state officers on pain of suffering grave consequences. Stalin did not give this advice for nothing: it amounted to a prologue to the Slánský issue because, in his view, slack control was precisely what had allowed Slánský to make mistakes for a long time, which in turn allowed the hostile activity of others. The conclusions of Stalin's remarks were unequivocal: in view of Slánský's errors in organizational and personnel policy, he has to be recalled from the office of the party's general secretary.

Participants of the meeting agreed with Stalin's views and with the suggestion that they be written up as the position of the Soviet politburo and sent to Gottwald. The official discussion was over.

Stalin then invited Čepička and the politburo members to dinner. It was served in his dacha, in the Usovo-Arkhangelsk area, about an hour's drive from Moscow; prior to the 1917 revolution, the spacious and simply appointed villa had belonged to a gold-mine owner. Many Soviet policy decisions were made here; Stalin delighted in organizing dinners, film screenings, and other distractions for politburo members and other guests. He would often express his opinions and ideas, judgments, and personnel evaluations, which would then turn into official political directives. Stalin and his comrades would loosen up and frequently say what they really felt but otherwise couldn't, given their official position. They could, for example, hurl insults and crudities at leaders of Soviet-bloc countries. This time they targeted Czechoslovakia.

Stalin showed exceptional interest in the Prague government and Zápotocký, the prime minister. First he said that the Czechoslovak party leadership makes the correct decisions but that their implementation suffers because they are not backed up by "appropriate organizational measures. This weakness is particularly manifest in the work of the government." And he added sarcastically that heading the government must really have been a tough task if the prime minister could find time to write novels. (Several historical novels had been published under Zápotocký's name.) Molotov exclaimed: "Long live the prime minister, laureate of the State Prize!" Stalin then turned to Čepička and asked him whether he, too, intended to write novels, which seemed to be all the rage in Czechoslovakia. Čepička tried gently to defend Zápotocký, pointing out that he set an example for younger officials, but Stalin's reaction was quite the opposite: "When one writes novels, one doesn't have time to do what needs to be done." In one of his many toasts, his criticism became even more acute: ". . . It would be desirable that the government become truly a governing body which does its job in a responsible and timely way. Only such a government, permeated by a militant spirit of decisiveness, management, and control, is more than a bunch of fools."

Stalin was also interested in General Ludvík Svoboda: deputy premier and former defense minister. He was amazed that Gottwald would keep him in the government even after he had lost Moscow's confidence. Stalin said he would make Gottwald responsible if Svoboda was not uncovered as an enemy. (Svoboda was subsequently stripped of all his offices and ended up as an accountant on a farm.) Stalin concluded with some critical remarks concerning several points of Czechoslovakia's policies. Corresponding changes were implemented soon after that.[18]

The letter that Čepička brought back and gave to Gottwald on July 24 was instrumental in developing the second concept of the great conspiracy. Stalin wrote:

Comrade Čepička has briefed us in detail and has reported about the activities of comrades Slánský and Geminder.

We still believe that statements of offenders, with no supporting facts, cannot serve as a basis for accusing leaders known for their great positive work. Our experiences in struggling against the enemy suggest that proven offenders often resort to slandering honest people, thereby trying to sow mutual mistrust among party leaders (this is how they struggle against the party). You are therefore correct to proceed cautiously, mistrusting the statements of experienced offenders concerning comrades Slánský and Geminder.

Considering what we have received from our Soviet personnel it is clear to us that comrade Slánský has committed a number of errors in promoting and posting leading personnel. He has shown himself to be shortsighted and too trusting. As a consequence, conspirators and enemies have freely and with impunity gone rampant and harmed the party and the people. Therefore, it seems to us that the post of the general secretary cannot be occupied by a man who understands people poorly and who makes frequent mistakes in posting personnel. I therefore think it would be correct to relieve com. Slánský of the office of general secretary.

As for your positive evaluation of comrade Boyarski's work and your desire that he continue working as an advisor to the Czechoslovak ministry of national security, we have a different opinion of this matter. Experience with Boyarski's work in Czechoslovakia has shown that he is not qualified well enough to discharge responsibly the obligations of an advisor. We have therefore decided to recall him from Czechoslovakia. If you really do need an advisor in matters of state security (and that is for you to decide), we would try to find you a stronger and more experienced one . . . At any rate we still believe that our advisor has to be guided and strictly controlled in his work by the CC KSČ leadership and under no circumstances should he substitute for the [national] security minister.[19]

Stalin's letter and Čepička's report were something of an unpleasant surprise for Gottwald. He had hoped that Slánský would end up completely exonerated and never even thought of dismissing him. He also felt Stalin's criticism of Slánský was also directed against himself as the party chairman. He reacted to the voice of Moscow as he always did in such circumstances: he followed Stalin's recommendation and limited his contacts with Slánský. He and Zápotocký then arranged for appointing Slánský a deputy premier.

Gottwald immediately drafted a response to Stalin:

> *Dear Comrade Stalin*: I have received your letter of July 24. Comrade Čepička has also reported about his meeting with you and about your valuable remarks and advice for which I thank you from my heart. I informed comrade Zápotocký today about your letter. I admit that your advice in re: the organization with respect to the matter of comrade Slánský [his dismissal as general secretary] follows from his political and, to a point, personal responsibility for the selection and posting of personnel. Nevertheless, I'll admit I had not anticipated such a measure. I had actually figured that a wholesale, top-to-bottom reorganization of the party's work would prevent a recurrence of errors to this extent: all the more so because, one, I believe in the political and personal honesty of com. S., and, two, I don't see very well who could successfully take com. S.'s job. Finally, I myself don't feel blameless and free of responsibility for certain mistakes. All this is to explain my position before receiving your advice. Now I ask for another piece of advice: How should your recommendations be carried out. According to the party's organization charter (par. 54), the general secre——

The draft abruptly ends. Gottwald didn't have the courage to finish it, let alone send it. He was scared of having admitted his own responsibility. Instead, a different letter went to Moscow on July 26, which included the following:

> *Dear Comrade Stalin*: I have received your letter of July 24. I informed comrade Zápotocký about it today. (1) I agree with the organizational measures which you suggested concerning comrade S. We think we should appoint him member of the government when we reshuffle it, probably next September, and in this context relieve him of his current office. I assume that comrade S. should continue in a responsible position, albeit in a different sphere. Please let us know what you think of this solution.

Gottwald also pressed for a new advisor to immediately take Boyarski's place.[20]

Stalin's opinion had entirely different consequences from what the Moscow security center and the Soviet advisors had intended. Stalin not only did not order Slánský's arrest, but he actually sharply criticized the advisors and, indirectly, their Moscow bosses. The setback was compounded when Gottwald reiterated the ban on interrogations against Slánský.[21] Engineers of the new conspiracy concept saw its very foundations endangered. Pursuing their objective now became not only an important political matter but also a matter of prestige.

While Gottwald and Stalin were corresponding, preparations were under way for Slánský's fiftieth birthday, which fell on July 31, 1951. It was celebrated just as the party had decided several weeks earlier. Gottwald awarded Slánský the Order of Socialism, the highest state decoration; the press published laudatory articles; a large factory was renamed after Slánský; and his collected works were published, with a fiery preface by Kopecký, who spoke at a gala assembly about this "shining example of a revolutionary" whom the central committee "recognizes in gratitude for his great contributions to the party, the working class, and the working people of Czechoslovakia." Delegations from several factories and cities congratulated him.

Gottwald, at the last moment, edited the congratulations of the Czechoslovak leadership, deleting some formulations that emphasized his cooperation with Slánský: "He is among the closest collaborators of comrade Gottwald; he is among the leading members of the Gottwald leadership of the KSČ; he is modest as a Bolshevik; he is energetic and implacable toward class enemies."[22] The message was still very laudatory: "Dear comrade, our entire party and all our working people greet you as their faithful son and warrior, suffused with love for the working people and fidelity to the Soviet Union and the great Stalin."

Slánský received dozens of greetings from communist parties—but Moscow was silent. Only after the celebration did some leading Communists realize the political significance of Moscow's silence. They didn't know what had caused it, though. Slánský was particularly shaken. He knew Moscow well enough to realize that the omission was no accident or oversight but an intentional and well-thought-out measure and could figure out the possible consequences. He became even more nervous when security almost completely stopped sending him reports about the Švermová-Šling conspiracy investigation. Kopřiva continued to visit Slánský privately, although less frequently than before. He later wrote that Slánský often asked about the investigation, and whether suspicions had surfaced concerning other officials. Kopřiva kept his counsel. As for Gottwald, Moscow's attitude turned his caution into fear, which informed his further decisions about Slánský.

Although Stalin had interfered with their plans, the Moscow security center interpreted two signals as favorable. Slánský's anticipated dismissal and Moscow's silence during his birthday indicated that he was indeed being held politically responsible for the "erroneous" personnel policies. All that was needed now was merely to reinterpret political responsibility as power ambitions. The advisors and their Moscow superiors ignored the continuing ban on targeting Slánský during interrogations and secretly continued to do so. London, Šváb, and others kept on writing their statements, and the advisors secretly got hold of whatever concerned Slánský, mostly from the Náchod group. However, interrogations yielded nothing new. If, after the first setback, the new concept was to come to fruition, it was all the more urgent that security get their hands on Slánský.

This was difficult though. Gottwald would have to lift the ban on direct interrogations, and Stalin would have to think of Slánský as the head of the conspiracy. The Moscow security center and the Prague advisors pursued these two avenues.

Interrogators Smola, Kohoutek, Mozola, and Holvek met in early August with deputy Jan Souček who delivered a package of their secret reports concerning Slánský directly to the Soviet embassy in Prague. They also blamed Kopřiva, describing him as Slánský's man who intentionally curbed investigations targeting Slánský.[23] It appeared as though they mistrusted the advisors as well; but in reality, the advisors were clued in and actually instigated this move. They wanted Moscow to receive "evidence" directly from the interrogators, not from the advisors.

However, this plan misfired as well. The Soviet embassy informed Kopřiva, who took strict measures against the complainers. Smola and others were transferred to secondary posts. Holvek, who was preparing a self-criticism, committed suicide on August 13; some investigators who worked on the case thought it was murder.[24]

Kohoutek was the only one to save his skin—or rather, the advisors were interested in saving it. His wartime history placed him squarely in their hands, and he served them very loyally.[25]

Kopřiva's disciplinary measures against the security personnel who complained to the Soviet embassy finally resolved the simmering conflict between the Doubek and the Náchod groups of interrogators. Doubek's position was strengthened and as he later stated, "relative calm now prevailed in the interrogations."[26] Elimination of the Náchod group weakened Taussigová's position in security, inasmuch as it included most of her informers, and she couldn't save them. The Soviet advisors didn't try to save their loyal sidekicks either. Their job was done, and they were dispensable. The advisors had needed them to accumulate secret information and to get authorization for targeting Slánský, countermanding the orders of people who advocated the original concept of the conspiracy—Doubek, Košťál, and Minister Kopřiva. However, influenced by the advisors, by early August the first two also believed, as Doubek later wrote, that "Slánský really was conducting hostile policies."[27]

Advisors Galkin and Yesikov therefore easily persuaded Doubek and Košťál of the value of a second report that would review new findings from the interrogations. They hoped it would lead to lifting the ban on targeting Slánský. Its authors focused it on Slánský and Geminder, in effect expanding their earlier report of July. Doubek later explained: "The material was gathered and summed up in a comprehensive report which went through ten drafts or so. The drafts focused on the political formulations, not the content itself. It was intended to persuade Gottwald that Slánský is an enemy."[28]

With this in mind, its authors paid a sudden mid-August visit to vacationing Kopřiva. They submitted the report and tried to persuade him that not Šling and Švermová, but Slánský headed the conspiracy. They counted on easy success, but the minister disappointed them. In his view, "Geminder, who manages everything from behind the scenes, is probably the head of the conspiracy." They were equally unsuccessful in getting permission to target interrogations at Slánský. Kopřiva did not dare directly countermand Gottwald.

However, the following day he left for Lány, the president's summer resort near Prague.[29] Upon returning, he told Doubek, Košťál, and the two advisors that Gottwald was considering the material very seriously. As for the main objective—targeted interrogations—the result according to Doubek was this:

> When Košťál and I asked whether we can question the suspects directly about Slánský and other high officials, he didn't respond directly but repeated that in order to uncover the head of the conspiracy, we ought to use all means at our disposal. Yesikov said that would be quite sufficient and that that was exactly what they were looking for. When Kopřiva left, the advisors were very satisfied and immediately instructed that some suspects be interrogated again.[30]

Interrogations targeted at Slánský were thus indirectly sanctioned. However, nothing suggested that they would unearth good enough grounds for his arrest, which is what the advisors were really after. More promising in this respect was the way Slánský was dismissed as the party's general secretary. The CC KSČ discussed this on September 6, 1951. It abolished the office of the general secretary and approved Slánský's appointment as vice premier. Gottwald explained the change by pointing out that during Slánský's tenure as the person responsible for organizational and personnel policies, enemies had become very active high up in the party and government apparatus.[31] This was a refrain that was first voiced by members of the Soviet General Staff when they talked to Čepička in January 1951. Czechoslovakia, according to them, was economically and strategically a particularly important member of the Soviet bloc. Strategically, though, it was the weakest because high-level positions in the army, security, government, party, and the economy were occupied by people whom Moscow didn't fully trust. In July 1951 Stalin had stated essentially the same thing, in harsher form, to Čepička and in his letter to Gottwald.

Stepping down from head of the party apparatus cast a shadow of doubt and suspicion over Slánský, but it wasn't a complete political downfall. It was even presented as a proof of the party's confidence in him. He got the important position of first deputy premier, in charge of the national economy. More importantly, he kept his seat in the all-powerful seven-member CC KSČ political secretariat.

The reshuffle changed the power positions of the leaders. The conflict over the Number Two position in the country ended with Zápotocký's victory; Čepička and Karol Bacílek also joined the top ranks of power. Both became members of the KSČ presidium and of its political secretariat. But Kopecký, Slánský's old nemesis, still didn't make it among the top seven.

The September CC KSČ session affected the new concept of the conspiracy in three ways. First, there was Slánský's self-criticism. Slánský didn't stop at admitting all the errors he was charged with but, as a Communist trained by the Comintern, he himself recalled Soviet experiences in struggling against enemies within the party:

> I am responsible for erroneous personnel policies which allowed the posting of so many malefactors, enemies and conspirators in important positions . . .
>
> I am responsible for the improper methods of work of the secretariat and for its overall incorrect orientation . . .
>
> This shows, comrades, the great danger the party was in as a result of so many malefactors penetrating the party apparatus and how great a responsibility for this matter falls directly on me . . . Let us consider the experience

of the Soviet CP, how they uncovered Trotsky, Bukharin, Zinoviev, and Rykov. They were not immediately uncovered as conscious spies and agents of the enemy.

As for my person . . . these measures will contribute to heightening my vigilance. The class struggle will exacerbate and Western imperialists will continue dispatching their agents . . . I am grateful to the central committee for giving me the opportunity [to make amends].

Second, the new concept acquired a precise political and organizational shape—in Gottwald's presentation. Gottwald stated that "abusing their positions in the CC KSČ apparatus, enemy agents selected and posted their people not only throughout the party but also in the governmental and economic apparatus . . . These are the beginnings of two centers, so to speak," of power. Kopecký further developed the "two power centers" idea: "The CC KSČ secretariat was turning into a second center, separate from the center that corresponds to the principles of our party's Bolshevik task . . . The fact is that the secretariat had turned into a second center, the decisive one. That is how it appeared to people in the party and outside . . . And there is no doubt that a second leading formation did exist."[32]

The advisors and the interrogators found the idea of two centers very handy. They latched on to it right away, for it provided their conspiracy concept with a solid grounding. Suddenly they viewed all the arrested Communist officials as members of this center, at the head of which they positioned Slánský.

Third, the conspiracy concept now had its own ideological-political line. Its main feature was struggle against Zionism or Jewish bourgeois nationalism, also described as "cosmopolitanism." In reality it was anti-Semitism pure and simple. It made its first appearance during the Rajk trial, though only as a secondary, peripheral phenomenon. With the arrival of Soviet advisors in Czechoslovakia, though, anti-Semitic tendencies rapidly gained ground among security personnel and among politicians: "[In early 1951 Boyarski asked Taussigová] who is our greatest enemy. I responded, the Western imperialists. Boyarski, however, said I was mistaken, for our greatest enemy is international Zionism . . . he had in mind the most elaborate espionage organizations.

In 1955, Doubek related how the advisors trained him and his colleagues in anti-Semitism:

They pointed out the growing influence of Jewry in the international political arena. They pointed out Rockefeller, Rothschild, and Du Pont and put this in connection with what Slánský and the Jews were doing here, saying there's a danger that the Jews will end up as masters of everything . . . They also pointed out the role of the State of Israel and tried to prove that precisely the Jews are the main representatives of international imperialism. [The advisor] com. Boris even said that Jews are not interested in political offices in capitalist countries lest their intentions of mastering the world become apparent.

In 1954 and in 1963, Taussigová mentioned two examples of anti-Semitism exhibited by high officials. "In early June 1951, I talked with Forman, an aide to [CC KSČ Secretary Josef] Frank, who told me word for word: 'Slánský is an enemy because he's a Jew.' " At about the same time she protested to Čepička about the dismissal of several military attachés, most of them Communists—Jews. Čepička attacked her, saying that "the Party Control Commission is a haven for Zionists and enemies."[33]

After the arrest of Šváb, the advisors pressed for the appointment of Andrej Keppert as head of the department for seeking out enemies in the party. On their recommendation, Keppert established a division for Zionism. Keppert was a long-time collaborator of Soviet security and an obedient executor of their instructions. He was also one of Taussigová's informers. She was particularly obliged to him for supplying unverified reports about Spanish veterans and other officials. He never hid his violent, rabid anti-Semitism. He used to tell his co-workers that when he saw someone with a big nose, he immediately started a file on him or opened the prison gate. He was also notorious for his limitless mistrust of everybody. He would say that "the fish rots from the head" and collected compromising information on every member of the KSČ leadership except Gottwald. In mid-1951, he moved a resolution for Communists in his workplace to express their mistrust in the CC KSČ "where there are also enemies and spies" and stated that consequently, only Communists in the security can purify the party.[34]

Keppert would not have dared make this attack without the backing of the advisors. They also protected Dr. Mudra, another rabid anti-Semite, who already in 1949 had provided the Soviets with scandal-mongering information about Gottwald's wife Marta. At the time, the Soviets were not interested. The wave of anti-Semitism carried Mudra back up, and he became notorious for quoting Malenkov's statements about Jews to people he was interrogating.[35]

The advisors paid great heed to Josef Vondráček's creations concerning a supposed Zionist agency. On Smola's instigation, Vondráček prepared two extensive "papers": one was a "Strategic Plan for Combating Trotskyism and Titoism," the other concerned a supposed British-American agency in Czechoslovakia which included a Zionist branch headed by Slánský. Doubek and Košťál did not believe Vondráček's confabulations and discussed them with their superior, Antonín Prchal. "I told him straight out," Doubek recounted later, "that we don't believe Vondráček's deposition, and why. I think Prchal didn't believe it either, but in front of us he acted as though there could be something to it. He was aware of Vondráček's deposition from the comrade advisor before we even saw him." The advisor actually insisted that Vondráček's statements be taken in all seriousness and that they be treated as verified facts—although Vondráček himself admitted to Ivo Milén in January 1951 that he "had made everything up." (Milén was arrested a week after this episode.[36])

Karel Šváb also volunteered a statement about Zionists. He stated that two groups of Jewish experts had penetrated the top management of Czechoslovakia's economy and that they were struggling for power. One group supposedly consisted of people who had spent the war in London and included Ludvík Frejka, Evžen Löbl, Josef Goldmann, and others. The other group consisted of people who had stayed at home, like Milan Reiman.[37]

At the September 1951 CC KSČ session, Václav Kopecký provided the ideological underpinning for anti-Semitic tendencies in the party and the security which by now had become fairly prominent, and artfully linked them with a criticism of Slánský. Gottwald actually was the first to mention that "an overwhelming majority [of the Communists under arrest] did not grow from the roots of our country and our party." For him, though, this was a peripheral matter, whereas Kopecký turned Zionism into a central topic of his presentation. Characteristically, Kopecký anticipated the intentions of Soviet security and political circles: he appeared as something of an ideological prophet. His September 1951 attack on Zionism also foreshadowed things to come:

> It is in my opinion a grave and unforgivable error to ignore the principle that cosmopolitans should in principle not be posted in leadership positions. This truly is an issue of cosmopolitanism, not a racial question . . . In the past we had to struggle with bestial anti-Semitism. Today, by the same token, we have to suppress Zionism because we know that many people of Jewish origin have changed their attitude toward the working class. Hitler persecuted Jews because they had joined us. Now, however, they have an affinity to Anglo-

American imperialism which supports Israel and counts on Zionism as a vehicle for internally disintegrating parties of the people's democratic regime and socialism . . . Do not underrate these things . . . Do understand what grave danger this is . . . This is exactly how it went in Yugoslavia . . . Something absolutely dreadful might have occurred . . . [the enemies] could have taken the people's democracy and yoked it around our necks as a Fascist dictatorship. These things should not be underrated in today's situation, they have their power aspect. Comrade Slánský has to admit that.[38]

All levels of the party then discussed the official report about the September 1951 CC KSČ session. They also received a confidential letter from the center, which included Slánský's self-criticism. Altogether 1,031 resolutions voiced agreement with the decisions of the leadership. The majority appreciated Slánský's self-criticism and reaffirmed their confidence in him. Other voices were heard as well, though, mostly from among party officials. Some asked that Slánský be dealt with more harshly. Isolated voices even called him an enemy. Overt anti-Semitism appeared at party meetings, manifest in statements such as "Jews sit in high positions and do nothing," or "Slánský brought into offices people of his own origin," and in drawing attention to all the places where Jews were employed.

The course of the party discussion gratified the engineers of the new conspiracy concept. Its head, whom they had selected, became the target of public criticism and the object of many doubts.[39] Once the CC KSČ accepted Slánský's self-criticism, the advisors and interrogators abandoned the original Švermová-Šling concept for good and focused completely on the new version.

The difference between the two concepts was fundamental. According to the first one, the Švermová-Šling group intended to eliminate Slánský who, according to the second one, actually headed the entire conspiracy. The first featured a group of alleged Trotskyites recruited among Spanish volunteers and wartime London exiles who were employed in the power apparatus, whereas the second focused on a power center headed by Zionists, in which Trotskyites played an auxiliary, secondary role.

In September, interrogations targeting Trotskyites among Spanish volunteers and resistance fighters ended, and all questions were directed at cooperation with Slánský, Geminder, and the nonexistent center. At the same time, an advisor asked Taussigová to gather materials for him concerning Slánský, Geminder, Frank, Frejka, and others, and took them to Moscow.[40]

The suspects, too, had to be reoriented toward the second concept after six months of being worked over. They had to realize that, in fact, they had never wanted to eliminate Slánský but that he had headed the conspiracy all along. Doubek and Košťál handled those who originally were to be defendants in the Švermová-Šling trial and "educated" them about this new view. Švermová later described the motives that inspired her first "confession" (the intention of overthrowing Slánský) and the second one:

> After a long inner struggle—I still didn't feel comfortable with the idea that prevarication could serve the party—I decided to make a "confession," so that show-trial preparations could go on. It became a task I had to fulfill in the interests of the party. We had been trained since youth to put the party's interests above everything else and to sacrifice everything, including one's self, for the party.
>
> After writing my "confession," I told the case officer that everything I had written was a lie. I said I would testify in court in line with what I had written down, because I considered it a party task, but that sooner or later, the truth would emerge, nevertheless.
>
> I then anticipated further preparations of the court proceedings but for weeks I wasn't interrogated. Then the second phase of investigation started, with R. Slánský picked out as the conspiracy leader. The same interrogators who used to call him a true Bolshevik whom I and my faction wanted to eliminate now forced me to confess that I had aided him in his criminal activity against the party and the state.[41]

Šling was being "reoriented" by Košťál, in stages. Košťál first suggested that Slánský had been aware of Šling's activity; Šling agreed. Košťál then specified that Slánský was the main culprit in the hostile activity Šling was involved in. In the third phase, they both described Slánský's activity as criminal. Košťál all along made use of the information coming from Šling's cellmate, a security agent. Šling apparently believed that in addition to Taussigová and Köhler, Slánský, too, was interested in his arrest, so that he "couldn't talk about [Slánský's] political errors."

Šling saw his own position improving with the switch in the conspiracy concept. He realized that he was no longer the head of the conspiracy and figured that his case would become a peripheral one. He even confided to his cellmate plans for a counterattack and listed several matters he meant to use against Slánský. Still, several more weeks passed before Šling's handwritten statement included the following:

It is clear that Slánský was fully aware of all of these matters [hostile activity], on the part of everybody, and that he was coordinating [their] activity. What I did in the [Brno] region was done under various ruses in the central bureaus and institutions and, naturally, in other regions as well.[42]

STALIN'S SECOND INTERVENTION: SLÁNSKÝ'S ARREST

Slánský's case continued to unfold along both political and security lines. Politically, his dismissal from the top party post officially closed the issue; however, the advisors and interrogators surreptitiously kept on trying to get Slánský arrested—the decisive step for unfolding their new conspiracy concept.

At issue was winning Gottwald's and Stalin's approval. Interrogations now freely targeted Slánský, but they merely expanded already familiar facts, none of which contained a "proof" serious enough to warrant his arrest. Time was of the essence: two months had passed, and the engineers of the new concept were treading water. Their plan had reached a critical point. There was only one way out, only one way to win rapid approval for detaining Slánský. If it failed, the entire concept might collapse.

The "smoking gun" came in the form of a letter to the "Great Street Sweeper." A letter, again, just as in Noel Field's and Otto Šling's cases.

In the wee hours of November 9, 1951, a certain Rudolf Nevečeřal crossed the border from West Germany to Czechoslovakia. It would be his last time. Nevečeřal was a Czechoslovak military counterintelligence agent. Originally he had been a member of an intelligence network working for the United States, led by General František Moravec, formerly a leading Czechoslovak military intelligence officer who now lived in exile. The Prague military counterintelligence had nabbed Nevečeřal during an earlier border crossing, turned him around, and then used him as a border-crossing agent in its espionage games with Moravec's service.[43]

Jaroslav Skřivánek, his controller, met Nevečeřal at the border, received material he had brought with him, and took him to a hotel in Carlsbad; Skřivánek then left for Prague. Nevečeřal was taken to Prague the following day. He requested that the intelligence agency do as promised, release him from their services and take him home. The agency assured him that he had indeed returned from his last trip, but insisted that he was still needed in Prague for a few days. He was put up in the Meteor Hotel, near the city center.

The material that Nevečeřal brought back from Germany included letters addressed to Josef Barfus and Daniela Kaňkovská. The latter contained a separate cover labeled "For the Great Street Sweeper," and a message requesting that the addressee forward the envelope to "the Great Street Sweeper." Nevečeřal was instructed to deliver the letters to Barfus and Kaňkovská personally.

On November 10, military counterintelligence copied the letters, resealed the envelopes, and passed them on to State Security. Two facts ought to be mentioned here. After the arrest of General Bedřich Reicin, military counterintelligence (which he had headed) was reassigned as a separate unit from the ministry of defense to the ministry of national security. It consequently cooperated very closely with State Security. Second, Soviet authorities had had considerable influence over Czechoslovak counterintelligence since 1945: Reicin and other commanders closely cooperated with their Soviet colleagues and often did their bidding.[44]

The letters reached State Security's Kamil Pixa, but he and his coworkers paid little attention to them. In content and form, they seemed to be a juvenile hoax, and the security personnel set them aside; however, to their great surprise, advisor Smirnov exhibited unusual interest in the letters. It is not known how he learned about their existence, but he repeatedly asked his interpreter, K. A., whether the letters had already arrived and wanted them immediately translated. The translator eventually had to hunt the letters down personally. Only then, on Smirnov's insistence, did they reach State Security's commanders. The advisors immediately met with Prchal, Doubek, and Košťál, to establish to whom the Great-Street-Sweeper letter was addressed.[45] The letter read in part:

> We hear that your situation is getting more and more difficult. One hears of fears and speculations, based on information from well-informed circles, that you are being set up for a trial such as Gomułka's. I hope this letter reaches you in time.
>
> We offer you a secure way out across the border. Based on statements from most reliable places we can offer you [political] asylum, a safe hiding place, and a future livelihood, though not a political career.
>
> You will receive instructions for your departure in the same way. Be careful and don't confide in anyone. Not even the courier knows what this is all about.[46]

Participants of the meeting figured that Slánský was the Great Street Sweeper. It is not clear who first suggested it; Prchal later stated that he heard it from advisor Galkin. They all feared Slánský might flee across the border. They planned their next steps, and once again, Nevečeřal entered the stage; he would now deliver the letters he had brought from "Herbert."[47]

Both addressees confirmed that "Herbert" referred to Herbert Kauders, with whom they were acquainted. Kaňkovská had known him since 1947. Two years later Kauders was in prison, sentenced to several years for black marketeering. They met again unexpectedly in 1951: Kauders had apparently escaped from prison and was getting ready to cross the border illegally. He promised Kaňkovská that he would send her information and instructions she should carefully follow, and that would eventually get her to Canada. On this occasion he mentioned the CC KSČ general secretary who covered up such matters and swept over his tracks. He called him the Great Street Sweeper. Soon after this last conversation, Kauders was in West Germany.[48]

Nevečeřal first delivered the letter to Barfus; however, local police in Prague had him under surveillance in another context. They were unaware of the letter game played by their headquarters and arrested both Barfus and Nevečeřal. The advisors were terrified, and the two suspects were immediately released, but Barfus won only a few days reprieve.[49]

Nevečeřal failed with the second letter as well. He was supposed to arrange a meeting with Kaňkovská. More importantly, though, he was to persuade her that the Great Street Sweeper was none other than Slánský and that she should deliver the letter to him. They met on November 14. By this time, she had been under surveillance for five days, and a couple of security officers had actually talked to her. She confirmed that she had met Kauders and recalled his comment about Slánský as the Great Street Sweeper. She also told Nevečeřal, though, that she simply couldn't deliver the letter. She had only seen Slánský once, fleetingly in a factory, and had never spoken to him. When Nevečeřal insisted, she agreed to think it over and to meet him again five days later.

Security's interest in Kaňkovská mounted after this meeting. She and her boyfriend realized they were being followed. Two men tried to start a conversation with her. They asked her strange questions, including whether she knew Slánský and whether she'd have an opportunity to meet him. She became nervous and afraid and decided to forget the whole matter. She burned the letter and skipped the November 19 meeting. When Nevečeřal called her the following day, she refused to see him and told him she had burned the letter.

The plan failed. The advisors had intended to nab Kaňkovská, letter in hand, in Slánský's office suite. Now the original letter was gone and the courier had failed completely. (Kaňkovská and her friend were arrested on November 25. In 1953, they were sentenced to thirteen and twenty years, respectively.)[50]

After this setback it appeared that the letter would not play its role. The advisors expected one thing from it—Slánský's arrest. Doubek later tried to persuade Beschasnov and Yesikov that the letter would not prove Slánský's contact with foreign countries anyway and, since it was never delivered, it couldn't be considered all that important. He was told, however, that "this doesn't matter; the important thing about the letter is that it will help get Slánský arrested," which in the end it did, although along different lines than originally intended. However, before tracing it any further, let us consider its origins.

Available information suggests that it was a joint creation of Czechoslovak and Soviet intelligence and security personnel:

1. Herbert Kauders was an agent of Czechoslovak military counterintelligence. This was confirmed by Karel Košťál who, in 1955 and 1956, had Leon Vondrák investigate the matter. In a handwritten deposition of January 28, 1963, Košťál stated that "Leon Vondrák researched the background of Kauders and established that he had worked with military counterintelligence before escaping." Kauders actually did not escape from prison but was released after serving a short part of his sentence. His court file was pulled by the ministry of national security and was lost. Rather than escaping to West Germany, he was sent there. Prchal stated in 1968 that Kauders was supposedly somewhere in South America.[51]

The fact that Kauders described Slánský as the Great Street Sweeper already in the spring of 1951, in his conversation with Kaňkovská, shows how early Slánský's show trial was being prepared in Prague and Moscow. This would have been only a few weeks after the Moscow military meeting of January 1951.

2. Three aspects of the Great-Street-Sweeper letter indirectly indicate Soviet participation in its authorship: First, Moscow knew about the letter, indeed had a copy of it, at least as early as Prague did, if not earlier. Second, Smirnov and Galkin not only knew about the letter's existence but searched it out. They took care that it not be ignored, and considered it very significant. Third, the text contained certain Russian expressions otherwise foreign to the Czech language.

Alexei Beschasnov was newly appointed to head the group of Soviet advisors in Prague. He arrived in early November and was immediately received by Gottwald who wanted to know about Moscow's views on the Slánský case. Beschasnov didn't have much to say but told Gottwald he would call again after reviewing the file. This conversation took place just before Nevečeřal arrived in the country with the Kauders letters. Beschasnov either wasn't aware of them or was told to keep quiet.

The letter traveled much faster in Moscow. It was in the hands of the Moscow security center on the very same day that it reached Czechoslovak military counterintelligence. It seems very likely that Moscow knew about it even earlier and had a photocopy at their disposal. On the following day, November 10, it was submitted to Stalin who readily believed that Slánský might flee the country. He immediately dispatched a special emissary to Gottwald—Anastas Mikoyan, a member of the Soviet politburo—with a recommendation that Slánský be arrested immediately.

There are two hypotheses as to when Mikoyan actually arrived in Prague. One argues for November 11 and is based on confirmed data: Gottwald's secretary, Milena Köhlerová (Bruno Köhler's wife), stated that the visit took place on a Sunday morning (November 11) and that Mikoyan recommended that Gottwald be treated by Soviet specialists rather than by Dr. Vladimír Haškovec, his personal physician. (Physicians were changed in mid-November.) Gottwald's appointment book features a note for November 11, "M. from M." (Mikoyan from Moscow). Further, the flight registry of the Prague airport recorded a special plane from Moscow arriving early on November 11, without listing the passengers.

The second hypothesis dates Mikoyan's visit at November 22, based on Gottwald's decision to have Slánský arrested on November 23; a twelve-day delay in fulfilling Stalin's order doesn't seem probable.[52] I prefer the first hypothesis.

Mikoyan was welcomed at the airport by Antonín Zápotocký who escorted him to the Soviet embassy, but Mikoyan refused his company when seeing Gottwald. He met Gottwald in less than an hour, alone in the president's residence. Mikoyan conveyed Stalin's message, namely, that Stalin was afraid Slánský might escape to the West and recommended taking immediate measures to strengthen surveillance, and especially to have him arrested.

Gottwald, who otherwise acted on Stalin's recommendations with no reservations, hesitated. He had no evidence; he requested it, but Mikoyan didn't furnish any. The conversation broke off over Gottwald's doubts. Mikoyan returned to his embassy and telephoned Stalin. Gottwald called in Čepička and told him about the purpose of Mikoyan's visit.

The conversation then resumed, with Čepička present. Mikoyan repeated Stalin's message, emphasizing that Stalin would hold Gottwald responsible if Slánský fled. He still didn't submit any evidence, though. Gottwald was alarmed and observed that Stalin had always counseled him well and that no doubt he had important evidence which the Czechoslovaks didn't have and which he could not share. He then ended the conversation. Mikoyan was to tell Stalin that Gottwald agreed.[53]

Mikoyan left for Moscow the following day and reported to Stalin. Gottwald meanwhile, according to Čepička, was to inform Zápotocký and decide about Slánský's immediate arrest. That meeting, however, didn't take place for another eleven days, and only after Gottwald had had another meeting with Beschasnov, on November 22. (Whether Beschasnov visited Gottwald more frequently cannot be established. Security excised many sections of Gottwald's appointment book.) Mikoyan's visit added urgency to this meeting. Gottwald wanted to find out what was new in the Slánský case. Beschasnov (according to his 1962 deposition) picked up a file for Gottwald, including a copy of the Great-Street-Sweeper letter, from Antonín Prchal. This was the day after Kaňkovská had burned the original. Gottwald was also assured that Radio Free Europe had broadcast the code mentioned in the letter. Gottwald didn't doubt that it was addressed to Slánský. Beschasnov recalled Gottwald's serious reflection over Slánský's impending arrest. He emphasized domestic-policy implications and Slánský's efforts to grab power. On the other hand, Gottwald considered Slánský's contacts with foreign countries merely a possibility.[54]

Gottwald informed Zápotocký about the developments only the day after meeting Beschasnov (November 23) in Čepička's presence. According to Čepička, "comrade Gottwald told comrade Zápotocký that he hadn't yet reached a final decision; he hadn't consented to an immediate arrest; he hesitated. During this conversation comrade Kopřiva called on the phone and asked to be received in an important matter." Kopřiva and Beschasnov appeared, with the Great-Street-Sweeper letter in hand. The minister had only just learned about it that morning from Beschasnov, who "also informed me [Kopřiva] that he had already seen com. Gottwald with the letter and that everything had already been decided, that they were waiting only for my return" from a business trip.[55] Čepička's report picks up the story:

The party leaders then decided that this document, intercepted by Czecho-slovak counterintelligence, confirmed an earlier finding of the Soviet intelligence which comrade Stalin had been aware of and which brought comrade Mikoyan with his recommendation to Prague.

[Kopřiva, on January 29, 1963:] There was talk [at the meeting concerning the arrest], com. Gottwald said, How far did that Slánský carry it . . . There was no long reflection when I was there, perhaps half an hour or forty-five minutes.[56]

Four years after the fact, Zápotocký explained his decisions to the CC KSČ politburo:

How did the arrest take place? Comrade Gottwald received a warning from Moscow that Slánský might flee. A few days later we received information from security about an intercepted letter *whose sense led one to guess* that Slánský might be escaping. The letter was from Kauders. Comrade Gottwald and I figured that it wasn't the Americans or the French who promised Slánský asylum but that the initiative came from Israel. I still believe so.[57]

It was Gottwald's custom that once he made a decision, he followed through resolutely and ruthlessly. He demanded that Slánský be arrested immediately, on the very same day (November 23). There was a suitable opportunity for it. Zápotocký was hosting a party to which Slánský had been invited. He agreed to inform Kopřiva when Slánský left the apartment, at which time he would be arrested. Kopřiva and Čepička also arranged for undercover military service vehicles to patrol at Slánský's villa.[58]

Kopřiva and Beschasnov left the president's residence at the Prague Castle for the national-security ministry on Wintrova Street and organized a group to arrest Slánský. It consisted of Doubek, Košťál, Prchal, and Josef Čech. The last two were not members of the operational command but were included because "they deserve to be present at this historic moment because of their work on this case." The minister asked them all to stay at their desks after work. Doubek was recalled from a brief vacation.[59]

Zápotocký was hosting a farewell party for a group of Soviet advisors who had been introducing Soviet methods for organizing and managing the economy. Slánský had, since September 1951, been the deputy premier in charge of economic matters, so his presence was natural. Zápotocký, usually an excellent host, was restless: Široký noticed that he was less attentive to his guests. He frequently left the room only to return even more troubled.

The arrest squad and two Soviet advisors met around 8 P.M. in Minister Kopřiva's office. In something of a pep talk, the minister confirmed that targeting the investigation at Slánský was correct, and discussed the circumstances of the Great-Street-Sweeper letter. He pointed out that being selected to participate in a historical event—the arrest of the former general secretary—was a high honor. He concluded by reviewing the technical and organizational aspects of the operation.

Before midnight Zápotocký left the room yet again to inform Kopřiva that the party was breaking up. The minister instructed the arrest squad to leave for Slánský's villa. The squad used a password for the military patrol to let them inside. Shortly after midnight, Zápotocký saw Slánský and his wife out. He phoned Kopřiva to tell him they had just left.

At about 1 A.M. Slánský entered the hall of his villa. He was about to turn the lights on when the arresting officers, covered in darkness, handcuffed him. The surprised Slánský asked: "Gentlemen, what does this mean?" He got no response. He immediately realized the horror of his situation. He asked "that he be allowed to sit down for a moment and kept repeating: 'Jesus Maria.'" The officers routinely searched him and then transported him, handcuffed, blindfolded, and gagged, to the Ruzyně prison in the outskirts of Prague.[60]

They headed for Doubek's office. They searched him again, thoroughly, and issued him prison garb: a shirt, knee-length underwear, a jacket and pants made of thick, coarse material, and house shoes, all without buttons or laces. He was taken to his special cell. He had his own guard and was watched constantly.

On November 24, 1951, at 1 A.M., the man who had just recently been the KSČ general secretary and the second most powerful person in the country, was transformed into inmate number 2359/865.

The arrest squad gathered in Doubek's office and reported over the phone to their minister: the task had been accomplished with no complications. Kopřiva reported to Gottwald, who had meanwhile impatiently called three times, and to Zápotocký.

After 2 A.M. Doubek summoned Slánský back into his office. The guard brought him in blindfolded, according to regulations which by then were routine. The two men were not total strangers: after 1945, Doubek worked in the economic and later in the personnel department of the CC KSČ secretariat that Slánský headed. He had no direct contact with the general secretary; but he knew him, admired him, politely listened to him, and conscientiously executed his directives and instructions. He had trusted him unconditionally and saw in him the personification of the party and its leadership. In October 1949 Doubek transferred to the newly created department of state security, which was in charge of uncovering enemies in the party, and was eventually promoted to chief of interrogations. In this position he met Slánský several times as his subordinate.

The relationship was now quite the reverse. The former factotum of the party apparatus was now the chief facing his prisoner, the former general secretary. Doubek's first interrogation of Slánský didn't last long. It was more of a conversation, really. Doubek asked Slánský to write a statement abdicating his seat in the parliament, thereby giving up his parliamentary immunity. He gave him a piece of advice combined with a warning: according to his later deposition, Doubek told Slánský that surely "he sees clearly that his role is over and that the only thing left is to decide to testify about all his hostile activity." Slánský obediently abdicated from the parliament and asked permission to write a letter to Gottwald. Doubek didn't have the authority to grant such permission but promised to pass the request on to Minister Kopřiva. Slánský returned to his cell at about 3 A.M.[61]

Geminder and Taussigová were arrested the same day. Relatives and close collaborators followed over the next few days. Geminder's name was now almost always linked with Slánský's. The masterminds of the new concept kept Geminder in reserve as a substitute head of the plot, if their first plan were to fail.

The arrest of Taussigová, one of the most active and consistent warriors against enemies within the party, seemed illogical. There were many such apparently illogical cases,[62] but in every instance there was a specific rationale. At issue in the case of Taussigová was the old power struggle between her as the main representative of the Party Control Commission (KSK) on the one hand, and Köhler, Novotný, Doubek, Čepička, and others on the other hand. The authors of the conspiracy concept intended to include her among Slánský's closest collaborators. On top of that, Geminder and Taussigová were not popular in the party.

On November 24, the CC KSČ political secretariat heard Kopřiva's report on Slánský's hostile activity and on his arrest, which discussed the second concept of the conspiracy, buttressed by statements of the communist officials under arrest and by fabrications of people like Vondráček. Slánský, according to Kopřiva, headed a group of enemies that included Spanish volunteers, Slovak nationalists, and London exiles. Furthermore he headed a Zionist group and intended to usurp power in the country. All those present agreed and listed additional instances of "Slánský's hostile activity."

Zápotocký suggested that Slánský probably wasn't "directly in America's pay but in the pay of the Zionists." Čepička argued that "the situation in the party and in our economy is not accidental. It is caused by wrecking activity." Široký said, "We erred in not reflecting hard enough about the Rajk trial. We underestimated it." Bacílek and Dolanský spoke in a similar vein. Concluding the discussion, Gottwald attempted to explain that the concept of the show trial had changed because, "In their first statements, people under arrest confessed to activity directed against the party and the state but tried to assert that the immediate objective of their [planned] coup within the party was to substitute Švermová for Slánský. They had agreed on this line. Most of them have now abandoned this argument and say that it is in fact not true, that they tried to sidetrack us. Now it makes more sense."[63]

A similar scene followed the next day at a meeting of the CC KSČ presidium where Kopecký shouted that "the people have long demanded Slánský's head." Only Zdeněk Fierlinger asked whether Slánský's espionage had been proven.[64] On December 6, CC KSČ members reacted similarly when Gottwald spoke of Slánský as the proven enemy, agent, criminal, and traitor:

> Further investigation of various previously unmasked conspiratorial groups and of all the circumstances has revealed new, previously unknown facts. These new discoveries prove Slánský's direct, active and, one might say, leading participation in the conspiracy against the party and the state, which we started to uncover a year ago with the arrest of that traitor and spy Šling.
>
> One other very serious fact completes the picture of Slánský's true role. We have acquired irrefutable proof that the espionage service of Western imperialists was organizing and preparing Rudolf Slánský's escape to the West. The whole Slánský affair is now being examined and investigated on a new basis. Understandably . . . the details of the investigation cannot be made public yet.

The participants did their best. They blamed everything possible on Slánský; they kicked and pummeled the political carcass of the man who six months earlier made them tremble and whose favors they curried.

> *Bareš*: We feel . . . we are looking down a deep abyss. We are amazed and angry to see a nest of adders hissing at us, jeopardizing all our hopes.
>
> *Baśťovanský*: Slánský gave the impression of a strict, dogmatic iceman, lacking warmth and kindness. His behavior was cynical, insincere, and moody . . . comrades feared him.
>
> *Fierlinger* [repeating his doubts, but toning them down considerably]: Of

course, a lot is still unclear in the Slánský matter, but I hope that eventually light will be shed on behind-the-scene secrets and that treason will be fully unmasked.

Most remarkable was the speech of Václav Kopecký, the party ideologue of show trials. He elaborated again upon the ideology of the coming show trial, Zionism:

> While unmasking the Šling malefactors it was pointed out that most of them come from wealthy Jewish families . . . Our party hasn't yet grasped seriously enough the problem of struggling against cosmopolitanism. The cosmopolitan thinking of the great part of people with a Jewish origin has been forgotten . . . Zionism has become a very serious danger in recent years . . . it has become an important instrument of American and British imperialism.
> The international Zionist organization is linked with the Jewish State of Israel . . . Advocates of Zionism figure that in the people's democracies, Zionism can be transformed into a species of Titoism . . . they have talked about Jewish Titoism . . . Connections with Zionism have been uncovered in Hungary and Poland . . .
> [Slánský and others] formed a second center. They figured that one day they would detain us, imprison us, put us on trial . . . But instead of their grabbing us by the neck, we have grabbed them.[65]

CC KSČ members condemned their general secretary before he could take the stand.

Communists were informed about Slánský's arrest in a special memorandum. The press reported on it, immediately inspiring a wave of meetings and resolutions approving the measures. From the end of November to December 19, the CC KSČ received 2,355 resolutions, and there was no end in sight. They expressed agreement and satisfaction with the arrest and belief in Slánský's treason and crimes; but many also called for blood, death sentences, investigations of all of Slánský's collaborators and of other people, including Kopřiva, Zápotocký, Dolanský, and Frank. Some even demanded the removal of Jews from all public offices.[66]

Slánský's arrest sent a tremor through the entire Communist party, affecting its officials most strongly and opening the floodgates to universal suspicion; the witch hunt escalated. Gottwald's appeal for every official to help unmask Slánský's hostile activity inspired thousands of denunciations, self-critical flagellations, fingers pointed at possible enemies and enemy lairs. Letters of people who had working contact with Slánský reflected fear for their lives.

Štefan Bašťovanský [CC KSS general secretary]: I ask that when considering my blame, it be taken into consideration that my wife—though a prewar party member—is of bourgeois origin.

Antonín Gregor [foreign trade minister and CC KSČ presidium member]: When the CC KSČ political secretariat dealt with supplies to the USSR, I should have recognized that there were doubts about my sincere attitude toward the USSR.

Today, however, I realize that com. Gottwald expressed his doubts about the correctness of my [trade] dealings with the USSR most clearly, if only in interjections. Whatever happens to me, I will not feel and think differently. Under all circumstances I shall remain true to the USSR and to com. Stalin.

General Jaroslav Procházka [chief of staff and CC KSČ member]: On January 11, 1952, I was informed about the decision of the CC KSČ political secretariat that I be dismissed, effective immediately, as chief of staff because of my political responsibility for the military policy of Slánský and company and for not reporting my attitude toward Slánský. I then wrote a report for com. Gottwald in which I requested that the party restore the confidence which I had lost through my incorrect behavior.[67]

Many of these letters and denunciations reached a special task force of an StB evaluation group, which submitted findings about 2,077 people. Interrogators thus gained a vast reservoir of "evidentiary material" and future witnesses.[68]

Slánský's arrest triggered a personnel merry-go-round. His co-workers lost their jobs, as did his acquaintances, people whom someone had fingered, ministers, CC KSČ secretaries, government officials, people from the economic and the party apparatus. This allowed for the advance of Slánský's former opponents and of people who suddenly turned into his opponents. The changes generated a significant group of officials who owed their career to "uncovering the enemies." It included, for example, Václav Kopecký and Antonín Novotný who (in December 1951) finally joined the CC KSČ political secretariat, the most powerful group in the country.

Most important for preparing the show trial was the change of the national-security minister. When Kopřiva took the job in mid-1950, Gottwald enjoined him strictly to follow the instructions and the opinions of the advisors. Kopřiva obeyed and turned into a mere figurehead, leaving the advisors in charge of the main security and intelligence areas. In addition, from the very beginning, Kopřiva faced some opposition from the Náchod group. Smola considered the minister a potential enemy; and after Slánský's arrest, he stated that Kopřiva would be next. Kopřiva's employees even collected material against him, and one such document accidentally (or intentionally?) reached his desk. After six months on the job he complained about the situation and considered resigning. Doubek later confirmed this, "I know that Minister Kopřiva felt hard-pressed by some of the circumstances at the ministry and that the office didn't suit him well. I think that deep down he didn't even agree with everything he was doing. I remember visiting him with Košťál one morning and he said, 'I'd just love to run away from this slaughter-house.' "[69]

Toward the end of December 1951, Gottwald asked Kopřiva to pre-pare a critical analysis of his own and his ministry's work and to draw some personal conclusions. Kopřiva did so, mentioned his own close relationship with Slánský, and submitted his resignation. Gottwald opted for this formal procedure in order to comply with Stalin's instruction. He wrote:

> In Stalin's opinion, we should relieve com. Kopřiva of the job of minister and replace him with a completely reliable and sensible (conscientious) party comrade. Kopřiva has to be released because he didn't manage to stop an entire train from crossing to West Germany [in September 1951]. Such matters cannot be forgiven. Also, I think Kopřiva is Slánský's man. It would therefore be dangerous for him to be in such a position.[70]

Stalin didn't know Kopřiva and was only relaying the wishes of the Moscow security center, which had already picked out a successor—their long-time collaborator Karol Bacílek, whom they recommended to Gott-wald. Bacílek hesitated, but Gottwald reminded him of his duty "to go where the party needs him" and hailed him as "a veteran party member, not linked with Slánský." Bacílek agreed and took the job intending to do it "without reservations; the party needs it."

Gottwald reemphasized that he should follow the instructions of the Soviet advisors. "Com. Gottwald personally introduced me to Alexei [Beschasnov] when I took office," Bacílek wrote. "I was told that he was one of the most able officials of the Soviet interior ministry . . . hand-picked by Stalin himself."[71]

Antonín Prchal, a collaborator of Soviet security since 1945, joined Bacílek in January 1952 as deputy minister and StB chief. He took over the job from Josef Hora, who had been installed less than a year earlier by Taussigová.

5

SLÁNSKÝ'S INTERROGATION

INTERROGATION METHODS

CZECHOSLOVAK STATE Security cooperated with Soviet advisors in developing an entirely integrated interrogation system, a critical element in preparing show trials. Interrogations constituted the basis for all investigation, so it was imperative that their results correspond to the political concept of the trial. Strict rules were followed in order to achieve this.

The interrogation system consisted of three elements: interrogations and protocols, physical duress, and psychological pressure. The interrogation started with the drafting of a plan and ended with a protocol that was approved by the advisors and accompanied by the interrogator's report on the status of the interrogation.

Interrogation plans covered a certain time period or topic for each interrogation session. The first ones were approved by the minister of national security who, accompanied by Beschasnov, occasionally took them to Gottwald for approval. The plan included the main point that the questioning should lead up to and a list of specific questions to be asked verbatim, with appended documentation when appropriate. The most important point was the interrogation objective, which determined the testimony or confession to be extracted from the suspect. Interrogators tried to meet, or at least approximate, these objectives because their own performance was measured against them.

The final protocol was reviewed by the advisors who had drafted the interrogation plans in the first place and who controlled how they were being met. If the protocol didn't achieve the stated objective, it was returned to the interrogators. The advisors either changed its text, and the interrogators then had to get their victim to sign it, or the advisors demanded that the interrogation continue until the protocol matched the objective. As a result, a suspect may have been interrogated for several hours, but the session would yield only a few pages or just a single page of protocol. Most of the session would be taken up by pressure to follow the interrogation plans, and a few paragraphs were enough to capture all the interrogator needed.

All interrogators and national-security ministers later confirmed that Soviet advisors drafted or approved the interrogation plans and directed the interrogations. Thus Jan Musil stated, "We were instructed about the interrogations. Their objectives and the issues to focus on were decided by comrade Alexei [Beschasnov]. Additionally, we received instructions about interrogating Slánský and advice on procedure from another advisor, comrade Georgi [Gromov] . . . We prepared plans for interrogating Slánský. We used them only after comrade Alexei OK'd them."[1]

After five years in the leadership of the Communist party, Minister Bacílek explained, "According to the procedure I prepared interrogation programs with the Soviet advisors. Comrades Gottwald and Zápotocký also received them. They were also copied on the protocols from the interrogations . . . The interrogation programs were OK'd by Alexei and myself, sometimes by comrade Gottwald."[2]

The advisors had all the protocols translated into Russian, by a special team of translators. In addition, Beschasnov and his deputies had their own interpreters. The head advisor dispatched the protocols to the Moscow center and, in turn, received comments or even fully formulated questions that were then included in the interrogation plans. Doubek mentioned that Beschasnov "quoted questions for the defendants from a piece of paper with a stamp of the Soviet foreign ministry."[3]

Once approved by the advisors, many of the interrogation plans and almost all the protocols were forwarded to Gottwald. Gottwald read them carefully, but his role went beyond that: the minister or Beschasnov sometimes asked him to consider questions they were interested in and to decide whether they should be put to Slánský. Košťál mentioned, "In meetings concerning Slánský's interrogation, I was told that comrade Gottwald decided all principal questions, and I was frequently asked to pick out all questions that called for his review. These concerned issues such as whether comrade Gottwald was aware of a particular offense of

Slánský's, whether a particular document may be used, whether Slánský was right when referring to comrade Gottwald, etc."[4]

The objectives of the interrogation plans were usually attained in a complicated and—for the suspect—painful way. Various forms of physical duress and psychological pressure were used. Between 1948 and 1954, Czechoslovak security developed these methods into an entire system. Only people of exceptional resistance and willpower managed not to succumb; and even these exceptional individuals gave in at least at first, and only later retracted their statements, refused to make any further "confessions," and refused to sign protocols. They included Jarmila Taussigová, Gustáv Husák, and Josef Smrkovský from among Communist officials.

The interrogators used a variety of forms of physical duress, and a wide scale of severity. This depended on what was customary as well as on the personalities involved: of both the interrogator and the suspect. Physical duress was not introduced by Soviet advisors in 1949; it had been employed even earlier, right after World War II, and became prevalent after the Communist takeover in 1948. Certain institutions and certain interrogators were notorious for their exceptional brutality. Some went too far and were fired or sent to prison or labor camps for a time. In some cases, interrogation methods were fatal. The exact count is not known because murders were sometimes reported as suicides, but many were actually admitted or proven.

The most frequently used, indeed almost routine forms of physical duress were beating, throttling, banging the inmate's head against the wall, and kicking. Josef Smrkovský was slapped eighty times one afternoon session, not counting fist blows, kicks, and banging his head against the wall. In a complaint to the party authorities, Gustáv Husák related, "During the interrogation I was hit, throttled, and abused in every possible way. I was physically completely exhausted and almost unconscious when on February 13, 1951, under brutal physical duress, I was forced to sign a false protocol." Taussigová complained about physical duress to Zápotocký, after he became president, saying that the interrogators tossed her around and pinched her breasts. Talking to Bedřich Hájek, an interrogator boasted, "In this very room we spun [Záviš] Kalandra around. Sure, we took turns while he was here all that time. When he could no longer stand on his feet [he wasn't allowed to sit down for seventy-two hours] and lay on the floor, he signed. So think it over, Hájek."

There were thousands of such cases, and of much worse ones. They became a routine feature of the interrogation process. Other highly prized and equally effective methods included night interrogations and incessant ones, continuing for several days. An outline of a lecture that Minister Kopřiva gave to interrogators in 1951 includes, "Break the [suspect] with a long interrogation. Four hours will bring no results. Short interrogations allow time for reflection. Long interrogations [leave the suspect] tired, distressed; he cannot think things through in peace. Ten, twelve hours yield better results than a shorter time."

Equally brutal and exhausting methods kept the suspect on his feet or even standing at attention. A special type was the "merry-go-round," with the suspect walking in circles and beaten with a wet towel. When he collapsed, he was drenched with cold water and slapped back to consciousness. On August 1, 1951, Husák refused to sign a protocol. He later wrote, "Three more months of brutality and violence followed. I spent hundreds of hours standing up. I was beaten, throttled, and injured [by a higher officer]. During the last three weeks in October [1951] I was interrogated, brutalized, humiliated, and intimidated incessantly, day and night, including weekends, sleeping perhaps two hours a day." Smrkovský testified, "On two occasions they didn't let me sleep for four days in a row. I was interrogated nonstop, and when I was nodding off, they slapped my face to wake me up."

Physical violence continued in other forms in the cell. Hunger and a ban on smoking were routine if, in the opinion of the interrogator, the prisoner didn't deserve more food or cigarettes because of his "stubborn attitude." Exercise and medical attention (which was particularly miserable) were denied for the same reasons. "Insubordinate" prisoners were deprived of their glasses and dentures; they could use them only at certain limited times (during meals). Gloves constituted a frequent punishment: prisoners had to wear them for weeks on end so that their fingertips would practically rot away. Thus on June 25, 1951, one interrogator ordered prisoner No. 2063 to put gloves on; he wore them until July 19.

The punishment cell (described above, in connection with Otto Šling) was a particularly cruel measure. It represented punishment for insubordination (for refusal to make a required statement). Torment frequently continued in the cell between sessions: the prisoner had to march around the cell and wasn't allowed to sleep or even to sit. He developed swollen feet, excruciating pain, and unbearable fatigue. The prisoner couldn't sleep because in regular intervals, usually of fifteen minutes, he was awakened to report. Thus on August 24, 1951, inter-

rogator Jaroslav Sedláček ordered prisoner No. 2057 into the punishment cell from 6 A.M. the following morning until 8 A.M. of August 27,
during which time he was not allowed to sleep. The same prisoner's
"insubordination" got him back into the punishment cell from September 1 through 3. He was awakened every ten minutes and had to walk
around for ten minutes.

Husák complained:

> I was on my feet nonstop for three days and three nights (seventy hours)
> and in the course of seven days and seven nights I had four two-hour periods
> of sleep, during which I was periodically awakened and brought to my feet
> again. My feet were swollen, and I wasn't allowed to sit. [In later months:]
> For dozens of days and nights I had to walk around my cell (I was forbidden
> to sit), I had to stand during interrogations, I was often in the punishment
> cell sleeping on bare ground, sleep was limited to one or two hours in a twenty-
> four-hour period . . . During the first 500 days of my detention I was allowed
> only one fifteen-minute walk in the yard. Over the next 300 days, there were
> only fifteen such walks. I was allowed to use glasses in my cell only after
> eighteen months, and my eyesight deteriorated considerably. I was allowed a
> sweater after twenty-three months . . . For six months now I have not been
> allowed to smoke.

A report for the KSČ leadership about the 1951 interrogations of
Smrkovský, dated August 27, 1955, mentioned that he hardly slept from
early May to the end of June, that a five-day nonstop session started at
the end of May, and that he suffered from hunger.

Psychological pressure complemented physical duress. The Soviet
contribution was particularly prominent in this area. Many prisoners felt
victimized even before their arrest: they were conspicuously shadowed
and their phone was tapped to make them nervous. Provocations cooked
up by security, which led to many arrests, had a similar effect. A particularly effective form of psychological pressure was the system of total
isolation. After his arrest, the prisoner met with no one except his interrogators and his cellmate. There was no contact with the outside
world, with the family, or an attorney. There was no access to the press
or radio. One could write to one's family only after several weeks in
prison, and "insubordinate" prisoners were often forbidden to write and
receive mail altogether, frequently for long periods. The suspects were
escorted to the interrogation offices blindfolded and handcuffed. The
interrogators stressed that no one was interested in them, that their wives
were unfaithful, and that their children had repudiated them. Isolation
was to evoke a sense of abandonment and uncertainty. Interrogators used

a very effective array of threats, including the punishment cell, ever-harsher interrogations, reduced food rations, and most effectively, threats that the families would be arrested or persecuted in other ways. Personal affronts and humiliation were routine. The prisoner ceased to be a person. He was known by a number which substituted for his name. The interrogators insulted the prisoners' nationality, race, political beliefs, and their humanity. The addressed them as "villains," "thugs," "agents of imperialism," "Trotskyites," "bourgeois nationalists," "traitors," "Zionists," "Jewish swine," "Jewish liars," "Jewish murderers." Taussigová wrote Zápotocký that during her five years in prison, no one ever addressed her as "Mrs.," but only "whore," "swine," "Gestapo tart"; "this whore gave birth to a bastard," they would say. Anti-Nazi resistance fighters were insulted by being identified with their adversaries as SS-men, Gestapo agents, murderers. General Václav Paleček, as another example, was interrogated in an SS uniform he was forced to wear.

Security agents, planted as cellmates, reported on the prisoners and were instructed to gear the conversation to rattle them, and to emphasize their isolation and the hopelessness of resisting. They kept reminding Communists that it was their party duty to confess and thereby to help the party struggle with enemies; the interrogators acted as deputies of the party.

Party officials arrested prior to February 1951 were under tremendous physical duress, and their confessions were literally beaten out of them. Later the degree of physical abuse noticeably abated while psychological pressures escalated, including appeals to party obligations. Many indeed "recognized" this obligation and fulfilled it.

The system of interrogations and protocols was organized to meet the interrogation plans and objectives. Interrogators usually started their work not knowing what the charges were and without any evidence. It was their job to extract the evidence (false confessions). One of them, Karel Kudrna, later stated, "We felt like demagogues. Instead of getting evidence we were told that they were villains and that we had to break them . . . Kopřiva said that he had the party's confidence and that they were enemies who had to be neutralized."

Class and political consciousness and party loyalty were to help the interrogators extract "evidence." Kopřiva challenged them, according to a transcript of a lecture, "to fill your hearts with hatred for the class enemy and his agents, to always bear in mind that people who have betrayed the party and the sacred cause of the working class are capable of anything, of any crime, any turpitude. Of all criminals, these are the worst." Kopřiva actually saw the result of the interrogation and the question-and-answer protocol as a reflection of the interrogator's political maturity.

Several forms of interrogation were practiced. One focused on the suspect's biography: as the suspect related it, the interrogator uncovered "dark spots," starting points for further questioning. Another form focused on self-criticism: it was used with officials who previously had publicly—or, indeed, in writing—admitted their political errors to party authorities. The interrogator's task was to translate these political errors into punishable crimes and to "persuade" his victim about the correctness of this procedure.

Yet another form focused on a compromising document, real or forged, that was shown to the suspect who then had to explain it. The objective of focusing on a person was to generate charges or evidence against another suspect. The forced testimony, further doctored by the interrogators, then served in interrogating another victim, in an interrogation focusing on a confession. The suspect's task was to refute false accusations.

The interrogators thought very highly of confrontations, either one-on-one or in groups. During a confrontation, two suspects were kept in separate spaces, and one recited a statement prepared by the interrogators that he had learned by rote. He couldn't be questioned and was then taken away. During a group confrontation, several witnesses recited their statements.

Soviet advisors introduced "question-and-answer" protocols. Prior to that, it was customary for the suspect to make a statement concerning the charges, which the interrogator would record. Question-and-answer protocols, however, included the entire dialogue. This method had several advantages. First, it allowed the interrogator to expand the charges: one answer became the starting point for the next question. The suspect would surrender and make one "confession," believing that would bring his torments to an end, but that confession became only another link in an entire chain of questions and confessions, the length of which was determined by the interrogator. Second, question-and-answer protocols allowed the interrogator to adapt the responses as required. The interrogator ignored everything the suspect had to say in his defense, arguing that "these are known matters, you'll present this at the trial; we're investigating your criminal activity, not your merits." The actual wording of the answers, formulated by the interrogator, led to even more serious distortions. He included only what he found useful and what was in line with the interrogation plan and slanted the wording to the suspect's disadvantage. He formulated the answers so as to bring them in line with the Penal Code's terminology: sabotage, high treason, and so on. As Minister Kopřiva explained in a lecture:

> In drafting the question-and-answer protocols we get the prisoners used to formulations that qualify as criminal activity. For example: "our subversive organization," "my hostile attitude." The question-and-answer protocol captures real activity, which the courts have to know in order to gauge the defendant's guilt. These protocols are more suitable for the courts. The court then knows in advance what the defendant stated.

Consequently, the protocols substantially differed from the actual statements, even from the forced statements and confessions. In some cases, the interrogator demanded that the prisoner sign a protocol that included statements the prisoner had never made. Again, Gustáv Husák recalled:

> [After I refused to sign a protocol,] the interrogators tried another method: dishonestly twisting, even literally falsifying the protocol . . . During confrontations in 1951, I wasn't allowed to say a word or write anything. During confrontations in 1953, I was not allowed to comment on a vast majority of the statements. Even when I could make a point, my interrogators recorded incorrect, abridged, even completely fabricated statements in the protocol. I therefore refused to sign it, seeing that it was incorrect and completely or partially fabricated. In my absence, the interrogators changed and distorted it further and didn't even submit it for my signature. These illegal methods were also employed with protocols written in February and March of 1954.

The system of interrogations left physical and psychological scars on all who were exposed to it for any length of time. Many suspects suffered fractures, lost teeth, impaired hearing or eyesight, headaches, frostbite, swollen feet, and other ailments. The mental health of many prisoners was impaired: there were cases of schizophrenia, loss of orientation, psychoses, and frequent suicide attempts. All prisoners indicated a loss of willpower and of the ability to resist the pressure of the interrogators and their false accusations.

There is no evidence that shots or other medication were used to weaken the defendants' willpower. In the weeks preceding the trial and during the trial itself, some of them received sedatives or stimulants; but once the effect passed, defendants reverted to resignation and passivity.

In addition to extracting a "confession," in itself a short-term objective, the perpetrators of physical abuse and psychological pressure had a long-term objective in mind as well. They wanted the prisoner to realize his own helplessness and the hopelessness of his position, and to see his only way out in confessing just about anything the interrogators wanted; to reach a moral breakdown when the pliant suspect fully cooperated with the interrogator. Once this point was reached, the worst forms of physical abuse ceased, other types of abuse were limited, and the psychological pressure significantly abated.[5]

FIRST WEEKS IN PRISON

The arrest of the conspiracy's head launched the second phase of the show-trial preparations. It focused on maximizing its political effectiveness (on defining its political orientation) and on selecting and preparing the appropriate group of defendants. The most pressing task was to elicit from Slánský a confession of truly shocking crimes. The trial itself, not to mention its success, depended on such a confession. The path toward it was not easy: progress was measured in tiny steps and encountered unexpected obstacles. Slánský resisted for six months. On November 25, 1951, two days after Slánský's arrest, Gottwald said, "I'm sure Slánský will talk," but it wasn't nearly that simple.

As soon as the CC KSČ presidium meeting of November 25, 1951 was over, Kopřiva briefed Doubek and Košťál about it. He emphasized Gottwald's belief that "in our country, Zionism is headed by Slánský. We shouldn't forget that even an old vixen can have kits." He also informed them that Slánský was entitled to write a letter.[6]

He did write one, dated *November 26, 1951*. Little did Slánský realize it would be his last:

To the CC KSČ presidium

Dear Comrades:

I realize that my arrest must have been spurred by some serious reasons of which I am unaware. I realize, too, that we have learned from experience that a person must be arrested if he is suspect, because an offender seldom confesses while at liberty.

However, any suspicions against me, suspicions of any crimes against the party, must be the result of some tremendous error.

Never in my life did I betray the party, consciously damage it, or collude with agents.

I realize that others who at first protested their innocence eventually turned out to be villains.

But this is not and cannot be my case. No one can know it better than I, because even in my most secret thoughts I have never been untrue to the party.

I know I bear a heavy responsibility for errors, above all in personnel policies because I was shortsighted and trusted bad people, I grossly neglected vigilance, I was flighty, and I was inconsistent in the field of ideology.

I have committed many other grave errors in organizational work, and these have harmed the party. But never, ever did I harm the party consciously.

I have one request: please do not condemn me as an enemy publicly and in advance. I am absolutely confident that the charges against me will turn out to be false.

Rudolf Slánský
November 26, 1951[7]

Interrogations began on November 27 and continued for a year. They were conducted by Department 6-A of the State Security's Interrogation Bureau, specifically by Doubek, Košťál, and Musil.

In his position as bureau chief, Doubek later supervised the interrogations but did not conduct them directly. In reality, though, they were directed from behind the scenes by Soviet advisors. A special three-member group consisting of Georgi Gromov, Grigori Morozov, and Ivan Chernov arrived from Moscow, with a single special task: to "do" Slánský. Alexei Beschasnov, the leader of Soviet security advisors, his deputy Yesikov, and Galkin also took an active part. The Soviets didn't actually interrogate the prisoners and weren't even present. Their role was different: since they were the only people in security with detailed knowledge of the concept of the trial under preparation, they could steer the interrogation in the right direction, control it, and advise the interrogators.

In the afternoon of November 26, 1951, Minister Kopřiva met with advisors and interrogators to discuss objectives of the first series of sessions. The minister had just returned from delivering Slánský's letter to Gottwald. He mentioned with satisfaction that both Gottwald and Zápotocký read the letter with a smile. The meeting participants decided to tell Slánský that Gottwald had returned the letter with the advice that "Slánský speak about all he did rather than write letters" and expected that Slánský would be profoundly shaken by this message.[8]

The meeting decided on a course of action: they would reiterate to Slánský that he had been unmasked and would ask him to confess his hostile activity. If he refused, they would initiate a detailed interrogation focusing on the self-criticism he made at the September 1951 CC KSČ session. "The interrogation will focus on the specific points of the self-criticism, arguing in every case that these are not political errors as he [Slánský] stated but intentional hostile activity." Long, ten- to twelve-hour interrogation sessions were to start on Sunday morning.

Gottwald's message was relayed to Slánský on *November 27*, but it didn't have the anticipated effect: it did not break the defendant. The actual interrogation started out by challenging Slánský to "Testify about your activity which has harmed the interests and policies of the KSČ."

Slánský at first refused to admit causing any damage but eventually the protocol recorded, "I harmed the party by committing a number of serious errors in organizational work and particularly in personnel work." It was his fault, he expanded, that many enemies had insinuated themselves into leading offices in the country and caused a lot of damage. "I therefore realize that my errors are far graver than I had originally believed." "Does this mean," the interrogator continued, "that your self-criticism at the September CC KSČ session was not as penetrating as you pretended?" And Slánský's response was "Yes." The session continued:

> *Interrogator*: Who were these bad elements, hostile to the party and alien to the working class, that penetrated the party and which you feel responsible for?
>
> *Slánský*: They were elements with capitalist origins, nationalists of various kinds, including Zionists, and also people who *later* turned out to be enemy agents.

The interrogators now felt close to the planned objective, which was for Slánský to admit (or come close to admitting) that his errors were not unintentional but were the result of hostile intent; however, their hopes of attaining a "confession" diminished as they shifted to the second phase. The questions gradually bore in this direction:

> *Interrogator*: So far, you have discussed your hostile activity in terms of very grave errors. Discuss now the roots of your hostile activity which you describe as grave errors.
>
> *Slánský*: I object to the question. I do not consider my errors to constitute hostile activity . . . The roots of my errors lie in my opportunistic tendencies

and leanings, in conjunction with improper work methods and lack of self-criticism.

[This admission of responsibility led to a follow-up question:]

Interrogator: Of course, you describe everything as a serious error. Why don't you discuss manifestations of your anti-Soviet attitude?

Slánský [a resolute refusal]: I demonstrated no anti-Soviet attitudes!

Interrogator [continues to attack]: Do you consider the activity of Trotskyites, who were involved in sabotage, as hostile?

Slánský: I do.

Interrogator: And facilitating this activity is also hostile activity?

Slánský: Not always.

Interrogator: Is facilitating this activity a criminal offense?

Slánský: Yes.[9]

For the following three days, *November 28 through 30,* the sessions revolved around the same issues. Slánský admitted political errors but not hostile activity. On *December 1,* an interrogator wrote in a summary report that "He testified that his own opportunistic errors allowed hostile elements to penetrate various areas of the party and the state apparatus in order to promote the restoration of capitalism in Czechoslovakia."

The results so far didn't satisfy the advisors. Gottwald, too, was demanding specifics to report to the central committee. The interrogators, therefore, intensified the pressure. On *December 2* Slánský was asked:

Interrogator: In which additional areas, other than those you've already discussed, did you sponsor policies hostile to the party and the state?

Slánský: I sponsored no hostile policies.

Interrogator: Don't you believe that your lies will protract the investigation.

During every interrogation, often more than once, Slánský was asked to "testify about other ways in which you harmed the party," but he usually remained silent. "He continuously tries not to speak and waits for evidence," an interrogator complained.[10]

No questioning took place on *December 6.* The CC KSČ was in session, discussing the Slánský affair, and Soviet advisors insisted that Doubek and Košťál be invited. They were to witness what Slánský's former close collaborators thought of him and use these as arguments.[11]

This had a great effect on Slánský. Nevertheless, he still didn't substantively change his statements. He admitted more political errors, but he continued to resist the main objective—that he qualify political errors as hostile activity. The initial phase of the interrogation was dragging on with little to show.

In mid-December, the advisors decided to employ the tactic of Slánský's "political and moral profile." They would continuously bring up his treason, call him a political swindler and liar, criticize his alleged immoral personal life, and highlight the opinions of the party leadership and ordinary citizens by quoting passages from the press and various resolutions.

But this tactic was also fruitless: Slánský still didn't change his position. On *December 22*, an interrogator reported that "Slánský was then interrogated without presenting evidence. When his political and moral profile is outlined to him, he is very depressed. Nevertheless, he still will not admit hostile intent."[12]

By early 1952, the investigation seemed to have reached an impasse. Slánský admitted a series of political errors and responsibility for having posted a variety of officials who *later* turned out to be enemies, foreign agents, and traitors. He intentionally named only people who had been arrested while he was still in office and who had already been labeled as "enemies." As most other victims in the first period of incarceration, he believed in his own innocence but in the guilt of others.

Slánský based his defense on the self-criticism he had presented to the September 1951 CC KSČ session, for two reasons: First, he had consulted this self-criticism with Gottwald. Second, he admitted political responsibility for errors and shortcomings in it but not for hostile activity; and in this form the self-criticism had been approved by the central committee. However, after his arrest, all party organs declared this self-criticism to have been insincere and deceitful; they condemned it and qualified all his errors as having hostile intent.

Slánský requested two days of peace to think things over. The request was relayed to the minister, who took it to Gottwald. Both Gottwald and Kopřiva believed that a change in Slánský's attitude was imminent and that he would confess. They instructed that this "historical moment" be taped, so important did they feel it to be.[13]

Slánský got his two days of peace (*January 5 and 6*), but he also got a cellmate, a "plant." Slánský kept quiet, sitting or walking around, lost in thoughts. Only now and then did he say something. He was interested in the life of convicts in the notorious Bory prison near Pilsen. His questions indicated that he counted on being convicted but not on losing his life.[14]

SLÁNSKÝ'S INNER STRUGGLE

Slánský spent five weeks in isolation before getting a cellmate on *January 3, 1952*. The agent was planted precisely when the interrogators thought that Slánský was close to a moral breakdown. In the mechanism of interrogations, a cellmate had not only a passive role (reporting the suspect's reactions to the interrogations) but also the active role of keeping him off balance and, in effect, continuing the interrogation in a different guise.

The interrogators and advisors debated on several occasions whom to select for Slánský. Their requirements were high: it had to be a former high official of the party who could match the former general secretary's knowledge of the working milieu and intelligence. It had to be someone who knew Slánský and had had some bad experience with him, yet not a former co-worker. Eventually they selected Bohdan Benda.

Benda had worked until the fall of 1948 in the Prague regional KSČ secretariat as a secretary for security and the military. After the split with Yugoslavia, Slánský heard that Benda maintained contact with Yugoslav diplomats and had even passed on some classified documents. This was a rather routine provocation in those days. Slánský decided that Benda should be arrested. His mother, sister, and wife were later detained as well. Benda himself was sentenced to many years in prison and thus had many reasons to hate Slánský. The interrogators counted on that and reminded him of Slánský's part in his own tragic fate.

Benda's controller was František Škorpík, a State Security commander, who in turn was directly handled by the Soviet advisor Georgi Gromov. Benda received his instructions from Škorpík and used his office to write daily reports. Later Benda testified:

> My main task was this: above all to keep an eye on [Slánský] when he wasn't being interrogated (in the cell) to make sure he didn't hurt himself in any way or simply didn't somehow evade interrogation. That was my main task. During the investigation I had other tasks as well, of course. I was to exert certain psychological pressure on Slánský to make him confess . . . as instructed by the interrogators, I was also to attack him in discussions, vex him . . ."[15]

Benda's reports corroborated the interrogators' belief that Slánský verged on a moral breakdown. The very first report of *January 4* expressed his astonishment over Slánský's state of mind:

> He is terribly shaken and gives the impression of being totally destroyed . . . I tried to start a longer conversation, but he told me he'd probably be a poor companion because he had too many worries and would not talk much. He said I had to understand that he was in a tough struggle with himself. I told him there was no point in thinking too much.
>
> [The following day, *January 5,*] he staggered about the cell and said that

his head was swimming because he was so terribly tired. He said that he couldn't sleep at all in this cell because he had to lie on his left side [to face the spy-hole], and he would request a change of cells. Then he asked me what the punishment cell is like, and I gave him a detailed description, as I know it from hearsay. He's clearly afraid of it.[16]

Slánský's two days for reflection were up on *January 7*. The advisors and interrogators impatiently anticipated his conclusions, which they expected would amount to their own triumph. Doubek's leading statement, formulated the day before by the advisors, started off the conversation:

> *Doubek*: You requested two days for reflection and said that after these two days you would talk about your hostile activity directed against the party and the state.
> *Slánský*: I thought through all the circumstances and have decided to testify about my activity differently than before. I don't want to conceal anything, and I want to confess how and where I engaged in hostile activity in various areas of work for the party and the country. After the past few days I want to talk especially about my hostile activity in the areas of personnel work and organizational-political work. I further want to talk about hostile activity in the economy and in all other areas I was involved in. I will also declare that my activity jeopardized the people's democratic regime in Czechoslovakia and elaborate on that in detail.

Slánský's step toward a full confession only partially satisfied the advisors and the interrogators and the minister and politburo members who listened to it on tape. Slánský had indeed qualified his own political errors as hostile activity, but the main confession was still lacking—a subjective hostile intent. Slánský invented a different motivation, which he felt was more moderate: Trotskyite vacillation, as first demonstrated back in 1927.[17]

However, this led Slánský onto even thinner ice. As Musil later wrote, the advisors and interrogators followed Stalin's line in considering Trotskyism not as a political deviation but as outright hostility. Trotskyites were automatically described as enemies of the party, socialism, and the Soviet Union.[18] Slánský would now be considered a Trotskyite, for which there was additional "evidence," consisting of Trotskyite literature discovered in his library. Photocopies of one book with underlinings served as a proof of his complete turn to Trotskyism.

Trotskyism dominated the interrogations of *January 8*. Slánský admitted Trotskyite vacillation but refused to confess any deliberate Trotskyite activity, including the posting of Trotskyites and cooperating with them. He held his ground even after confrontations with several pliant prisoners (Evžen Klinger, Vilém Nový, and Václav Vlk) whose prepared statements contradicted him.

Yet this line of interrogation was not entirely fruitless. In Communist terminology, Trotskyism amounted to hostility to the party and to the Soviet Union. The interrogators managed to get Slánský to discuss hostility toward the party along these lines. According to the protocol of *January 12*, Slánský was asked to "describe the evolution of your hostile attitude toward the party." He responded, "My hostile attitude toward the party started developing in 1927 when I was regional secretary for Ostrava. I then manifested serious Trotskyite deviations. At this time, Zinoviev and his comrades came out as Trotskyites in Moscow."

In this spirit he requalified many specific events which a month ago he had considered mere political errors, "As a result of my antiparty activity, we were not adopting Soviet experiences in constructing socialism. We did not invite advisors and specialists in various fields of socialist construction."[19]

Slánský counted on "confessing" only a fraction of what the interrogators were after. The sessions, however, formed a chain; and every day and every week, another link was added. Slánský confessed one thing, assuming it would be the last, but it turned into the starting point for the next one.

These confessions were still only partial, though important to the masterminds of the interrogation. Since January 7, they had been expecting a complete, or "spontaneous" confession, but they didn't get it. On *January 21* they decided on a vehement attack to achieve Slánský's moral breakdown. When Slánský repeated his Trotskyite vacillation line and unintentional hostility, they interrupted him:

> *Interrogator*: That's not all. Seven weeks ago you were asked how and with whom you conspired against the republic, and you still haven't answered.
> *Slánský*: I didn't prepare any conspiracy.

This question was the pivot of the interrogations for four days and nights. There were other charges as well, but they all led to this main point. This was the most important shift in the interrogation to date: a shift from hostile activity to a conspiracy.[20]

The interrogators mobilized Benda, Slánský's cellmate, as well: he was instructed to frustrate Slánský and to suggest continually that he make a "full confession." Their conversations illuminate Slánský's reaction to this critical phase of the interrogation. He knew he would be convicted yet hoped to deflect the worst of what his tormentors wanted.

His inner struggle escalated. It included first signs of resignation, as he assured himself, "I have to overcome this and reconcile myself to a confession." On *January 21,* Benda recorded that

> [Slánský] is trying to dodge political questions any way he can. . . . He's very interested in convict life . . . He asked me how I think convicts in Bory receive former party officials. He tries to put on as calm a front as possible, but evidently it is costing him a lot of effort. In reality, he is very nervous and depressed.
>
> On *January 22*: He was very sleepy but tried to overcome it by walking. Every ten minutes or so he staggered so badly that he might have collapsed . . . He said he saw some children playing outside and people walking. He found that very sad, and it disturbed him very much.

Three days later, on *January 25,* Benda saw that "talking about the family bothers him terribly, so I stuck to this topic." Their conversation continued:

> *Slánský*: You're telling me you're a criminal, but all I can say is that I'm here for crimes against the state as well, so I can't reproach you for anything . . . I have to struggle with myself and reconcile myself to it, and therefore there's nothing you can tell me. Let's make this clear, I know the workings of this company and all their methods . . .
> *Benda*: If I can advise you from my own experience about your struggle with yourself, as you call it, I tell you it's best to settle it once and for all and to confess everything right away, because confessing bit by bit is much worse, and the interrogators have got to think that there's even more you're guilty of.
> *Slánský*: I know all these methods; I even signed off on using them several times. Of course now I'm experiencing it all myself, and it's that much worse.
> *Benda*: See? If you know that, you also know the results of the methods; and you certainly know it's hopeless to struggle here for anything.
> *Slánský*: I know all that, but it doesn't work that fast.[21]

SLÁNSKÝ'S SUICIDE ATTEMPT

The most difficult week of Slánský's year-long incarceration started *January 26*. Extended and all-night interrogation sessions turned into incessant ones that were to end only after he confessed to conspiring against the state. Benda was instructed to keep demoralizing Slánský during his short periods in the cell, to outline his "moral and political profile," and to underscore complete confession as the only way out. He took the offensive right after a night-long session.

Benda: I simply have to see you in the same light as the entire party and nation does: as a traitor and an enemy. And I'm telling you again, the way I feel about you, and thus our life here together, can be good only if you reconcile yourself with everything and confess all.

Slánský: I know that everybody's got to detest me now; but I'm telling you, this is my affair, and I have to reconcile myself to it on my own. It's me who's being interrogated and charged here, and it's my duty to discuss these things only with the case officers. I can't discuss them even with my cellmate.

Benda instigated another conversation after lunch. He raised the issue of families again, a topic he knew affected Slánský particularly strongly since he learned that his wife, Josefa, had been arrested. Slánský mentioned that he had a sixteen-year-old son and a daughter of two-and-a-half and that his son had chaired the youth union in his secondary school, which definitely would no longer be the case.

Slánský: You see, now I have to shoulder this entire burden as I face the party and the nation. I realize how they must all hate me and that I don't have a single friend out there. It's difficult to cope with that.

Benda: That's exactly why it's so important to fully fess up to that responsibility and settle it as fast as possible. There's a good old Czech proverb about that.

Slánský (interrupting): I know: The way you make your bed is the way you'll lie in it. You have your whole life ahead of you and a good perspective, whereas there's only one thing ahead of me . . . And Slánský made the sign of the cross in the air.

Benda reported: I contradicted him and said that surely [the end] depended on his attitude to the whole matter, but he interrupted me again: "I know it's not quite as tragic, but my outlook is hopeless nevertheless."

The conversation continued, and ended with Slánský's repeated assertion that he knew all the methods, he had approved them all, and now he was experiencing them all himself.[22]

Reports from the cell suggested that the advisors had selected the right moment for the final blow. Slánský was uncertain about his own situation: he saw it as hopeless, the sign of the cross surely meant that he thought about death, but the next moment he felt it wasn't quite so tragic.

Doubek and Košťál started off a nonstop session in the morning of January 26. They singlemindedly pursued the questioning in one direction: to elicit a confession that Slánský had headed a conspiracy against the state, to which end he created a network of people whom he intentionally placed in high offices where he managed them. Slánský rejected

Slánský with his son, Rudolf, Jr., on his 50th birthday, July 31, 1951

the idea, but the interrogators ignored his resistance. After two hours they said:

> *Interrogator*: List who specifically was involved in your conspiratorial organization.
> *Slánský*: I did not prepare a conspiracy.
> *Interrogator*: We'll confront you with Evžen Löbl.

Confrontations substituted for nonexistent evidence and served to extract confessions from recalcitrant suspects. They were, therefore, pre-

Slánský with his daughter, Martha, 1951

pared very carefully. The prisoners were not allowed to talk; and after the recitation, the witness was taken away. Slánský knew the role confrontations played and realized his own powerless and hopeless position, as his cellmate reported:

> He said that such a confrontation cannot end well for him because everything is prearranged, and there's nothing he can do. He said that one does indeed recall additional details; but usually the people one is confronted with simply lie, either to diminish their own responsibility or to earn some favors here. When I asked him why the interrogators would do that, he said that's the way things are; they already have an entire investigation framework and try to fit everything into it at any cost . . . The points that they go over during confrontations are, in effect, the highlights of the entire investigation, and the whole framework would be damaged without them.

Doubek and Kohoutek took care of Löbl's side of the confrontation: they wrote out his text; Löbl memorized and recited it. It was based on his deposition of April 1951, according to which Slánský gave him instructions concerning international trade negotiations that had already been labeled as hostile. Löbl's confrontation statement, however, went beyond that in declaring that Slánský headed the conspiracy for which he had recruited Löbl. When it was over, Doubek asked Slánský:

> *Doubek*: Are you still going to deny organizing a conspiracy against the state?
> *Slánský*: I do indeed deny organizing a conspiracy against the state.[23]

Since the confrontation yielded nothing specific, the interrogation proceeded nonstop, even more intensively. Doubek reported:

> Košťál, Musil, and I continued the questioning all afternoon and into the evening, but with no result. The Soviet advisors invited Košťál and me to an ice-hockey game, to give us some diversion and said that right after the game we'd return to Ruzyně to continue with the interrogation. Musil would be in charge during our absence, and we'd continue all night . . . Toward the morning, Košťál repeatedly told Slánský, "You have to confess, you have to!" Slánský leaned against the wall, his eyes popped, his face turned red, and, veins on his neck bulging, he clenched his hands and screamed in an insane voice, "I cannot!" He repeated that about a dozen times in an ever-higher pitch. After a few minutes this attack passed, he sat down and, depressed, held his head in his hands.[24]

The psychological crisis culminated in a nervous breakdown. The interrogation was adjourned, and Slánský was dragged off to his cell. Not for long, though. Early on *January 27,* the interrogators reported these events to the advisors, who were angry that the interrogation had stopped. They viewed the attack as a very favorable rather than an unfavorable moment, one which ought to be used to extract a confession. The interrogation resumed but Slánský resisted all afternoon and into the night.[25]

He returned to his cell for a while in the morning of *January 28,* only to feel the pressure from his cellmate. Benda, focusing on Slánský's repeated comments, said that "he is very troubled to see people walking around as he looks out of the window and wonders, 'Why can't I be among them?' to which I said that if I were in his place, I wouldn't even want that."

> *Slánský*: That's exactly why this thought is so awful: all those people, the granny crossing the street or anyone else, they all hate me. You know something, my tragedy is a dreadful one. You can't even imagine a worse one.
> *Benda*: You're a traitor and an enemy of the party and of the whole nation;

and instead of heaping scorn on you, here I am actually showing you some kind of false sympathy.

Slánský: Right, I understand you; I'm a criminal and certainly a much worse one than you. The crimes I've been accused of are so great and of such a character that you can't even imagine them. I can't even tell you what I'm being charged with. You're not allowed to know it; but you gather that if the party decided to arrest its general secretary, it wasn't for anything petty. Today I face a very difficult decision. I'm being investigated and naturally they don't let me sleep, and I'm not even mad at them for it. If I turned against the party here in the cell you'd have every right to curse me, but that won't happen. My investigation is a matter of time. I still feel, for example, that I did not commit some of the crimes I'm being accused of; but the interrogators will probably manage to persuade me, perhaps as early as tomorrow, that in fact I did commit them. The thing is, I have to sort it out for myself.

The report ended: When the conversation turned to the possibility of suicide, he stated that he certainly wasn't even thinking about it because he was burdened with so much now that he definitely wouldn't want to leave the scene with it all.[26]

Early in the next phase of the nonstop interrogation (in the afternoon and night of January 28) Slánský still refused to confess. The interrogators once again brought in Löbl, who counseled Slánský to confess as he himself had and tried to persuade him that denials wouldn't help him. Still there was no direct result. Only late at night, actually toward the morning, did Slánský agree to say that the hostile elements whom he had allowed to infiltrate into high positions in turn placed other enemies and thus formed a dangerous grouping.

Although this was just another partial confession, it was exceptionally important for Slánský. On *January 29,* when Benda badgered him again about confessing, Slánský responded:

Slánský: It's no longer a matter of confession because I have confessed. I know, you can sit here and reproach me, and I won't be mad at you. I'm a criminal. What the party has accused me of is true. Yes, I have sunken into the mire of opportunism; I have adopted an ideology hostile to the party and have caused so much damage that I must face the music. I'm not evading my responsibility. On the contrary, I take it all on myself, but believe me, I did it all unconsciously and I believed that I was doing good work in the party's interest. This is exactly the problem . . . Surely I cannot admit knowing that Reicin was a spy when I didn't know it. He never told me, and I myself also never was a spy. So how could I have known . . .

Benda: You think anyone will believe that?

Slánský: I know no one will believe me. I know everyone believes that everything was exactly as the party published it, that I am a conscious traitor, and yet that's not how it was. I really had been wearing dark glasses and didn't see anything. I also know that confessing is not a mitigating circumstance because I'll get the highest sentence anyway, since the degree of my guilt will not be measured by the degree of subjectivity or objectivity but by the damage I have caused, and that damage is tremendous.

Benda: Nevertheless, a true confession would still make it easier for you.

Slánský: But I cannot admit to what I didn't do. They can keep me here as long as they want, without sleep, and eventually they will perhaps believe me after all.

Slánský continued to deny deliberate hostile activity. Nevertheless, he had shifted his line of defense another step toward the demands of the interrogators: "Subjectively I wasn't an enemy," he argued, "but I became one objectively, and that was my main offense."

The sessions of *January 29 and 30* focused on activity with hostile intent, but they yielded no significant result. Benda argued "in every possible way and variation that he's a coward, traitor, and enemy, if he continues to cause damage by his attitude even here,"[27] but Benda's pressure didn't lead anywhere either.

The afternoon and night sessions of *January 31* were conducted as usual by Doubek and Košťál. Late at night the exhausted Doubek took a break. Soon after he left, Slánský told Košťál he needed to go to the toilet. Košťál got up to escort him, opened the door, and carelessly started out first. Slánský shoved him out, shut, and bolted the reinforced door. He then looked for the service revolver that the interrogators usually kept in the writing desk. It wasn't there or in Košťál's briefcase. The suicide plan collapsed but not the idea. Slánský ripped out the telephone cord and hanged himself on the window latch. The terrified Košťál meanwhile mobilized his colleagues and maintenance workers who managed to force the door, just in time to save Slánský.[28]

Everything suggests that Slánský had planned his suicide. His psychological state influenced it too, but he also considered it a part of his defense. Suicide would have been a natural event, his last resort. He was counting on capital punishment and the "voluntary step" would have spared him further physical and mental torment. More importantly, it would have spared him the public humiliation of making himself out as a traitor, spy, and murderer.

But Slánský wasn't allowed to choose the moment of his death. His life was to end not in investigative custody but on the gallows. From the moment of his arrest in November 1951, that was the only role he could play for the Communist party leadership, the interrogators, and the advisors. He, therefore, had to be returned to life, to fulfill his greatest party task.

He was immediately put in the care of the prison physician who used all his skills to save him without any side effects. He was in the prison clinic from *January 31 to February 2*. He had another nervous breakdown that escalated into an attack of frenzy. The attack was so powerful that he was straitjacketed and spent time in the hospital tied to his bed.

On February 2, Slánský returned to his cell, which had been bugged. Benda welcomed him, asking him where he had been all this time: "At first he didn't respond, but then he said he was really bad off; he had been hanging. I asked him how it was possible, and he said: 'Quite simply—I was hanging, and I was long in agony. Now they'll probably take me everywhere in handcuffs.' When I asked him why they'd do that, he said, 'I just did something so stupid.' "[29]

PIECEMEAL CONFESSIONS

Slánský changed after his failed suicide attempt: the realization that there was no way out pushed him to the point of a moral breakdown, which did not escape the attention of the advisors. He resisted with less and less energy. He admitted what they wanted, while still denying any subjective hostile intent. Toward the end of February, though, he started weakening even on this point. He still didn't confess everything that was demanded, though. Liberation through death was still on his mind; but in February, this was a wish rather than an intention.

Interrogation resumed as soon as he returned from the prison hospital. These were special sessions with no protocols, in a special room. Following the recommendations of the advisors, it was equipped with an iron ring, a collar of sorts, which would be affixed to Slánský's neck when he had a breakdown. His leg was tethered to another iron ring.

Interrogations without protocols went on for four days. They were to wear the prisoner down and to prepare for the next important step. As Benda reported on *February 5*, they were effective: "Once he sits down, he starts nodding off. He once started shaking violently in this semiconsciousness. When I asked him what was wrong, he said that the moment he closes his eyes he hallucinates."[30]

A three-week series of intensive interrogations started right after that, on *February 7*. They focused on two points: on admitting the existence of an antistate center, and on Slánský's role in intentionally creating and leading it. The interrogators achieved their first success quite soon. Slánský agreed that he had been responsible for posting officials who formed a group of enemies within the party, but he rejected the characterization of this group as an alternative power center. The interrogators didn't yield, and toward the end, the protocol gave them what they wanted:

> *Slánský*: It is true that these hostile elements that I had allowed to penetrate high offices of the CC attracted other elements not only in the party apparatus but also elsewhere, and that they formed a dangerous grouping.
>
> *Interrogator*: This situation was caused by the hostile activity you have testified about, especially since it was you who placed all these agents and other hostile elements in these high positions . . . Correct?
>
> *Slánský*: Yes, that's how it was. *Through my hostile activity I caused the formation of a second center in the party and the state* [emphasis added].
>
> *Interrogator*: You insist on minimizing your activity. What else did the formation of this second center lead to?
>
> *Slánský*: It led to seriously jeopardizing the people's democratic regime in Czechoslovakia.

Slánský's statements still lacked that all-important feature: that he formed and led the center intentionally and that the objective of his activity was to liquidate the existing political system. Two more days of harsh interrogations culminated on *February 9* in another small step: "Speak directly! You headed the conspiracy!" shouted the interrogator, and recorded the response, "Though I found myself [*sic*] at the head of a hostile antistate center, formed within the CC KSČ apparatus, I had no intention of organizing a conspiracy."

The "I found myself" formulation wasn't satisfactory, and the interrogators and advisors organized another confrontation. They brought in Hanuš Lomský, a veteran Communist official. In a memorized statement, he declared that he had belonged to a group of Slánský's collaborators that had conspired against the state and that Slánský gave him instructions. Slánský denied Lomský's statement.

Hours passed; the pressure mounted. It started in the morning when the interrogators extracted another piece of confession from their exhausted, wretched, and desperate victim—namely, that he had headed preparations of the enemy center. The interrogators were not satisfied. They wanted more—they wanted the principal and intentional organizer of the conspiracy. The pressure escalated further, and after several hours, they recorded:

Interrogator: The confrontation has already demonstrated that you were the main organizer of the conspiracy against the party and the republic. Forget all your evasions now and tell us the whole truth!

Slánský: I don't want to deny anything, and I want to speak the whole truth. I conducted my hostile activity from the position of an enemy. That is where I ended and where I stood. In other words, I acted as an agent of the bourgeoisie in the working class, as an enemy of the Communist party and of the USSR. My hostile activity created conditions and circumstances for developing a conspiracy against the state. I conducted this activity as a conscious and intentional enemy.[31]

The required confession of the leading organizer of the conspiracy still wasn't forthcoming. This last step seemed so close, yet it was so difficult. The adversaries struggled over it for several more days and nights. Every day of the struggle affected Slánský's state of mind: his despair mounted; his helplessness and hopelessness made him yearn for death.

Returning from the afternoon interrogation of *February 10,* Slánský was "again very quiet and kept on mumbling to himself. I tried to figure out what he was saying, but I could make out only one word, without any context: 'Death.'"

The following day, *February 11,* after a night-long interrogation, "he was clearly very disturbed, but he controlled himself. As he was falling asleep, in semi-consciousness, all of a sudden I clearly heard him sigh deeply and mutter twice the word 'gun.'"

After he returned from the afternoon interrogation of *February 13,* Slánský "was greatly disturbed; he kept on sighing, grabbed his head in his hands, and muttered something. When I asked him what was wrong, he said he was feeling sick. I asked him whether it was the stomach and he said, 'No, I feel sick generally, I feel so bad, it is so hard.' He paced incessantly, nervously pounded the walls, and sighed terribly."[32]

The strenuous effort of the interrogators and advisors led nowhere. In the *second half of February* they had to settle for the formulation that Slánský had headed the center and that his activity made the conspiracy possible. They abandoned their effort for the moment and worked their way around the incomplete confession by composing the following sentence from Slánský's statements: he headed a center which was preparing a conspiracy against the state.

Toward the end of February, though, the advisors again felt Slánský was experiencing a moral breakdown. Benda was to stop telling him to make a full and spontaneous confession. Their last discussion on the topic took place on February 28:

Benda (B): You won't save anything now.

Slánský (S): Nothing will save me now.

B: Well, no one will give you more than what you've earned.

S: That's hard to say.

B: The most disgusting thing is cowardice. I'm only interested in the essence of the matter; that's got to interest everyone. Surely the party didn't put you here for nothing.

S: That sure cuts deep, but you know I don't want to talk about it.

B: I can easily imagine it from a suspect's point of view.

S: To abdicate responsibility.

B: You've got to realize that the longer it lasts, the further it grows.

S: What I have to reconcile myself with, I have to keep inside.

B: I'm just being human toward you. A person tries to judge others but not oneself. One sees what someone did and judges it by one's own yardstick, like, this is good, this is bad—but this seems to be bad. But I believe that if you wanted to talk, everything would be quite different. Look how you humiliate yourself here. Everybody used to feel a certain respect for you but now, with what has happened, with what you've done, everybody rejects you, and you must feel that inside as well.

S: I'm dozing off.

B: You see it best in yourself. Instead of having a positive attitude toward the interrogation, you doze off; you won't sleep.

S [Saying something about the brain, that he doesn't know anybody who could take all of this . . .]: Surely everyone has the right to his own point of view on the matter, and to defend other people's point of view when they're charged with a criminal offense.

B: You'd want this to have a simple outcome, that's what you'd want.

S: I know that I never intentionally sided with any enemy against the party.

B: I figure that if there were some objective reasons, the party would have opposed it.

S: Yeah, but I'm responsible for my actions.

B: Yeah, but everyone will say, he couldn't have been so stupid as not to see it. Everyone must be responsible for his actions . . . People look at your responsibility . . . Their belief is the belief of the party, and that's as it should be.

S: But they didn't see the problems. There are no mitigating circumstances here for me. I know what kind of a party official I was. An awful lot of people are suffering terribly.

B: I don't understand why you all made such a circus out of it.

S: But I cannot confess such things, some things I absolutely cannot confess.

B: I just wonder what you could have not known about.

S: It's not just one thing with me. I was responsible for everything.

B: And like it or not, you'll bear all the consequences.

S: The greatest problem is to see what I did consciously.

B: Yeah, the thing is, you aimed at everything working out for the worst.

S [is reconciled with nobody believing that he didn't know Šling would turn out to be a traitor]: I know I'm responsible for not having seen that; it's no excuse that I failed as a Communist, that my judgment failed me. I know that, but I wasn't the only one; there were others in high positions who didn't see it either.

B: I know, you've got to eat what you cooked up.

S: Yeah, slop it up.

B: Whether you admit it or not, you'll be an intentional traitor.

S: In my own mind I never betrayed intentionally; all these circumstances just came together. There are people in the party apparatus and in high positions I could point my finger at, and others believe they are doing their job well. I'll take on myself an antiparty, opportunistic position; but I'll take on nothing more, even though this cannot be enough—what can I do—I'm trying to identify with my new position.

B: You'd have to be stupid, and I think it's out of the question.

S: So long as the party had confidence in me, I could make mistakes. And that's what happened. As soon as there is serious suspicion [he whispers], we'll turn the page. [He sighs that he wants to be kept alive, as he said yesterday during the interrogation.] Tough is the life of a Canadian lumberjack; tough now is the life of a general secretary. [Slánský would like to find something he could admit to; they wanted a confession during interrogation.] If they let me sleep till doomsday I couldn't confess. In essence they are right, but one cannot admit every last iota.

B: This is not a matter of iotas.

S: The party was right when it said it's not a subjective matter with me, but let's wrap it up.[33]

It took the advisors and interrogators three months of intensive questioning, using physical duress and psychological pressure, to break Slánský. Even then, his breakdown was superficial and incomplete: only a prisoner who confessed anything the interrogators wanted, with no resistance—and who followed all other instructions as well—was considered really broken. The question was: Had Slánský reached the state of complete resignation? Would he now confess anything, anything at all?

THE NEW PLAN: FOCUS ON SPECIFICS

Toward the end of February 1952, Gottwald summoned Doubek and Beschasnov to report on the state of the investigation; Zápotocký was also present. As Doubek later related, Gottwald liked what he heard.

He said that the interrogations should continue as planned, following the instructions of the advisors, and that nothing should be done without their consent.[34]

The advisors decided soon after this meeting to change the format of the interrogations. Instead of general topics concerning the head of the center and of the conspiracy, they would focus on details of the center's activity and on the conspiracy's objectives. Since there simply was no evidence about the organized center or about Slánský's antistate activity, the center's composition and its "criminal activity" would be developed later, from this new line of interrogations. Nevertheless, the advisors were not empty-handed: they had extracted from their victims an assortment of false statements. The defendants were first forced to admit hostile intent and then that they followed instructions of the center and of Slánský, or at least that they acted with his connivance. It was therefore not difficult to charge the general secretary with criminal activity. Advisors and interrogators dealing with Slánský worked out a general plan of interrogations focusing on all the main areas of "hostile activity."

Its first issue was foreign policy, which took up almost a month of questioning. The initial focus was on posting hostile elements in the foreign ministry. On *March 3,* Slánský admitted that "he knew that enemies in the foreign ministry, headed by Minister [Vlado] Clementis, were engaged in hostile activity [and, *March 4*] that his own [Slánský's] activity concerning the foreign ministry, including his approval of foreign postings for people who later deserted to the enemy, served the interests of imperialist intelligence services."

There was little resistance in these matters. Resistance was only a little stiffer when the posting of "enemies" abroad was directly linked with conspiring against the state. On *March 8* Slánský "confessed that hostile activity of his own and of enemies he had promoted into important positions, as well as the activity of people who openly deserted to the services of foreign enemies, was directed toward conspiring against the state and restoring capitalism in Czechoslovakia."[35]

The next phase concerned espionage: Slánský's participation in or support of "espionage activity" of diplomats such as his brother Richard Slánský, a diplomat in Poland and Iran, and his brother-in-law Antonín Hašek, the Swiss correspondent of the Czechoslovak Press Agency and later envoy to China. Slánský resolutely rejected these charges and held his ground for more than a week. The focus on espionage upset him terribly. He felt this was a tremendous insult; he was angry and enraged, and after a three-week break he again contemplated death. On *March 20,* his cellmate recorded:

> Yesterday, Tuesday, he returned from the interrogation very upset and didn't even want to talk. After a moment of contemplation and reflection, he was more communicative. He said he agreed with the party that it's better to finish it all fast, even if it hurts. He said, "This is how I feel: better to end the horror than horror without end. I know that the longer it lasts, the worse it will get. There will certainly be many more confrontations because there are still many contradictions."[36]

On *March 26,* after several days of an impasse, confrontations were resumed. Jaromír Kopecký was brought in: a former diplomat in Switzerland who had been imprisoned for more than three years. He spoke of Hašek's espionage link with U.S. intelligence, stating that Slánský used him as a contact to send intelligence reports to Allen Dulles. Slánský immediately and resolutely denied this. He was then confronted with Artur London, who since the war had met Slánský only twice. The advisors expanded an insignificant conversation they had in 1946 into a meeting with an antistate character, during which they allegedly established conspiratorial contact. London's medical treatment in Switzerland in 1947 and 1948 yielded testimony about Hašek's espionage.

As soon as London finished reciting his part, the interrogator asked Slánský:

> *Interrogator*: Do you confirm this [1946] meeting with London?
> *Slánský*: I do.
> *Interrogator*: Was that when you established conspiratorial contact with London?
> *Slánský*: There was no conspiratorial contact, it was only a conversation.

It took another two days before the interrogators abandoned their fruitless effort to link Slánský with espionage. Then they shifted to another issue. London was supposedly a member of a circle of Slánský's close collaborators whom he coached in the conduct of hostile activity. In the last two days of March, Slánský was to corroborate this part of London's testimony. Results were expected from another confrontation with London, but as an interrogator wrote on *March 31,* Slánský still didn't give in:

> He was confronted with London. London testified that Slánský had recruited him for the work of the conspiratorial organization which he headed and gave him direct instructions for conducting hostile activity. Slánský denied

managing London's hostile activity but during the confrontation, he admitted once again that he had engaged in hostile activity himself and that he had headed the antistate center.[37]

Getting Slánský to admit that he knew about espionage activity of his relatives was not the ultimate goal of the interrogation plans. It was a stepping stone that, in due course, would lead to Slánský's admission of his own espionage.

FOCUS ON ESPIONAGE AND THE ANTISTATE CENTER

The advisors budgeted three weeks in April for extracting a confession of Slánský's own espionage. They decided to start off by asking Slánský to freely discuss his espionage activity, "about which there is a lot of evidence." But on *April 1,* Slánský resolutely rejected them: "I was involved in no espionage." Nevertheless, this new tack affected him strongly. Benda reported that Slánský raged and banged his head against the wall. In an effort to throttle himself, he clutched his arteries until he made himself red in the face and made his eyes bulge.

More confrontations followed. On *April 2,* Slánský was confronted with Josef Vondráček: an agent of the British Intelligence Service before the war and of the German Sicherheitsdienst during the war; after the war, he was sentenced to many years in prison. Vondráček had an uncanny ability to pick up the slightest clues as to what the interrogators were after, and they used him as a "universal witness," suitable for all occasions. He had also testified against Šling. Now he stated that Slánský had maintained espionage contacts with certain U.S. intelligence officers who were also organizing an international Zionist movement in Czechoslovakia and mentioned one Geiringer-Grannville.[38]

Slánský argued from the outset that he never knew this person and never heard the name. The advisors, however, insisted on making this intelligence connection. The interrogators did their best to extract a confession, but to no avail. Slánský deflected the second attempt to turn him into a spy.

Another attempt followed. The interrogation plan spelled it out briefly as "the espionage connection with Konni Zilliacus." However, before following this line, the interrogators had National Security Minister Bacílek ask Gottwald "whether Slánský ever informed him about his dealings with Zilliacus." Gottwald said he didn't. Considering the close professional and social ties between the two men, his response doesn't seem credible.

Konni Zilliacus was a British member of Parliament and a leader of the Labour Party's left wing. After World War II he maintained contacts with left-wing politicians of the Czechoslovak Social Democratic Party, particularly with Zdeněk Fierlinger, who worked hand-in-hand with the Communists. Zilliacus also had close ties with various East European Communist leaders.

In 1947, Fierlinger copied Slánský on two letters from Zilliacus, which security later found in Slánský's files. Marginal notes made it clear that Slánský had read them. Slánský had also received some letters through diplomatic means. From 1946 to 1948 he met with Zilliacus three times in the presence of others. Interrogators later extracted statements from four other prisoners about the intelligence nature of the Slánský-Zilliacus correspondence. Further, there was Clementis's statement that Slánský instructed him in the fall of 1947 to receive Zilliacus, give him information, and to maintain contact with him. They met once again; and in June 1948, Clementis received four documents, each several pages long, amounting to position papers of Zilliacus and his political associates on various United Nations issues. A few hours before his execution, Clementis wrote to Gottwald, "Zilliacus and nine other Labour Party members saw me [in 1947] without Slánský; and as for his so-called position papers, which he had sent me in June 1948 to Paris, I copied [Andrei] Vyshinsky [Soviet deputy foreign minister]."[39]

The advisors embellished these data into a vast construct of Slánský's extensive intelligence activity, and turned Zilliacus into an agent of the British Intelligence Service. At first Slánský rejected these charges as resolutely as he had the two previous efforts to make him a spy. He was therefore confronted with Bedřich Geminder.

Geminder worked before the war for many years in the Soviet Union, mostly for the Comintern. For some time, he was also the secretary to Georgi Dimitrov. After returning to Prague, he headed Slánský's secretariat and the CC KSČ international department. High Communist officials called him a "gray eminence"; he knew a lot about the background of the Soviet purge trials and, once arrested, he didn't believe in resisting. Consequently, as Kohoutek later stated, "Geminder was unusually ready to testify, from the moment of his arrest. He directed his statements particularly against Slánský." His protocols furnished the interrogators with "evidence" about Slánský's hostile activity.

At first they focused on the connection between Slánský and Tito; but during the *April 3* confrontation, Geminder discussed the espionage character of Slánský's conversation with Zilliacus, which he had witnessed, and his own role as a conduit for correspondence between the two.[40]

Slánský rejected both charges and insisted that he never had any correspondence with Zilliacus. On *April 4,* Benda wrote, "I asked him why he denied it when it was based on testimony of someone else, and he said: 'It's tough, I know how it is, they torment a man so long until he signs off, whether it's true or not, just to get some peace. Clearly I cannot admit it when I am one-hundred-percent sure there's nothing to it.'"

The interrogators agreed with the advisors that a show trial without espionage wouldn't have the necessary effect. They felt it was their party duty to "do Slánský in for espionage." After two days of unsuccessful interrogations, they organized a group confrontation, on *April 5.* Slánský was confronted with Geminder, London, and Eduard Goldstücker. Geminder repeated his earlier statements; London said he used the foreign ministry's courier to deliver Slánský's secret letters to Zilliacus; and Goldstücker, who had worked in London from 1947 to 1949 as a Czechoslovak diplomat, talked about arranging correspondence between Slánský and Zilliacus and about meeting Zilliacus on Slánský's instructions.

Immediately after the confrontation, the interrogator homed in:

> *Interrogator*: Three confrontations have clearly demonstrated your espionage ties with Konni Zilliacus. Tell us when you started sending intelligence reports to this British spy.
>
> *Slánský*: I never sent him any such reports, and I never received any.

The interrogation continued late into the night. Only on *April 6* did the exhausted Slánský sign the following formulation:

> *Interrogator*: Thus the information you transmitted to this veteran British spy was of an espionage character.
>
> *Slánský*: The information that Zilliacus departed with served espionage objectives and thus had an espionage character.[41]

This was a good beginning. Now it was a matter of expanding this confession and of extracting additional ones. From *April 7 to 12* harsh interrogations continued incessantly. The interrogation plans called for Slánský to qualify his conversations with Zilliacus specifically as intelligence cooperation and, above all, for an admission of written contact. Without this shift, Slánský's "espionage" would have lost its meaning: it would have shrunk to a couple of conversations between 1946 and 1948.

The report of *April 12* indicates that after a week of incessant pressure, Slánský's masters were still treading water: "The only thing he is admitting so far is that when he met with Zilliacus, which, as he admitted during confrontations, happened twice, he discussed information of an espionage character. He continues to deny any written contact with Zilliacus."

Something quite unexpected surfaced during this line of questioning. Slánský mentioned meeting Moshe Pijade, a leader of Tito's Yugoslavia, in the spring of 1948 in Prague. It is not quite clear why he brought this up. He possibly wanted to deflect the interrogation away from espionage, or he thought that the struggle against Titoism was still the main objective and that his trial would be Czechoslovakia's counterpart to Hungary's with László Rajk. In any event, the interrogators welcomed this voluntary and surprising statement. They reported right away, "While interrogated about his connections with Zilliacus, Slánský confessed that in spring 1948 . . . he met at the Yugoslav embassy in Prague with the Titoist agent Moshe Pijade."[42]

The meeting with Pijade was immediately ascribed espionage characteristics, and the following few days focused on developing the details. It didn't become the main facet of the espionage activity, though: that was reserved for Zilliacus. *April 14* started off another week of interrogations along these lines. For three days Slánský refused to expand his earlier statements. Thus on *April 16,* the following interchange occurred:

> *Slánský*: I have, true, admitted that in conversations with Zilliacus I passed on information of an espionage nature; but I maintained no written contact with him.
> *Interrogator*: The investigation has revealed that you, Geminder, and Goldstücker were involved together in espionage for the [British] Intelligence Service.
> *Slánský*: I was involved in no espionage with anyone.

The focus on written intelligence contacts continued. Two pieces of evidence were submitted: letters from Goldstücker and from Karel Šváb. They showed only one thing—that the two senders copied Slánský on letters Zilliacus had sent to third parties. The interrogators, however, presented them as evidence of written contact, notwithstanding their trivial content and disregarding the fact that these "espionage messages" passed through several hands.[43]

Written contact was thus established, but only in one direction: from Zilliacus to Slánský. The opposite direction, far more important, was missing. Any espionage obviously required that messages be transmitted to Zilliacus as well. Efforts at filling this gap dominated the interrogation plans for *April 21 through 25,* but to no avail: Slánský resolutely refused to make the required confession. This of course devalued even the uni-directional contact he already had admitted because the substance—the specific content of the espionage cooperation—was missing.

This important gap was to be bridged by a general concept of Slánský's and Zilliacus's shared objective of shaping Czechoslovakia in the image of Tito's Yugoslavia. Slánský seemed to like this. He expanded on it at length, focusing especially on its ideological underpinning, a theory of Czechoslovakia's specific path toward socialism.

The interrogators considered Slánský's exegesis of Czechoslovakia's path to socialism very important. They reported on it in detail on *April 26*:

> As Slánský has admitted, Zilliacus started this cooperation by sending him various documents via Goldstücker, whom Slánský helped disseminate his hostile ideology and propaganda in Czechoslovakia. Slánský further admitted that his hostile activity and the activity of the entire enemy center, which he headed, had the same objective as Zilliacus: the objective which imperialists, with the help of the Titoist clique, managed to pull off in Yugoslavia. Slánský further elaborated the hostile ideological concept that was the basis for his hostile activity. He stated that this ideological basis consisted of an anti-Marxist concept of a specific Czechoslovak path toward socialism.[44]

However, Slánský's explanation did not satisfy the higher-ups: for an espionage matter it was quite unsatisfactory because it was too theoretical. Gottwald was also dissatisfied—but for a different reason: it was he who in 1946–47 had promoted the theory of Czechoslovakia's specific path toward socialism. He therefore feared the advisors might be using Slánský's thesis to aim at him. This must have been why he instructed that this line of questioning be dropped. Slánský's effort to infuse the espionage charge with an ideological dimension thus failed.

After three weeks of incessant pressure, Slánský's espionage confession still amounted to a paltry two conversations with Zilliacus and two letters addressed to third parties. The interrogation was stalemated. The advisors decided to abandon this line for the time being and to turn to other matters.

On *April 23,* when they started questioning Slánský about domestic activities of the antistate center, his resistance suddenly melted away. In the course of ten days he freely admitted a variety of "crimes." On

May 2, he was asked again about intentionally conspiring against the state, which he had previously denied. An interrogator reported:

He now qualifies his and the entire antistate center's hostile activity, which he testified about previously, as specific preparations of an antistate conspiracy. Slánský admits that the antistate center was in fact a conspiratorial organization.

[Slánský also admitted that] he tried to keep the party chairman [Gottwald] from decision-making and to isolate him from the CC KSČ secretariat, so that he himself [Slánský] could become the decisive factor and could influence decision-making to serve the enemies. [Slánský further admitted] that while involved in hostile activity under his leadership, members of the antistate center secured and expanded their positions. They appointed additional hostile elements into the state administration and economic bodies.[45]

From *May 3 to 11*, interrogations focused on expanding earlier protocols even further. The advisors and interrogators wanted Slánský to admit that for a long time he had been conspiring with non-Communist politicians, especially leaders of the former Social Democratic Party. They particularly wanted an admission of cooperation with Bohumil Laušman, that party's last chairman, and Blažej Vilím, its last general secretary. Slánský resolutely refused, as noted on *May 7*:

Interrogator: As usual, you're not telling the truth. It is not natural that you would have conducted your hostile activity against the people's democratic regime only with the help of your accomplices in the KSČ. You conducted it with the help of other reactionary elements as well. Tell us the truth about it.

Slánský: I am unaware of having cooperated as an enemy with any of the mentioned politicians.

Interrogator: Nevertheless you persist in your ridiculous lies, denying your cooperation with Laušman.

Slánský: I stick to what I said.

Interrogator: That corresponds to your hostile attitude. Nevertheless, it will be proved.[46]

Slánský's resistance concerning Social-Democratic politicians eventually weakened. Authors of the show trial scenario inserted a brief mention of cooperation with both politicians into Slánský's testimony in court.

FOCUS ON ZIONISM AND BACÍLEK'S VISIT

Interrogations then shifted to what politically was the most important area—Zionism, which would provide the show trial with its basic ideological underpinning of anti-Semitism. Anti-Semitic outbursts were far more frequent in State Security since the arrival of Soviet advisors, and in the rest of society since Slánský's arrest. They were to culminate in the trial. Anti-Semitism had been apparent in earlier show trials organized by the Soviets in other people's democracies. Unlike in the Slánský trial, though, it had never been a dominant feature (the main motive and focus) of the trials. This was an important difference between the Slánský and the Rajk trials.

On *May 12* Slánský was asked to discuss the organization of the Zionist organization he had supposedly managed in Czechoslovakia. Slánský categorically denied even knowing of any such organization. The issue was debated long into the night but both adversaries stuck to their initial positions.

The following day, *May 13,* the advisors suggested administering a major "psychological blow"; raising the question of Slánský's nationality. The interrogators then insisted that Slánský's nationality wasn't really Czech, but Jewish. He vehemently denied this, but they continued to use the term "Jewish nationality" throughout and eventually included it in the protocol. Slánský refused to sign it.

This did not satisfy the advisors. They insisted that the expression "Jewish nationality" be used and handed the protocol back to the interrogators, with firm instructions that they extract a signature. They tried on *May 14,* but with no success. In the end, they had to settle for the formulation, "Czech nationality, Jewish origin." The psychological blow actually heightened Slánský's vigilance and resolve. For two days, *May 15 and 16,* he denied the charges of aiding and abetting Zionists. Then he admitted them in the cases of certain comrades of Jewish origin or victims of Nazi persecution. He still, however, refused to qualify his support for these people as intentionally favoring Zionists. The week-long interrogations yielded meager results. On *May 17,* the report read, "Slánský's interrogations have started focusing on Zionist activity in Czechoslovakia and the activity of the Zionist organization that he headed. However, he continues to pretend that he knows no details of the Zionist organization."[47]

His own resistance didn't exhaust Slánský nearly as much as the continuous anti-Semitic tenor of the interrogations, including crass insults of Jews. In his cell, he angrily compared this "fight against Zionism" to the anti-Semitism of the Nazis, and recalled the fate of his parents and of his brothers, Josef and Zdeněk, whom the Nazis had murdered. He repeated his determination "not to give in, in this matter, and to carry on resisting."

The interrogators planned to link Slánský with Anglo-American imperialists during the second week of the Zionist-oriented interrogations. On *May 19*, they suggested that by placing Zionists in high positions, Slánský supported imperialist interests. He denied it; however, he accepted this formulation the following day. During the next three days, *May 21 through 23*, the interrogators went after an admission of direct contact with imperialists. Once again, Slánský rebelled. His answers were angry, he turned red in the face, his whole body shook, and his helpless anger turned into a rage. On *May 24* he was confronted with Geminder, who played the role of a leading Zionist and Slánský's conduit to the imperialists. Even though Slánský flatly denied Geminder's statements, the interrogators continued treating them as established facts.

The original intention of taking care of the entire Zionist angle within two weeks did not work out. The protocol of *May 25* reads:

> *Interrogator*: Relate how you were linked via Zionists with British and American circles and to their intelligence operations. Whose interests were you working for in Czechoslovakia?
>
> *Slánský*: It is true that my support and protection of Zionists amounted to support for American and British imperialist interests as well. However, I did not use Zionists to maintain any connections with American and British ruling groups.
>
> *Interrogator*: You were linked with Western imperialists not only via Geminder but also via other Zionists. Elaborate on how you maintained contact through these channels.
>
> *Slánský*: I maintained no such contact.
>
> *Interrogator*: Your denials won't help you.
>
> *Slánský*: I have already confessed my connection with Konni Zilliacus. I maintained no other connections with imperialists.
>
> *Interrogator*: This of course is a lie! We'll prove it.

Zionist-oriented interrogations were interrupted for the moment. On *May 26*, as planned, the question of espionage cooperation with Zilliacus was resumed.[48]

In mid-May the advisors and interrogators reviewed their six-month progress. They had dealt with all the main political topics that were to constitute the criminal structure of the trial under preparation: the existence of an antistate center and a conspiracy, Trotskyism, Titoism, Zionism, and espionage. There were still a few gaps, though: some aspects needed fleshing out, and a few more details were required; but Slánský was unwilling to confess anything else. The report of one of the commissions which later investigated the entire trial quotes Musil, one of Slánský's interrogators:

> When we insisted on specifics, Slánský exploded in fits of hysteria . . .
> When we focused on unmasking his accomplices, he didn't name anyone and stubbornly resisted. He resolutely refused to mention any specifics and accepted only protocols with general statements. When the interrogating officers forced him more intensively to specify the criminal activity which he had admitted, he had fits of rage during which he screamed: "This is not true!" and such, like a madman. He banged his head against the wall and shook all over. These fits were taken to be provocations and the advisors instructed that the interrogations continue.[49]

Minister Bacílek, his superiors, and the Moscow security center were not very satisfied with the six-month results either. The advisors recommended intervention along party lines, that is, that the minister himself speak to Slánský. The meeting was prepared by the advisors, who settled its agenda with Beschasnov. Bacílek was to counsel Slánský that he confess and stop dragging out the investigation.

The meeting can be reconstructed only on the basis of later recollections of its participants. At 8 P.M on *May 27,* Minister Bacílek entered the interrogation room. A group confrontation, programmed as carefully as ever, was scheduled. It was to demonstrate Slánský's effort to hinder the investigation. The four witnesses, Geminder, London, Goldstücker, and Pavel Kavan, merely repeated their earlier statements about Slánský's espionage links with Zilliacus. Bacílek then gave something of a speech, mixing reproaches with advice:

> Your entire activity has been uncovered and the party knows all about you. You have no choice but to admit everything, yet you refuse. Your denials cause the party difficulties: you want to harm the party even from your position today. You should realize how senseless it is to deny the facts when we know everything. The preceding confrontation, during which you were nailed by no fewer than four people, was one example of how senseless such an approach is.

In conclusion, Bacílek again appealed to Slánský "that he confess and stop hindering the investigation."

Slánský "answered [the minister] fairly positively," stating that he had no intention of hindering the investigation. He took a different tack, though, when the conversation switched to his supposed activity as an enemy and an intelligence agent. His general tenor was this: I realize that my activity caused the party great harm. I had, however, never realized that I was acting from the position of an enemy. I started admitting this only in prison, because I wanted to help the party. A participant recorded the statements which discomfited the minister the most:

> [Slánský] said that while he has been admitting hostile activity, it is not true: he never did engage in any hostile activity but made mere mistakes which cannot be viewed in the same light. He said he had no interest in concealing anything but that he simply never was an enemy. What he wrote in the protocols isn't true either, and he did it only to be accommodating and to demonstrate that he wants to cause the party no difficulties.

This was an unpleasant surprise and a shock for the organizers of the meeting. The interrogators hadn't imagined Slánský would dare speak out so openly. The minister was confused and dumbfounded for a moment. Then he said that there was evidence of Slánský's hostile activity and asked him to state unequivocally "whether or not he is an enemy."

Slánský responded without hesitation: "I am not and never was an enemy."

Bacílek waved his hand and indignantly said that "one can't get anywhere with him and that there's no point in talking any more. He now saw that Slánský is far more obstinate an enemy than he had ever imagined. He interrupted the session and left."[50]

Slánský was escorted back to his cell. He was awake long into the night and mentioned to Benda that he had had a hard day. Little was left of his original hope that he could alert his former comrades to the falsity of his own statements and of the interrogations. Slánský apparently realized this immediately and started fearing the interrogators' revenge. Benda related on *May 28*:

> All he said was that the minister came over just to chew him out, that they're unhappy with him, and that it's very bad for him now. When I tried to calm him down, he said, "You're right, one can even get used to the gibbet . . ." After a while he started shaking all over, he moaned and clutched his heart. He looked up at the ceiling as though he had lost his senses and muttered under his breath, "Up there . . ." He said he felt awful and helpless and he acted insane.[51]

Bacílek reported to Gottwald and discussed his visit with his closest friends. These included Jozef Való who later recalled: "Comrade Bacílek came over and said: 'You know, Való, that swine Slánský won't admit anything more than what they can prove to him.' I said to him: 'Karol, a party that needs a political police and courts to enforce its line is ripe to be disbanded. It's no longer a party.' "[52]

SLÁNSKÝ'S BREAKDOWN

In June and July, the interrogations focused on the three main political themes of the trial: cooperation with Zilliacus, Titoism, and Zionism. The point was to fill in the gaps: to extract missing confessions, flesh out the statements, add further specifics about "hostile activity," and name more accomplices.

Interrogations about Zilliacus actually started on *May 29*, when Slánský was confronted with Ludvík Frejka, President Gottwald's chief economic advisor, who used to see Slánský very frequently. He was to testify that, during a 1947 meeting at which he had been present, Slánský gave Zilliacus confidential economic information and that Slánský gave Frejka the task of maintaining espionage contacts with Zilliacus. Frejka thought the confrontation with Slánský was very important, as he wrote to Gottwald a few hours before his own execution, "I pointed out during interrogation that in 1947 I actively contributed to uncovering K. Zilliacus . . . Having twice incriminated Slánský in very important matters, . . . I hoped that my good intentions would be believed and that I would be given a chance to help atone for what I had committed, either alone or with others."[53]

Efforts of this second cycle of interrogations focusing on Zilliacus didn't yield much new. Slánský added a few insignificant details to his earlier confession but refused to confess the "outbound direction" of written contacts (sending reports to Zilliacus). This "outbound direction" did eventually appear in trial proceedings but only in the statements of Geminder and others; not of Slánský. Intelligence cooperation with Zilliacus became a prominent part of the indictment.

On *June 9*, interrogations shifted to contacts and cooperation with the "Yugoslav-Titoist agency." The weekly summary of *June 14* lists a number of details that Slánský had confessed:

> The line promoted by the anti-state center headed by Slánský was this: while they tried to isolate the [Czechoslovak] Republic from the Soviet Union and disregarded experiences of the Soviet Communist Party, they frequently

organized various trips and visits to Yugoslavia and then promoted Tito and his regime in Czechoslovakia. Slánský admitted that he and Tito followed the same line also in selecting hostile elements.[54]

In the second week of June the focus once again shifted to Slánský's May 1948 interview with Moshe Pijade, and especially on the antistate center's cooperation with Yugoslavia "along party, foreign-policy, economic, military, and security lines." Slánský agreed with a variety of outright fabrications or bizarre interpretations of facts. The report for *June 16 through 21* is full of such expressions as "stated," "confessed," "elaborated on."

The last weeks of June focused on economic aid that members of the antistate center provided to Yugoslavia. Now Slánský faced Ludvík Frejka, for the second time, and Vilém Kún. The weekly report for *June 23 through 26* states, "Confrontations with Vilém Kún and Ludvík Frejka proved his [Slánský's] active support for Titoist Yugoslavia and promoting Titoism in Czechoslovakia. Slánský agreed with most of the statements by Kún and Frejka."[55]

The Yugoslav-oriented interrogations ended on *June 29*. With insignificant exceptions, Slánský confessed everything: both the common objective and espionage links with Titoists, and the details. The "Yugoslav-Titoist agency" featured very prominently in the indictment and in the trial.

On *June 30* the third main topic was broached again—Zionism. The interrogation zeroed in on the deliberate posting of Zionist members of the antistate center in important positions. Slánský rejected the charge. Later in the day he was confronted with Geminder. After the confrontation, an interrogator kept insisting on the following question:

> *Interrogator*: Your accomplice Bedřich Geminder has now reminded you of certain facts in confrontation with you. Will you confess to what your accomplice Bedřich Geminder has stated?
> *Slánský*: I deny it.

The weekly report dated *July 5* stated, "He discussed intentionally posting Zionist personnel in the apparatus of the party and state administration. He expanded his earlier statements concerning this issue."

For the following week, *July 7 through 12,* the advisors planned a confession of support for alleged Zionist organizations in Czechoslovakia and of espionage connections with Israeli diplomats. The former were legally sanctioned organizations; as for the diplomats, the focus was on

Ehud Avriel who headed the Israeli legation in Prague. The week's results were summed up on *July 13*:

> He admits supporting the Zionist movement and its activities but denies direct connections with Israeli spies. Geminder proved that. He admits that he was in contact with Israeli diplomats, agents of Western imperialism, via Geminder and certain other accomplices.

Slánský continued to deny direct espionage links with the diplomats in the next session as well.[56]

Zionist organizations were taken up again in the week of *July 14*. The interrogators wanted Slánský to expand his confession and to admit that he had maintained contacts with these organizations even before World War II and that he and the antistate center had maintained contact with imperialist circles via these organizations. On *July 15* Slánský responded to the first question:

> I do not recollect maintaining connections with Zionists before [the 1938] Munich [Treaty].
> *Interrogator*: Which other Zionists were you in touch with during the First [prewar] Republic?
> *Slánský*: I wasn't in contact with any other Zionists before the war.

As for the second question, the weekly report of *July 19* states:

> He elaborated on other ways in which he supported the hostile activity of the Zionist organization in Czechoslovakia and on his support for [André] Simone, a Zionist and a Trotskyite. He further confessed that Zionist organizations were an important link between the antistate center headed by Slánský and Western imperialist circles.

Even before filling in all the details about Zionism, the advisors decided to throw Free Masons in with the "reactionary organizations" Slánský was supposed to have cooperated with. On *July 26*, Slánský confessed: "In the course of interrogation Slánský furthermore admitted that through him, the antistate center used the additional support of Free Masons for its hostile activity."[57]

The indictment eventually treated Zionism in a separate chapter. All the aspects of the interrogation protocols were featured in Slánský's statements at the trial.

In June and July, Slánský admitted practically everything he was asked about. His resistance crumbled, and he stopped fighting over every formulation. He didn't volunteer anything but he agreed with just about anything the interrogators submitted. This new attitude resulted in an overall change in his prison regime. The harshness of the sessions abated, and the interrogators showed a kinder face. He returned to the cell calmer and more composed. He suffered nervous breakdowns only exceptionally. Conversations with Benda also became friendlier, and they dealt with personal and family life as well as with prison stories.

Slánský had only now reached the point of a complete moral breakdown. He resigned himself to the role assigned by the masterminds of the trial. This transformation was the natural result of the six months of harsh interrogations—which proved the futility of any resistance—and of Minister Bacílek's visit. Several interrogators independently observed that during this second cycle of interrogations, Slánský would repeatedly ask them, with only a hint of irony, whether they are satisfied with his answers. He was reacting to the "dissatisfaction of the higher-ups," which he heard about first from the interrogators and later from Bacílek himself.

6

REHEARSING THE SHOW

LEADERSHIP OF THE ANTISTATE CENTER

THE SECOND phase of preparing the show trials focused on touching up the conspiracy concept, bringing its political emphasis up to date, so to speak. Slánský's arrest was broadly and even enthusiastically accepted throughout the country, with some good reasons. Communists and non-Communists alike felt the country's mounting economic difficulties, suffered political discrimination and persecution, or were upset by the absence of democratic procedures in the party. They readily believed that these problems resulted from the deliberate activity of an "enemy gang," and expected radical improvements since this "gang" had been identified and eliminated. The economic aspect of Slánský's "hostile activity" was, therefore, highlighted far more than in other show trials to date.

One other factor played a role: an unexpectedly strong wave of anti-Semitism in Czechoslovakia and its ascendancy in the Soviet Union added emphasis to the Zionist argumentation in the trial under preparation.

Changes in the concept of the grand conspiracy had immediate consequences. It was necessary to arrest people who would fit its new framework. These included: Rudolf Margolius, deputy minister of foreign trade (arrested on January 1, 1952); Otto Fischl, deputy finance minister; a number of leading business executives, including Josef Goldmann, Jiří Kárný, František J. Kolár, Jaroslav Jičínský, Jaroslav Bárta, František Fabinger, Zdeněk Rudinger, Otto Eisler, Matyáš Lewinter, Ivan Holý, Eduard Outrata; and Josef Frank, CC KSČ secretary in charge of the economy (arrested May 25, 1952).

196

Ludvík Frejka, Gottwald's chief economic advisor, was arrested on January 31, 1952. Gottwald's secretary noted that prior to the arrest, "Gottwald discussed Frejka with Köhler, saying that they want to take him away and that he doesn't feel comfortable about it, but what can he do?"[1]

The last victim, arrested on June 19, 1952, was the journalist André Simone, an international-affairs commentator of *Rudé právo*, the KSČ daily. Moscow had long considered him a spy; for example, Geminder's notes from a July 1948 interview with Soviet ambassador Silin reported that "Comrade Geminder informed com. Silin about a remark com. Molotov had made about A. Simone to com. Slánský during the Paris conference [of 1946], and asked that com. Molotov be queried about the specific grounds for this remark." And Karel Šváb testified later that "Geminder reported that according to Soviet information, A. Simone works for the French intelligence."[2]

When Bacílek took over the ministry of national security, Gottwald made the trial with Slánský and others Bacílek's first priority, in order "to restore peace." The advisors and interrogators were also interested in a rapid and successful conclusion of their efforts. They went for broke: interrogations of people selected as members of the antistate center continued at full speed, according to the rules and customs which had become routine by then.

These included physical duress, psychological pressure and, with Communists, appeals to party loyalty. This last method took on various forms: threats that the party would abandon and condemn the victims; challenges that presented the required confession as a party task; reproaches for unwillingness to help the party; warnings that leading comrades were dissatisfied with their statements; and promises that their willingness to talk would determine how the party would gauge their guilt, etc.

Applying these three forms of pressure, the interrogators gradually managed to break down all their victims, which in turn was an indispensable condition for confessing whatever was needed. The motivations for Šling's, Švermová's, and Slánský's "confessions" (discussed earlier) indicate how similar they were. Other instances only confirm this pattern:

> *Clementis* [in his farewell letter]: My protocols and my statements in court resulted first from duress ("I'll have you beaten up so bad that blood will spurt") and then from resignation.

Frejka [in his last letter to Gottwald]: After four days or so, I saw that you, esteemed Mr. President, obviously regarded me as a villain and a traitor, and that this, too, was the opinion of security who in my eyes represented the working people. At that point, I figured that my subjective ideas as to who I am and what I had wanted must be false. From that day on I acted like the thirty-year veteran of the labor movement that I am and—please believe me, Mr. President—I sincerely and mercilessly adopted the objective position of the Czechoslovak working people. I forced myself to view all my activity through the eyes of my interrogators. I then testified along these lines, being as strict as possible with myself.

Geminder [in his last letter to the CC KSČ political secretariat]: Immediately after my arrest I realized the tremendous political significance of this step. I said to myself: My life is over and the only thing left to do is to embark on the path of truth and . . . help the party unmask imperialist plans, help it turn the plots they had been hatching into a weapon against them.

Simone [writing to Gottwald before his execution]: I was flabbergasted when I was told, immediately after my arrest, that I was a member of Slánský's conspiracy and a spy. This was so far-fetched that I hoped I might establish my innocence. I gave up that hope after three days, though, on account of what I was told by my case officer and his immediate superior, a staff captain.

The case officer told me I had been expelled from the party. He said my arrest implied that the party had already condemned me, that I had no right to present evidence, that if I didn't confess, he and his colleague would take turns interrogating me all night, and that if I collapsed they'd drench me in ice water. He threatened me with the punishment cell and with beatings. That scared me; but one particular threat affected me tremendously, namely, that my wife would be arrested if I didn't confess.

Nevertheless, I stuck to the truth and protested my innocence. After two weeks, though, I realized this was futile. The case officer ignored everything I said and turned everything, including my recognized accomplishments, against me . . .

I have to add that the staff captain told me that if my two case officers failed to extract a confession, another team would come, and a third, a fourth, and so on, if it were to take five years.

I reflected on this perspective. I reached the conclusion that only the intervention of higher authorities could turn the situation around. I therefore decided to confess whatever the case officer wanted, in statements so preposterous that they were bound to catch his superiors' attention, make them investigate the case, and give me a chance to prove my innocence. Unfortunately, this hope—and I realize today how naive it was—didn't work out.[3]

Only very few individuals managed to resist the pressures and refuse to confess. They included some who had been fingered as leaders of the antistate center, such as Taussigová. The day before her arrest Köhler told her: "Remember the party is right even when it is unjust." This, she recalled, "fortified me for the fate that would come." She was tormented no less than her comrades and suffered several nervous breakdowns in prison. At first she believed she would manage to prove her innocence and viewed her case officer as "a representative of the party." Cruel realities, however, eventually stripped away her illusions. She told her cellmate on June 2, 1952,

> that she felt it in her own skin how criminals are made. They are blameless people who were falsely accused and sentenced. Now it is clear to her why so many people are in prison since so many of them are innocent. They use false documents and protocols here; and by putting her under tremendous physical duress, they have managed to extract some initial false protocols which will now be used against her.
>
> Five weeks later, on July 7, Taussigová decided that if she ever went to trial, it would indicate that there was an obstinate enemy in State Security who wanted honest people to be sentenced. She will therefore use all the means at her disposal to unmask in open court this great enemy whom her case officer faithfully serves, just as Dimitrov did [in the 1933 Reichstag trial]. Originally she didn't want to defend herself, for fear that Voice of America would capitalize on it and turn her into a martyr; but now she sees it's the only way the public can realize there's an enemy in State Security.[4]

So much progress was made by mid-1952 that the producers of the show started considering the indictment. They discussed the title for the show and the cast for the antistate center. Doubek, who participated in these discussions, later wrote:

> The suggestion was made that the group be called the Espionage-Conspiracy Center or the Conspiratorial Espionage Center. For a long time, the favorite was Espionage and Conspiratorial Center. According to one suggestion, the title somehow was to indicate that [the center] included Zionists and that the activity of the defendants was similar to Tito's in Yugoslavia. Other suggestions included Conspiratorial Zionist Espionage Center and Espionage Zionist Center. No good suggestion was ever found to capture the Titoist line. The final approved name was the Antistate Conspiracy Center Headed by R. Slánský. This was approved by all authorities and accepted by all the defendants, including R. Slánský himself.[5]

The nonexistent center was construed as an extensive organization, with branches in all important aspects of political life, party institutions, and state apparatus. The composition of its leadership had to correspond to this concept. Every sphere of activity which constituted an important power nucleus had to be represented, preferably by a person "of Jewish origin." As Doubek later stated, the selection was also influenced by "how well a person confessed, what guarantees there would be that he would do a good job in court, what impression his statement would make, and how close he was to R. Slánský." Specifically:

> Šváb was included in the main group because he talked well and because he was connected with Slánský. He represented the security line in the center.
>
> Reicin was included because he represented the army line. There was espionage, a murky past (Gestapo, Fučík), and direct contact with Slánský. [Reicin was charged with causing the death of Julius Fučík, a wartime Communist resistance operative.]
>
> Frank was arrested with the intention of including him in the main group.
>
> Hajdů talked eagerly and had a rich espionage history, an aspect in which other members of the center were weaker . . . but not all of it could be verified or documented and a great part of it was therefore supported only by his own testimony.
>
> Frejka talked well.
>
> Fischl: there was a strong Zionist line, sabotage, millions-worth of speculation with property, and a connection with Slánský.
>
> Simone was a cosmopolite who talked well, was extensively involved with espionage, and had direct links with Slánský.[6]

The center furthermore included Šling (the party line), Clementis (the line of Slovak bourgeois nationalism and foreign policy), London (Trotskyism, foreign policy, Spanish volunteers, and espionage), Margolius and Löbl (Zionist and foreign-trade lines), and Geminder (Zionist and party lines).

The advisors, interrogators, and prosecutors knew full well that no center, let alone its leadership, ever existed. Constructing it was nevertheless an important condition for producing the entire great conspiracy. Beschasnov presented the construction of a nonexistent center as an important special feature of the future trial. In September 1952, he explained in a letter to Josef Urválek, who would be the chief prosecutor, "that no specific *collusion* in antistate activity has been uncovered, yet it is obvious that all the defendants acted in harmony. They knew and supported each other, and therefore it wasn't even necessary for them to conspire. That only heightens the sophistication of their association and the difficulty of uncovering it."[7]

THE JUDICIARY

The country's judiciary started preparing for the upcoming trial in mid-1952; or rather, that is when security authorities started preparing the prosecutors, judges, attorneys, witnesses, and expert witnesses. The special mechanism for producing show trials had been functioning for almost four years. Many of the officials who eventually fell victim to it had helped construct it in the first place. Ministers of justice Alexej Čepička and, after May 1950, Štefan Rais, took great care that the judiciary obediently play its ignoble role. Čepička was among the most active in developing the whole mechanism.

In October 1948 a separate State Court was created to deal with criminal offenses against the state and other cases with political motivation. Its several sections operated in various parts of the country, as needed. The procedure with all show trials was as follows: State Security authorities submitted (directly or via the ministry of justice) the political objective of a forthcoming trial to KSČ authorities for approval. (The approval came from the CC KSČ political secretariat and, in the center and in the country's regions, from the KSČ security committees.) The minister of justice (or his deputy or, locally, the prosecutor) reported to the same KSČ authorities on the indictment and the proposed sentences. Party decisions were absolutely binding for the prosecutors and judges; the minister of justice was responsible to the party for implementing them.

On May 11, 1950, the KSČ leadership approved directives for the work of "regional security groups of five." These directives also dealt with political trials.

> The regional security group of five will discuss political and security preparations of important trials (or as instructed by higher authorities) and will prepare appropriate recommendations for the presidium of the regional KSČ committee.
>
> A representative of the regional prosecutor's office will inform the regional security group of five about all judicial issues bearing on security.
>
> The regional security group of five will evaluate the reports of the prosecutor and approve recommendations, as appropriate.
>
> The regional security group of five will decide on particularly significant specific cases autonomously. A well-informed representative of the state prosecutor will report on cases handled by the State Court, particularly on cases involving capital punishment. In cases where capital punishment has been proposed, the regional security group of five will solicit a report from basic and district organizations concerning the defendant's behavior, the danger he poses, and his family background. The group of five will then submit its recommendation to the CC KSČ security commission.[8]

When he was minister of justice, Čepička and his deputies, especially Karel Klos, introduced changes in the judiciary that guaranteed its smooth subordination to political authorities. The prosecutor, rather than the judge, became the main protagonist in trial proceedings. The prosecutor stood above the court but below State Security interrogators and the justice ministry's special department for political trials. Sentences were decided by political authorities, and Deputy Minister Klos passed these decisions on to the state prosecutor, the president of the State Court, and to the deputy president of the Supreme Court, who in turn passed them on to the appropriate prosecutors and judges. The proposed sentence could not be changed without Klos's approval.

Leading officials of the justice ministry never stopped emphasizing this subordination, and punished cases of its violation. On November 21, 1949, Čepička addressed a conference of leading district prosecutors and judges: "The district and regional prosecutor simply has to be the focus of administration and specialized knowledge for everything concerning criminal justice."

The justice ministry instructed prosecutors' offices to report on the progress of individual proceedings, and to request approval of anticipated procedures. State prosecutor Bohumír Ziegler made the following point at a staff meeting on December 7, 1949: "In serious instances, we have to solicit the opinion of the criminal department of the justice ministry. The instructions of the ministry have to be followed in any event."

On January 25, 1950, Hugo Richter, president of the State Court, instructed, "The prosecutor's recommendations made during the main hearing are under all circumstances binding. If the court senate does not intend to follow them, this has to be decided in advance by the presidium."

Elsewhere Richter said, "The senate of the State Court has to inform the prosecutor about its intentions concerning the case and request an opinion as to whether the state prosecutor considers these intentions correct and appropriate to the situation, inasmuch as the prosecutor usually knows more. The prosecutor's opinion should prevail."

The state prosecutor's office in Bratislava enjoined prosecutors on February 10, 1950, to participate in the court's conference about sentencing and, "prior to handing down the sentence, to check by phone with the state prosecutor's office in Prague, so as to eschew handing down sentences that would be quite intolerable."

A judge of the State Court stated at a meeting on December 5, 1950: "We realize that we frequently sentence people against the will of the working class [i.e., the sentences are too mild], but we hand down such sentences because we have no way out."[9]

Thus the State Court handed down sentences that had been decided by political, nonjudicial, authorities. But its subservience was even more extensive: the State Court was effectively a servant of State Security. Judges coordinated the political effect of the trials with State Security. They followed a script, they asked questions that security had drafted and recorded responses that security had drummed into the defendants.

The only elements that marred this perfect production were defense attorneys. Leading authorities of the justice ministry attacked them early in the game. Thus Čepička lamented, on November 21, 1949, "It seems that some defense attorneys have developed a thick hide. They have restored the old sharp practices of acting as though there was no difference at all, even in very serious matters, between the defendant's and the defense counsel's attitude toward the state."

Similarly Otakar Heráf (Čepička's deputy), on June 12, 1949, addressing a conference of judges and prosecutors, said, "We [the justice ministry] follow matters of defense attorneys and are aware of their mischief . . . Do not let them abuse quotes from Marx and Lenin, do not let them attack national-security authorities or the correctness of administrative protocols."[10]

The law about practicing law was being changed at the time. Only defense attorneys from an approved list of politically reliable ones were allowed to practice at show trials. Security authorities, rather than the defendant, selected the defense attorney: the defendant actually met with his attorney only once, just before the trial. On top of it all, most of the selected attorneys cooperated with the StB.

Political authorities, the KSČ leadership above all, took particularly careful precautions in all important political trials, and especially in all trials with Communist officials. One reason no doubt was the fact that the justice ministry and the administration of justice was one of the few areas without Soviet advisors. On June 16, 1952, National-Security Minister Bacílek approached Čepička with the following request:

> In a personal interview about the preparations of the Slánský trial, comrade Gottwald suggested I consult with you about selecting prosecutors for the trial. [Minister of Justice] comrade [Štefan] Rais recommends comrade [Václav] Aleš as the chief prosecutor. Comrade Široký recommends com. [Jan] Fejéš as one of the prosecutors, especially for party matters. In essence we are really looking for our own Vyshinsky.[11]

On August 27, the CC KSČ political secretariat approved Bacílek's recommendation that Josef Urválek be appointed chief prosecutor. He had solid experience from a former position as deputy prosecutor general. Even more importantly, he had successfully acquitted himself of several earlier important political trials, and had headed the office of the regional prosecutor in České Budějovice for several years. Bacílek's recommendation highlighted Urválek's experience and his party loyalty, as well as the fact that "as a regional prosecutor he is conscientious and systematic. He has a particularly good attitude toward young working-class personnel in the judiciary, to whom he relays his experience. He is valued in his job for having adopted the techniques of Soviet prosecutors."[12]

Bacílek told Urválek about the decision of the CC KSČ political secretariat. Urválek later recalled:

> He told me that I was given the responsible task of prosecutor in the Slánský trial, which, he said, was a great honor and a manifestation of the party's trust in me. He said that the investigation was being conducted by the best security personnel the party had, with the help of experienced Soviet advisors and that the trial was managed by the party and personally by comrade Gottwald.[13]

The political secretariat asked Bacílek to recommend additional prosecutors, judges, and defense attorneys. This selection was discussed at several meetings involving Bacílek, his deputy Antonín Prchal, Doubek, Košťál, Milan Moučka and the advisors, and Minister Rais. Bacílek submitted his recommendations on October 25, 1952. Václav Aleš, František Antl, and Miloslav Kolaja were appointed prosecutors, and they too were told what a great honor this was.[14] Antl later wrote:

> I arrived in Prague for a regular meeting of regional prosecutors. I was told first to stop by the justice minister's office. When I got there, his deputy Karel Klos was present, too. They invited me to sit down. [Minister] Rais paced the office and finally asked me whether I knew why I had been invited. I said I didn't. With an air of importance he informed me, "You will make your mark in history because you will be a prosecutor in the trial of Slánský and others." We then all left for the meeting of the general prosecutor's office. I was surprised and amazed when the minister almost fawningly opened the door to the elevator for me . . . Kolaja and I didn't even have our degrees yet. We graduated only after the trial.[15]

Jaroslav Novák was appointed president of the court tribunal. Its other members included František Stýblo and Karel Trudák (whose place was later taken by a military judge, Jiří Štella), and Justices of the People Václav Jareš and František Doušek, with Václav Petr as a substitute.

Novák was an experienced judge; he had been a jurist since 1924. He got this job even though—or perhaps precisely because—his own political background would have been enough to get him in trouble. The recommendation listed the following: "His attitude to the people's democratic regime is *outwardly* positive"; his attitude toward the USSR "*appears to be* positive"; before joining the KSČ, after February 1948, "he had a rightist orientation"; he needs "a stronger class consciousness . . . his petit-bourgeois upbringing still affects him"; his wife behaves "as a lady." Other factors decided his nomination, however: "He is very good technically," he had successfully handled several major political trials, he did his job well, "and is therefore considered a seasoned old master."[16]

Stýblo was the very opposite of Novák. He was only twenty-eight years old but already headed a department of the State Court in Brno. He had no legal training whatever. He completed nine grades of school and, in 1949, a course in political education. However, "he is very self-assured in handling trials . . . he was given important trials of a political nature . . . which he managed successfully."[17]

The CC KSČ approved the defense attorneys only on November 13: Vladimír Bartoš for Slánský and Margolius; Vojtěch Pošmura for Geminder, Šváb, and Löbl; Jiří Šťastný for Frank, Clementis, and Reicin; Václav Synek for Hajdů, Fischl, and Šling; and Jaromír Růžička for Frejka, Simone, and London. With one exception, they all collaborated with State Security.[18]

Once the advisors and the interrogators turned to preparing the indictment, they realized that their information about the defendants' "criminal activity" couldn't be proven. All they had in hand were the forced confessions and not very persuasive "evidence" produced by a documentation group. The gaps were to be patched up by expert depositions. The masterminds of the trial hoped that expert witnesses would calculate the actual damages caused by members of the antistate center. Thus the idea of a commission of experts was born.

On June 3, Bacílek approached several government ministers with a request that they nominate members for such a commission. Its task was outlined clearly: "To develop in a short time, as needed, the necessary background for documenting the sabotage activity of the enemies in custody." Bacílek's letters detailed some of the specific requirements. Thus the State Planning Office was to support the following construct:

It is well known that the Five-Year Plan was developed without considering an expansion of mining, although it was later established that mining could be expanded by 300 or 400 percent. The mining of nonferrous metals decreased, especially of copper, zinc, nickel, cobalt, wolfram, molybdenum, and others. As a consequence of this sabotage, the plan did not propose mining iron and nonferrous ores in several places [where mining had been uneconomical for decades].[19]

Four months later, on September 27, Bacílek recommended that the CC KSČ political secretariat approve the formation of five expert commissions: for the ministry of defense (headed by General J. Tchoř); ministry of foreign affairs (Jan Souček); finance ministry (Otakar Pohl); the State Planning Office (Zdeněk Púček); and for industry (Antonín Rydrych). Originators of the whole idea wanted to invest the commissions with considerable authority, and persuaded Bacílek that they should be government commissions. Zápotocký refused that and suggested that "the interior ministry take over the expert commissions."[20]

PERFECT HARMONY

By the fall of 1952, all three elements of the show-trial production (security, political institutions, and the judiciary) were operating in perfect harmony and at full speed. This increased the demands on coaching the victims. Both the producers and the victims shared one overriding ideal: service to the party. The advisors and the interrogators controlled every step and every technical detail of the preparations.

In October, after several discussions with the advisors, Doubek started drafting the indictment. Beschasnov and Yesikov returned the first draft with a number of suggestions. The second draft was more successful, but it still didn't meet with full approval. The advisors changed a number of points in the Russian translation and added some suggestions. The third draft, which Doubek prepared with Prchal, satisfied them. The prosecutors had a brief opportunity to comment on it, and then it was sent to Moscow. On November 11, Bacílek submitted it to members of the CC KSČ political secretariat.[21]

The court proceedings were drafted ahead of the indictment. They served as the script for the show trial and were also developed by the interrogators and the advisors. The last draft was shaped by Doubek and Beschasnov. The script consisted of the existing question-and-answer administrative protocols which contained the sequence of questions to be asked during the trial, as well as the defendants' answers. While the script was being prepared, Beschasnov flew to Moscow with the whole package for one final consultation.

The defendants learned the questions and answers by heart. They were tested daily. The interrogators asked the questions and checked the answers, which had to follow the script word for word. Depending on their performance, the victims were favored or penalized. The interrogators competed among themselves in how well "their" actors mastered the text. The texts could still be adjusted so as to maximize their impact in court.

However thorough the preparations, the producers were still not sure about the outcome. They could not rule out that a defendant might fail them in court and intentionally digress from the script. They had triple insurance. First, the cellmates (StB agents) emphasized the significance of sticking to the protocols and reported any inclination of the defendants to veer from them. Second, the interrogators escalated the psychological pressure, particularly appeals to party discipline. They told their victims that their performance would reveal their true attitude toward the party, or that it would earn them a place with the vanguard of fighters against imperialism or that this was their contribution to the victory of socialism.

The third and safest guarantee was taping the script. A general rehearsal of sorts was staged. In a specially equipped room, Doubek asked questions; and the defendant answered, believing he was being tested. In an adjacent room, František Škorpík, an StB commander, taped the responses. The real intention was this: if the defendant "failed" in court, as Traicho Kostov did in Sofia, the microphone would be turned off and the tape with the appropriate answer would be turned on. Bacílek was aware of the purpose of the taping and had some of the tapes played for Gottwald and other leaders.[22]

Learning the answers by heart was a method introduced in 1950 by Soviet advisors. The interrogators, prosecutors and judges all thought it proper. Thus Antonín Prchal stated on November 8, 1955, that the advisors "argued that this is being done so that [the defendants] don't stutter in court and so that the trial proceeds smoothly." And Urválek said, "I accepted that questions would follow the protocol because I realized the need to avoid a situation in which the defendants might refer to high officials, and I would not be able to rebut their arguments. I acknowledged the need to focus the questioning, in a trial with such wide publicity, on the main issues. However, I did not expect that during the trial, the defendants would repeat their answers practically word for word."

František Antl said in 1968, "At the time I saw nothing perverse about it. I firmly believed that it was appropriate, that it was in the defendants' best interest to know what questions they were supposed to answer. During the trial I realized that even if the prosecutor omitted a question or two, the defendants would still respond as though the question had been asked."[23]

Witnesses were prepared similarly. They were handpicked by the interrogators and the advisors. Thirty-five were actually summoned, with many others on standby. All but three were behind bars: either in prison or in investigative custody. They included two former Gestapo agents and three "universal witnesses," whom security used in several political trials. Security didn't even have to talk these witnesses into perjuring themselves: they took it as a matter of course that it would yield favors in their prison routine. All others were subject to psychological or physical pressure until they succumbed. They, too, learned their testimony by rote. Marie Švermová wrote that "the interrogators assured me that the party is giving me an opportunity to prove my attitude: that I'd be testifying at the trial. They said K. Gottwald was fully informed about this. I learned by heart my witness testimony that they had drafted. It contained both the questions of the court president and my answers, in which nothing could be changed."[24]

Bedřich Hájek wrote:

> How did I end up testifying against Slánský? After the very first few sessions, the interrogator emphasized my cooperation with Slánský, the enemy. . . . For several months I truthfully stated all about my absolutely proper contacts with him. The pressure mounted as the case officer suggested issues he would like to hear about. When I could no longer tolerate the constant threats, I thought of a plan . . . I concocted statements which, I thought, would at first sight be clearly outrageous. My fabricated testimony actually contained what the interrogator wanted to hear. I surrendered to the pressure and agreed to testify as a witness—just a few words, as I had practiced it. When it was ready, I was summoned several times to the office of another security officer where I was to learn it by heart. The officer sat there with me, although sometimes I stayed alone for quite some time (locked in). I was tested so often that I ended up really knowing it to the last iota. Every mistake, every change of word order, every word I dropped was pointed out, and I was warned not to deviate from the prescribed text in the slightest. I was even bribed: I got black coffee several times. I remember that a member of the court panel, who had my testimony in front of him, several times nodded approvingly as he saw that I had learned my part well.[25]

Antonín Prchal was in charge of the expert commissions. At a joint meeting he and Bacílek explained what their role was: to enumerate the damages that the defendants had caused. Commission members were assured that their working papers would be for internal use only, just for the interrogators; and that depositions for the court would be prepared by other expert witnesses. All the commission members signed a statement formulated by Prchal according to which they would "prepare the depositions only on the basis of established facts." Several of the members, however, later stated that at the same time "they were instructed both by comrade Urválek and by comrade Prchal to make depositions that would corroborate statements of the defendants." They certainly followed this instruction.

Doubek testified that these depositions were "based on the defendants' statements." Ludvík Frejka, for example, qualified something he did as sabotage. The protocol stated that this was corroborated by an expert deposition, which was quoted to that effect. "This was done so that [proof of] certain activities deemed hostile would be based not only on the statement of the defendant but also on a deposition of the expert commission."[26]

The experts were diligent. They prepared sixty specific depositions and three summary ones. Not in a single case did they contradict the forced statements of the defendants. Nevertheless, they still went through several drafts because the show-trial producers demanded more and more.

State Security officer J. Hovorka stated:

> Officers of the interrogation bureau required that the expert depositions not only postulate the responsibility of some of the detainees but also qualify their activity as having criminal intent. Depositions that merely stated the responsibility of the detainees were returned by the interrogation bureau with a request that criminal activity be qualified as well.[27]

Thus the experts followed the requirements of the show-trial producers to the letter, corroborating intentional economic and other sabotage and enumerating the damages caused. The depositions were replete with numbers in the billions of Czechoslovak crowns which were to astound the population. These numbers represented imaginary amounts of imaginary damages, but also reflected actual economic difficulties resulting from an economic policy enforced by Moscow. Making the defendants responsible for all the economic difficulties of the country heightened the political impact of the trial. The depositions were a conscious collection of half-truths, lies, fabrications, and artificial constructs that nobody checked. In this form they reached the court. The originally projected commissions of court experts never existed.

Participation in an expert commission turned out to be an important career move for some. Before long five members were appointed ministers. Some individuals were particularly active. Zdeněk Púček anticipated the wishes of the interrogators already in his preliminary notes, and took it upon himself to determine what constituted criminal activity: "On the one hand there was the official line, the line to reconstruct Czechoslovakia's economy and socialist industrialization; on the other hand there was the line as actually executed, the line of wreckers, directed against socialist industrialization."

In fact, on December 9, 1952, after the trial closed, the expert commission that Púček headed prepared an extensive document drawing Gottwald's attention to even further "enemies": "We therefore consider it our duty to share with you our opinion concerning the responsibilities of additional comrades for the activity we reviewed, so that you can decide how this responsibility should be clarified."

This was followed by a list of "sabotage activities" and a list of high-level officials who were at liberty, including ministers Jozef Púčik, Jaromír Dolanský, and Gustav Kliment and several general managers of industry.[28]

Prosecutors started preparing for the trial in September 1952. They were under Doubek's supervision, as were the judges. For more than two months they were kept in complete isolation in a security villa in Prague and were driven every day to the Ruzyně prison. Their living and working quarters were bugged. Prosecutor František Antl later reminisced, "Work started at 8 A.M. At noon we had a one-hour break, and then we continued until 6 P.M. when we had an hour for dinner. Then we worked from 7 P.M. until midnight when we were driven back to our quarters."[29]

Doubek explained their duties and tasks right away, and later elaborated on them in several meetings, as he wrote in August 1955, "The prosecutors and the judges were told to strictly follow the material they had received and to change nothing in it. This went for their role in the trial as well."

Beschasnov also told them at the outset that "the case has been well prepared" and that they were to follow the protocols exactly as they had been prepared because they "have been approved at the highest places." Similar remarks were made during the weekly meetings of the advisors and the prosecutors.[30] Prosecutors also confirmed the existence of these instructions, which they followed to the letter. Thus Václav Aleš wrote on November 24, 1955:

We familiarized ourselves with the various interrogation depositions of various people . . . which were in final draft and signed . . . As for the actual indictment, as prosecutors we really had nothing to do with it and, therefore, did nothing, except make some technical legal adjustments to its conclusion. We were explicitly forbidden to ask [during the trial] any questions that were not included in the question-and-answer protocols. [Doubek's argument was that all the protocols] had been discussed politically in advance . . . analyzed by the Soviet advisors . . . that an additional question could interfere with the course of the trial and could then impair other matters which will come to trial in connection with the Slánský case.

Prosecutor František Antl said, "Our task in Ruzyně was to study and to care for nothing else. For example, even when the justice minister wanted to visit us, we had to go meet him at the gate, otherwise he wouldn't have been allowed into the prison."[31]

Several defendants were allocated to each prosecutor, who questioned them in court. This corresponded to Soviet practices in trials with Trotskyites of the 1930s when the prosecutor was largely in charge of questioning. The victims were assigned jointly by the advisors and the interrogators, who also decided which questions would be asked by the judge. Except for a brief meeting Urválek had with Slánský, the prosecutors did not even meet the defendants until the trial. The interrogators played segments of the defendants' taped confessions for the prosecutors, to assure them that the confessions really existed and that the protocols corresponded to their statements. Antl stated:

We wanted to see what the defendants looked like before the trial started. We were not allowed to participate in the interrogation, we were not allowed to see them, to know them. We didn't hear their statements directly but only from a tape recording. State Security played over the statement of one of the defendants for each of us, the four prosecutors. We figured that everything was in order, that their criminal activity corresponded to what they were to stand trial for, and that in essence they were confessing everything without reservations.[32]

The interrogators and advisors had fewest problems with preparing the defense attorneys. They adhered strictly to the principle that in a show trial, a defendant cannot defend himself but can only confess. The defense attorney was not allowed to go beyond the limits of the indictment. He could ask no questions that would weaken the credibility of the indictment or of the trial proceedings; this went for his concluding statement as well. Prchal quite intentionally gave the defense attorneys the impression that their participation was only a formal matter, for decorum alone. He emphasized that the defendants had confessed to the fullest extent; and that since the defendants would not defend themselves anyway, any defense would be superfluous. The defense attorneys could read only the part of the indictment that concerned their particular clients. Some were allowed to meet their clients before the trial date, in the presence of two security officers. The concluding arguments for the defense were reviewed in advance by the interrogators.

COACHING SLÁNSKÝ

The defendants were of course the most important participants of the trial. Their statements and their behavior in court would determine the trial's political impact, which was the real issue at this late stage of the game. Slánský was, as always, the center of attention. By July 1952, the interrogators had brutalized him to the point of breaking him. Interrogations concerning the three main topics of the trial had been completed. In the following four months they fine-tuned his performance so as to maximize its stage effect.

They wanted to root his "hostile activity" deeper in the past. It would be more logical, they figured, to demonstrate that Slánský was actually born a traitor. This would make a great impression on the country. But all they had in hand were a few doctored or misinterpreted documents and depositions. Thus a photo of Slánský's parents' house served as evidence of his bourgeois origins. A photocopy of his prewar request that he be allowed to postpone serving his sentence for a political offense was presented with the following commentary: "The document proves that Slánský was an opportunist, coward, and a bootlicker of the bourgeoisie that ruled the First [prewar] Czechoslovak Republic." Slánský's statements about his Trotskyite vacillation in 1927 were supplemented by a doctored document from the police files.[33]

The producers of the trial did not think these offenses were impressive enough. They needed to demonstrate his cooperation with the bourgeoisie and his betrayal of the nation in a tangible, shocking form. They decided that Slánský's wartime activity might fill the bill, particularly his participation in the Slovak National Uprising: in September 1944, the

Communist leadership in Moscow dispatched him to join the uprising as a political commissar of the partisan headquarters.

When dealing with the Uprising (*August 14*), the interrogators had the security minister ask Gottwald "whether Slánský had the right to inform General Heliodor Pika [commander of the wartime Czechoslovak military mission in the USSR, executed in 1949 in Czechoslovakia] about certain issues of the Slovak partisan movement that was organized from Moscow." They were told that "Slánský did not have that right." Interrogations about the Uprising were to recast Slánský's participation in the resistance into deliberate treason and indirect aid to the Nazis.

The interrogators didn't have much trouble extracting a variety of "confessions" during the first week. Slánský's statements were summed up in a report of *August 9*: "Slánský has so far confessed that he did a poor job of fulfilling the tasks concerning the Uprising which the Moscow KSČ leadership had given him, and was bureaucratic about it . . . He also admitted having extensively briefed the traitor General Pika in Moscow and the [Czechoslovak] government delegation from London about the origins and course of the Slovak Uprising."

More confessions followed in the following week. On *August 17,* the interrogators reported that Slánský's activity "aided the hostile plans of British imperialists. He also admitted betraying the cause of the Uprising and the KSČ leadership's interests in Moscow, so that he actually departed from Slovakia as a traitor."[34]

The indictment and Slánský's statement in court eventually discussed his activity during the Uprising in terms of betraying the interests of Czechoslovakia's people and as executing the plans of American imperialists to enslave Slovakia. Cooperation with General Pika was qualified as an espionage connection.

Interrogations continued throughout August with few hitches. Slánský was no longer nervous when returning to his cell, and sometimes even seemed happy. The interrogators were satisfied and rewarded their victim with favors, especially books. After the afternoon session of *August 22,* his cellmate Benda reported, "In the evening he returned to the cell in very good spirits and told me right away that we'd have *The Good Soldier Švejk* to read for Sunday. It was clear from his behavior that his position in the interrogations had improved." But the next day, *August 23,* he reported a sudden change: Slánský "returned at night very exhausted and clearly disturbed. He rolled about on the cot and kept on sighing."[35]

The sudden change occurred when the interrogators decided to turn Slánský not only into a traitor, spy, and Zionist, but also into a murderer. That would have had a particularly shattering impact on the public. They wanted Slánský to confess to the intent of eliminating Jan Šverma.

Jan Šverma, the husband of Marie Švermová, had been one of the prewar leaders of the KSČ. He was generally considered Gottwald's closest aide and possible successor. The Communist leadership in Moscow exile sent him as their political emissary to join the Slovak Uprising. Slánský was the political officer with the partisans, Šverma with civilian authorities. When the Uprising was defeated, Šverma retreated with other partisans to the Tatra mountains but succumbed during the ordeal.

Slánský denied feeling any hostility toward Šverma, who had, in fact, been a close personal friend. On *August 22,* a group confrontation was staged. Four prisoners were to testify that Slánský hated Šverma, and that he intentionally neglected him during the retreat into the mountains. When it was over, the interrogator asked, "Do you confess that your true attitude toward Jan Šverma was that you saw him as a rival and an obstacle in your effort to achieve a high position in the KSČ?"

> *Slánský:* I deny it.
> *Interrogator:* Your denial is of course ridiculous. These four people who testify against you offer such strong evidence that it will nail you. Further denials are therefore useless. Your hostile attitude toward Šverma has been proven.
> *Slánský:* I maintain what I have said about my attitude toward Šverma.[36]

The interrogation then focused on the motivation: on admitting guilt in Šverma's death in order to eliminate a political rival. Slánský resisted. He had another nervous breakdown and repeatedly screamed in fits of fury: "You will not turn me into a murderer! I will not let you make a murderer of me! I am not a murderer!" But on *August 25,* the interrogators recorded their first success: "He admitted he gave Šverma no help to save his life, even though he saw that Šverma was completely exhausted and was begging for help. He confessed that his part in Šverma's death amounted to a major crime against the KSČ and was a part of his hostile activity."

The advisors were probably not satisfied with a formulation admitting a role in Šverma's death because of mere neglect. It lacked the intent, the ingredient needed to show Slánský as a murderer. However, Slánský did not give in on this point. On *August 26,* his cellmate Benda reported that "on Saturday afternoon he returned from the interrogation very angry and told me that he's once again in trouble upstairs, so that they didn't even lend him anything to read. In the evening he came back still very angry and even though he brought a book along, he said he still hadn't reached an agreement with the people upstairs and that the tension continues."[37]

The interrogators got nowhere with the concept of intentionally murdering Šverma and abandoned it on *August 28*. The indictment eventually stated that Slánský deliberately created conditions that led to Šverma's death.

The advisors, however, did not abandon their original plan. When the trial itself was in session, they summoned two former partisans to testify against Slánský on the issue of Šverma's murder. This, however, led to dangerous complications.

> When the case officers told him [Slánský] that after the break, two partisans would testify against him as the murderer of Jan Šverma, he got another attack. He declared that he would not let anyone make him out as a murderer and begged that they immediately report, to someone responsible, his request that those witnesses not be admitted. He said that he didn't want to ruin the trial but that's what could happen if the two appeared. The advisors didn't want to give in; they stated that Slánský would not dare ruin the trial. The case officers, however, weren't so sure. In the end they decided to telephone K. Gottwald at the Castle, and he decided against calling the witnesses.[38]

Once Šverma was no longer an issue, the tensions abated, and Slánský calmed down again. On *August 29*, Benda reported, "in the evening he returned in a better mood. He said he had had a schnitzel and that he's receiving better care. He was talkative and in a good mood."[39]

Writing the script and coaching Slánský for his court appearance started in September. Interrogations were no longer as intensive and were peppered with jokes and laughter. There was more free time, which Benda filled by reading aloud. Conversations of the two prisoners were more relaxed. They swapped stories. Slánský would hear a joke from the interrogators and tell it to Benda, who recorded it in his report for the interrogators. Nevertheless, the changes in the ambience did not calm Slánský down.

The interrogators were recasting the interrogation protocols into a question-and-answer form, eliminating any ambiguities. They molded the questions and answers so as to follow their own ideas and intentions, achieving what the actual interrogations had often failed to achieve. They organized the protocols so as to make the criminal activity appear in the worst possible light. Slánský was horrified when he first saw this version. Hundreds of pages of forced statements and confessions were processed and reconstituted into perhaps a tenth of the original, but it was a damning tenth. Slánský was shocked, even though—or because?—he had signed off on almost everything the new version contained.

As the script was being written, Slánský went through another crisis. This time it was marked not by nervous attacks but by permanent nervousness, rage from impotence, despair, and apathy. It is possible that during this time Slánský was given sedatives and a lot of medication to soothe his headaches in order to reinforce his apathy and weaken his mental agility. Benda recorded his moods during the first half of September:

> *September 1.* He was nervous again as he returned at lunchtime from the interrogation. He was snapping his fingers, feeling his throat, and didn't talk much. He complained of a headache again.
>
> *September 3.* He was very disturbed yesterday when he returned from interrogation. This, however, was very different from his usual nervousness and one could call it suppressed rage. He was red in the face, and his eyes flashed with rage.
>
> This morning his rage mounted further. He walked about, periodically banging the wall with his fist, he kept on mumbling something as though he couldn't suppress his rage, and at one point he even uttered a long muted roar.
>
> *September 4.* Yesterday evening he was still very nervous. He kept complaining of a strong headache. He actually moaned in pain from time to time. He also said that he hears illusions, that everything he hears is very distorted. At times he just gazed absentmindedly into space with a demented expression. About an hour before he was taken to the interrogation, he drifted back into apathy.
>
> *September 9.* His nervousness exploded again when he returned from interrogation in the afternoon. He is now mostly in a state of resigned despair rather than rage.
>
> *September 12.* He returned very upset from the afternoon interrogation. We still read *By the City Gates,* though. We read the ending which is very poignant and tragic, and he suddenly started crying and asked me to stop, saying that he couldn't handle it any more. He said he felt awful when he heard how people sacrificed themselves and then realized the situation he was in himself; it broke his heart. Then he just sat there and stared with a look of despair.[40]

In a few weeks his nervous attacks recurred, triggered by the advisors' second attempt to present Slánský as a would-be murderer, this time of Gottwald. Gottwald was chronically ill, and Slánský had been the only one to receive his medical bulletins. Doing away with Gottwald would be presented as removing the greatest obstacle the antistate center faced in reaching its objectives, and as a demonstration of Slánský's aspiration to be the country's top man.

Technically, the advisors tried to show that Dr. Vladimír Haškovec, Slánský's brother-in-law and Gottwald's personal physician, was a member of the antistate center, and that he deliberately treated Gottwald so as to shorten his life. Haškovec had already been arrested. He was branded an enemy and later sentenced.

Interrogations related to Gottwald's health started suddenly on *September 15,* and became very pointed the very next day: Slánský, the argument went, intentionally monopolized Gottwald's health care, didn't do what was necessary, and failed to inform Gottwald about Haškovec's strange past—fabricated of course by security. Slánský was on high alert again, especially when the interrogators offered him various favors for a confession. Benda wrote:

> He was very nervous when he came back from the afternoon session. He told me right away that he was in great trouble upstairs and that he had to do some thinking . . . He started jogging about the cell and said he was very nervous and kept on saying that he had to think something over. He sighed and pounded the wall. When he sat down, he banged his head against the wall. He mentioned several times that they were offering him all kinds of things.

At first he resolutely rejected the charge. The protocol of *September 17* includes the following:

> *Interrogator*: All your statements indicate that you tried to formulate [Gottwald's] health bulletins in your own favor.
> *Slánský*: I formulated them according to realities.
> *Interrogator*: This of course isn't true. Did you really do all you could to improve the health of K. Gottwald?
> *Slánský*: Yes.

The report of *September 20,* however, had a different tone: "Although he states that he had not thought through how exactly to eliminate K. Gottwald, he admits that he counted on the possibility that the president of the republic might die."[41]

The interrogators kept up the threats-and-promises routine for another week, but Slánský resolutely refused to accept the role of murderer. His resistance exploded into attacks of hysteria. On *September 24,*

Benda wrote, "He is still very irritable. He slept poorly and kept on sighing and moaning. At one moment he got red in the face, and it sounded like he was weeping. He flips between rage and despair."

This line of interrogation ended on *September 27,* with partial victory for both sides:

He admitted calculating that if the conspiratorial antistate center had usurped power, he would have taken over K. Gottwald's position . . . He further admitted that while he relied on K. Gottwald's death, he also figured that if he came to power he would get rid of him in some other way . . . He concealed from the president that Haškovec is an enemy . . . Slánský confessed that Haškovec didn't treat the president as he should have, thereby contributing to shortening his life, that is, accelerating his death.[42]

When he read this report, Gottwald believed—or, to soothe his own conscience, acted as though he believed—that Slánský really had tried to get rid of him through Haškovec. He commented to his secretary, "Those were the days when they sent policemen with batons against us. Now they send doctors."[43]

The indictment eventually mentioned Slánský's effort to isolate Gottwald from political decision-making. The section about shortening his life corresponds to the report of September 27.

Slánský was called in every day until the end of September; however, with one exception, these were not real interrogations. Now he was studying his part for the trial. The pressures ceased almost entirely. Nevertheless, it was not a time of inner peace. Slánský's nervousness, pensiveness, resignation, his absent staring into space even when talking to Benda or to his interrogators were only now and then punctuated by moments of real calm and joy or by eruptions of tears or rage.

The advisors and interrogators carefully monitored Slánský's state of mind, lest some last-minute complications tangle up the last phase of the trial preparations. Benda had to give detailed reports about Slánský's reactions, recording the slightest indication of any possible intention to resist in court or to hurt himself. We can thus follow Slánský's moods right up to the eve of the trial:

October 1. He's in the same mood. He's not particularly excited, but he's very nervous and tense. He's quite talkative and kind of forcibly happy. Only now and then does he fall into melancholy. He says nothing about the interrogations.

Slánský's mood was relatively calm, if nervous, for only four days. Then came a change:

October 6. This afternoon he complained that his headache grew worse
and that he wasn't feeling well. He staggered about, evidently weak. He was
all kind of broken down. He was really pale in the face and dragged himself
about very slowly.

The next day was even worse:

October 7. He's not eating much and he's sleeping poorly. He complains
of constant headaches and says that the pills don't help him. One can see a
kind of physical collapse. He drags about all hunched up and jerks nervously
every now and then.

Slánský felt really bad for another two days. At the end of the week,
on *October 10 through 12,* he was quite calm and even unusually happy.
But on *October 13,* "he went to interrogation before lunch and returned
after a while all red in the face and clearly excited. He walked about
and kept on mumbling, 'Jesus Maria.' "[44]

This change was caused by interrogation targeted on the letter to the
Great Street Sweeper. The advisors cooked up a scenario according to
which U.S. intelligence was to have offered Slánský a way out of the
country, as "one of theirs." Slánský, however, insisted that he maintained
no contacts with U.S. intelligence, that he never received any letter, and
that he didn't know the people who were supposed to have sent it. On
October 15, Benda recorded that Slánský had calmed down; but on
October 16,

in the morning and especially in the afternoon he relapsed into his earlier
state, that is, into silence and melancholy. He kept on mumbling something
under his breath.

October 17. He was in the same melancholy mood. He wasn't particularly
agitated or excited but was depressed.

Interrogations about the letter to the Great Street Sweeper ended on
October 18 with no success for the advisors. An interrogator wrote that
Slánský "states that he didn't know anything about any offer of U.S.
intelligence and received no letter."[45]

During the last month before the trial, Slánský's outbursts of nervousness alternated with moments of apathy, resignation, and occasional
despair. His nervousness erupted when the sedatives lost their effectiveness. On Sunday, *October 19,*

he was very melancholy from the morning on. He walked about like he was
mute, sighed, and didn't react to my approaches. He has been like this all the
time these past few days. He isn't particularly nervous or agitated. He just

stares like he's dumb and looks feverish. Occasionally he falls into despair and then he starts muttering to himself, "Jesus Maria, this is driving me crazy." *October 29.* His mood has not changed. He's a little calmer in the evenings but very nervous in the afternoons. At times he has a look of absolute despair. He starts jerking and tossing his head and it takes a moment before he regains control.

The weekend of *November 1 and 2* had a calming effect, just as the previous weekend had. Both days "were calm; his mood doesn't change. He's rather calm and quite normal. He did complain, though, that he slept poorly these last two nights because he cannot get rid of heavy thoughts.

His Sunday mood didn't change much, until *November 6*:

He was still rather calm after the afternoon interrogation. But he went back to interrogation in the evening and, after about an hour, returned very agitated and nervous. He laid down but couldn't sleep for quite a while (about an hour), even though he had taken a pill. He kept on sighing, covered his face with his hand and one could see his hand twitching nervously.[46]

After the afternoon session of *November 7,* he was calm again. But the weekend of *November 8 and 9* was not like the previous ones. Books and sedatives didn't help. Slánský repeatedly jerked about, wrung his hands and went red and white in his face, which went on until 6 P.M. on Sunday. On Monday, *November 10,* "he was once again calmer in the morning." He indicated he was expecting the trial to start soon.

His changing moods settled in the last week before the trial, which he looked forward to as a liberation, especially once he was told its exact date.

November 12 and 13. He was calm but he still didn't talk. One can't detect any nervousness except that from time to time he utters a deep sigh or goes red and white in the face. Usually he seems absentminded, though. This is no normal calm, though, but apathy and depression of some sort.

While yesterday he was quite calm with just hints of nervousness, today [*November 14*] he's entirely calm and even in a good mood.

In the evening he returned from interrogation kind of puzzled and quiet. One felt that this crisis, which showed in the way he paced the cell, how he was red in the face and in his monosyllabic answers, was caused by helpless rage.[47]

He woke up on Saturday *November 15* quite calm and stayed in a good mood until the evening. "He was actually happy and told jokes." Then he was taken to a short but important interrogation. He had visitors: Josef Urválek, the chief prosecutor, and Jaroslav Novák, president of the court senate. They read him the indictment and told him the trial would start the following Thursday. He returned "still a bit agitated and nervous, but he cracked a few jokes." The next morning, on *November 16*, he discussed his visitors.

> During and especially after that whole conversation, he was very nervous. Tears welled up in his eyes at one moment, when he said, "Well, everything will be over by Christmas." And he repeated: "Everything." I tried to tell him that he sees things too darkly but he just smiled bitterly. He was very nervous. Then he stated that he's glad it will be over because waiting is the worst part of it, and added sarcastically: "You'll no doubt be glad too when it's all over, and you get out of here." After the afternoon interrogation, he told me right away, "Well, the trial starts on Thursday at 9 A.M." He sighed a bit but was generally calm.

Slánský accepted the indictment without a murmur, without a single reservation, silently. He had resigned himself to whatever would come.

The next day, *November 17*, he "didn't even mention [the trial]; he was quiet and pensive. He was as usual self-absorbed and silent but quite calm." He returned from the afternoon session "in the same mood, and told me right away that he still hasn't seen a defense attorney but expects him tomorrow. He took a pill and fell asleep rather fast but kept waking up all night and was very restless. He kept moaning 'Jesus Maria.'"

On *November 18*, "he was very nervous and stone silent" all day, even after the visit from Dr. Vladimír Bartoš, his defense attorney. Their brief and very formal conversation strengthened Slánský's belief that he should expect the worst. All he told Benda at first was that "his defense attorney was here, but that was all." Only later did he elaborate:

> He saw his defense attorney in the old building and in civilian clothes and said that the attorney wouldn't be coming again and that their conversation took place in the presence of two case officers. He emphasized that part and grimaced sarcastically. At night he kept thrashing about and couldn't fall asleep.

On *November 19* his constant nervousness gave way to thoughts about the remaining ten days of his life. Slánský "kept repeating: 'Ten more days.' When they took him in for questioning, he was more nervous than usual and said: 'I have to go there. I have to talk with them.' Other than that he spent the evening pacing the cell."

The advisors and interrogators opted for interrogations until the last moment, in order to prepare their victim for the trial psychologically and to monitor whether he intended to wreck the production of the show. Slánský returned from his last session "at night and very disturbed. He kept on tossing about on his cot, sighed, and couldn't fall asleep."[48]

THE FINAL WORD: THE POLITICAL AUTHORITIES

Security completed its trial preparations around November 10. The final word was now up to political authorities. In late October 1952, Stalin discussed the upcoming trial with Gottwald, Zápotocký and Široký, at the Nineteenth Congress of the CPSU.

They were invited to join Stalin in his dacha outside Moscow. Georgi Malenkov and Nikolai Bulganin were present as well. They started out by discussing economic matters. Gottwald requested credit for purchasing military hardware. Stalin agreed and moved on to the Slánský trial. He showed detailed familiarity with the matter. He didn't miss the chance to make a joke at Zápotocký's expense and rebuked him for spending more time on his writing than on government work, which in turn allowed Slánský's "rampage." The Czechoslovak politicians must have felt out of sorts: they didn't know what Stalin was after.

Gottwald had yet another reason to feel uneasy. He had hoped for a private conversation with Stalin, but that never materialized. He wanted to settle a certain matter that disturbed him greatly: he had discovered that his apartments were bugged and believed it was the doing of Moscow. Stalin's criticism of Zápotocký and the absence of a private audience only heightened his insecurity.[49]

Gottwald returned from Moscow quite disturbed. He didn't know whether Stalin's behavior was accidental or intentional. This uncertainty influenced his attitude during the final phase of the trial preparations. He tried more than ever to avoid anything that could possibly cast any shadow on him, especially in determining the sentences and how they would be carried out.

The CC KSČ political secretariat discussed the trial on November 13, 1952. The meeting was attended by all members, as well as by Justice Minister Štefan Rais and the Soviet advisor Alexei Beschasnov. The main point on the agenda was the draft indictment. The meeting resolved: "To approve the draft of the indictment, subject to a commission consisting of Bacílek, Čepička, Kopecký, and Rais putting it into final form in accordance with points raised during the discussion." Čepička argued that "from the expert [legal] point of view, the indictment is weak," that it contained incomprehensible sections, that it didn't persuasively formulate the objective of the plotters, and that "it doesn't elaborate on the means that the conspirators wanted to use in attaining their objective." Novotný recommended that greater attention be paid to Slánský's efforts to gain control over the party, the army and security. Kopecký called for greater emphasis on international aspects—on the intentions of imperialists who recruit agents from among the "Western exile" and Jews. Široký found the concept of the indictment correct but argued that "the defendants talk too much."

Gottwald made most of the comments, which reflected—or indeed were inspired by—his self-defense. He suggested that the indictment should "persuasively prove how they got to that platform, and particularly Slánský's camouflage, two-faced nature, and perfidy." He instructed that the section about sabotaging the national five-year economic plan be reworked so as to emphasize that the party and government decisions were correct but that they were corrupted by the enemies—yet that the five-year plan was being met regardless. He disagreed with Novotný, Kopecký, and Široký, arguing that the defendants' "activity in the party should not be a subject of the indictment because they had been thrown out of the party for that," and had that part eliminated. Gottwald pinpointed two other sections that ended up being eliminated. One concerned the role of the International Bank and the International Monetary Fund. The other, which made Gottwald feel particularly vulnerable, read as follows:

> They [the defendants] rejected experiences of the Soviet Union in constructing socialism [and] tried to hoodwink the Communist party and Czechoslovak people by underhandedly disseminating the detestable Trotskyite theory of Czechoslovakia's specific path in constructing socialism, without the dictatorship of the proletariat.

Gottwald also substituted the expression "of Jewish origin" for "Jews" in the description of eleven of the defendants.

The CC KSČ political secretariat decided that the trial should open on November 20 and should last seven days, as opposed to Bacílek's recommendation that it last ten days. It appointed a political commission (Bacílek [chairman], Široký, Čepička, Kopecký, Rais, Novotný), a press commission (Kopecký [chairman], Prchal, Klos, Vladimír Koucký, Josef Vorel, Doubek), and a commission for managing the trial. Novotný was given the job of organizing attendance in the courtroom, with the help of the CC KSČ apparatus. Bacílek, Kopecký, Rais, and Novotný were

in charge of arranging it so that members of the CC KSČ political secretariat could listen in on the trial directly from their offices.[50]

During or immediately after this meeting, Gottwald instructed Bacílek to interview all the defendants except Slánský. This was originally
an idea of the advisors which Gottwald adopted. The advisors expected
that these interviews would strengthen the defendants' determination to
play their appropriate role in the courtroom. It was a sort of a party
guarantee, an effort to minimize the risk of unforeseen events.

The interviews took place in Doubek's office. Doubek and the case
officers, who brought in their wards one by one, also attended. Doubek
later wrote that Minister Bacílek "didn't promise anything, but he hinted
that their courtroom behavior would influence the sentences. He also
guaranteed to each one that his family wouldn't suffer in any way. Of
course, everything was tied to how the defendant would behave in court."

František Homola, Frejka's case officer, corroborated Doubek's rec-
ollection:

> Com. Bacílek talked to Frejka generally about his criminal activity and in
> conclusion told him that he expects him to make a good presentation during
> the trial and to follow the [question-and-answer] protocol. I recall that Frejka
> answered that he would indeed follow the protocol because what it says is the
> truth.

After the interview Frejka commented to his cellmate "that it's not
so bad with him yet, they're still counting on him."

Meetings with the minister met the expectations. All defendants
promised to follow the script. Thus Clementis said, "I'm a lawyer and
a politician, I know what to expect. I have no illusions in this respect.
I will behave in court so as to give no pretext for any campaign against
the party or the republic."[51]

The interviews had two other results. Hinting that the sentence and
the fate of the families would be influenced by discipline in the courtroom was a particularly strong psychological weapon. On the other hand,
it gave the defendants some hope that they might be spared.

On November 15 and 16 the appropriate commission put the final
touches on the draft of the indictment. Its meeting was attended also by
Beschasnov, Yesikov, Urválek, Doubek, and Prchal. The commission
made thirty-three changes. The first class of changes sharpened the formulations, for example: "Trotskyite-Titoist, Zionist, bourgeois-nationalist traitors"; "perfidious traitor"; "son of a wealthy merchant" (Slánský). The second class added phrases, sentences, or entire paragraphs,

for example: "Governed by fanatical hatred of the USSR, they sabo-taged our relationship with the USSR"; sections about Clementis's bour-geois nationalism and about his contacts with Konni Zilliacus. The third class of changes were deletions, such as: Slánský "aided Hitlerite gangs in spilling the blood of the Slovak people"; or, "the particularly thievish commercial agreement with Britain."

Toward the end of the meeting, Urválek asked about the sentences that he, as prosecutor, should call for. Nobody opposed Kopecký's opin-ion: "Every one of them has three scaffold's worth." Urválek took this as an instruction.[52]

The political commission met on November 17, with Beschasnov attending. Its agenda consisted of the following: (1) changes in the text of the indictment; (2) attendance in the courtroom; (3) security measures during the trial; (4) the suggestion that representatives of other people's democracies be invited to take part in the trial; (5) the trial schedule (with Novák and Urválek attending); (6) certain suggestions of the press commission.

Debate about point (1) concerned mostly the designation of some of the defendants as being of Jewish origin. Beschasnov pressed his original proposal that the term Jewish nationality be used. The argument ended in a compromise. Šváb and Frank would be described as Czech, Cle-mentis as Slovak, and all the others as "of Jewish origin." After these changes the text of the indictment was submitted to Gottwald who made some final minor changes.

The recommendation concerning point (2) featured organized par-ticipation of KSČ officials from all regions of the country. The spectators would rotate daily and would be selected by KSČ district committees. An entry ticket was to be considered an honor and a reward for accom-plishments.

The security plan [point (3)] outlined the responsibility of leading security officials for various aspects of the trial: political (Bacílek, Prchal, Doubek), organizational (Milan Moučka), and technical. It also dealt with supervising the behavior of the defendants and witnesses dur-ing the trial.

As for point (4), the commission decided "to invite editors of fra-ternal parties." Foreign Minister Široký was to decide himself about participation of journalists from the West.

As for the trial schedule, the committee changed the resolution of the CC KSČ political secretariat and decided that "the trial will last eight days. The sentence will be pronounced at 5 P.M. on the eighth day of the trial at the latest, and will be formulated in the Soviet fashion, that is, first the justification and only then the sentence." Novák and Urválek were to prepare a detailed time schedule for each day. The committee also discussed Urválek's closing speech. The advisors had recommended that Urválek "study closing speeches from the trials of the Trotskyites and of Rajk" and draft his speech after discussing it with Rais. The committee approved the speech and even commended Urválek for it. Gottwald himself lauded it later.[53]

The press commission planned an extensive press campaign. It included publishing a book, actually the script of the show, with an 80,000-copy printing in Czech and in four world languages. The first press release was to be issued on the evening of the opening day. However, on November 19, the CC KSČ political secretariat decided to announce the trial already the following morning. Novotný and Köhler, who proposed this change, wanted to forestall "that people first learn about the trial from Western radio."[54]

On the same day Gottwald received an exact schedule of all eight days of the trial, prepared by Urválek and Novák. The trial would start on November 20 at 9 A.M., and the sentences would be handed down on the eighth day, between 9 and 11 A.M.[55]

7

THE TRAGIC END

POLITICAL MURDERS

J AROSLAV NOVÁK , president of the State Court Senate, opened the trial of the Leadership of the Antistate Conspiratorial Center in the Palace of Justice in Prague exactly on schedule. He would preside over one of the most tragic shows of postwar Czechoslovakia and of the Soviet bloc as a whole, which would end with a series of political murders. The trial was actually produced as a show; its scriptwriters, directors, and actors designed it, prepared it, and produced it with this intent.

State prosecutor Josef Urválek charged Rudolf Slánský (born 1901), Bedřich Geminder (1901), Ludvík Frejka (1904), Josef Frank (1909), Vladimír Clementis (1902), Bedřich Reicin (1911), Artur London (1915), Evžen Löbl (1907), Vavro Hajdů (1913), Rudolf Margolius (1913), Otto Fischl (1902), Otto Šling (1912), and André Simone (1895) with the crimes of high treason, espionage, sabotage, and military treason. The forty-page indictment contained the political concept of the trial: it depicted Slánský and his accomplices as seasoned traitors of the Communist party and as agents of Western espionage centers. Following the example of Yugoslavia, they allegedly wanted to tear Czechoslovakia out of the Soviet camp and restore capitalism. To achieve this they created a second power center, they conspired, placed their people in leading posts, subverted the policy of Socialist construction and of alliance with the Soviet Union, and planned to remove Gottwald and his leadership. The anti-Semitic aspect of the trial was particularly prominent: of the fourteen defendants, eleven were described as being of Jewish origin: one section of the indictment dealt with their support of Zionist orga-

227

nizations, and other places discussed their support for Israel.

The trial proceeded exactly as scripted. The prosecutors and the judges asked the prescribed questions, the defendants and the witnesses recited the answers they had memorized. Bacílek, Prchal, Beschasnov, and other advisors followed the trial from a special room. The interrogators, in another room, monitored the proceedings to make sure they corresponded to the script. In the case of any deviation, they were to alert the president of the court senate immediately via a special signal mechanism installed in his desk, unplug the microphone, and play a tape. It wasn't necessary. The trial proceeded without a major glitch. The most serious complication was Slánský's refusal, discussed earlier, to testify about the death of Jan Šverma. The producers were also unhappy when Vilém Nový, a witness, couldn't recognize André Simone, with whom he had worked after the war in the Communist press. There were also heated comments when Otto Šling's pants fell down during his cross-examination: they thought it was intentional. They also sharply rebuked prosecutor Miloslav Kolaja for twice skipping a scripted question; the defendant ended up giving an answer that did not match. They even threatened that another prosecutor would take over the case.[1]

Each day, prosecutors, judges, interrogators, and advisors met after the court session was over. Advisors evaluated the progress and gave instructions for the next day. Interrogators reported on the defendants' reactions to the trial. Every interrogator monitored his "ward." He spent breaks with him in a specially constructed temporary cell in the corridor of the court building, and spent the night with him in the prison cell. The interrogators didn't observe any particular distress of the victims The strong sedatives administered by the prison doctor obviously worked right up to the verdict.

On the second day of the trial, Gottwald circulated a proposal concerning appeal procedures to members of the CC KSČ political secretariat. Although he didn't really wish it, it was possible that some of the defendants might appeal. Gottwald proposed the composition of the senate of appeals, the public prosecutor, a time-schedule, and the results of the appeal. It would take place on December 4; it would last one (!) day, with the participation of "the particularly well-qualified public" from the ranks of defense, security, justice, and the party apparatus. The appeal would confirm the verdict of the State Court. Members of the CC KSČ political secretariat approved the proposal *per rollam* (without actually meeting).[2]

The media reported on the trial from day one. Live coverage from the courtroom focused on the most shocking aspects of the defendants' statements. The media also reported "voices of the people." For one reason or another, the terrible crimes shocked most of the population. The public-opinion machinery was revved up. Lower-level Communist authorities were instructed to organize meetings of the party, labor unions, and the public which would kindle "the flames of the people's justified wrath against the infamous traitors and enemies." A wave of protests swept the country.

Resolutions poured in, addressed to the CC KSČ and to the State Court: by December 5, 8,520 arrived from units of the party, the labor unions, the government, non-Communist parties, schools. They mostly featured angry denunciation and hatred for the defendants and called for their death. Anti-Semitism was also very strong. The trial inspired an avalanche of snitching. This time around, lower party personnel and even groups from factories pointed their fingers at hundreds of people whom they described as protégés of the conspirators, Zionists, or as people of "suspicious origin."

The general character of the indictment, the thoroughness of the trial preparations, and its anti-Semitic character provoked some doubts and questions as well. Such private doubts, however, were seldom voiced in meetings, and appeared only in isolated cases in the resolutions. Many of them were reported by party organizations to the CC KSČ.

The first overwhelming enthusiastic wave of approval turned into a nagging question: How was all this possible? How could the conspirators have caused damages in the billions? What had the government been doing? The deputies? These questions were voiced at meetings and on other occasions. They were followed by expressions of mistrust in the government ministers, including Zápotocký. The questions went beyond responsibility for economic damages. How was it possible, people asked, for Gestapo and imperialist agents to penetrate the leadership of the party and the state? Who actually controlled the highest officials of the country? From here, it was only one step to the demand for control from below.

The wrath of the people, once unleashed, turned into a crisis of confidence in the leading national and party institutions and personalities—with the exception of Gottwald. His authority actually increased, and his cult reached its peak. He was presented as the only trustworthy leader and as the savior of the country from machinations of the enemies and saboteurs.[3]

The seventh day of the trial featured the concluding remarks of the

Prosecutor Urválek delivering his final speech on the last day of the trial, November 26, 1952

prosecutor, the defense attorneys, and the defendants. Urválek concluded his almost four-hour speech:

> Citizen judges, in the name of our nation, whose freedom and happiness the conspirators opposed, in the name of peace, against which they infamously conspired, I demand the death penalty for all defendants. Let your verdict come down as an iron fist, without the slightest mercy. Let it be the fire which will extirpate the roots of this infamous canker of treason. Let it be a bell which will ring all over our beautiful motherland, calling for new victories in our march toward the sun of socialism.

Defense attorneys also acquitted themselves successfully of the mission outlined for them by the advisors and interrogators. They confirmed

Slánský listening to Urválek's speech, November 26, 1952

the correctness of the indictment and of the trial. They stated that the defendants' "guilt has been clearly proven, their activity cannot be defended . . . from the legal point of view the indictment cannot be contested."

Finally, the defendants. They spoke briefly, reciting a text prepared by the interrogators. They confessed to all their alleged crimes and commented on the proposed verdict. None of them defended themselves or protested.

Slánský: I deserve no other end to my criminal life than that proposed by the state prosecutor.

Geminder: I realize that even the severest verdict, which will always be just, will not allow me to personally compensate and make up for the great damages I have caused.

Frejka: My guilt is so great that I accept in advance any verdict of the court as the just verdict of Czechoslovakia's working people.

Frank: I beg the State Court to gauge the depth and extent of my guilt strictly, and to hand down a strict and severe sentence.

Clementis: The verdict concerning my activity, which the court of the nation will hand down, can only be just, however harsh it may be.

Reicin: I realize that for these crimes of mine I deserve the harshest penalty.

Šváb: I therefore beg the State Court to judge and condemn my treason as harshly and as mercilessly as possible.

London: I know that the verdict will be a just one.

Löbl: I realize that I deserve a harsh and strict penalty.

Margolius: I cannot but ask for the strictest possible penalty.

Šling: I am rightfully being scorned, and I deserve the highest and strictest penalty.

Simone: Therefore I beg the court for the strictest penalty.[4]

As the defendants were making their closing remarks, Gottwald suddenly convened members of the CC KSČ political secretariat to decide on the sentences. There is no record of this meeting. Ten years later, Čepička wrote about it:

There was some hesitation at first as we were deciding the sentences for these people; but once the case was clarified, there was a unified opinion about the verdicts. Whoever proposed the verdicts didn't act alone; they had been reviewed ahead of time. I don't think prison terms were even discussed. The verdicts were discussed in an atmosphere of the great responsibility that everyone, including com. Gottwald, felt; and I don't think it took too long.[5]

Čepička's description agrees with statements of other participants—Novotný and Široký—only in one aspect: that the discussion didn't last long and wasn't particularly extensive. Novotný and Široký stated independently that, in fact, there was no discussion and that the meeting was over in a few minutes. Gottwald proposed "eleven ropes" and life for Hajdů, London, and Löbl. The others tacitly agreed.

The court handed down these sentences the following day, *November 27,* exactly as instructed over the phone by Gottwald.

The defense attorneys were to discourage their clients from appealing, arguing that not appealing would improve their chances for a pardon. Nobody appealed. The eleven condemned defendants asked the president of the republic to be pardoned. Gottwald originally didn't even intend to convene the party leadership to discuss this. In the end, though, members of the CC KSČ political secretariat did meet to discuss the requests. Viliam Široký later reminisced:

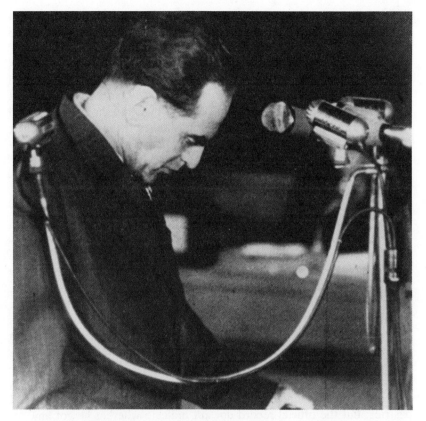

Slánský hearing his death sentence, November 27, 1952

After the verdict was handed down, with many capital punishments, comrade Gottwald summoned us to a meeting. He told us about the verdicts and said that some of the defendants had written him asking for a pardon. The letters with the requests were not distributed. Com. Gottwald did not recommend granting pardons; he was in favor of carrying out the sentences. And that was it, apart from our deathly silence and tacit agreement with com. Gottwald's opinion. It's hard to say much today. I myself don't know whether none of us opposed his suggestions because we really believed in the justice of the verdicts or because we didn't have the courage.[6]

On December 2, all eleven were informed about Gottwald's decision and told that the verdict would be carried out the following morning. The doomed men met their families for one last time, amid heart-rending scenes. The reunions were attended by the interrogators, and the families were separated by a wire partition. Josef Lédl, who attended Slán-ský's meeting with his wife, reported: "He clung to the wire mesh and cried loudly, which gave the impression of a well-rehearsed theater."[7] The meeting of Frejka with his wife was the most dramatic. She was probably the only one of the condemned men's next of kin who believed in the trial and in her husband's treason. As they parted she gave vent to her feelings: she had always believed her husband, he had never lied to her before, and she believed he hadn't lied to the court either. Their last meeting was filled with loud recriminations and her harsh condem-nation. Both had to be escorted away by the interrogators.

All except Slánský wrote their last letters: Clementis, Reicin, Si-mone, Šling, and Šváb wrote to their families and to Gottwald; Fischl, Frank, and Margolius wrote to their families; Frejka and Geminder wrote to Gottwald alone. Their last lines, written after so many cruel experiences and with no further fears of the consequences, are surpris-ing. They reveal their belief in their own guilt (albeit different from the guilt established by the court), in Slánský's treason, and in the happy future of the regime. Some declared that they never were traitors, agents, or enemies of the party and wished the party, the Czechoslovak people, and Gottwald many more successes. Letters to their families were filled with solicitude for their fates. Bacílek forwarded them to Gottwald after only ten days. The families themselves received them only after ten years.[8]

In the last hours before the executions, the attitudes of the guards relaxed. The condemned expressed their final wishes. Slánský requested pastries; but the official record doesn't indicate whether he got any.

The eleven men were hanged on December 3. Starting at 3 A.M., they left for the gallows, one by one. The executions were witnessed by an interrogator, a physician, and the assigned prosecutor, who gave instruc-tions to the hangman. The last one to hang was Slánský: the physician declared him dead at 5:45 A.M.

They all appear to have met their death with resignation. Šling's last words were, "Mr. Chairman, I wish the Communist party, the Czecho-slovak people and the president of the Republic every success. I never was a spy!" Šváb exclaimed, "Long live the Soviet Union, long live the Communist Party of Czechoslovakia!" Clementis simply said, "Thank you." And Slánský declared, 'I've got what I deserved." The official report listed asphyxiation as the cause of death.[9]

The bodies were cremated; StB personnel put the ashes in paper bags and scattered them in a field outside Prague.

Some of the interrogators did not anticipate the executions. They thought that Gottwald would pardon at least some of the defendants; even Doubek thought so. But they later accepted the rationale which an interrogator later presented to Bedřich Hájek, who reminisced:

> Sometime after the New Year of 1953, I asked my interrogator whether the defendants had been pardoned. He told me that the trial had provoked a firestorm of anger among the people, especially in the factories and that thousands of resolutions insisting on the death penalty had poured in.[10]

More than that. Thousands of resolutions actually expressed lack of confidence in the judges because they let three defendants off with their lives. Indeed, several delegations from factories arrived at the State Court to express the mistrust felt by "workers" and demanded an investigation as to whether the judges weren't intentionally covering up for the enemy.

The party held a national conference from December 16 to 18, 1952, to wind up the issue of the trial politically. Gottwald discussed it as a great victory of socialism and drew political lessons from the uncovering and sentencing of the "conspirators." The tragedy was not over, though. On April 7, 1953, the CC KSČ political secretariat approved Gottwald's proposal concerning "accommodations, labor assignments, and other issues concerning the next-of-kin of the condemned criminals of the antistate center." The resolution included the following:

> 1. Move the next-of-kin of the condemned traitors and criminals into two or three districts. They will be permitted to take along essential furnishings and clothing.
> 2. Employ adult members of the families in these districts in small factories of light industry, in agriculture, cottage industry, etc.
> 3. Arrange that these exiles be under permanent supervision of the ministry of national security.
> 4. The next-of-kin of the condemned criminals are stripped of their party membership.

In early 1953, so-called "follow-up trials" started; they continued for over a year. They were construed as trials of various parts or branches of the antistate center in security, the military, the party apparatus, the economy, the foreign-affairs ministry, and in Slovakia. Over 250 high-level Communist officials were victimized.

On the other hand, the CC KSČ political secretariat approved on February 17, 1953, a "Recommendation to Decorate State Security Personnel." Fourteen officers, including Doubek, Košťál, Musil, and

Moučka received the Order of the Republic. Six others received the Order of Labor, and forty-seven were decorated for valor. Doubek was promoted to lieutenant-colonel, Košťál and Musil to majors. Doubek, Košťál, and Kohoutek received an award of 30,000 crowns while another sixty people received 8,000 to 15,000 crowns apiece.[11]

FINAL QUESTIONS

We have traced the staging of the political show trial up to its tragic end. Two questions are of particular importance: What motivated this particular show trial, and why did the actors accept their tragic or infamous parts?

The question concerning the root causes for producing postwar Europe's largest political trial with former Communist officials, and specifically for its anti-Semitic orientation, calls for a consideration of changes in Soviet great-power politics.

The final collapse of the great-power alliance in mid-1947 foreshadowed a long-term presence of the United States in European politics. This was becoming apparent in the spring of 1947, and Moscow was fully aware of it in July, especially as the Marshall Plan was launched. Soviet expectations that the USSR would be the only great power in Europe, free to expand its sphere of influence further, collapsed. From this moment on, the Soviets assumed the possibility of a third world war and started preparing for it. The war was initially contemplated as a defensive one; but starting in 1951, the Soviets foresaw the expansion of socialism over all of continental Europe by having Soviet-bloc armies occupy other countries.

Politically, Czechoslovakia appeared to be the weakest link in this military strategy: top positions in the army, security, state administration, and the party were occupied by people whom Moscow either didn't trust or who knew too much (such as Šváb, Reicin, Osvald Závodský, and others).

Eliminating one group of Soviet collaborators in the security apparatus and substituting another group for it (Bacílek, Prchal, Keppert, and others) may have been a result of conflicts and changes within the Moscow security center itself. This question, however, cannot be answered definitively.

In the course of 1950, these motives were augmented with yet another one, which eventually became most prominent: anti-Semitism. A massive wave of anti-Semitism swept the Soviet Union at this time. In

1948–49, the Jewish Anti-Fascist Committee was dissolved. Many cultural institutions were disbanded. After the death of Andrei Zhdanov, anti-Semitism informed the purge which followed the "Leningrad affair." In the "Crimea affair" of 1952, twenty-four Jewish intellectuals were executed: they were condemned in a secret trial for their alleged intention to turn the Crimean peninsula into a Jewish region that would serve as a U.S. military base. A few months later the "doctors' plot" was cooked up in Moscow. Several physicians were accused of planning to eliminate certain leading Soviet politicians on instructions of Western intelligence agencies, prominently including international Jewish charitable organizations. The struggle against Zionism culminated in the early 1950s. Why?

The spring of 1947 saw the beginning of changes in Soviet Middle-East and Near-East policies, especially concerning Palestine. Moscow had tried to penetrate this area earlier but now escalated its efforts for two reasons.

One reason was the Truman Doctrine of March 1947, which Moscow viewed as endangering its own great-power aspirations and the potential germ of a great military conflict. Inasmuch as the Middle East could have served as a staging point for a campaign against the Caucasus oil fields, its strategic location suddenly grew in importance.

The second reason was the changing posture of Britain in the Middle East. Britain had always been an obstacle to Soviet efforts to gain a foothold there. However, British positions weakened after World War II. Palestine became the weakest element in the British sphere of influence. Growing unrest led Britain to request in April 1947 that its League of Nations mandate be terminated, and the UN General Assembly took up the issue in April and May of 1947. Britain's steps created a power vacuum that the Soviets were ready to exploit in order to penetrate the area.

The only politically significant force that existed in Palestine and the Middle East was the Zionist movement. It was anti-British; on top of that, it had the Haganah—a well-prepared military organization. Zionists struggled for an independent Jewish state that would result from dividing Palestine into a Jewish and an Arab section. This went against British plans. On May 14, 1947, Andrei Gromyko, the Soviet delegate to the UN, unexpectedly backed the division of Palestine and the creation of a Jewish state. This surprised even the Palestine Communist Party—which on that very day was still working for an Arab-Israeli federation and was denouncing Zionist plans for an independent state.

Gromyko's proposal was well received around the world and evoked Jewish sympathies toward the Soviet Union, especially within the left wing of the Zionist movement.

Britain, on the other hand, escalated its persecution of Zionist activists, especially of Haganah members, precisely because it feared possible Soviet influence. Britain offered political, financial, and military support to the Arab movement and to other countries which resolutely opposed the formation of a Jewish state. It was evident that if the territory of the Palestine Mandate were divided, the new Jewish state would face an Arab military offensive. The Jewish Agency, leading the Zionist movement, realized it wasn't prepared to face such a campaign: Haganah had only 10,000 rifles, 2,000 submachine guns, five hundred light machine guns and two heavy ones at its disposal.

Meanwhile, since 1945 Czechoslovakia had opposed the persecution of Jews and tried to help Jewish victims. In August 1945, the government denounced anti-Jewish demonstrations in Slovakia and brought their instigators to justice. In July 1946, Czechoslovakia gladly acceded to a request of the Jewish community and granted passage through the country to Western Europe to some 100,000 Jews escaping pogroms in Poland. In August 1946, Gottwald promised help for representatives of the Jewish religious community in resettling Jewish children from Poland.

Foreign minister Jan Masaryk strongly favored the formation of a Jewish state. On August 27, 1947, the Czechoslovak government discussed Masaryk's candidacy for the post of chairman of the UN Political Committee. Communist members argued that Masaryk could hardly advocate a clear Slav (pro-Soviet) policy. Masaryk answered that "he couldn't promise that as chairman he would always act in accordance with the wishes of the Soviet bloc . . . Considering his policies and views of thirty years standing concerning Jewish matters, he could hardly be expected to side with Ibn Saud against Jews in the Palestine question."[12]

In August 1947, however, Moscow's very definite preference concerning the Palestine question was the establishment of a Jewish state. In mid-August, the Czechoslovak leadership discussed a report about a Warsaw meeting of the Soviet-bloc communist parties that called for all-around material and political support for Jewish efforts to establish an independent state.

In the United Nations, Czechoslovakia favored the partition of Palestine. Czechoslovakia was represented on the UN Special Commission on Palestine (UNSCOP) and actually chaired the commission which car-

ried out UN Resolution No. 181/II of November 24, 1947, concerning
the end of the British mandate, the establishment of the State of Israel,
and delineation of its borders. Czechoslovakia was one of the first countries to recognize the new state, on May 20, 1948. President Gottwald
received Israel's first minister to Prague, Ehud Avriel, who emphasized
on this occasion that "the government and the people of Israel and all
Jewry hold Czechoslovakia in cordial esteem for its sincere friendship
for a nation struggling for its freedom . . ."

Even before Israel's independence, though, in the summer of 1947,
David Ben Gurion, chairman of the Jewish Agency, dispatched his representatives to several Western countries to purchase weapons for the
Haganah. He was not successful. Western governments embargoed the
sale of weapons to the Middle East, and they considered Haganah an
illegal organization operating on the territory of the British mandate,
that is, on the territory of an ally.

Ehud Avriel (formerly Überall) was one of Ben Gurion's people sent
to Europe with this mission. Avriel met in Paris with Robert Adam
Abramovici who represented the import-export firm of Joseph Nash.
Before the war, this firm had operated in Romania representing, among
others, Czechoslovakia's Zbrojovka Arms Works. General Heliodor
Pika, at the time Czechoslovakia's military attaché in Bucharest, had
met both Nash and Abramovici, who in 1939 funneled financial support
to Czechoslovakia's anti-Nazi resistance through him (Pika). After the
war, General Pika, appointed deputy Chief of General Staff, was responsible for Czechoslovakia's arms industry. He renewed his contacts
with Nash and Abramovici, who were now in Paris, again representing
the Zbrojovka Arms Works.

Bedřich Reicin, commander of defense intelligence, recommended
the sale of arms to Haganah via the Nash firm. The Czechoslovak government approved. General Pika was very instrumental in arranging this.
The arms in question were nonmoving inventory: weapons built for the
Germans during the war but which were now useless. The Prague government was happy to unload them. On December 1, 1947, the Zbrojovka Arms Works signed a contract to sell more weapons than Haganah's entire arsenal at the time. The next task was to deliver the weapons
to Israel. This was the job of Pika, Reicin, Clementis, and Masaryk.
The Polish government refused to allow transshipment, and the weapons
were therefore sent down the Danube River through Hungary to Yugoslavia, and then clandestinely through Italy to Tel-Aviv. They arrived
in April 1948.

Meanwhile, further arms negotiations had started in March. Czecho-slovakia suffered a dire shortage of hard currencies and offered Haganah a considerable additional amount of hardware from its own surplus, valued at about $18 million. One of the main instigators of this project was Antonín Zápotocký, then a deputy premier. He discussed the pos-sibility of additional weapon sales with Mordechai Oren, an officer of the left-leaning socialist Mapam party. Zápotocký even promised to train Israeli fliers and paratroopers in Czechoslovakia. The government pre-sidium had Reicin negotiate details of the arrangement with Avriel, who represented the Haganah. The military airport in Žatec was put at Ha-ganah's disposal for moving the weapons. The transport, ostensibly a sale of scrap metal to an Addis Ababa company, was taken care of by a Panamanian air company, under code name Operation Balak. In April and May, the Prague government released eighty-five aircraft to Ha-ganah but refused to sell tanks and cannons. The aircraft were flown via an air-bridge from Czechoslovakia's Žatec to Yugoslavia's Titograd (then called Podgorica) to Ekron in Palestine. Some eighty Haganah fliers were trained in military schools, and another group was undergoing paratroop training at the training center in Stráž pod Ralskem.

At this time, too, a Czechoslovak military brigade for Israel was being formed. Its members were being trained in Velká Střelná, in the Libava military area. Its formation was proposed by Shmuel Mikunis, general secretary of the Communist Party of Israel. He originally wanted to create an international brigade from Jews of the people's democracies. Moscow approved, and Mikunis, armed with Malenkov's approval, vis-ited Communist leaders of the bloc. In Prague he dealt with Slánský and Geminder who were, however, not particularly enthused by his requests.

Mikunis calculated that the presence of this brigade would strengthen his party's influence in Israel. He assumed that most members of the brigade would be Communists. However, the entire plan changed after the split with Yugoslavia, which had been particularly receptive to it. Only a Czechoslovak brigade was created, which included a few dozen Hungarian and Romanian Jews. Instructors and commanders were se-lected by Šváb's records department of the CC KSČ secretariat, partic-ularly Osvald Závodský. The position of brigade commander went to Antonín Sochor, a decorated Hero of the USSR, who in 1948 made two secret trips to Israel where he participated in developing the operation plan for the attack on Gaza.

After the British government protested in October 1948, Czechoslo-vak authorities decided to stop the training and accelerate the brigade's transfer to Israel. Preparations, however, dragged on. In addition, the Israeli government, while interested in the influx of Jews, was less enthusiastic about an independent Communist military unit. The transport took place in parts, starting in December 1948, with the last contingent of some five hundred people leaving in April 1949. By then the Arab-Israeli war was over, and the brigade was not needed.

Mikunis's calculation that members of the brigade would strengthen the hand of his Communist party did not work out. Only seven volunteers joined it. Leading Israeli Communists declared this sabotage and inferred that those responsible in Czechoslovakia must be Zionists. Mikunis suggested as much to Malenkov, whom he met again in Prague in May 1949 during the Ninth KSČ Congress.

Czechoslovakia was the only member of the Soviet bloc to provide Israel with military assistance, and Israel's leaders expressed their satisfaction and thanks to Gottwald. There was a rub to the whole matter, though. Czechoslovakia's position evoked the displeasure of Britain, which protested the air-bridge and twice protested the training of the brigade. On January 10, 1949, the CC KSČ presidium discussed the British campaign against Czechoslovakia.

Arab countries protested as well. Hitherto friendly relations were greatly affected and turned into hostility that soured even further when Czechoslovakia cancelled existing agreements to furnish military hardware and refused to sign new ones. This was a result of a Soviet intervention, after Gromyko promised Israel's UN representative in February or March of 1948 to arrange that Prague not sell weapons to Arab countries. In the following three months, Clementis reported to his government about very sharp protest notes received from Syria and other Arab countries and about the loss of important traditional customers for weapons.

In 1948, Arab countries and Israel had an equal share of Czechoslovakia's exports of hardware. In addition, Lebanon arranged for Czechoslovak purchases of strategic minerals. In the following years trade with Israel and Egypt decreased, but trade with Saudi Arabia and with Arab parts of French Africa increased. Czechoslovakia's trade with Israel considerably decreased after 1948 but continued for another couple of years: in March 1950, the two countries signed a one-year trade agreement. Israeli companies were also instrumental in arranging for Czechoslovak purchases of strategic minerals in 1948 and 1949; additionally, Israeli diplomats tried in 1949 to mediate Czechoslovak efforts to get U.S. credits. By then, however, the former friendly relations between Moscow and Israel had deteriorated, a trend which accelerated after the 1950 outbreak of the war in Korea.

Moscow's plans to secure influence in the State of Israel by supporting the Zionist movement didn't pan out. The elections were won not by leftists who viewed the USSR with favor but by pro-American parties. On top of that, the USSR found itself isolated in the Arab world. Moscow tried to break through this isolation in the fall of 1948 by making overtures to Syria but with no great success. At the same time, anti-Zionist campaigns in the Soviet Union metastatized into anti-Semitism. The Soviet press carried articles describing Israel as the aggressor in the Arab-Israeli war of 1948. The campaign against Zionism, which reflected the shift in Soviet policy toward Israel and its efforts to break through the isolation in the Arab world, culminated in the Slánský trial in Czechoslovakia, the country which militarily helped Israel the most.[13]

The second important question is this: What motivated the actors in the show trial to accept coresponsibility in the political murders?

There were general and personal motivations, and not all can be captured. Nor can we examine the motives of all participants. I shall focus on four of the most important—and possibly the most typical— personalities. In analyzing their motives, we frequently have to make do with the testimonies of others or with self-serving depositions the protagonists made several years after the fact.

All except for members of the Communist leadership testified that they followed the wishes and orders of the party which they served. Almost all, except for the victims and the interrogators, stated that they believed the indictment and the testimonies and that they had no reason not to believe, seeing that the victims freely admitted everything. This begs the question: Did they believe or not? Did they know the truth or not? Did they want to know it?

The victims of the show trial listed in their final letters and in discussions with their interrogators three motives for their decision to accept and play out their assigned part. One was fear of physical and psychological brutality and recognition of the hopelessness of any defense. Second was the belief that they would save their own lives and spare their families further troubles. The third was service to the party, which required their confessions in the interests of the victory of socialism. The interrogators counted on this motive; characteristic of their attitude was Košťál's well-known dictum, "He'll confess, he's got a good attitude toward the party."

The trial, however, evolved differently than its victims had expected.

Those who fulfilled party orders and wishes as its good and faithful foot-soldiers, those who confessed to the most heinous (albeit nonexistent) crimes were dispatched by the party leadership to the scaffold. Those who—also in the party's best interests—refused to follow the orders and wishes of its highest leaders managed to save at least their own lives. The party's reward for the obedient and the loyal was the gallows. They expected clemency, at least. They were late to realize their error but even that didn't cure some, and they behaved as good party soldiers even under the scaffold.

Many Communists clung to their belief in Gottwald's and Stalin's justice. Thus Bedřich Hájek wrote about his feelings:

> [During interrogations] I would often glance up at that well-known picture of Stalin with his benevolent expression, and I would think, If only there were some way of letting him know what's happening here. Surely he would help . . . I know I wasn't the only comrade in that frame of mind.[14]

Slánský's year in prison was typical for most of the high party officials. At first he believed he would manage to prove his innocence and resisted the demands to confess, but then he became resigned and, in the end, decided to do as the party wished. Some even believed in the grandeur of their mission and in the righteousness of their self-sacrifice. In 1955 and 1956, Slánský's interrogators reviewed how he changed over time:

> *Karel Košťál:* Slánský struggled over every word and every formulation, and he confessed new facts only when they were proven to him. At all times he stayed at the level of the confessions he had already made but as new issues were addressed, he had to be incriminated again and again and he would give in only one step at a time . . . At first he talked only about errors, then about hostile activity in some amorphous form, later he confessed to hostile intent—but he always strove to objectivize his activity. It was far easier for him to talk about objective aspects of his activity than about his own participation, intentions, and guilt. In the course of the interrogations, he referred from time to time to his earlier confessions, as though he were trying to suggest that we know what he thinks about them . . . Toward the end of the interrogation process he found it far easier to talk about his participation in all activities under review, except for the intention to eliminate J. Šverma and accelerating the physical demise of K. Gottwald.[15]
>
> *Jan Musil* [describing Slánský's nervous attacks]: He would scream things like "I didn't do that!" or "That's not true!" etc. Once we said to him that he would have agreed with dropping an atom bomb on Czechoslovakia if it were in the interests of imperialists, and he screamed, "Give me an atom bomb!" . . . Virtually every problem had to be proven to him, he didn't want

to admit anything voluntarily. Thus whatever he did confess, we considered as verified and didn't check its veracity any further.[16]

Bohumil Doubek: During the interrogations, Rudolf Slánský always tried to maintain the dignity of a general secretary. He recognized his activity as criminal only after he was directly pushed into it, but he always made it clear to the interrogators that he did so out of his own good will and because he didn't want to cause any further harm to the party, which had already publicized the case. He would frequently qualify some activity as criminal and hostile for the protocol although earlier he had explained it to us quite differently, as nothing special. Then he would say, "Well, I'll say it whatever way you want, but that's not how it was." Toward the end of the interrogation, when he was at peace with everything and was in a good mood, he often asked whether his answers were satisfactory and added ironically that no one could accuse him anymore of trying to harm the party by his attitude toward the whole case . . . However, he resolutely refused to be shown as a common criminal (as Šverma's murderer); he still saw himself as a political leader. He was very sensitive to any mention of his Jewish origins . . . Toward the end he didn't battle over formulations anymore . . . Just from time to time, when he was asked for a particular phrasing, he would say, "Please, don't ask me to say that, people would laugh at it, and no one would believe it . . ."[17]

Among political leaders, Klement Gottwald, KSČ chairman and president of the Republic, was most involved in engineering the trial and in the judicial murders. Did he believe the indictment?

His secretary later stated, "Nobody could talk to him while he was following the Slánský trial. He believed all the statements. He said that Soviet security personnel have information which we don't have, information dating back to the Comintern, which made him believe completely in the correctness of the charges.[18]

Alexej Čepička discussed Gottwald's anxiety and surprise when he learned about the extent of Czechoslovakia's economic contacts with Israel. Both he and Gottwald's secretary admired Gottwald and defended him.

But other statements suggest other conclusions. Gottwald's secretary also stated that he did not believe in Frejka's guilt; that he laughed about the trick played on Clementis in order to arrest him; that he didn't believe that Leopold Hofman, commander of his bodyguards, was a criminal when he was arrested; that he knew about the provocations staged by security; etc. And he simply had to realize that decisions and activities which he himself had approved or knew about were paraded at the trial as criminal offenses. He received information about the interrogations, including the protocols, and therefore had to know about the interrogation methods. It is unlikely that as seasoned a politician as Gottwald would have fallen for that collection of lies and half-truths.

Why then did he condone the political murders? He was afraid: he was afraid of becoming the fifteenth defendant in Slánský's trial, or the first in the next one. He knew that the trial was produced by advisors who represented the interests of Moscow. He feared that he himself would be in danger if he resisted their witch hunt. Instead, he obediently joined in staging the trial, as the leading personality. He must have told himself in self-justification and in the search for his own peace of mind that nothing could be done against Moscow anyway; and for the same reason, he must have said that he believed the indictments.

Once he took the lead in staging the trial, he had to follow its rules, which included the need to show the "plotters" in the darkest possible colors, as absolute outcasts. Most terrible crimes were dreamed up and attributed to them, crimes which could be punished in one way only, lest the trial lose the desired political effect. The bloodthirsty mass hysteria whipped up by the Communist leadership added to the effect. Not to mete out capital punishment or to grant clemency would have undermined the credibility of the trial, and Moscow would have seen it as protecting the plotters. Gottwald would have come under suspicion. Čepička actually suggested that the proposed sentences had been the subject of consultations. He didn't say with whom, but no doubt they were consulted with Moscow.

Fear and self-preservation were the main motives for Gottwald's decisions about the murders. They only increased his awareness that Moscow was interested in him as well. He believed his apartments were bugged by the Soviet security center. He knew that several Soviet security agents operated in his immediate environment and tried to limit his contact with them to office necessities. His secretary recalled his angry dissatisfaction with the bodyguard commander appointed after the arrest of Hofman: "[Gottwald] said that they should put him in the Pankrác prison, then they'll have some peace."[19] He was not aware that Arnošt Kolman had been interrogated in Moscow about him.

Nevertheless, Gottwald could have prevented a lot. He enjoyed the necessary authority in the country, and Moscow didn't ignore his opinions entirely. However, he acted as a weakling and feared Moscow more than he needed to. Fear not only stopped him from helping the victims but forced him to take on an active and conscious part in their murders. He presided over a system that he helped build and which offered a Communist politician only two alternatives: to sacrifice others and save his own skin, or to face the current, stand on the side of truth and justice, and risk his own life. Gottwald opted for the first alternative.

The motives of other members of the political leadership were similar to those of Gottwald, though not perhaps as pronounced. Additionally, their attitudes were colored by their earlier conflicts with Slánský over power and policy. This was not a factor in Gottwald's case.

As for the judiciary, consider the chief prosecutor Josef Urválek, who on August 16, 1956, stated to a CC KSČ commission:

> I felt the party had entrusted me with a very responsible task. I believed that the investigation of such an important case was being conducted by the best cadres of security, that people were arrested only after the party had carefully considered the matter, that their criminal responsibility had been established before responsible comrades discussed it at the CC session, and that com. Gottwald was personally monitoring the investigation.
>
> There was one general directive: the entire investigation was in the hands of security, and we were to cooperate fully with the security authorities investigating the matter, who enjoyed the full confidence of the party.

On November 21, 1962, he made a deposition for the KSČ leadership. He repeated that he had believed the documents. Several facts influenced his position: The interrogation was managed by Soviet advisors whom he viewed as "seasoned cadres of Soviet security who were passing on their experiences." Another factor: "He hadn't the slightest inkling that illegal methods had been used during the interrogation . . . that the defendants made false statements under duress." He was "especially" swayed by the expert opinions. If he didn't believe in the truth of the indictment, he would have had to "personally face up to the thought that he was surrounded by a gang of criminals who quite openly perpetrated most heinous crimes."[20]

It appears that he believed in the truth of the indictment and fulfilled a party task as well. Still, Urválek had his doubts and even official reasons for them: in September 1952 Beschasnov discussed the peculiarities of the trial with him and admitted that an actual antistate center— the fulcrum of the entire indictment which Urválek would recite so passionately—never really existed. On November 2, 1955, Václav Aleš, one of the prosecutors at the trial, described Urválek's feelings just before the trial opened: "Comrade Urválek had some doubts as to whether certain statements of the indictment will stand up, or whether Slánský won't deviate from the question-and-answer protocol."[21]

Less then three years after the trial, Urválek admitted to his friends in an unguarded moment that he never believed the full scope of the indictment. This statement was recorded by State Security.

The most important personality among the interrogators was without any doubt Bohumil Doubek. In depositions, which he voluntarily wrote in 1955 and 1956, he stated that he believed in the hostile activity of Slánský and his associates. He also mentioned doubts that he had shared with his superiors and the advisors. He was intimately familiar with the interrogation methods, with the extraction of confessions, the fabricated and provoked criminal offenses. What then were his motives? There were two: service to the party and belief in the Soviet advisors, and the lust for and fear of power.

He elaborated about the first motive at length in his deposition:

> I joined the interrogation bureau and immediately was in contact with comrade advisors for whom I had great respect, who taught me, and for whom I did everything they asked. I declare that in some instances I might have resisted suggestions of our own responsible officials; but I did without objection whatever the comrade advisors told me to do. I spoke about this with Košt'ál, Brůha, and Musil, who can corroborate it, I always figured that the comrade advisors knew what they wanted, that, as they suggested, they knew the Soviet plan corresponding to the international situation, which we were not privy to. They were in contact with our highest leaders, even with com. Gottwald, who as far as I know agreed without the slightest reservation to everything the advisors recommended. On some issues, I sometimes doubted the guilt of the suspects, or even believed in their innocence; but I still thought it served a higher goal and recalled what com. Vladimir [Boyarski] once told me: Splinters will fly when you chop down a forest. And the main argument of com. advisors, when they gave us shots, was this: Can you imagine what a blow this will be to the imperialists? I was also flattered when the comrade advisors shared certain matters with me which they didn't share with the minister. I reciprocated.
>
> I believed that what was being done was in the interest of the party and of the international peace-keeping movement, just as comrade advisors told me when I sometimes vacillated just a little bit. I believed them blindly, and they knew it. They were really the first Soviet people I had met (other than in May 1945), and we were in daily contact for several years.

As for the second motive: Lust for power and fear of power resulted from Doubek's sudden rise to power. Virtually overnight, this factotum of the party apparatus became a master over the fates of a number of high officials. People whom he used to fear were now afraid of him. He dealt with advisors and ministers and was even received by Gottwald. He was obsessed by power. Yet he had to struggle for his position: by faithful service, obedience to the advisors, by implementing their methods, developing fabricated charges, by provocations, trials. Once he climbed the ladder, he had to stay up there. He knew that his fall could land him in prison and could even cost him his life. He took seriously a dictum of the advisors that one often leaves security work before one's time is up, and feet forward. He also knew that many critics and competitors vying for his job were pointing to his friendly relations with some of the "plotters" in prison. Thus self-preservation was also among his motives. Nevertheless, "it is true that several times I wanted to leave the interrogations [bureau], and I even discussed it. But I always let myself be talked into staying and continuing with the job."

Surprisingly, Doubek was the first among the trial's engineers who was shocked by its ending. He tried to resign in 1953 and was allowed to leave a year later. The following year the tide turned, and he was arrested for illegal interrogation methods. Although Kohoutek, and later Košťál, Prchal, and others, had to be presented with proofs of the illegal interrogation methods they employed, Doubek volunteered a long account about them while in custody. He detailed the production of the show trial very specifically and asked the question,

> Why did I do all this, even though I didn't think it correct? I have already mentioned that I believed some matters . . . On the other hand, there were methods and procedures that I considered improper even then, and still I used them. I will try again to explain this briefly and hope that it will not be considered self-justification or avoiding responsibility.[22]

He then described his concept of service to the party and his limitless belief in the advisors, quoted above.

I conclude this discussion of the Slánský show trial with one of Doubek's most significant statements in his August 1955 confession which concerned not only the "head of the conspiracy" but the entire trial:

> Whatever Slánský's guilt may have been, the truth is that his role in the conspiracy had been developed in advance and that his interrogation followed this predetermined line.[23]

APPENDIX A

BIOGRAPHIES AND LAST LETTERS OF THE CONDEMNED

DR. VLADÍMIR CLEMENTIS (September 20, 1902–December 3, 1952)
An important Communist official before World War II. Greatly influenced Slovak intelligentsia. Expelled from the party as the war broke out because of his criticism of the 1939 Nazi-Soviet Pact. During the war active in Czechoslovak exile in London. After the war readmitted to the party and appointed state secretary at the foreign ministry. Appointed foreign minister after the 1948 death of Jan Masaryk. In 1950, dismissed from all offices and later arrested.

I.

12/2/1952

My dear Olga, Boža, and all my loved ones,
    I have just been told that your appeals for clemency have been turned down. I have a few hours of life left. I know how dreadful and unbelievable this is for all of you. If anything can make it easier for you, it may be this: during these two years in prison I have reached my peace with everything. It might now be even more difficult to remain in this world and to relive all the torments I had to go through during these last two to three years and especially these last two weeks. During those endless days I frequently thought about you, about Father and Mom, about my happy childhood and my teenage years. It was all too gentle and too good, too trusting. I wasn't ready for the hard life, full of evil and full of traps to fall into. If I were different, I might even believe in fate. You'll remember that one of my favorite songs which Mom used to sing went like this: "Whose are those sheep grazing up the mountainside?" How these words came true! It's like Mom's last sigh over me.
    I know you don't want to and will not forget me. But do forget the pain of these last two or three years and of these last days. In spite of everything, a better time has been born, even if the journey toward it is hard and often cruel. If there's anything I have lived for, it is this. This is a bitter consolation in these last hours.
    Your grandchildren are sure to live a happy life, without all the anger

249

and evil that was our portion. You too will feel better if you look at the world in this way and don't look back too much.

The most difficult moments of my life will come in the following hours: saying good-bye to Lída, who is suffering through all this more painfully than any of us. You know what we have meant for each other. And I know that you'll *do* everything humanly possible that you [the letter breaks here]

I just returned to the cell after having seen off Lída and I don't have the words to express what I feel for her. Loving her, loving her terribly, this is so little to give in return for what she means to me in these last hours.

Once again: forget this recent evil history and live your life with your children, whom I think about and to whom I wish all the best.

I embrace you, my Olga and my dear V . . . and all of your kin.

Yours, Vlado

II.

12/2/1952

Lída, my only one,

I told you just a moment ago that I am at peace with everything. I thought it was true. Only after seeing you did I realize that without you and without reliving with you all that holds us together my peace of mind is a mere posture forced by rationality and will. You gave me all you ever could when you said that you know everything and that you understand. I know it could not be otherwise—I never doubted it. Yet I still needed to hear you say so. I will take that with me.

Before meeting you I wrote Olga and Boža that the toughest moments of my life are still ahead of me—saying good-bye to you, my Lída, my only one. I am not going to rewrite that letter, even though in this case I expressed myself hopelessly inadequately.

You know I have always shied away from grand words. And what words would be grand and stately enough to express what your eyes spoke of? We never were as close, we never belonged to each other as completely as we did a moment ago, separated by this wire mesh. What terrible suffering you must have gone through, Lída, my eternal love, to make yourself so beautiful, so pure and so grand that you could inspire what I now feel for you but cannot put into words.

Now I believe that you'll have the strength to face the hard life ahead. That is another great consolation in these last hours. I believe you yourself will manage to answer the question that I let pass, How is one to live? I believe, I know, that you can only live the life of a dignified human being, the life of a person who in my mind was the goal and the meaning of all my activity until the very end.

I believe you will live to see a Socialist Europe—in ten or fifteen years—and you will welcome it on my behalf, too. For that, if for nothing else, you have to persevere and find a positive attitude toward life and toward our times. You know better than anyone who and what I was, what I felt and believed in, and what caused my shortcomings, errors, and my ugly behavior and actions, judged by their consequences. In a world free of tensions, dangers, reversals, and the sultry air of the last battle, others will manage to see this as well.

Your eyes assured me of all this as they spoke to me. I keep seeing them, I feel you are with me, I feel you know how much I love you. A long time ago, anticipating this moment, I said to myself I wouldn't reminisce, I wouldn't look back—I had two years for all that. It is easier to depart while looking into the future.

Yet I do reminisce. With no bitterness, with no anger—and that explains what I'm thinking about: about what little good I've done to others, about helping usher in a just future that I have never ceased to believe in. About meeting real people in life. About finding and having you.

Well: I got right into it, and it's so hard to get out—and why should I? I gave in to this pleasant weakness; after all, it gives one some strength. I feel at this moment as though I could wander about the Hron river, have all those good talks with people close to me, [I think about] Uhlisko and relive so many of the troubles and joys we shared?!

12/3

I'm drinking a lot of black coffee. I slept a little, I'm writing intermittently—but you know what fills the pauses, you know that nothing has been left unsaid between us, whether or not we said it in words.

My wife, and my dear Hádička, I know you will be bathed in the love and care of Dad and Mom and all my family who will help you suffer through the worst.

I'm finishing my last pipe and I'm listening. I hear your clear voice sing Smetana's and Dvořák's songs and I am, I remain, I always will be with you.

Your Vlado.

III.

12/2/1952

A little over an hour is left of my life, and these words will not influence my fate. Surveying this world free of bias or anger, I feel it my duty to state the following:

I. I understood from the very beginning the political inevitability of my sentence. Nevertheless, I had nothing to do with Slánský's conspiracy. I thwarted more of his intentions than I carried out. At one of the first meetings of the [party leadership's foreign-policy group of] Five, Minister Kopecký categorically declared that I was a foreign minister only in appearances but that Ruda [Slánský] would in fact instruct ambassadors, etc. If it weren't for that statement, not nearly as many of Slánský's people would have penetrated the foreign ministry.

My protocols and my statements in court resulted first from duress ("I'll have you beaten so bad that blood will spurt") and then from resignation. [French ambassador Maurice] Dejean never reminded me of my obligation. I never talked to him about matters as preposterous as diminishing the influence of the USSR in Czechoslovakia, etc.

I received Zilliacus and the nine Labour party M.P.'s without Slánský. I copied [Andrei] Vyshinski on his [Zilliacus's] "position papers" which he sent me in 1948 to Paris. My conversations with Beneš were completely invented rather than reproduced, etc.

Nevertheless, I clearly recognize my guilt and don't intend to minimize it, even though I am not guilty in the sense and to the extent of the charges against me.

II. I have to force myself to write this: After I resigned I was told that a member of the former anti-Communist department of the Bratislava police headquarters (he can be identified as the largest and fattest man there) was spreading a rumor in Prague that [Viliam] Široký was in their service in 1918–20. I did not report this, because I don't believe it and think Široký is being confused with his brother.

However, when I was first questioned about Slánský's criminal activity, I felt it my duty to report this matter to the interrogating staff captain and to mention a number of facts concerning Široký.

III. I thought I would have the opportunity to talk to Minister Bacílek before the sentence is carried out and to make good in this conversation for at least a little of the damage I caused. When the lieutenant on duty told me I would be talking to no one, I mentioned these doubts to him. He asked me to write it all down. I did so at least in outline.

IV. My final statement was sincere and I stand behind it fully. Today more than ever.

OTTO FISCHL (August 17, 1902–December 3, 1952)
A veteran Communist party official. From 1946 headed the CC KSČ economic department. After February 1948 appointed deputy minister of finance.

IV.

12/2/1952
My dearest Maruška and Helenka,
I know what you have been through since January 16, 1951. Now you have to drink up the cup of bitterness for all I have done to you. Please, forgive me for the times I may have treated you unjustly or improperly. Remember only the beautiful and the good in our life.

As a man, husband, and father, I have one last request to make: Don't mourn for me, don't let your suffering and pain break you. Defend yourselves and protect your health, live as happily as you can, don't wear mourning. Helenka should go to the theater and do whatever will amuse her, strengthen her nerves, and give her the strength to overcome all that pain caused first by Eva, now by me, and by Grandma's passing away.

I'm leaving with courage and at peace with everything. I'm leaving with love for all who have loved me, including Eva whom I don't reproach for anything. I'm at peace with the world and worry only that the three of you find life bearable and that time sets everything right. Helenka, you're young, you don't know what life has in store for you—you may yet be very very happy. So don't give any quarter to those who are hostile. Be courageous, hold your head high, and protect your health and your frail nerves.

You, my darling Maruška, have always been an exemplary wife, and you surpassed yourself as a mother. Support Helena; you're the only one left. To say or write this is easy, I know. Life has already asked so much of you, during the war and at other times. You always stood courageously by my side; be equally faithful to Helena, help her overcome everything, however tough it may be. You know yourself that though one often feels there's no way out, life straightens and sorts everything out.

Even though your and Helena's lives are now in total chaos, someone will turn up to help you a little. Even though you're getting on in years, you'll live to see Helena give you a lot of joy. I'm relying on Pepa and Hanuš, and I'm writing to Fred. I won't mention others because I don't know how they behaved while I was in detention. Do not turn down Fred's help, I can't believe that being my brother he wouldn't fulfill my last wish. Forget everything there was between you and him. Now I see most clearly how petty many things are that one considered so important.

Recall our last trip with Eva to Berlin, how nice it was and what I said at the time. I have often thought about it. I generally think back to pleasant things and how good our family life was. Surely we don't need to recall the unpleasant moments I caused you during our twenty-five years of marriage. Carry me in your hearts, both of you, and I will carry on living with you.

Talk to Helenka often about our life together, how we met, about our wedding, about Královice, about Prague before and during the war, and finally about Berlin after the war, where Eva ended it and where we lost her, as you once wrote, worse than if she had died.

I hope to see you yet today, although the law doesn't allow Helena to visit. I will probably be out of sorts: it will be the first and the last time that we will have seen each other in a long time.

Believe me, though, I am leaving calmly, at peace with everything. After all that has happened, this is the only way out. Otherwise I'd just keep on complicating your lives. As it is, my guilt will be expiated, and you will embark on a new life in difficult circumstances. Try to manage with me in your hearts and souls. That would fulfill my most ardent desire.

I recommend that Helenka study linguistics and literature. In detention I saw full well what support, help, and consolation one gets from a good book. With her frail health she can devote herself to these studies undisturbed and without her health being an obstacle. She can study privately and by herself. She should also get involved with sports. That will strengthen her health, focus her interests, and she can accomplish a lot as a team captain. Just don't let her abandon her interests. Life has served her enough bitterness, let her seek whatever is beautiful, nourishing, and helps overcome even the greatest difficulties.

Please take to heart this wish: Spare yourselves unnecessary mourning and sorrow, live a firm and robust life, do not succumb to the attacks of pain, take life's pleasures as they come, and don't give up hope.

I think about all my friends. I won't mention any names lest I leave someone out. Remember me to those who have treated you well since my arrest, for they are the true ones. I beg these friends to try to understand me and forgive me for all the trouble I may have caused them. Would they please try to understand whatever I did not or could not explain. I beg the same of you as well. Give them all my last greetings.

As I leave this world, I will be thinking about our leave-taking at the railroad station. I was leaving for the Krkonoše Mountains from where I never came back because I was arrested. I will recall all the love between us, all that your eyes told me. I think you read everything in mine as well. Let my love for you and for the children support you in the life to come. Believe me, I have always loved you both more than anything. I am only sorry, dear Maruška, that I went to bed so soon on the eve of my departure.

I am limiting myself strictly to personal matters. I don't want to discuss and burden you with my aberrant political path. Helenka, you should firmly join the ranks of Czechoslovakia's youth, *march with it resolutely and sincerely.* Nobody will reproach you on my account, because you have had an entirely different upbringing, you are in a different environment, and you are growing up in the people's democratic regime.

I recommend and beg you to *immediately* request a change of names and to use only Mother's maiden name, Topinková. The new legislation makes it easy. It is not necessary to have constant difficulties just because of my name.

Do not be guided by false sentimentality. Join the ranks of labor on behalf of the whole, do not shirk from anything. Neither of you—unlike me—carry any burden.

Seek consolation in fruitful work: you, Helenka, at school, and you, Maruška, in production. The course you're taking about *khozraschot* [a Soviet accounting method] will certainly benefit you: your accounting work is also important. Work will provide consolation, the satisfaction of being useful and, indeed, your livelihood.

The people's democratic society will not ostracize you. On the contrary, it will help you, for it does not punish a wife or a child for the faults of a husband. I have paid my dues, and you will not suffer for me. Personal relations and family relations with a father and a husband are different than one's political opinions. As much as I loved you both, politically I have committed offenses against you as well.

You must not pretend otherwise, to yourselves or to others. The name change will give you the proper distance. Don't try to faithfully defend me—the indefensible.

After the visit: Thank you, my dear Maruška, for your courageous stance. When you read the words above, you will see that we have truly merged into one, sharing the same thoughts and the same words. I am happy that Helenka, too, is behaving so well and so courageously. I am very grateful to her and beg her to carry on like that. I also thank Hanuš especially for being such a help.

Once again, good-bye to you all, to the whole family and to friends who have remained faithful to you. I am to suffer the supreme penalty, but I will leave in peace because I have seen, dear Maruška, that you know everything I would have wanted to tell you but didn't have the time. Keep me in your memory the way you said you would, follow my advice, and be brave.

I was sorry I couldn't kiss you. I do so now and I'll be kissing you in my mind in my last moment. I will think only about the spiritual harmony between us, Maruška, and about Eva and Helenka, the two fruits of this harmony.

After all my wandering I will, following Comenius, search for the depths of the soul in you. Remember me, do not weep and wail, go through life calmly and bravely, seek support in work and in creative activity in our people's democratic society. My heavy offenses notwithstanding, society will help you find your place and make your contribution as its sincere members, which will give you satisfaction and happiness.

Be very well. You'll have to be healthier than ever: you will need more strength.

Read this letter when you feel at your worst and remember that I would implore you to be strong.

My last good-bye. Your loving
Otta

V.

Prague 12/2/1952

Dear Fred,

I will no longer be alive when you receive this letter, and you will be the only one left of our family. You know well that I never burdened you or troubled you with anything while I was in investigative custody.

Now, a few hours before my death, I have a big request. Please look after Maruška and Helena. They are both in poor health and have no support. You know full well what they have been through. If you fail to look after them and if something happens to them, you too would be in part to blame.

Please let bygones be bygones. No decent person would understand if you didn't. I'm not asking for any material support but for human and moral support. They have to know that there is at least a brother-in-law and an uncle left.

Good-bye to you and your family. I am calm and at peace with everything as I leave. If ever I hurt you or your family, please forgive me. I reproach no one for anything.

Perhaps I'll yet get to talk to you today, but I'm writing anyway because I don't know what state of mind I'll be in during the visit.

Do not mourn for me and do not be angry. Be brave, just as I have been all this time. I have to atone for my guilt.

I kiss you all, remembering all the good times. Remember me as well.

Your Otta

P.S. I'm sending the letter into your own hands for you to tell the others about my execution, should you not know about it yet.

JOSEF FRANK (February 15, 1909–December 3, 1952)
Prior to World War II active as a Communist official in consumer cooperatives. Spent six years in Nazi concentration camps. After the war, a leading official of the Communist party, ending his career as CC KSČ deputy general secretary.

VI.

Prague, 12/2/1952

My dear Jiřinka,

Thank you so much for your lovely visit, which was also our last reunion. A sad reunion, true, but it filled me with great strength because I heard directly from you that you had forgiven me. Someone at least understands me.

Believe me that ever since I left the family I have been thinking about you as never before. A night seldom passes without my dreaming about you and reliving over and over all we've been through over the years. I have been taking stock of our life all this time. After years of a miserable childhood my real life started only with you. It was wonderful and happy, especially in the early years when I was nobody and nothing. Those were our loveliest times. And then of course when little Zdenka and Jirka came. Yes, I was happy and content. I didn't even realize it at the time, not until now. It's too bad I didn't spend more time with you, my love, that I didn't appreciate you and your words and comments even more. I'm particularly sorry that I didn't listen to you after I returned in 1945, and didn't devote myself to something else, where my silly qualities, my trustfulness, my ardor, and on the other hand my peaceful nature and my weak character would not have shown up as they did. Of course, no what-if's will help today.

I know you're the only one who can understand me because only you know me well enough to realize what's in me. I was a fool, and one has to suffer and pay for foolishness. What really hurts, though, is that you, who has nothing to do with all this, have to suffer as well. That our children have to suffer. Even though my fate is not pleasant, it's easier because I won't know anything. You, on the other hand, will live on, and my case will cast a shadow over you for quite some time to come. That is the difficult part. I fully realize and appreciate that. Therefore I implore you, my dear Jiřinka, be brave and steadfast. Persist and see it through even if it's tough. All the pain will abate in time, all will pass. The case will be forgotten and you and our children will once again manage to live in peace and happiness. In this case, too, the son and the daughter can't be blamed for the father. You do have someone to live for. You have our children, our healthy, smart, talented, beautiful children. They are full of life and, therefore, you will find oblivion and a new meaning, a new content of life in their lives. Carry on bringing them up as decent people, better and also happier people than you and especially I have been. Be kind to them so that your love can substitute for their father's absence. I hope that in your future which, I realize, will not be an easy one, you will find a balance again, that life will become normal again, and that you and the children live happily and decently. Please, try to forget. If you do think about me, think about the good. Finally, I want to ask you to remember me to all our relatives and friends. I ask them, too, to forgive and pardon my offenses and to forgive me if I ever hurt them.

As I conclude, I beg once again your forgiveness and especially that you pardon me if I didn't always treat you right in the past.

I can do nothing but beg your pardon, nothing else is left. I lived with you for almost twenty years, albeit with a six-year interruption during the occupation, and it was a full and beautiful life. I did not live in vain. I am leaving behind two children and even though they will cause you many worries and a lot of work, they will, nevertheless, help ease the burden of fate which has fallen on you. On the other hand, though, this end is better, both for you and for me, than if I were to languish for years somewhere in prison and still not return. Seeing how this has ended with me, I wish for my sake and yours that such cases are never repeated, that people learn something from it, if nothing else. I wish that you soon live again quietly and especially in peace, that you benefit from the new order, that you and our children don't have to experience the suffering of another war.

My dearest Jiřinka, my children, I wish you all the best. May you soon be content and, if possible, happy again. I wish this truly and sincerely, from the depth of my heart, so long as it is beating. I wish this because I have loved you above everything. Thinking about you all I take leave of life which I loved but which I didn't know how to live.

My dearest, my dear wife and children, I kiss you affectionately in my heart for the last time.

Your loving Pepa and Daddy

P.S.: I have also written a few lines to my parents and my siblings which are attached. Please deliver them to them.

VII.

Prague 12/2/1953

My dear Jiříček,

I was so much looking forward to seeing you and hugging you one last time. Alas, it wasn't possible. I'm very sorry about it. You were my little boy, my joy, my life. I was always making plans, especially these last few months, for us to read together, go for walks, go places and so on. It is not to be. You of course stay here, you'll grow, you'll study, you'll graduate, you'll go to work, you'll join the army, and you'll form your own life.

Dear Jiříček, now that you have only Mommy and Zdenička, you have to be especially good. You always were a good boy, tidy and obedient, which is why I loved you so much and why others love you, too. Mommy is now all alone for everything. She will have to earn money alone, look after the household, cook, clean up, sew, and look after you so that one day you will grow up and turn into a fine man. Please obey her in everything and be good to her. Carry on studying as well and as diligently, perhaps even better, so that you grow up into a proper man. You promised me you would before you even started school.

You are still very small, and you don't understand what has happened to me and why. You'll understand it when you grow older. Mommy and Zdena will explain, so that when you're grown up and an adult, like I was, you don't commit the kinds of acts I committed.

I firmly believe that will not be the case. You are living and growing up in different times and in a different society than I did. In this new society, cases like mine will not be repeated.

Therefore, study all the time, everywhere. Study at school and at home, learn from Zdena and from Mommy. Study as you enter life and keep in mind what you will have learned when you work; don't forget it and behave accordingly. Be strict with yourself and with others, be principled and implacable, be firm and uncompromising, be always direct, open and aboveboard, and always rely on yourself above all. Adopt these qualities in your life. I lacked them and, therefore, ended up the way I did.

I wish you well, my dear son. May your life shape up better than mine.

You have all the ingredients for it. In closing: when you're bigger, look after Mommy, help her, and love her. She deserves it for the hard life she leads.
A thousand greetings and hugs,
Your Daddy

VIII.

Prague 12/2/1953

Dear Zdenička,
I wanted to see you so badly, to stroke your hair one last time and to exchange a few last words. Alas, it was not to be. I'm writing at least a few lines to say good-bye. Although you're fifteen, we really didn't know each other well because that's the way it was fated. You grew up by yourself and without me during the six years I spent in the concentration camp. All that time I thought of you as a baby of two-and-a-half, and you had meanwhile turned into a child with your own mind, your own opinions and judgments. Therefore, I often didn't understand you, which created the impression that we were not close, that we didn't understand each other. It was only an impression, though. I really loved you a lot, even though I couldn't show it and express it. I saw you as a good and exemplary child, and I was very proud of you. You were a good, smart girl and gave your parents a lot of joy.
I especially appreciated your political maturity and interest. I'm therefore sure, Zdenička, that you understand what has happened and why. You see that I have committed acts I should not have and, therefore, have to bear the consequences, however heavy.
What really hurts is that you, too, will suffer because of it. You, who were certainly facing a bright life and future. You are, of course, sensible enough to realize that under these circumstances you won't be able to study anymore. You wouldn't even have the necessary peace and quiet. But you're young, and there's no reason to lose hope. Your whole life is still ahead of you.
I have a request to make, and please try to fulfill it. Try to help Mommy in every possible way, so that she can find her way out of this and so that for a long, long time you have at least her. You understand that she'll now have lots of work and many worries . . . She's not alone; Jirka is there, too. Try to make her life easier for her. Help her all you can, be considerate and, please, listen to your mother. Perhaps you'll like your job. You'll help her earn some money and use your time to continue studying. You'll always need it in life. I'm sure that after a while you'll be able to sit for the exams and accomplish your objective. Surely children can't suffer for their fathers. When I write that you should listen to Mommy, I don't mean just that you should help her clean up and so forth. I especially mean that you should consider her advice and comments about life in general. They may sound

old-fashioned and passé to you, but remember that Mom speaks from experience, the way life taught her. It is extremely important to draw from it and learn. Learn from me as well and draw your own conclusions for your life. Be a good girl, carry on being diligent and steadfast. I wish you a lot of success in your life ahead, which is beautiful and will get better and better. Of course, one has to know how to live it. Thousands of kisses for the last time from your
Daddy

IX.

Prague, 12/2/1952
My dear parents and siblings,
I send greetings, in the last moments of my life during which I'm constantly thinking about you all and about the time we spent together.
I beg you all to forgive me for what I have committed, and for the fact that you, who had nothing to do with it, will end up suffering as well. Yet I believe it will pass and that my case won't hinder you in your lives.
I have one request. Please remember that Jiřinka and the children are left behind and that their fate is much harder. Please try to help them as best you all can, so that their heavy destiny weighs a bit easier on them, so that they, too, can get out from under it and can build at least a relatively decent and bearable life.
For one last time, hugs and kisses to all,
Your Pepa

LUDVÍK FREJKA (January 15, 1904–December 3, 1952)
Before World War II an economic correspondent for the Communist press. During the war active in Czechoslovak resistance in London where he also dealt with economic issues. After the war, chairman of the CC KSČ commission for national economy and economic advisor to Prime Minister Klement Gottwald. Later headed the national-economy department of the Office of the President. Participated in drafting all major economic decisions.

X.

12/2/1952
Prague, Pankrác
From Ludvík Frejka
Dear Mr. President:
In the last hour of his life a man doesn't lie and therefore I beg you to believe what I have to say here. These lines will at any rate reach you when I will no longer be here, so why should I write anything but the truth?
I write especially to beg your forgiveness for having deceived you so often, especially for using assorted so-called "professional" arguments to

advocate measures which supremely harmed the construction of socialism, in discussions concerning the Two-Year Plan, the Five-Year Plan, and other economic decisions. In my last hour I beg you to believe that subjectively, I was not trying to deceive you. I realize that the important thing is what a person objectively does rather than what he subjectively wants. Consequently nothing I write now can detract from my tremendous blame. Writing this is important mostly for me, and perhaps a little for you: so that you understand why you didn't see through me sooner.

I held on to this false subjective consciousness of who I am and what my intentions were ten months ago when I was first arrested. I couldn't understand it at the beginning. But after four days or so, I saw that you, esteemed Mr. President, obviously regarded me as a villain and a traitor, and that this, too, was the opinion of security who in my eyes represented the working people. At that point I figured that my subjective ideas as to who I am and what I had wanted must be false. From that day on I acted like the thirty-year veteran of the labor movement that I am and—please believe me, Mr. President—I sincerely and mercilessly adopted the objective position of the Czechoslovak working people. I forced myself to view all my activity through the eyes of my interrogators. I then testified along these lines, being as strict as possible with myself. Indeed, I felt I managed to uncover a lot during the interrogations.

As the interrogations progressed, I also came to appreciate that what subjectively I had thought of as errors were objectively [crimes,] as indeed is every type of reformism and Trotskyism. With the bourgeoisie influencing the working class and particularly in today's situation, with Anglo-American imperialists influencing the peace camp, this was their intention which I pursued, albeit unwittingly.

Subjective consciousness of course counts little in the face of history and therefore, I intentionally started talking about myself as an agent of Western imperialists and of Beneš's clique. I only ask, Mr. President, that you believe this: I did so not because this subjectively was the case but out of good will, because I realized that only thus will the righteously enraged people and the party relatively quickly repair all the damage I had caused.

I knew that this is the only way in which a heavy blow could be administered to the Western imperialists. I acted accordingly, to contribute at least a little to the preservation of peace.

Once I grasped that in the interests of peace I have to oppose as strongly as possible all my malfeasance, I left it up to others to apportion my share of those evil deeds, and of any good I may have done, especially in recent years.

Of course I assumed—and it was repeatedly emphasized during interrogations that my attitude was considered positive—that my good intentions and my effort to help as best I could would be taken seriously; and that, therefore, even after handing down the sentence, I would be given the opportunity to atone at least a little for the terrible damage I unwittingly did, by continuing to uncover saboteurs in Czechoslovakia's economy. I thought that for other reasons, too, my good intentions would be taken seriously. My testimony implies that my gravest crimes—in posting personnel and in drafting the Two-Year and the Five-Year plans—date back to 1945 through 1948. I hoped that my intentions today would be gauged by my—mostly positive—activity in recent years. My testimony also indicated that I never had anything to do with Zionism and with Zionist dirty tricks. I also pointed out during interrogation that in 1947 I actively contributed to uncovering K. Zilliacus, and in 1949 to the uncovering of Milan Reiman and Gen. Š. Drgač, former chief of general staff. I assumed that this, too, would be weighed as evidence of my subjective intentions. Having twice incriminated Slánský in very important matters during interrogation would, I thought, have the same effect. For all this I hoped that my good intentions would be believed and that I would be given a chance to help atone for what I committed, either alone or with others.

I'm sure this did not happen for very serious reasons.

I just hope that my attitude during interrogation and in court, in uncovering all I knew about myself and others in what little time there was, contributed at least somewhat to getting economic planning back on track and accelerating the construction of socialism. I hope I thereby contributed at least minutely to the struggle for peace, and that my behavior in the last ten months will be evaluated as my best activity.

I ask you, esteemed Mr. President, to believe at least this, that over the past ten months I did my best to discharge my obligations to the working people and to the KSČ. Others will judge how successful I was. It was my best intention.

Once more I beg your pardon and I beg you to believe that I sincerely repent.

Ludvík Frejka

BEDŘICH GEMINDER (November 19, 1901–December 3, 1952)
Long-time employee of the Comintern. Before returning to Czechoslovakia in 1945, he worked as Georgi Dimitrov's secretary. In Czechoslovakia, he headed the CC KSČ international department.

XI.

To the CC KSČ political secretariat
To the hands of Klement Gottwald, the party chairman

I did not manage to live, serve, and work as well as I could have and as I wanted to. I always lived alone. This was my problem, my fault, because I never confided in any one. I never sought out my comrades for support, counsel and help; and they just let me live the way I did, believing that I was happy and that all was in order.

The party chairman was the only one to warn me on one occasion, and he said, *mea culpa.* I wanted to visit with him at the time and tell him what troubled and bothered me. I didn't find the courage to do so. I don't want to paint myself better than I am, but at the time—in the summer of 1950—I wanted to point out the prevarication, the behavior and the methods of Slánský, as I experienced them personally and as I observed them in his personal life. I did not do so—maybe I feared taking this step—and therefore I'm greatly to blame in the eyes of the party. However, there are people to whom I suggested this and whom I warned about Slánský.

Why do I mention this? I don't want to sound better than I really am or than the party justifiably describes me. I only want the party to believe that if I hadn't ended in Slánský's hands, I would not have ended up committing crimes and treason. But I alone am responsible for my actions. I have been a party member for long enough, witnessing historical events both in the Soviet Union and in our own country, to realize that my methods and behavior amount to the greatest crime against the working class and the party. I will pay for it properly, with the death sentence.

It is too late for regrets. I have just one wish, that I be forgiven posthumously. I ask this *especially and above all of those who were close to me and had good intentions.* It pains me that I have disappointed them so much.

I go to the gallows with a heavy heart but with a relative peace of mind: in my person, one of those who caused so much damage will be eliminated, the air will be purified, and one of the obstacles to the victory on the road to socialism will be removed. The party is always right and my case proves it once again.

I do not feel shame for addressing you with my last words. A man condemned to death has the right to meet and talk to his dearest, his next-of-kin. That is you. I thank you, that is, the party, for looking after me like your own son. I did not deserve it, and you were right to expel me as a disloyal and ungrateful person from the midst of honest people.

What more can I say? Immediately after my arrest I realized the tremendous political significance of this step. I said to myself: My life is over and the only thing left to do is to embark on the path of truth and—in this particular situation which my guilt led me into—to help the party unmask imperialist plans, help it turn the plots they had been hatching into a weapon against them.* In this way I wanted—belatedly—to make up for part of the great damage I had caused. I know it's not my achievement,

---

*I have to add: This is why during interrogation I confessed even to matters which are not connected with me directly and personally, but which, nevertheless, are political facts and thus sacred truths.

because my liquidation is all in all the achievement and victory of the party, and thus a defeat of imperialism.

You may think of these lines as empty clichés. Before ascending the gallows, though, a man doesn't lie. This is what I feel, and with these thoughts I depart. The party has been and will be victorious.

Geminder Bedřich

Please give my personal effects that haven't been confiscated to political exiles.

The written documents in the hands of State Security include important documents, valuable for the Institute of Party History. Note in particular Georgi M. Dimitrov's handwritten notes in his diary from the Leipzig trial. They should be handed over to the Bulgarian party.

Thank you.

RUDOLF MARGOLIUS (August 31, 1913–December 3, 1952)
After 1945, when he joined the KSČ, he was member of the CC KSČ national-economic subcommittee for foreign trade, and worked in the Czechoslovak Union of Industry. After February 1948, appointed deputy minister of foreign trade.

XII.

My dearest, most beloved Heda,

A few hours ago I saw you for the last time, I spoke with you and saw a picture of our little darling Ivan. My thoughts have been with both of you almost all the time throughout this separation. I retraced my life many times, step by step, from my first childhood memories up to our last days together. There was not a moment, not a second of the life we shared, my dear Heda, which I did not review and relive. I reconstructed your present life from your letters and from Ivan's charming child artwork, and imagined our future, more recently only your future.

What a wretched sight my past offers. I have wasted my life. I was always a weakling, a single child, the apple of my parents' eyes, leading an easy and comfortable life. My weakness, my petit-bourgeois life, my ambition, careerism, and my submission to people just like me have generated all this evil that I created, and that has led to this end.

You, darling Heda, were the only beautiful person I ever knew in my adult life. Whatever beauty I ever knew—perhaps with the exception of my childhood in Podušice—I got from your ardent heart and from your love, which I deserved so little. Yes, I did love you and do still; why, my feelings for you and for little Ivan are the only positive thing in my soul. But everything else in me, my weakness, my petit-bourgeois attitudes, etc., and my criminal activity it generated, all this betrayed my love. How can a person who helped destroy the wonderful future of his own child and of his wife, how can a person who marred the happiness of millions, who helped the warmongers, how can such a person talk about love?

I was not worthy of the deep feelings which you bestowed upon me during our life together and which you expressed yet again only today during your visit. Yes, I am not worthy of you, and you and little Ivan have to blame me. You don't want to believe this yet, but later you should analyze me thoroughly, cast a critical eye, study my opinions, my life with you, reread with an objective eye—the eye of any other woman or mother—my testimony in court, the statement of the prosecutor and the verdict. You will find I am telling you the truth today, you will find justice in statements of the prosecutor, the court, and thus of the entire Czechoslovak people.

It is good that all is ending this way. It is good for Czechoslovakia and for the entire peace camp, and it will be good for me and for you. Even if the verdict had been different, I would have written you the same letter and said the same things about myself. Eventually you are bound to see that I'm right. And I beg you to draw the necessary conclusions. My end must be the beginning of your new life, a beautiful life both for you and for little Ivan, a life that will take part in the progress of Czechoslovakia's people and of all mankind toward a glorious Socialist and Communist future.

If I were to live any longer, it would be a tremendous burden on you; you would be tied to me and to my past. My departure amounts to a liberation. Live a full life. Bring up little Ivan so that he turns into a good, honest man; a loyal and faithful citizen of people's democratic Czechoslovakia; a strong, educated, and diligent fighter for the progress of mankind. Let him not grow up isolated but rather in a good peer group, in the Young Pioneers and the Youth Union. When he is older, explain my fate to him, truthfully and with no adornments. Let it serve him as a lesson, a warning, and an incentive to work even harder for the benefit of society, so that he may repair the damage caused by his father. I beg you, my darling Heda, to look after your health and your nerves. You will need them to guide little Ivan toward a beautiful future. Work with joy and with love, as you always have. Commune with nature and enjoy its beauty. Don't shut yourself off in solitude. On the contrary, seek out the company of good, honest people; enjoy yourself, go to the theater, cinema, and to concerts. Enjoy life, for it is beautiful. I am sure that you yourself will recognize the truth about me as I have written about it, and that later you will find the occasion to fully and beautifully develop those deep feelings which you are full of. I would hope so, for both your and Ivan's sakes. And I am sure that your choice will be the right one, unlike when you chose me.

I beg you never to fall for the opinions and gossipmongering of reactionary people and to resist all remnants of petit-bourgeois attitudes in yourself and in people you deal with. Maintain unswerving faith in the party and the government. Believe the teachings of Marxism-Leninism. Every deviation, however slight, leads to disaster. Bring up little Ivan in the same spirit. You have an excellent mind, education, and broad knowledge; and I'm sure that in this respect, too, you will be a good teacher and friend of your son.

It would please me if Ivan leaned on Ruda and Eva as he grows up. He must have gotten close to them when he stayed with them in Bratislava, and they like him, too. Their firm character and political attitude will surely help Ivan to grow up properly, too.

Ivan will be going to school next year. I am quite certain that school and, later, the Young Pioneers will help him turn into a good man. His teacher should definitely know that I am his father. Nevertheless, I believe that neither Ivan nor you should suffer on account of my accursed name. Therefore, abandon my name as soon as possible. This of course does not mean that your relationship with me should be kept a secret. In due course, Ivan has to be properly told everything. Chance encounters before he understands the whole matter could cause depressions and inferiority complexes in a child, which could embitter him for the rest of his life. I want to spare him this. Please bear it in mind as well.

A few more words about myself. The time in detention was a great education for me, though it came too late, alas. All the personnel with whom I was in contact, wardens and interrogators, behaved impeccably. I was an enemy, but they always treated me as someone who wasn't born an enemy but who turned into one as a result of class relations. Only here did I finally recognize the futility of my petit-bourgeois life, in contrast to the strength and the purposiveness of the working class building a new life.

My dearest Heda, I thank you from the bottom of my heart for all the beauty you have given me. I don't know a more beautiful, a more wonderful person. I thank you for your love, your sacrifices, your care; for all those beautiful moments and the entire period in the past that was suffused by the warmth of your sentiments; for your belief in me, unwarranted though it was, and for your hope in a further life together. I thank you for all your kisses and tender caresses which I still feel today; I thank you for little Ivan and for the able-bodied good man you will bring him up to be.

We said good-bye a few hours ago. You are so beautiful, my love! The image of you, and the dear image of little Ivan's face, is firmly etched in every nerve of my retina, in every last vein of my brain and of my heart. They will remain with me till the end and perhaps for eternity, if there is such a thing.

I wish you good health, strength, courage. I wish you love and happiness. I wish that you live to see the greatest joys and successes, the filial love of your Ivan.

I embrace you, my darling Heda, I hug and kiss you both.

Your Ruda

12/3/1952

XIII.

12/3/1952

My dear Ivan,

Many years will have passed before you receive this, my first and last letter to you. By now you are an adult and you correctly understand the life and the end of your father. Your mother will have explained my fate to you, and you will have learned about it from the press and from literature. You surely don't remember me any more; your mind will have erased all memories of us playing and jumping about and cuddling, at home and outside in nature, by the Líšeň pond and in the mountain snows. You don't remember, and that's as it should be. You can evaluate my life and draw your own conclusions soberly.

I have grievously offended society and was justly condemned for it. There are no excuses, not even for you; you, too, should condemn me harshly. Blame is not hereditary, though, and a son cannot be reproached for the offenses of his father. On the contrary, the Socialist order in which you are living will help you become a proper citizen and to develop differently than did your father, who grew up in a capitalist world.

I would wish that knowing my fate will give you strength in life, that it will help you become better than others, that you will always act in the interests of society and progress and devote all your energies to the construction of a Communist world.

Study hard, continue expanding your knowledge, become a master of your vocation. Enjoy nature, music, poetry, creative arts. And love people! Help them to be better, to eradicate whatever bad is still in them. The world is beautiful, Ivan, and you have a chance to make it even much more beautiful for yourself and for your fellow citizens.

Ivan, cherish your dear mother. She is a lovely and wonderful person. She is a woman who has suffered a lot and lives for you alone. Make her happy with your love, devotion, and your successes. Best wishes, Ivan!

Your father

BEDŘICH REICIN (September 29, 1911–December 3, 1952)
From age fifteen active in the Communist movement: first in the Komsomol (Communist Youth Union), later in the party. Returned to Czechoslovakia after World War II as an officer of the Czechoslovak Army Unit in the Soviet Union. After February 1948 appointed deputy defense minister.

XIV.

Prague, 12/2/1952

My beloved Jožinka,

Only a few days ago I wrote about minor daily worries and now I face an extremely hard task: to write you my last letter.

First of all I beg you to forgive after my death all this unspeakable sorrow which my activity has caused you, turning your entire life into one great tragedy.

Yet I did and I do love you so terribly much. Memories of our entire life together, from that memorable May 1, 1930, until our separation in February of last year, have been going through my mind; and the thought of all those wonderful things so criminally dissipated rends my heart even as I prepare to see you for the last time, my love.

I wish, and this will be my dying wish, that you forgive me all of this and that you preserve memories of the better part of me, both for yourself and for our Vlád'a.

I wish that you will manage to keep a cool head through this terrible catastrophe, that you realize there is still reason to live, and not to become despondent, that there is meaning to your future: namely, our son, our dear Vlád'a, who mustn't suffer for my offenses, who mustn't suffer at all, because he's innocent. And I believe he will not suffer because, on the one hand, I have talked to the highest authorities who have assured me that they will not allow the innocent to be harmed in any way, and, on the other hand, because his mommy is here, who will not lose heart and will take care of him. My dear Jožinka, bring up our boy as a simple but worthy and able-bodied member of our people's democratic society, and preserve all your strength and abilities for this goal. This is the main thing, in fact virtually the only thing I beg of you at this moment, and this, too, will help you overcome all the dreadful difficulties which my guilt has caused you.

When you do think of me, I beg you to think of the modest positive aspects which I used to show, however few there were, and to try to preserve them in our Vlád'a's mind as well.

I will write Herta and Hilda separately; I have asked them to come with you to visit me. In any event, tell them I'd like them to honor my memory by helping you cope with Vlád'a, as far as they can.

Now a few practical matters: I was told by National-Security Minister Bacílek that families of the condemned will not be permitted to suffer from the hands of irresponsible persons. If you have any difficulties at your workplace, or Vlád'a in school, turn for help to the ministry of national security or directly to the minister.

After some time, decide for yourself according to circumstances whether it is necessary that you apply for a change of your surname. If necessary, let Hilda do the running around for you.

I have written to Anda Skleničková and all your family asking them to help you. It would be good if you and Vlád'a spent Christmas with my family. You should hear from them as soon as Anda calls on them.

I have written to František Engl asking him to assist you in bringing up our boy. Given his current school performance, I'd like Vlád'a to take up a trade of his choice after finishing his compulsory education, unless he improves considerably. Later, if he shows some ability and diligence, he can always continue studying, in a trade school, for example. I don't want to force this idea on you because there's plenty of time for it, depending on how the boy makes out. I'm writing to assure you that I'm not dead set on further studies for the boy. Speaking as a man who didn't complete his own education, I would like Vlád'a to avoid the difficulties and consequences it caused me.

Dispose of my personal effects as you see fit. Save the watch, which is among my personal effects here and which the security personnel will surely return to you, as a memento for the boy.

My beloved Jožinka!

Forgive me for this terrible bequest, this tremendous worry and sorrow which I leave you with, because I loved you so much. Forgive me and think only about the good.

Love from your Bedřich

Dear Vlád'a,

Listen to your Mom, study hard, and see that you can soon work and help Mommy and look after her in her old age.

Love from your daddy.

XV.

Mr. Klement Gottwald,
President of the Czechoslovak Republic
Prague Castle

Dear Mr. President,

The undersigned Bedřich Reicin, sentenced on November 27, 1952, to death by the State Court in Prague, makes the following request before his execution:

I request that you show clemency in awarding my wife, Josefa Reicinová, née Barešová, b. February 23, 1909, profession and employment: worker, and my son Vladimír Reicin, b. June 9, 1941, a student, a widow's and an orphan's pension.

I realize that my criminal activity, for which I have been justly condemned, has resulted in my family losing any entitlement to a pension. Nevertheless, Mr. President, knowing your magnanimity and your goodness, I turn to you with this request, for which I offer the following argument:

My wife, Josefa, is the daughter of Karel Bareš, a [Communist] mining official from Nové Strašecí. He was persecuted for his Communist beliefs during the 1920 Kladno strike and as a consequence died soon after. My wife has since her youth worked as a worker in various factories in Prague.

She is still working, and meets and exceeds her quota. However, her health is poor. Before I was detained, physicians (Col. Dr. Pešek and others) recommended that she be assigned only light duty. After my arrest she started working on a machine, but she collapsed after a short time. She was on partial disability and later was given lighter work in a knitting cooperative of disabled persons. I am quite sure my wife's diligence will never allow her to abuse the pension you might award her and that she will continue to earn her living and to support her son with her own labor, as her strength permits.

As I make this request, Mr. President, I beg you to believe that my wife, formerly a party activist in Prague 19—Bubeneč, doesn't bear the slightest responsibility for and didn't in the least participate in my criminal and hostile activity against the people's democratic order, and that she is bringing up our son as a worthy member of our people's democratic republic.

I beg you, Mr. President, out of the goodness of your heart and sense of justice to accede to this request.

Bedřich Reicin
Prague, December 2, 1952

ANDRÉ SIMONE (May 27, 1895–December 3, 1952)
Left Czechoslovakia in 1922 and worked for the Communist and left-wing press in Germany and later in Paris. Spent the war in Mexico where he was active in the anti-fascist movement. Returned to Czechoslovakia in 1946 to work as a Communist journalist.

XVI.

My dearest darling Ilschen,

As I now take my leave of you forever, I implore you never to forget how much I loved you. I devoted all the inner forces of goodness I had to our relationship. Remember that and forget everything else about me. Your life is ahead of you, there's a lot you can yet accomplish. Honest labor, the kind you always liked, is the best friend, the best aid in overcoming sorrow. Forget me and think about yourself, think about your future which will be different from this day which, because of me, amounts to such an awful blow to you.

I have had enough time to think about the future, and I saw it in all its glory. I saw a space reserved for you; I saw a measure of happiness for you, as for everyone else who sincerely participates in the great construction.

Hold on to that, that is the only path, and you always wanted to take it. Now that I have caused you such terrible sorrow, embark upon it with even greater determination. Look forward, not back.

You told me a moment ago that I should stay calm. I am calm. I am calm especially because I know you have the necessary strength to fashion a new life for yourself. With all my heart I ask you to focus on that task. Do not dissipate your strength by thinking about my fate. Spend the last drop of your mental strength on quickly shifting from today's situation to a normal life, so that all that has happened will recede fast.

My love, there are so many things I'd still like to talk about! How I wish I could find the words to really console and help you. But I keep seeing you misty-eyed with sorrow and realize that you can find consolation and help only in your own determination to go forward, forever forward.

You are the loveliest, the most honest, the most sincere person I have ever known in this world. That's how I recalled you these past six months, that's how I recall you in these last moments, that's how I'll keep recalling you until I stop thinking. I have come to realize these past months that all I ever thought of you falls short of reality.

Thank you, my dear Ilschen, for everything you have done for me, for the love you have given me. I returned it as ardently as possible. I loved you, I still love you and, therefore, I wish that you live your own life, without thinking about me, in an atmosphere of construction and of freedom. Be very well, my dearest; I wish you a long, happy, and successful life. I embrace you and kiss you one last time, my dearest Ilschen, with a love that in these last moments burns with the purest flame.

My love to Mařenka.

Your Otto*

My dearest darling Ilschen,

In the hour of our parting I beg you ardently never to forget that I loved you, and that I devoted all the inner forces of goodness I had to our relationship. The worst thing is that I cannot even lessen the tremendous sorrow which I saw in your eyes today.

Do not forget that you have a life ahead of you, that you can still accomplish a lot, and that in time, labor will bring you consolation and peace of mind. You have to live for that goal: to work, honestly and happily, the way you always liked to. Therefore it is necessary that everything concerning me

My dearest darling Ilschen,

There's so much I'd still want to tell you, but I see you before me as I saw you a moment ago, and the tremendous sorrow I saw in your eyes seems to have scattered the words. Not being able to lessen your terrible torment is worse than any punishment

My dearest darling Ilschen,

I keep seeing you before me as I saw you a few hours ago and

*Otto Katz was Simone's real name.

My dearest darling Ilschen,
    In the hour of our parting I beg you ardently, I always loved you, I focused all the inner forces of goodness I had on our relationship.

My dearest darling Ilschen,
    There's so much I'd still want to tell you in these last hours of my life, but I keep seeing you before me as I saw you a few hours ago

My dearest darling Ilschen,
    Good-bye forever. I see you before me as I saw you a few hours ago, and your look will follow me until the end.

XVII.

President Klement Gottwald

Dear Mr. President:
    I am writing this letter a few moments, a few hours perhaps, before my end, and I will live no more when you read it. In a moment like this, probably even the worst kind of person tells the truth. I am quite sure that you will believe me when I declare that every word of this letter is based on the truth.
    What truth do I want to tell you about? It is this: I never was a conspirator or a member of Slánský's antistate center. I never was guilty of high treason, never a spy, never an agent beholden to Western or other services. If you can muster the patience to read through this letter, you will see I am stating the truth.
    I realize that the question will immediately arise, why then did I confess to these crimes. Let me address that question first.
    I was flabbergasted when I was told, immediately after my arrest, that I was a member of Slánský's conspiracy and a spy. This was so far-fetched that I hoped I might establish my innocence. I gave up that hope after three days, though, on account of what I was told by my case officer and his immediate superior, a staff captain.
    The case officer told me I had been expelled from the party. He said that my arrest implied that the party had already condemned me, that I had no right to present evidence, that if I didn't confess, he and his colleague would take turns interrogating me all night, and that if I collapsed they'd drench me in ice water. He threatened me with the punishment cell and with beatings. That scared me; but one particular threat affected me tremendously, namely, that my wife would be arrested if I didn't confess.
    Nevertheless, I stuck to the truth and protested my innocence. After two weeks, though, I realized this was futile. The case officer ignored everything I said and turned everything, including my recognized accomplishments, against me.

Let me quote a few statements of the case officer: "[E.E.] Kisch was a Trotskyite and a spy and if he were alive, he'd be sitting here with you." "We know that your father was a member of Jewish organizations." (Father never did belong to any Jewish association.) "You made the rounds of the newspapers and hawked your stories like a salesman." (I never did anything of the sort. All my stories were written on request.) The case officer mentioned a specific piece of evidence which supposedly proved that I peddled stories: he said I had published an article written for *Literaturnaya gazeta* also in *Tvorba*. He described my book *Those Who Betrayed France* as imperialist propaganda, but later it turned out that he hadn't even read it. He barely scanned it during the last weeks of investigation when the staff captain insisted.

I want to mention three other statements of the case officer, because they indicate his lack of professionalism. He said: "The chief of Intelligence Service said to one agent that you are one of I.S's leading agents in Czechoslovakia. A leading Trotskyite has stated that you are one of the leading Trotskyites in Czechoslovakia. We have in hand receipts that you gave foreign intelligence agencies for monies you received for espionage."

At first blush all this seems inconsequential, yet it isn't and it cannot be: it indicates the spirit in which the case officer conducted the interrogation. I have to add that the staff captain told me that if my two case officers failed to extract a confession, another team would come, and a third, a fourth, and so on, if it were to take five years.

I reflected on this perspective. I reached the conclusion that only the intervention of higher authorities could turn the situation around. I therefore decided to confess whatever the case officer wanted, in statements so preposterous that they were bound to catch his superiors' attention, make them investigate the case, and give me a chance to prove my innocence. Unfortunately, this hope—and I realize today how naive it was—didn't work out.

Now to proofs of my innocence.

1. Membership in Slánský's conspiratorial group.

In my statement to the court I colored my interviews with Slánský according to the wishes of the case officer. Slánský decided I should work in *Rudé právo* even before we had met face to face. When Dolanský told him over the phone that Kisch and I had arrived, he said that he had just read a quote from my book in *The History of Diplomacy* and told me I could stay in Czechoslovakia. Slánský invited me over not when we were briefly introduced at the [Eighth KSČ] Congress [in 1946] but after the evening at your place, which I attended with Kisch. I wrote a story on Slánský after [Gustav] Bareš OK'd my idea to write capsules about our leaders for the election campaign. However, it was Bareš who decided whom I should write about; I made no recommendations. The May 1946 story about Slánský was the only one I ever wrote about him. It was not written in a spirit hostile [to the party]. Of course it highlighted Slánský, whom I knew only as the party's general secretary, but mostly it focused on the main planks of the party's election platform. In 1946 Slánský did not and could not have instructed me to exert a Trotskyite influence on *Rudé právo* because I wasn't even an editor then, just a stringer who was paid for each story. I came to *RP* perhaps twice a month and got to know casually perhaps three or four editors, apart from [Vincenc] Nečas, whom I had met before the war. This was the situation practically until the summer of 1948. Until then, [Vladimír] Koucký and [Gustav] Czaban visited me once and [Vilém] Nový came over twice with a larger group. Only in the summer did I start visiting the *RP* offices daily, for six months, after Nový, [Miroslav] Kárný, and Koucký suggested that I become an advisor to the foreign desk. At that time, though, I saw no more of Slánský and didn't talk to him even at receptions. How then could he have given me those instructions?

It is true that Slánský suggested I write a book about the February [1948] events, something like [John] Reed's *Ten Days That Shook the World*. I never dreamt, though, that this would have amounted to instructions to write the book in a Trotskyite spirit. That interpretation came about only after I told the younger of my two case officers that Slánský wished that I write a book modeled on Reed's. The case officer asked me what book that was. I told him about it and mentioned that Reed treated Trotsky favorably. The case officer then said that it was clear to him that Slánský wanted me to write a Trotskyite book. I pointed out in a discussion with the staff captain that Slánský could reasonably argue that to instruct anyone to write a Trotskyite book after February 1948 would have been sheer madness; but the point stuck, and I confessed to it just as the interrogation personnel wanted.

As for Slánský wanting me to maintain informal contacts with foreign journalists, instead of accepting the offer to head the press department of the ministry of information, this is true. However, Slánský didn't give me the slightest, not even the most cryptic, instructions to maintain espionage contacts. We were not alone: Dolanský, whom I saw before going to Slánský, was also present.

There is one other important question concerning my relationship with Slánský. The case officer and the staff captain told me that already in 1946, Slánský and Geminder had information in hand that I was a spy. During the break in the trial that followed my testimony, the case officer told me that this was information from the French party which [Artur] London passed on to Geminder in 1946, who then either gave it or showed it to Slánský. I don't know the document so I can't say anything about it. I wonder though why Slánský and Geminder did not tell me about it, if I was indeed a member of their center, especially since Šváb and others stated at the trial that Slánský used his knowledge of their crimes to bind his people, e.g., Reicin,

Šváb, Frank, and others, even closer to himself. Why did he act differently with me? Simply because I was not a member of his conspiracy. On the contrary, Slánský became more distant after 1946. I saw him twice in 1947: he was very reserved. In 1948 I saw him about the book. If I had been a member of his center, Slánský would have warned me, especially if I had been a member of the center's leadership, as alleged. I pointed this out early in the interrogation but was always cut short.

My past played a great role in the interrogation. The case officer stated in the court protocol that I had been undermining the labor movement for thirty years and that I advocated Trotskyite positions as early as in 1926. The fact is that in those days, I wasn't even interested [in politics], that I lived a Bohemian life, I knew no Trotskyites and very little about Trotskyism. I collaborated with [Erwin] Piscator in the theater for ten months in 1927/28, but he was no Trotskyite then. I don't know whether he turned into one later. I do know, though, that the official newspaper of the SED [the East German Communist party] published his statement on German unity this year.

The case officer formulated the protocol as though Piscator, [Wilhelm] Münzenberg, and I formed an inseparable trio. In actuality Piscator merely introduced me to Münzenberg, and even that was an accident. I met Piscator again in 1932, at the Mezhrabpom [International Workers' Aid] Film company where he was directing some movie. Since he was once again working without a plan and with an unlimited budget, I made a report to the Comintern. After that there were only chance meetings with Piscator in Paris and in New York. I never had a Trotskyite or any other hostile connection with him. Quite a few leaders of the German CP of those days would confirm that Piscator was no Trotskyite and that I therefore could not have learned any subversive methods from him. My case officer refused even to talk about this.

My relationship with Münzenberg was quite different from that stated in the protocol. In 1928 I took over the "Universum-Bücherei" publishing house which I headed until the end of 1929. During all this time there wasn't a single occasion when I talked to Münzenberg alone. There were others present during every one of our three or four meetings. Nor could I have helped him, contrary to what the case officer stated in the protocol, cover up profiteering, because I had nothing to do with financial arrangements: I was involved only with producing books, contacting authors, with publicity, and with editing the publishing house's monthly. Fritz Grauzow who at the time managed the publishing house's finances and who now lives in the GDR could confirm this. I pointed out all this early in the interrogation.

Toward the end of 1929 I left the publisher because I disagreed with Münzenberg's dictatorial attitude of accepting a book for publication without consulting me first.

In early 1931 Münzenberg invited me to join Mezhrabpom Film in Moscow as a script writer. I was glad to accept. Only in Moscow did I really come to understand the mission and the principles of the Communist party. As I look back at that period, now, during the last hours of my life, I can truthfully state that in Moscow, in the Soviet environment, I changed.

My connection with Münzenberg was accidental. I met him once in the presence of Kolen, when he visited Moscow, and later when I visited Berlin (on the occasion of the 1932 Amsterdam Congress and also when I was finishing the editing of the book *Fifteen Iron Steps*), always with others present. [Lazar] Kaganovich described this book at a meeting of the Moscow party committee as an example of good publicity for the USSR.

Thus contrary to what I said in my statement, I was not in touch with Münzenberg continuously from 1927 to 1932, and not for one second did I maintain Trotskyite or other hostile contacts with him.

The same goes for my collaboration with Münzenberg in France from 1933 to 1937. I always worked at home, never in the office. During this time I wrote or edited five anti-Nazi books, including *The Brown Book*. I was secretary of "Protaprons" in London and of various anti-Nazi committees. At this time I was in constant contact with the party leadership. [Franz] Dahlem, [Walter] Ulbricht, and [Anton] Ackermann could surely confirm that I wasn't involved in any of Münzenberg's intrigues, that I severed all contacts with him toward the end of 1947, and that I aided in the struggle against him. Let me add that I collaborated with him in France following instructions that the Comintern secretariat gave to Mision, who represented International Workers' Aid in Moscow, namely, that I go to Paris, contact Münzenberg, and pass on to him instructions to organize a committee for the aid of victims of Nazism. Let me also mention that when the French journalist [Geneviève] Tabouis intervened on my behalf with the Paris police in 1938, she was told that Münzenberg had denounced me as a Comintern agent.

The case officer put into the protocol that I undermined the labor movement in various capitalist countries, starting, with Münzenberg, in Germany. I have already described my relations with him. Let me repeat that in Germany I was not involved in any political activity. German Communist writers with whom I worked could back this up, as could members of Piscator's theater, some of whom are working in the GDR, and people who worked with the "Universum-Bücherei," a couple of whom also live in the GDR.

As for France, I knew [Paul] Vaillant-Couturier, [Gabriel] Péri, [Louis] Aragon, and two to three other Communist writers, including Jean Richard Bloch and [Victor] Pozner. The party had issued strict instructions that we not contact the French CP. I didn't know any rank-and-file party members, except for Jeanne Stern, an editor. She and her husband were awarded a peace prize at a film festival. How then could I have been undermining France's labor movement and the unity of the French working class?

Or take Great Britain. The only members of the British CP I knew were [Harry] Pollitt, [William] Gallacher, Isabel Brown, and Ivor Montagu, her husband, and one or two editors of the *Daily Worker*. As Isabel Brown would confirm, I was shadowed by the police from my first trip on and I refrained from all contacts with Communists other than those mentioned. They could confirm that my work in Britain involved anti-Nazi activity and later support of the Spanish Republic, but never any wrecking activity.

Let me address the question of my so-called contacts with other enemies of the working class. The case officer stated in the protocol that my main contact in France until 1939 was the Jewish bourgeois nationalist, minister [Georges] Mandel. What is the truth? I met Mandel and Tabouis at a luncheon at which Soviet Ambassador [Yakov Z.] Surits was present as well. Between 1937 and spring of 1939 I met Mandel perhaps a half-dozen times. On two occasions I asked him, on request of the Spanish ambassador, to intervene so that weapons for the Spanish Republic could be released. I visited Mandel at his ministry only once in my life, in 1938, when following an agreement with [Franz] Dahlem I asked him whether he could help the German CP to organize an underground broadcasting station. I shall return to Mandel later.

I worked with [Juan] Negrín in propaganda from 1937 until the end of the Spanish War. At that time the Spanish CP supported Negrín against the Trotskyite [Francisco Largo] Caballero, and considered him pro-Soviet. I have not seen him since 1939.

At the same time I was in contact with Louis Fischer, who worked in the USA doing publicity work for the Spanish Republic. Fischer was then considered a progressive journalist. He frequently visited the Soviet embassy, and was in close contact with Soviet delegations at every League of Nations conference in Geneva. His wife, who was a Soviet citizen, visited him in Paris in 1938 and then returned to the USSR. Fischer turned into a warmonger only after the war broke out, at which time I was no longer in contact with him.

I met Supreme Court Justice [Felix] Frankfurter in May 1939, on the recommendation of Thomas Mann. He arranged for me to meet James Roosevelt, the president's son, who then worked in Hollywood and helped raise $15,000 which was used to aid German Communists in French camps. I had never met or had the slightest contact with Frankfurter or J. Roosevelt until then.

Having been an editor of the Paris daily *L'Ordre* also played a great role in the interrogation. I joined the paper in 1938, with the approval of the German CP leadership. I represented the interests of the Spanish Republic because Negrín had contributed FF2 million to the paper. It was the only bourgeois paper in France which unequivocally favored the French-Soviet pact, supported the Spanish republic, and opposed Munich. As the staff captain informed me, Clementis stated that [Emile] Buré, *L'Ordre*'s editor-in-chief, was on the list of [Jan] Masaryk's and [Edvard] Beneš's agents. I knew that Buré received moneys from the Czechoslovak embassy, but he received moneys from the Soviet embassy as well, as the paper's manager told me. My job was to make sure that its foreign-political line opposed Munich and the Nazis, favored the French-Soviet pact, and helped the Spanish Republic. While I worked for the paper in 1938 and 1939, it didn't run a single story against this line. I suggested to the case officer that he have these two years of the paper analyzed. He just laughed in my face.

My contacts with Geneviève Tabouis were also frequently described during the interrogation as having a hostile intent. When I knew Tabouis, she favored the French-Soviet pact, the Spanish Republic, and anti-Munich policies. I supplied her with anti-Nazi information and with news items from the Soviet Union favoring the Spanish Republic. Soviet Ambassador Surits asked me more than once to influence Tabouis in a particular issue; more than once did I provide Péri with information I had received from Tabouis, which he then used in *L'Humanité*. The case officer described this as a gigantic whitewash maneuver benefitting the Chamberlain-Churchill policy. In reality, I frequently prevented Tabouis from using nonsensical information. I never maintained the slightest contacts with her or with Buré that would have had a hostile intent, and I used my influence on them strictly in the cause of peace and the anti-Nazi struggle.

I was told during the interrogations that my book *Those Who Betrayed France* used information from the secret military service. In fact, I had no connection with it and received no information from these sources. I used only what I had heard from visitors of the *L'Ordre* office that was frequented every afternoon by journalists and politicians, from Tabouis, and from their guests. I primarily used reports of the capitalist press. I stated that Joseph Bernstein, member of the CP USA, helped me organize the newspaper information. The case officer said that within three days he could get an answer from other Communist parties on any question; but when I suggested that he verify my statement concerning Bernstein, he didn't even respond.

I don't want you to think I don't realize the heavy blame I am laden with as a result of my false confessions. If I had steadfastly insisted on the truth, and if I hadn't made any false confessions, I would not have had to end this way. I really believed that my case officer's superiors would recognize that my statements simply couldn't be true and I believed that the information I provided would be checked. I bear the main blame for my terrible end. You and the court could not have acted otherwise; I myself blocked the path to a different ending.

I considered retracting my confessions in court. I didn't because I considered the tremendous damage I would have caused. Therefore, I memorized the protocol and played my part in court until the end. I think it was better that way.

Why am I writing you all this? I cannot bear the thought that you might believe that I would have linked up with an outcast who attempted your life, that I would have been in cahoots with the man who denounced [Julius] Fučik. The most unbearable thought of all is that I will end up in the company of criminals with whom I had nothing in common and who committed such terrible crimes.

I always held you in deep respect, esteemed Mr. President. I saw you as a shining example of a Communist, of wisdom, steadfastness, and humanity. My heart aches at the thought that you see me as an enemy of your great historical efforts. I therefore had to write this letter. I fear you may not have time to read it, but I hope you'll have someone summarize it for you. Excuse it being written so poorly, I'm writing it on a little stool, sitting on the cot.

I wish you all the best and a long life. May the Czechoslovak people reach Communism under your wise stewardship. And should you ever, during your rich and successful life, remember that somewhere in Prague a man is buried who caused his own end but who never betrayed the party, the country, or the Soviet Union, this letter will have accomplished its goal.

André Simone

December 3

OTTO ŠLING (August 24, 1912–December 3, 1952)
A member and official of Communist youth and the Communist party from age fifteen. Participated in Czechoslovak wartime resistance in London. After the war, regional KSČ secretary in Brno.

XVIII.

To the President of the Czechoslovak Republic:

Before my execution, I declare in truth that I have never been a spy. Václav Nosek and others could truthfully testify to my activity in England. I kept no secrets from them. I maintained no ill-intentioned connections with Beneš and his clique. I did not visit Beneš alone, without the party's knowledge. Nosek and others were familiar with my work for Young Czechoslovakia and in the Center for Czechoslovak Youth. I was not involved in this activity for the benefit of Beneš's clique.

I furthermore declare that I have never been a millionaire and did not try to get any compensation [for wartime losses]. I never owned any capital. My family is without means. I mention this lest they suffer on my behalf.

I was not aware of the criminal activity of the conspirators to the extent showed during the trial. I personally conducted no sabotage and was not aware of the sabotage activity of the Kuthan brothers.

One of my crimes was my conduct during the investigation of 1950. I submitted to Slánský and for all that I fully deserve the death sentence.

I declare that Růžena Dubová, [Vladimír] Lenc, and other people I worked with in Brno are innocent.

I regret my crimes, my cooperation with Slánský.

I wish the Communist Party of Czechoslovakia and the people's democratic Czechoslovakia all the best.

Otto Šling

XIX.

My dears,

May I even address you thus? I know I have caused you, my dear Marian, a lot of sorrow and unhappiness. I'm writing before my death to tell you that I have loved you and that during the last hours of my life I recall with thanks our life and our happy moments of love, and I think about little Jan and Karel. You have surely read my testimony. It served the cause of peace and the struggle against American imperialists, which consoles me. That is the only thing I can say for myself—I am sure you'll be allowed to take care of the children and bring them up. I was told not to fear anything in this respect. I think that if you were denied the opportunity to work and to secure your livelihood, you should turn to the president of the republic: the punishment should affect me alone, not you.

I had a wrist watch (Omega) and three (3) fountain pens. Request them as keepsakes for the boys and for you *I hope* as well, particularly remembering our days of happiness, despite all that you feel for me.

I would like you to save these few lines for Jan and Karel. Explain them to the boys when they grow up.

Tell them I loved them, and that before I died I cared most of all that they *thoroughly* master something useful in life (a trade, best of all), that they live honorably, believe in the great edifice of socialism, and honor and trust the Communist party. I'm sure that both Jan and Karel will give you in life what I did not, that they will make up for what I have caused you.

Give my love to Alinka and all whom I have loved. Ask her to remember me sometimes, if she can. If possible, have my ashes put on my mother's grave in Teplice.

I am dying happily, realizing that my death helps the cause of peace and the construction of Socialism. I wish you all the best, my dears, and to you, Marian, all the strength you'll need to bring our children happiness.

Once again many thanks, my love to Jan and Karel. May their future happiness carry you over the sorrow that I have caused you. I kiss them in my mind and hope they will live happily.

I embrace you and Alinka. Good-bye.

Yours Otto

XX.

My dears,

I hardly dare address you thus. I know I have caused you, Marian, a lot of bitterness and unhappiness; I understand that you hate me, I understand that Alinka hates me, yet I did hope that you would visit for one last conversation before the execution. I'm sure you read my testimony in court and believe that you will at least admit that it served the cause of peace and Socialism. That is my only consolation.

I have loved you and the children, and I thank you for the happiness you have given me.

I am writing this postscript after I was told that you refused to join me for a last meeting.*

I have been thinking, Marian, about the first film we saw together and about everything we have lived through. Only now, aware of your implacable hatred, am I happy to die. I believe, though, that you will see from my testimony that I never was a spy. I was not charged with sabotage.

Otto

Dear little Jan and Karel,

Many hugs and kisses. Be good to your Mommy, love her, and when you grow up, support her in her hard life.

Study, and master a trade thoroughly. Construct Socialism. That will help you find full happiness in life. Never act cowardly and bear in mind that only a pure attitude toward the party and the country can guide you to happiness. Sacrifice your life for this happiness, if necessary.

I am sure you will love and live for your Mommy who has always acted well and honorably. She is a beautiful person.

I embrace you and be happy.

Your father.

Marian, give them this letter or tell them its content after they've grown up and can understand it.

It was my bad luck that I didn't finish my education. May they avoid all my errors. If necessary, point out all my errors and all negative things so it may serve them as a *warning*!

KAREL ŠVÁB (May 13, 1904–December 3, 1952)
Grew up in a Communist family. Was a member of Communist children's and youth organizations since his early years. During the war imprisoned in Nazi concentration camps. After the war he headed the records department of the CC KSČ secretariat. In 1950 appointed deputy minister of national security.

*Mrs. Marian Šling was not informed about the opportunity to pay her husband one last visit.

XXI.

To Klement Gottwald
President of the Republic
Chairman of the CC KSČ

Hours before death one speaks the truth. I, too, want to share with you certain truths that I believe you should be aware of.

It is true that I recognized Slánský's rationale and his true intentions concerning his conspiracy, as I described them in my report, only after several months in detention. Early in the interrogations I was actually steered away from these thoughts.

However, the moment I realized that my idea was plausible and that I was not considered a provocateur, I did all I could to help unmask the conspiracy to its full extent, as it unfolded in court.

Mine was therefore not a case of confessing participation in the conspiracy but of recognition, albeit belated, that Slánský did in fact have such intentions.

I repeat: Before my arrest I was not aware of any conspiracy and I did not know Slánský's true intentions.

Thus if I spoke in court not only as though I had been fully informed about his conspiratorial preparations and had even willingly taken part in them, I did so because I considered it my duty and a political necessity.

In this respect then my conscience is clear: both during the interrogation and during the trial I did all that needed to be done, regardless of personal consequences.

I was also assured that after the trial I would have more opportunities to help clarify and uncover additional enemies and culprits who may still be hidden. I believed I could still be quite useful in this. This knowledge, too, gave me the strength to present myself at the trial the way I did. However, I will not manage to discharge this obligation.

On the other hand there is no doubt that before my arrest I had plenty of opportunity to recognize Slánský's true face and that I could have cut his malignant activity short by at least two years.

I am greatly to blame for not having recognized this *in time,* for I could have forestalled a whole lot if I had.

I therefore consider the sentence fully justified. I am leaving in peace, realizing that this solution was the only correct one.

My entire life had only one meaning—to serve the party. Too bad that instead, I served the villain and his masters.

I am happy that after removing this life-threatening cancer, the Czechoslovak people can progress under your stewardship faster and more joyfully, side by side with the Soviet Union, toward socialism and a happy future. In

this I wish you good health and full success.
Karel Šváb
executed as a traitor on 12/4/1952*

XXII.

12/4/1952

My dears,
     At first I thought it might be better to spare you the distress of a last meeting but now I see that would not have been right and I am glad that I saw at least you, dear Jarka and dear Vlád'a, and could tell you what I thought necessary.
     Thank you for your last words of consolation and for the courage with which you are bearing everything. I'm sure you need it, and you'll need even more courage before the pain subsides and before you get used to an immutable reality.
     Life will go on despite this personal matter, negligible in the scheme of things. You will carry on in life and take up your appropriate stations.
     To make life a bit easier, I beg you to trust the party, actively contribute as much as you can to all the tasks of socialist construction and believe that what happened, that is, the way all this has ended, is the only correct way, benefitting in every way the working class, and with it, you.
     Dear Jarka, I know I didn't give you many happy and joyful moments in life. On the contrary, they were mostly sad, full of worries and unpleasant consequences. Please forgive me and forget them. If you remember anything, let it be the pleasant moments: surely you'll find enough of those to recall. You know what I always put ahead of my own and our shared interest; nothing has changed about that.
     If you have the chance to look after yourself in addition to the children, I wish you all the best. If you need it, I hope you will not pass up such an opportunity.
     Other than that I know that your life's meaning will be to look after the children and that you won't let anything sidetrack you. I wish you all the best in that.
     Dear Vlád'a, once again, chin up. Do your best to courageously and confidently master your field so that you can pay back at least a part of my dues. Better to do less but all the more honestly. Forgive me for having burdened your young life so heavily. Nevertheless, I believe you can handle it, so long as you don't sever ties with your peers and with the working class. Always do what the people want, and you'll be on the right track.
     In addition to studying and preparing for your own task in life, don't forget to help Mother. You know how much she thinks of you and how she

*It appears that Šváb wrote the anticipated date of his execution.

cherishes you. Help her in every way. Give her your moral support now and later, when you're able to; help her materially and in bringing up your sisters. I wish you, dear Vlád'a, a very happy life and every success in all of your ventures.

My dear little Zdena, I'm sorry I didn't see you anymore. Mommy and Vlád'a will help you understand everything, and I am sure that you too will soon start studying happily and enthusiastically, so that you can help all the others live a life full of happiness and joy. Listen to Mommy and help her as much as you can because she really does have it tough. You will soon grow up to lead your own life: remember from time to time your daddy who truly loved you.

And all of you together, look after our Světlana. Make up for the fatherly love she will not know. May she be the sunshine of your old years, Jarka.

Dear Father: I realize I didn't give you much joy in your old days. But if you listened to my final speech, you'll know I remembered you and the shining memory of Mother, in a way that everybody must have understood. I wish you good health, and I am sure you understood everything.

The same wishes to Grandma, may she live a long life, and to all the others, Ruda and Nora, Vlasta and Mastřík, to Anča, to Růža and Bohouš, Franta and Kätin and all their children and Jůra and all our friends.

I embrace you all for the last time, my dears. Yours
Šváb, Karel

APPENDIX B

RUDOLF SLÁNSKÝ—BIOGRAPHICAL DATA

1901   Born July 13 to a tradesman's family in Nezvěstice near Pilsen.
1919   Graduates from high school in Pilsen.
1920   University student in Prague.
        Joins the left-wing Marxist Association.
1921   Joins the Communist Party of Czechoslovakia (KSČ), founded that year.
1923   Elected member of the Prague Regional KSČ Committee.
1924   Sentenced for a public speech in Prague to two months in prison.
        Appointed editor of *Rudé právo*, the KSČ national daily.
1925   Appointed editor-in-chief of *Dělnický deník* (Workers' Daily), the KSČ regional daily in Ostrava. Meets Klement Gottwald.
1926   Elected Regional KSČ Secretary in Ostrava.
1928   Appointed Regional KSČ Secretary in Kladno.
1929   Gottwald elected KSČ General Secretary at the Fifth KSČ Congress; Slánský elected member of the central committee and the politburo.
1930   Summoned by Gottwald to join the KSČ central apparatus.
1934   Gottwald leaves for Moscow and entrusts Slánský and Jan Šverma with the party leadership.
1935   Elected to the National Assembly (Czechoslovakia's legislature).
December 1935–January 1936   Leadership of the Comintern criticizes Šverma and Slánský for opportunism. The KSČ unleashes a campaign, headed by Gottwald, against opportunism. Slánský and Šverma make a self-criticism at a Comintern committee session and at the Seventh KSČ Congress. They are stripped of their leadership positions.
1936   Six months later, after the Comintern changes tack, both are recalled to leadership positions in the KSČ; their criticism, however, would never be rescinded.
1939   Summoned by Gottwald to exile in Moscow. Slánský joins the exile leadership. Appointed editor-in-chief of the Czechoslovak broadcast of Radio Moscow, editor of *Československé listy* (Czechoslovak Paper) published in Moscow.
1944   Leaves for Kiev as member of the main partisan staff of the Ukrainian Front, head of the Czechoslovak Partisan School. In September leaves with Šverma for Slovakia, where an uprising against the Germans has

erupted. Active in the uprising as a leading official of the partisan staff. After its defeat, he withdraws with the staff into the mountains, fights his way through to the front and meets up with the Soviet Army on February 19, 1945.

March 1945   Joins Moscow negotiations about the first postwar Czechoslovak government.

April   Returns to Czechoslovakia as the KSČ general secretary.

October   Appointed deputy to the Provisional National Assembly.

March 1946   Reconfirmed as the KSČ general secretary by the Eighth KSČ Congress.

May   Elected deputy to the Constitutional National Assembly.

September 1947   Heads Czechoslovak delegation at the founding meeting of the Cominform.

February 1948   Appointed commander of the People's Militia. Elected to the National Front's Central Action Committee presidium.

May   Elected deputy of the National Assembly.

June   Heads Czechoslovak delegation at the Cominform meeting which dealt with the Yugoslav CP.

January 1949   Heads Czechoslovak delegation at Comecon's founding meeting in Moscow.

May   Reelected to the KSČ central committee and as general secretary at the Ninth KSČ Congress.

November   Heads the Czechoslovak delegation at the Cominform meeting that drew political lessons from the Rajk trial.

January 1950   Negotiates Czechoslovak economic issues in Moscow. Received by Stalin, returns with his recommendations that Czechoslovakia switch its economic orientation.

May   Heads CC KSČ delegation at the KSS Congress, where he speaks about the group of so-called Slovak bourgeois nationalists.

January 1951   Heads the Czechoslovak delegation at a Moscow meeting of Soviet-bloc countries on military matters.

July   CC KSČ organizes fiftieth birthday celebrations for Slánský; laudatory articles in the press, congratulatory telegrams from the CC KSČ and public organizations, from delegations of workers, etc. Slánský's name is bestowed on selected factories. His selected works are published. Gottwald awards him the first Order of Socialism.

September   Criticized for errors in party work, recalled from office of general secretary, appointed deputy prime minister, responsible for economic ministries.

November   Arrested.

December   CC KSČ approves his arrest and expulsion from the party.

November 1952   Condemned to death as head of an antistate conspiratorial center.

December   Gottwald denies his clemency plea. Executed on December 3.

1963   Exonerated judicially.

APPENDIX C

COMPOSITION OF LEADING INSTITUTIONS, 1948–1953

Široký, Viliam
Slánský, Rudolf (until November 1951)
Zápotocký, Antonín

The CC KSČ Party Control Commission (KSK), 1948–51:

Benada, L'udovít
Bína, Antonín
Doubek, Karel
Kapoun, Josef
Klícha, Bohumil
Mestek, Karel
Pimpara, Adolf
Řípa, František
Růžička, Oldřich
Taussigová-Potůčková, Jarmila

LEADING BODIES OF THE CZECHOSLOVAK REPUBLIC:

President of the Republic:
Gottwald, Klement

Prime Minister:
Zápotocký, Antonín

Speaker of the National Assembly:
John, Oldřich

Interior and National-Security Ministers:
1948–53: Nosek, Václav, interior minister
1950–1951: Kopřiva, Ladislav, national-security minister
1952–1953: Bacílek, Karol, national-security minister

State-Security Commanders:
1948–50: Veselý, Jindřich
1950–Feb. 1951: Závodský, Osvald
Feb.–Dec. 1951: Hora, Josef
Dec. 1951–53: Prchal, Antonín

Justice Ministers:
1948–50: Čepička, Alexej
1950–53: Rais, Štefan

APPENDIX D

POLITICAL TRIALS OF LEADING COMMUNISTS

Defendants	Number of People	Trial Date	Prosecutor	Presiding Judge
Pavlík, Gejza, et al.	4	6/29/1950	Střída	Novák, Jaroslav
Slánský, Rudolf, et al: Clementis, Vladimír Fischl, Otto Frank, Josef Geminder, Bedřich Hajdů, Vavro Löbl, Evžen London, Artur Margolius, Rudolf Simone, André Šling, Otto Šváb, Karel	14	11/20–27/1952	Urválek, Josef	Novák, Jaroslav
Foreign Ministry Group: Goldstücker, Eduard, et al.	5	5/25–26/53	Havelka	Novák, Jaroslav
Hofman, Leopold	1	9/17/53		
Security Group: Černý, Karel Milén, Ivo Pich-Tůma, Miroslav Pokorný, Bedřich Šmolka, Vladimír Valeš, Oskar Závodský, Osvald	7	12/23/53	Kebort, V.	Podčepický, Vladimír
Pavel, Josef	1	12/30/53	Zdražil, D.	Štella, Jiří
Plaček, Štěpán	1	1/20/54	Putník	Hůle, J.

Party Apparatus *Group*: Fuchs, Vítězslav Hájek, Bedřich Landa, Mikuláš Lomský, Hanuš Polák, Ervin Švermová, Marie Taussigová, Jarmila	7	1/28/54	Švach, Emil	Novák, Jaroslav
The Trotskyite *Great Council*: Černý, Oldřich Holátko, Bohumír Hrubý, Pavel Novák, František Pluhař, Ladislav Roušar, František Vlk, Václav	7	2/23–25/54	Aleš, Václav	Trmáček, K.
Army Officers *Group*: Bulander, Rudolf Drgač, Šimon Drnec, Vladimír Hromádko, Ota Klapálek, Karel Kopold, Bedřich Novák, Zdeněk Svoboda, Antonín	8	3/30–4/1/54	Zdražil, D.	Štella, Jiří
Haškovec, Vladimír Haas, Ladislav	2	4/9–10/54	Dlouhý, J.	Stýblo, František
Slovak Bourgeois- *Nationalist Group*: Holdoš, Ladislav Horváth, Ivan Husák, Gustáv Novomeský, Ladislav Okáli, Daniel	5	4/21–24/54	Gešo, Ladislav	Uhrín, J.

Group of Industry   11   8/6–7/54   Aleš, Václav
  Managers:
Bárta, Jaroslav
Fabinger, František
Goldmann, Josef
Holý, Ivan
Jičínský, Jaroslav
Kárný, Jiří
Kolár, František J.
Lewinter, Matyáš
Rudinger, Zdeněk
Smrkovský, Josef
Outrata, Eduard (11/5/54)

ABBREVIATIONS

A MNP	Archive of the Ministry of Economic Planning, Prague
A ÚML	Archive of the CC KSČ's Marxism-Leninism Institute, Prague
A CC KSČ	Archive of the Central Committee of the Communist Party of Czechoslovakia
A CC KSS	Archive of the Central Committee of the Communist Party of Slovakia, Bratislava
CC	Central Committee
COMECON	Council for Mutual Economic Aid
CPB	Communist Party of Bulgaria
CPSU	Communist Party of the Soviet Union
HLP	Hungarian Labor (Communist) Party
IS	[British] Intelligence Service
KSČ	Communist Party of Czechoslovakia
KSK	The CC KSČ's Party Control Commission
KSS	Communist Party of Slovakia
MV	Czechoslovak Ministry of the Interior
NKVD	The Soviet secret police
OSS	Office of Strategic Services
SED	Socialist Unity Party of Germany (East German Communist party)
StB	State Security (Czechoslovak secret police)
USC	Unitarian Service Committee

NOTES

CHAPTER 1

1. Archive of the Central Committee of the Communist Party of Slovakia, Bratislava (A CC KSS), Bašt'ovanský collection: Notes from the founding meeting of the Cominform and from the CC KSČ presidium meeting, October 2, 1947.

2. Archive of the Central Committee of the Communist Party of Czechoslovakia, Prague (A CC KSČ), collection 02/1, meeting of June 28, 1948.

3. Ibid., minutes of the CC CPSU session of July 4–12, 1955 (Czech text).

4. Ibid., Political Trials, Commission I/I, vol. 16, doc. no. 404.

5. Ibid., collection 100/24, Stalin's letter of July 14, 1948.

6. Ibid., collection 02/1, meeting of June 26, 1948.

7. Ibid.

8. Ibid., minutes of the CC CPSU session of July 4–12, 1955 (Czech text). Khrushchev: "As is now becoming evident, [Beria] and his accomplices weakened the revolutionary forces by annihilating the personnel of our party and of other fraternal parties . . . They set leading party officials against each other until their destruction. Our intelligence agencies operated in this way not only in Yugoslavia but in all the people's democracies . . . To maintain an agency in fraternal parties and to gather intelligence about these parties and especially about their leaders violates most seriously the norms of conduct among fraternal parties and countries. Such a situation may lead to conflict."

9. *Zasedání devíti komunistických stran* (The Meeting of Nine Communist Parties), Prague 1947, p. 54. A CC KSČ, Political Trials, Commission III, Paper no. 6.

10. *Rudé právo,* September 7, 1948.

11. A CC KSČ, Political Trials, Commission III, Paper no. 6.

12. Ibid.

13. Ibid. *Rudé právo,* September 7 and 19, 1948. Bierut, B: *O straně* (On the Party), Prague 1951, p. 101.

14. Bierut, B., *op. cit.,* pp. 205–7; *For a Lasting Peace, for People's Democracy,* No. 27, 1949, p. 1.

15. *Nowe drogi* (Warsaw), 1949, special issue devoted to the session of the CC Polish Unified Workers' Party of November 11–13, 1949.

16. *Rudé právo,* November 16, 1949. A CC KSČ, Political Trials, Commission III, Paper No. 6.

17. Kořalková, K.: *Vytváření systému dvoustranných spojeneckých smluv mezi evropskými socialistickými zeměmi* (Creating the System of Bilateral Treaties of Alliance among European Socialist Countries), Prague 1966, p. 56.

18. A CC KSČ, Political Trials, Commission III, Paper no. 22.

19. Ibid., minutes of the CC CPSU session of July 4–12, 1955 (Czech text).

20. Ibid., Political Trials, Commission III, Paper no. 22.

21. *For a Lasting Peace, For People's Democracy,* no. 15, 1948, p. 1.

22. A CC KSČ, Political Trials, Commission III, Paper no. 22.

23. Ibid.; Mančcha, P.: *Albánie na cestě k socialismu* (Albania's Road to Socialism), Prague 1952, p. 88; *Rudé právo,* November 11, 1948.

24. Ibid.; *Rudé právo,* May 14, May 16, June 12, 1949.

25. A CC KSČ, Political Trials, Commission III, Paper no. 22.

26. Ibid., collection 100/24, vol. 105, doc. no. 1274.

27. Ibid., Political Trials, Commission III, Paper no. 4.

28. Ibid., collection 100/24, vol. 105, doc. no. 1274.

29. Ibid. The letter to Kolman also included the following: "After com. Gottwald returns, the party presidium will discuss your presentation again and final decisions will be made."

30. Kaplan, K.: "Moje rozhovory" (My Conversations), ms.; A CC KSČ, Political Trials, Commission I/II, vol. 16, doc. no. 404; Commission III, Paper no. 4.

31. A CC KSČ, collection 100/24, vol. 105, doc. no. 1274; A CC KSČ, Political Trials, Commission III, Paper no. 4.

32. Ibid., collection 100/24, vol. 105, doc. no. 1274.

33. Kaplan, K.: "Zamyšlení nad politickými procesy" (Reflections about Political Trials), *Nová mysl* (Prague), no. 8, 1968, pp. 1079–1081; A CC KSČ, Political Trials, Commission III, Paper no. 4.

34. Ibid.

35. A CC KSČ, collection 100/4, vol. 94, doc. no. 504.

36. Ibid.; Kaplan, "Reflections."

37. A CC KSČ, Political Trials, Commission III, Paper no. 39; Šváb's Archive, the Field Case, the T Commission.

38. Ibid.

39. Ibid., MV–1 31 and 110.

40. Ibid., Paper no. 17.

41. Ibid., Political Trials, Commission I/II, doc. no. 680.

42. Ibid., Commission III, Paper no. 39.

43. Ibid., Paper no. 17; MV–372–Z–82 MV.

44. Ibid.

45. Ibid., Commission I/I, doc. no. 752; Commission III, Paper no. 39; MV–327–Z–842 MV.

46. Ibid., Commission I/I, doc. no. 752.

47. Ibid., Commission I/I, doc. no. 639; Commission I/II, doc. no. 88; Paper no. 17; MV–327–Z–842 MV.

48. Ibid., Commission II: letter of Herta Field to Artur London of July 1949; Commission III, Paper no. 39.

49. Ibid., collection 100/24; letter of Oldřich Papež to Rudolf Slánský of August 25, 1949; Gottwald's report to Slánský of August 28, 1949; Commission III, Paper no. 39; Šváb's Archive, Field Case, T Commission.

50. Ibid., Commission III, Paper no. 42 (Archive of the Ministry of Foreign Affairs, Budapest, reports of August 19 and November 3, 1948).

51. Ibid. (reports of April 2 and July 7, 1949).

52. Ibid.; Népszava, October 14, 1956 (P. Justus).

53. Ibid. (report of June 8, 1949).

54. Ibid. (report for July 1949); Rudé právo, June 19, 1949.

55. A CC KSČ, Political Trials, Commission III, Paper no. 42 (reports of September 8 and 13, 1949).

56. Ibid., collection 100/3, vol. 110, doc. no. 375.

57. László Rajk and His Accomplices Before the People's Court, Budapest, 1949.

58. A CC KSČ, Political Trials, Commission III, Paper no. 42 (report of October 5, 1949); Rudé právo, September 12–16, 1949.

59. A CC KSČ, minutes of the CC CPSU session of July 2–14, 1955 (Czech text).

60. A CC KSČ, Political Trials, Commission III, Paper no. 16 (Archive of the Ministry of Foreign Affairs, Sofia 167567/II–2/48).

61. Ibid. (Sofia 109525/49–I–3).

62. Ibid.

63. Ibid. (Sofia 115047/49, report of May 5, 1949).

64. Ibid. (Sofia 109525/49, report of April 1, 1949); For a Lasting Peace, For People's Democracy, no. 8, 1949, p. 2.

65. For a Lasting Peace, For People's Democracy, no. 10, 1949, p. 2; Rudé právo, April 6, 1949, p. 2.

66. A CC KSČ, Political Trials, Commission III, Paper no. 16.

67. Ibid.; Rudé právo, December 11, 1949.

68. A CC KSČ, Political Trials, Commission III, Paper no. 16 (Sofia 122 454/49, report of June 15, 1949).

69. Ibid.

70. Rudé právo, December 2 and 3, 1949.

71. A CC KSČ, collection 100/24, "Report on the T. Kostov Trial," Political Trials, Commission III, Paper no. 16; Rudé právo, December 8, 1949.

72. Rudé právo, December 8–18, 1949; A CC KSČ, Political Trials, Commission III, Paper no. 16.

CHAPTER 2

1. A CC KSČ, Political Trials, Commission I/I, doc. no. 645; Commission I/II, doc. no. 603, MV–372–Z–842 MV; Šváb's letter to Gottwald of June 17, 1949.

2. Ibid., Commission I/I, doc. no. 648, MV–372–Z–842 MV.

3. Ibid.

4. Ibid., MV–373 KS StB Prague.

5. Ibid., Commission III, Paper no. 17.

6. Ibid., collection 100/24, doc. no. 947.

7. Ibid., Political Trials, MV–327, sub-vols. IV-1.123, IV–1.169a, and V–1.85.

8. Ibid., MV–327, sub-vol. V, record of Pavlík's interrogations of June 2, 25 and 27, 1949.

9. Ibid., record of Pavlík's interrogation, June 16, 1949.

10. Ibid., Commission III, record of an interview with Oldřich Papež, June 1948.

11. Ibid., Paper no. 17.

12. Ibid., collection 100/24, Mátyás Rákosi's letter of June 1949; Political Trials, Commission III, Paper no. 39, and the Final Report; Pelikán, ed., *Pervertierte Justiz*, Vienna 1970, p. 56.

13. A CC KSČ, collection 100/24, Rákosi's telegram to Gottwald of June 25, 1949; collection 100/1, Security's report to Slánský of June 29, 1949; also MV, the Pavlík volume (cited further as Pavlík).

14. Ibid., Šváb's Archive, Field Case, T Commission (report from Budapest about Pavlík).

15. Ibid., Political Trials, MV–39/2, vol. VII, and MV–39/1, vol. IV.

16. Ibid., collection 100/24, Šváb's letter of July 2, 1949.

17. Ibid., Political Trials, Pavlík, interrogation of July 6, 1949.

18. Ibid., Pavlík.

19. Ibid., collection 100/24, Report on the Investigation of V. Veselá, July 1949.

20. Ibid., Šváb Archive, T Commission, meeting of July 20, 1949.

21. Ibid., Political Trials, Pavlík interrogation of August 3, 1949; Commission II, Šváb's letters to Kopřiva of July 28 and August 4, 1949.

22. Ibid., Šváb Archive, T Commission, meeting of July 25, 1949; Šváb's report of August 5, 1949 (also in collection 100/24); MV–391, vol. V.

23. Ibid., Commission I/I, doc. no. 640.

24. Ibid., collection 02/2, doc. no. 201.

25. Ibid., also collection 100/24, doc. no. 947; Political Trials, MV–392, vol. VI; *Pervertierte Justiz*, pp. 56–59.

26. Ibid.

27. Ibid., Political Trials, Commission III, Paper no. 57; Šváb Archive, T Commission, minutes of meetings, September 1949.

28. Ibid., collection 100/24, doc. no. 947.

29. Ibid., Šváb Archive, T Commission, minutes of meetings, October 1949.

30. Ibid., collection 100/24, doc. no. 947.

31. Security envisioned the network of accomplices in national institutions and in Slovakia to include the following: the president's chancellery (Ludvík Frejka, Štefan Rais); the cabinet office (Milan Reiman, J. Fukátko, Kováčík); parliament (Bedřich Rattinger); ministries: of foreign affairs (Artur London, Evžen Klinger), transport (B. Burkoň), social welfare (J. Popel), information (Oskar Kosta, Rudolf Feigl, František Novák), industry (A. Trunec), defense (Jaroslav Šolc), nutrition (Brieger), foreign trade (Evžen Löbl, Karel Markus), commerce (Pavel Bock, J. Sedlák), agriculture (Glasserová), interior (Englišová, A. Šedivý), finance (Biel); Comecon (Josef Goldmann). The network in Slovakia: the CC KSČ secretariat (Vojtěch Jančík); the Club of KSS Deputies (František Komzala); Slovak National Council (Ladislav Holdoš); Slovak ministries: of agriculture (Michal Falťan), industry (Ján Púll), planning (Július Bránik), radio (Stahl); the board of the Bratislava *Pravda* (Eduard Friš): ibid., Šváb Archive, T Commission.

32. Ibid., collection 100/24, Šváb's letters of October 26 and December 28, 1949.

33. Ibid., doc. no. 947; *Pervertierte Justiz,* p. 59.

34. A CC KSČ, Political Trials, Commission II, Gottwald-Stalin correspondence; collection 100/24, doc. no. 947.

35. Ibid., collection Plaček, unorganized; Kaplan, "Conversations" (Plaček).

36. A CC KSČ, Political Trials, Commission I/II, vol. 6, docs. no. 67–72.

37. "Statement of Jarmila Potůčková (Taussigová) for the General Prosecutor's Office, Prague, Concerning Charges Against Her," n.d., (copy in author's possession); cited further as "Taussigová"; p. 2.

38. A CC KSČ, Political Trials, Barnabitky Commission, letter of Teodor Baláž of 1963; Commission III, Paper no. 32.

39. Ibid., Commission I/I, vol. 22, doc. no. 451; Commission III, Paper no. 19.

40. Ibid.

41. Ibid., Barnabitky Commission, Final Report, section 1948–1954; Commission I/II, deposition of Vladimír Kohoutek of October 4, 1955; Commission III, Paper no. 32.

42. Ibid., Commission III, Paper no. 19.

43. Ibid., Commission I/I, vol. 12, doc. no. 202: "Report on the Náchod Commission."

44. Taussigová, p. 40.

45. A CC KSČ, Political Trials, Commission I/II, vol. 49, doc. no. 884.

46. Ibid., collection 100/1, vol. 200, doc. no. 1282; Political Trials, MV-Šváb volume; Commission I/II, vol. 2, doc. no. 479.

47. Ibid., collection 100/24, letter of Czechoslovakia's ambassador to Moscow about his conversation with Bodrov (December 1949); Kopřiva's letter to Gottwald, November 5, 1949; Šváb's letter to Gottwald, December 14, 1949.

48. Ibid., Political Trials, MV-Šváb volume. Šváb wrote on October 26, 1949: "Interrogations to date indicate that we will not manage to make substantial progress in uncovering serious saboteurs through these people."

49. Ibid., Barnabitky Commission, Final Report and background, section 1939–1945; Kaplan, *op. cit.*, (Š. Plaček).

50. Ibid., collection 100/24, Šváb's letter to Gottwald, October 4, 1949; Kaplan, *op. cit.*

51. Husák, Gustáv, "Request for Full Party Rehabilitation, Addressed to the CC KSČ," May 1, 1963 (copy in author's possession); quoted further as Husák; p. 54.

52. A CC KSČ, collection 018, meeting of December 8, 1949.

53. Ibid., collection 01, meeting of February 24–26, 1950.

54. Ibid., collection 02/1, meeting of March 13, 1950.

55. Ibid., joint session of the CC KSČ and CC KSS presidia, March 14, 1950.

56. Ibid., Political Trials, Commission II, Gottwald-Stalin correspondence; Commission III, Paper no. 32.

57. Ibid., *CC KSČ Information* no. 10, March 24, 1950.

58. Ibid., collection 02/1, meetings of May 2, May 22, May 30, and September 5, 1950.

59. Ibid., Political Trials, vol. MV-Clementis.

60. Ibid., collection 02/1, meeting of June 28, 1950; A CC KSS, CC KSS session of September 27, 1948; cf. also Široký, V., *Za šťastné Slovensko v socialistickém Československu* (For a Happy Slovakia in Socialist Czechoslovakia), Bratislava 1952, p. 144.

61. *László Rajk,* pp. 131–32.

62. Husák, pp. 47–48.

63. A CC KSČ, Political Trials, Barnabitky Commission, minutes of the CC KSS Presidium meeting of February 5, 1949; Commission III, Paper no. 32.

64. *Porada Informačního byra komunistických stran v Maďarsku 1949* (The Hungary 1949 Cominform Meeting), Prague 1952.

65. A CC KSČ, Political Trials, Barnabitky Commission, Final Report, section 1948–1954; Commission III, Paper no. 32; Husák, pp. 51–53.

66. A CC KSČ, collection 01, meeting of February 24–25, 1950; A CC KSS, meeting of the CC KSS presidium, January 27, 1950.

67. Ibid., Political Trials, Barnabitky Commission, Final Report, section 1948–1954; Commission III, Paper no. 32.

68. Ibid.; cf. also vol. MV-Clementis; collection 100/24, Šváb's report of January 11, 1950.

69. Ibid., Political Trials, Commission III, Paper no. 32.

70. Ibid., collection 100/24, Šváb's report of March 8, 1950; Husák, p. 45.

71. A CC KSS, meeting of the CC KSS presidium of April 3, 1950; A CC KSČ, collection 100/24, doc. no. 835; Husák, p. 56.

72. A CC KSS, CC KSS session of April 6, 1950; cf. also edited version in Široký, *op. cit.*, pp. 184–86; Husák, p. 57.

73. A CC KSČ, Political Trials, Barnabitky Commission, Final Report and analyses, section 1948–1954; A CC KSS, CC KSS letter to the regions, April 26, 1950.

74. A CC KSS, minutes of the Ninth KSS Congress; Široký, *op. cit.*, pp. 246–52.

75. A CC KSČ, Political Trials, Barnabitky Commission, Final Report, section 1948–1954; Commission I/II, doc. no. 56 (deposition of Bohumil Doubek); Commission III, Paper no. 32.

76. Husák, p. 56.

77. *Nová mysl*, no. 5–6, 1950, pp. 516–525.

CHAPTER 3

1. A CC KSČ, collection 018, meetings of March 11, September 15 and December 8, 1949.

2. Ibid., collection 03/2, vol. 26, doc. no. 192.

3. Ibid., collection 100/4, vol. 37, doc. no. 235; collection 02/3, vol. 7, doc. no. 111.

4. Ibid., Political Trials, Commission III, Paper no. 5; collection 02/3, vol. 7, doc. no. 111.

5. Ibid., collection 02/3, vol. 7, doc. no. 112 and vol. 26, doc. no. 102; collection 02/1, meeting of May 2, 1949.

6. Ibid., Political Trials, Commission III, Paper no. 5.

7. Ibid., collection 100/36, doc. no. 303–2.

8. Ibid., collection 100/4, vol. 64, doc. no. 358.

9. Ibid., Political Trials, Commission III, Paper no. 5.

10. Ibid., also collection 13, doc. no. 2/3; collection 100/4, vol. 64, doc. no. 358.

11. Taussigová, p. 10.

12. A CC KSČ, collection 02/1, meeting of January 9, 1950; Political Trials, Commission III, Paper no. 5.

13. Ibid., collection 100/4, vol. 64, doc. no. 358; Taussigová, pp. 11–12.

14. Ibid., collection 100/4, vol. 64, doc. no. 358; Political Trials, Commission III, Paper no. 5.

15. Ibid., Political Trials, Commission I/I, vol. 4, doc. no. 41; Commission I/II, vol. 48, doc. no. 840.

16. Ibid., collection 100/45, vol. 12, doc. no. 209.

17. Ibid., Political Trials, Commission I/II, vol. 6, doc. no. 1067, and vol. 48, doc. nos. 931 and 839; Commission III, Paper no. 13; collection 100/45, vol. 12, doc. no. 209.

18. Ibid., Political Trials, Commission III, Paper no. 13.

19. Ibid., collection 02/3, meeting of June 20, 1950; collection 100/1, letter of KSK officials to Slánský, dated July 18, 1950; cf. also Commission I/II, vol. 60, doc. no. 1041.

20. Ibid., Political Trials, Commission III, Paper no. 13; collection 02/4, meeting of July 12, 1950, and vol. 18, doc. no. 137.

21. Taussigová, p. 30.

22. Ibid.; A CC KSČ, Political Trials, Commission I/II, vol. 60, doc. no. 1041.

23. Ibid., Commission III, Paper no. 13; Taussigové, p. 31.

24. A CC KSČ, collection 02/4, meeting of August 16, 1950; Political Trials, Commission I/II, vol. 48, doc. no. 838.

25. Ibid., collection 100/1, letter of Bohumil Ubr of August 17, 1950; record of an interview of Slánský, Köhler and Baramová with Ubr, of August 31, 1950.

26. Ibid., Political Trials, Commission I/II, vol. 60, doc. no. 1040.

27. Ibid., Commission I/II, vol. 14, doc. no. 237; Commission III, Paper no. 13. Köhler wrote to Bareš on September 21, 1950: "Here is my proposal concerning the Brno matter. One section is possibly too sharp, the other not sharp enough. I tried to capture the essence of what Brno means . . . We should discuss personnel consequences separately."

28. Taussigová, p. 32.

29. A CC KSČ, Political Trials, Commission III, Paper no. 13; MV, volume Šling; Pervertierte Justiz, pp. 71–72.

30. A CC KSČ, Political Trials, Commission III, Paper no. 13; collection 02/1, meeting of October 16, 1950. On January 29, 1963, Kopřiva stated: "When this letter surfaced, Vladimír [Boyarski] and I went to see Slánský, who recognized Šling's handwriting . . . Slánský called com. Gottwald and we then took it to the Prague Castle. Vladimír, Slánský, and I went to see com. Gottwald, and he said that [Šling] would have to be arrested."

31. Ibid., collection 100/45, doc. no. 176; Taussigová, p. 34.

32. Unless stated otherwise, information about Šling's interrogation and his time in prison is based on interrogation protocols, reports of the agent in his cell, and on reports about the progress of the investigation written for Kopřiva and Gottwald, in A CC KSČ, Political Trials, MV–1018–1024, vol. 2, vols. Šling.

33. A CC KSČ, Political Trials, Commission I/I, vol. 14, doc. no. 232.

34. Ibid., vol. 4, doc. no. 41.

35. Ibid., Commission I/I, doc. no. 56.

36. Ibid., vol. 60, doc. no. 1041; collection 100/2, vol. 58, doc. no. 663.

37. Ibid., vol. 45, doc. no. 1107; MV–1025, vol. 3, MV–1026, vol. 5; collection 100/2, vol. 58, doc. no. 663.

38. Ibid., Commission III, Paper no. 13; MV–103, 1012, 1480–81.

39. Ibid., Commission III, Paper no. 13.

40. Ibid., collection 02/1, meeting of November 13, 1950.

41. Ibid., Political Trials, Commission III, Paper no. 13; *Pervertierte Justiz,* pp. 77–80.

42. A CC KSČ, Political Trials, Commission I/II, vol. 48, doc. no. 838.

43. Ibid., collection 100/45, doc. no. 176; Taussigová, p. 36.

44. A CC KSČ, collection 02/1, meeting of December 14, 1950.

45. Ibid., Political Trials, MV-Švermová.

46. Ibid., collection 02/1, meeting of January 22, 1951.

47. Ibid., Political Trials, MV-Švermová; collection 02/1, meeting of January 29, 1951; *Pervertierte Justiz,* pp. 76–77.

48. Švermová, M., "Remarks about the Indictment," 1963, ms. (copy in author's possession). Cited further as Švermová.

49. A CC KSČ, Political Trials, Commission I/I, vol. 19, doc. no. 378; Commission I/II, doc. no. 479; Commission II, interview with Ladislav Kopřiva, January 29, 1963; Commission III, record of an interview with Ladislav Kopřiva of May 1968, Paper no. 19; Kaplan, "Conversations" (Bohumil Klícha).

50. A CC KSČ, Political Trials, Commission I/II, vol. 12, doc. no. 202.

51. Ibid., vol. 19, doc. no. 381.

52. Taussigová, pp. 38–39.

53. A CC KSČ, Political Trials, Commission I/II, vol. 19, doc. no. 381.

54. Ibid., collection 100/45, doc. no. 176; Taussigová, pp. 39–40.

55. Ibid.; Taussigová, pp. 40–41.

56. A CC KSČ, Political Trials, Commission I/II, vol. 19, doc. no. 380.

57. Kaplan, *op. cit.* (Bohumil Klícha).

58. A CC KSČ, Political Trials, Commission I/I, vol. 16, doc. no. 404.

59. Ibid., collection 100/24, Bedřich Reicin's letter to Gottwald, February 1, 1951.

60. Ibid., Political Trials, Commission II, interview with L. Kopřiva of January 29, 1963; Commission III, interview with L. Kopřiva of May 1968; Karel Kaplan in *Nová mysl* no. 7, 1968, pp. 922–23.

61. A CC KSČ, Political Trials, Commission III, Paper no. 29.

62. Ibid.

63. Ibid., collection 02/1, meetings of January 28 and February 20,. 1951; collection 100/24, Švermová's letter to Gottwald, January 26, 1951.

64. Ibid., collection 01, session of February 21–24, 1951.

65. Švermová.

66. A CC KSČ, collection 01, session of February 21–24, 1951.

67. Ibid.

68. Ibid., Political Trials, Commission III, Papers no. 14 and 23; MV–1018–1024, vol. 2, interrogation and reports of October 30 through November 11, 1950; *Informační bulletin ÚV KSČ (CC KSČ Information Bulletin),* March 1951.

69. Ibid., Commission I/II, vol. 4, doc. no. 43; vol. 41, doc. no. 613.

70. Ibid., vol. 4, doc. nos. 41–43; vol. 5, doc. no. 45, Kopřiva's letter to Zápotocký of January 9, 1952.

71. Ibid., Commission I/I, vol. 19,. doc. nos. 378 and 380; Commission III, Paper no. 19.
72. Taussigová, p. 37.

CHAPTER 4

1. Husák, pp. 38, 47, 50–51; A CC KSČ, collection 02/2, vol. 72, doc. no. 88; vol. 78, doc. no. 94.
2. Kaplan, "Conversations" (Štěpán Plaček).
3. Ibid., and collection 100/24, letter of Kopřiva, Gregor, and Jaroslav Procházka to Gottwald, January 1952.
4. Taussigová, pp. 43–45.
5. A CC KSČ, Political Trials, Commission I/I, vol. 2, doc. nos. 24 and 28; Commission I/II, vol. 4, doc. no. 41.
6. Ibid., Commission I/II, vol. 19, doc. no. 5; vol. 4, doc. no. 41; vol. 41, doc. no. 613; Commission III, Paper no. 20.
7. Ibid., Commission I/I, vol. 2, doc. nos. 24 and 28; Commission I/II, vol. 5, doc. no. 44.
8. Ibid., Commission I/II, deposition of Karel Arasin.
9. Ibid., Commission I/I, doc. no. 28 (interview with Josef Vondráček, May 22, 1953); Commission I/II, vol. 4, doc. nos. 1–43; vol. 41, doc. no. 613.
10. Ibid., Commission I/I, vol. 2, doc. no. 28; Commission III, Paper no. 20.
11. Ibid., Commission I/I, vol. 2, doc. no. 24.
12. Ibid., MV-Slánský.
13. Ibid., Commission I/I, Doubek's deposition written when in custody. (Cited further as Doubek).
14. Ibid., Commission I/I, vol. 2, doc. no. 24; Commission I/II, vol. 5, doc. no. 45; Commission III, Paper no. 20.
15. Ibid., Commission II, Gottwald-Stalin correspondence.
16. Ibid.
17. Ibid., collection 02/2, vol. 102, doc. no. 118.
18. Ibid.
19. Ibid., Commission II, Gottwald-Stalin correspondence.
20. Ibid.
21. Kopřiva: "Once com. Gottwald calls to ask me over and says, Stalin has written and tells us to quit these investigations targeted against Slánský, this could be the work of the class enemy who's trying to sow discord." Ibid., interview with Kopřiva on January 29, 1963.
22. Ibid., collection 100/24, vol. 108, doc. no. 1401.
23. Ibid., Political Trials, Commission I/II, vol. 5, doc. no. 45; Kaplan, *op. cit.* (Ladislav Kopřiva).

24. A CC KSČ, Political Trials, Commission I/II, vol. 4, doc. no. 43; vol. 5, doc. no. 45.

25. Archive of the Marxism-Leninism Institute, Prague (A MLI), "The Activity of the Underground KSČ Leadership, 1939–45," by V. Kahan.

26. A CC KSČ, Political Trials, Commission I/II, vol. 5, doc. no. 45.

27. Ibid., Commission I/I, vol. 2, doc. no. 24.

28. Ibid.; *Pervertierte Justiz,* p. 99.

29. A CC KSČ, Political Trials, Commission III, Paper no. 20.

30. Ibid., Commission I/II, vol. 5, doc. no. 25.

31. Ibid., collection 01, meeting of September 6, 1951.

32. Ibid.

33. Taussigová, pp. 41, 45, 46.

34. A CC KSČ, Political Trials, Commission I/II, vol. 2, doc. no. 479.

35. Štěpán Plaček's memorandum to the CC KSČ Rehabilitation Commission, dated August 13, 1968. (Copy in the author's possession.)

36. Ibid.; A CC KSČ, Political Trials, Commission I/II, Doubek.

37. Ibid., Political Trials, MV-Šváb.

38. Ibid., collection 01, meeting of September 6, 1951.

39. Ibid., Political Trials, Commission III, Paper no. 14; A MLI, collection Resolutions, September–October 1951.

40. Ibid., Commission I/II, vol. 41, doc. no. 613.

41. Švermová.

42. A CC KSČ, Political Trials, MV-Šling.

43. Ibid., Commission III, "Letter to the Great Street Sweeper," ms.; Karel Košťál, supplement to deposition, January 28, 1963 (copy in author's possession).

44. Ibid.

45. Ibid.; Kaplan, *op. cit.* (Antonín Prchal, Kamil Pixa).

46. *Pervertierte Justiz,* p. 102.

47. Kaplan, *op. cit.* (Antonín Prchal).

48. A CC KSČ, Political Trials, MV-Slánský, testimony of Daniela Kaňkovská; Commission III, "Letter to the Great Street Sweeper."

49. Kaplan, *op. cit.* (Antonín Prchal).

50. A CC KSČ, Political Trials, Commission II, deposition of Rudolf Nevečeřal, 1962; Commission III, "Letter to the Great Street Sweeper"; MV-Slánský, testimony of D. Kaňkovská.

51. Ibid., Commission III, Paper no. 23; Košťál, supplement to deposition; Kaplan, *op. cit.* (Antonín Prchal).

52. A CC KSČ, Political Trials, Commission II, Gottwald's roster of visitors for 1951; Commission I/II, vol. 16, doc. no. 404; *Pervertierte Justiz,* p. 101.

53. A CC KSČ, collection 02/2, vol. 102, doc. no. 118.

54. Ibid., Political Trials, Commission II, Beschasnov's answers to questions of the CC KSČ Rehabilitation Commission, 1962.

55. Ibid., collection 02/2, vol. 102, doc. no. 118; Political Trials, Commission II, interview with L. Kopřiva, January 29, 1963; Commission III, interview with L. Kopřiva, *Reportér,* no. 25, 1968, p. v.

56. A CC KSČ, collection 02/2, vol. 102, doc. no. 118; Political Trials, Commission II, interview with L. Kopřiva, January 29, 1963.

57. Ibid., vol. 78, doc. no. 94.

58. Ibid., Political Trials, Commission II, interview with L. Kopřiva, January 29, 1963; Commission III, interview with L. Kopřiva; Kaplan, *op. cit.* (L. Kopřiva).

59. Ibid., Political Trials, Commission I/I, vol. 2, doc. no. 24.

60. Ibid., cf. also Commission III, interview with L. Kopřiva and Paper no. 23.

61. Ibid., Commission I/I, doc. no. 24; Commission III, Paper no. 23.

62. Ibid., MV–111, investigations file no. 1480–106.

63. Ibid., collection 02/5, meeting of November 24, 1951; *Pervertierte Justiz,* pp. 104–112.

64. A CC KSČ, Political Trials, Commission I/II, doc. no. 614.

65. Ibid., collection 01, meeting of December 6, 1951.

66. Ibid., Political Trials, Commission III, Paper no. 14; Novotný collection 69, unorganized.

67. Ibid., collection 100/24.

68. Ibid., Political Trials, Commission III, interview with L. Šonka (May 1968); MV 1/13, correspondence 1953–54.

69. Ibid., Commission I/I, Doubek.

70. Ibid., Commission II, Gottwald-Stalin correspondence.

71. Ibid., collection 02/2, meeting of April 17, 1956; vol. 78, doc. no. 94; Kaplan, *op. cit.* (Alexej Čepička).

CHAPTER 5

1. A CC KSČ, Political Trials, Commission I/I, deposition of May 3, 1956.

2. Ibid., collection 02/2, vol. 78, doc. no. 94.

3. Ibid., Commission III, Paper no. 29.

4. Ibid., Commission I/I, doc. no. 28.

5. Ibid., collection 02/2, meetings of August 29 and November 15, 1955; collection 100/45, doc. no. 176; Political Trials, Commission III, Papers no. 29 and 38; Bedřich Hájek, "Moje vzpomínky . . ." (My Recollections), unpub. ms. (Cited further as Hájek.)

6. A CC KSČ, Political Trials, Commission I/I, doc. no. 28.

7. Ibid., doc. no. 16.

8. Ibid., and Commission III, Paper no. 23.

9. Ibid., MV–1/4, vol. Slánský (further: Slánský), protocol, November 27, 1951.

10. Ibid., internal memoranda, December 1, 2 and 3, protocol, December 12, 1951.

11. Ibid., Commission III, Paper no. 23.

12. Ibid., Slánský, int. memo, December 22, 1951.

13. Ibid., Commission III, paper no. 23.

14. Ibid., and Slánský, cell reports, January 5 and 6, 1952.

15. Ibid., Commission II, doc. no. 28 (J. Svoboda's interview of January 19, 1963, with B. Benda); Commission III, Paper no. 23.

16. Ibid., Slánský, cell reports, January 4 and 5, 1952.

17. Ibid., protocol, January 7, 1952.

18. Ibid., Commission I/I, doc. no. 28.

19. Ibid., Commission III, Paper no. 23; MV-Slánský, protocol, January 12, 1952.

20. Ibid., MV-Slánský, protocols, January 21–25, 1952.

21. Ibid., cell reports, January 21–25, 1952.

22. Ibid., cell report, January 26, 1952.

23. Ibid., protocol of January 26, 1952; confrontation with Löbl, January 26, 1952; cell report, July 7, 1952.

24. Ibid., Commission I/I, doc. no. 24.

25. Ibid., Commission III, Paper no. 23.

26. Ibid., MV-Slánský, cell report, January 28, 1952.

27. Ibid., cell reports, January 29 and 30, 1952.

28. Ibid., Commission III, Paper no. 23.

29. Ibid., and MV-Slánský, cell report, February 2, 1952.

30. Ibid., cell report, February 5, 1952.

31. Ibid., protocols, February 7 and 9; confrontation with Hanuš Lomský, February 9, 1952.

32. Ibid., cell reports, February 10, 11, and 13, 1952.

33. Ibid., recorded cell conversation, February 27, 1952.

34. Ibid., Commission I/I, Doubek.

35. Ibid., MV-Slánský, reports of March 3, 4, and 8, 1952.

36. Ibid., cell report, March 20, 1952.

37. Ibid., protocol, March 26, 1952; confrontation with Jaromír Kopecký and Artur London, March 26, 1952; int. memo, March 31, 1952.

38. Ibid., protocols, April 1 and 2, 1952.

39. Ibid., Commission II, last letter of the condemned: see Appendix.

40. A CC KSČ, Political Trials, Commission I/II, docs. no. 78 and 608.

41. Ibid., MV-Slánský, cell report, April 4, 1952; protocols, April 4–6, 1952; confrontation, April 5, 1952.

42. Ibid., int. memo, April 7–12, 1952.

43. Ibid., int. memo, April 14–19, 1952.

44. Ibid., int. memo, April 21–26, 1952.

45. Ibid., int. memo, April 23–May 3, 1952.

46. Ibid., protocol, May 7, 1952.
47. Ibid., int. memo, May 12–17, 1952.
48. Ibid., int. memo, May 19–25, 1952; protocol, May 25, 1952.
49. Ibid., Commission I/I, docs. no. 28 and 31.
50. Ibid., and Commission III, Paper no. 23.
51. Ibid., MV-Slánský, cell report, May 28, 1952.
52. Ibid., collection 01, meeting of January 3, 1968.
53. Ibid., MV-Slánský, confrontation with Ludvík Frejka, May 29, 1952; last letters of the condemned.
54. A CC KSČ, Political Trials, MV-Slánský, int. memo, June 9–14, 1952.
55. Ibid., int. memo, June 16–21 and 23–28, 1952.
56. Ibid., int. memo, June 30–July 5 and July 7–12, 1952.
57. Ibid., int. memo, July 14–19 and 21–26, 1952; protocol, July 15, 1952.

CHAPTER 6

1. Ibid., Commission I/I, vol. 16, doc. no. 404.
2. Ibid., MV-Geminder, Šváb.
3. Last letters of the condemned.
4. A CC KSČ, Political Trials, MV-Taussigová, cell reports, June 2 and July 7, 1952.
5. Ibid., Commission III, Paper no. 38.
6. Ibid., Commission I/I, doc. no. 24.
7. Ibid., doc. no. 28 (interview with Josef Urválek, August 16, 1956).
8. Ibid., collection 0/3, meeting of May 11, 1950.
9. Ibid., Political Trials, Commission I/II, vol. 21, doc. no. 483; vol. 30, doc. no. 507; Commission III, Papers no. 29 and 37.
10. Ibid.
11. Ibid., Commission I/II, Bacílek's letter to Čepička, June 18, 1952.
12. Ibid., collection 02/5, meeting of August 27, 1952.
13. Ibid., Political Trials, Commission I/I, doc. no. 28; Commission I/II, doc. no. 539.
14. Ibid., collection 02/5, meeting of October 25, 1952.
15. František Antl, "Zpověd' prokurátora" (A Prosecutor's Confession), in Rovnost (Brno), March 23–April 3, 1968, p. 2. (Cited further as Antl.)
16. A CC KSČ, Political Trials, Commission III, Paper no. 38.
17. Ibid.
18. Ibid., Commission I/I, doc. no. 31; collection 02/5, meeting of November 13, 1952.
19. Ibid., Commission I/II, docs. no. 531, 575a; Archive of the Ministry of National Economic Planning (A MNEP), collection VM SUP, doc. no. 177.
20. A CC KSČ, collection 02/5, meeting of September 27, 1952; Political Trials, Commission I/II, doc. no. 542.

21. Ibid., Commission III, Paper no. 38.
22. Ibid., Commission I/II, doc. no. 56.
23. Ibid., Commission I/I, doc. no. 28; Commission I/II, doc. no. 42; Antl.
24. Švermová.
25. Hájek.
26. A CC KSČ, Political Trials, Commission I/II, docs. no. 42, 542, Doubek.
27. Ibid., Commission I/II, doc. no. 41.
28. Ibid., collection 100/24, doc. no. 990/1; A MNEP, collection VM SUP, doc. no. 177.
29. Antl.
30. A CC KSČ, Political Trials, Commission I/I, doc. no. 24.
31. Ibid., Commission I/I, doc. no. 41; Antl.
32. Antl.
33. A CC KSČ, Political Trials, MV 1/11, docs. no. 1 and 4.
34. Ibid., MV-Slánský, int. memo, August 4–9 and 11–16, 1952; Commission I/I, doc. no. 28.
35. Ibid., MV-Slánský, cell reports, August 22 and 23, 1952.
36. Ibid., protocol, August 22, 1952; confrontation, August 22, 1952.
37. Ibid., int. memo, August 18–25; cell report, August 26, 1952.
38. Ibid., Commission III, Paper no. 23.
39. Ibid., MV-Slánský, cell report, August 29, 1952.
40. Ibid., cell reports, September 1, 3, 4, 9, and 12, 1952.
41. Ibid., int. memo, September 15–20; cell report, September 15, 1952; protocol, September 17, 1952.
42. Ibid., cell report, September 24, 1952; int. memo, September 22–27, 1952.
43. Ibid., Commission I/II, vol. 16, doc. no. 404.
44. Ibid., MV-Slánský, cell reports, October 1, 6, 7, 10, 12, and 13, 1952.
45. Ibid., cell reports, October 15, 16, and 17; int. memo, October 18, 1952.
46. Ibid., cell reports, October 19, 29, November 1, 2, and 6, 1952.
47. Ibid., cell reports, November 7, 8, 9, 10, 12, 13, 14, 1952.
48. Ibid., cell reports, November 15, 16, 17, 18, 19, 20, 1952.
49. Ibid., collection 100/24, record of a conversation with Stalin, October 1952; Kaplan, "Conversations" (Alexej Čepička); F. Ouředník, unpublished dissertation (ms, 1969).
50. A CC KSČ, collection 02/5, meeting of November 13, 1952.
51. Ibid., Political Trials, Commission I/I, doc. no. 24; Commission I/II, doc. no. 41.
52. Ibid., Commission I/II, doc. no. 29.
53. Ibid., doc. no. 28; Kaplan, op. cit. (Josef Urválek).
54. A CC KSČ, collection 02, doc. no. 129.
55. Ibid., Political Trials, Commission I/II, doc. no. 36.

CHAPTER 7

1. Ibid., doc. no. 41 (interview with Václav Aleš, November 24, 1955).
2. Ibid., collection 02/5, *per rollam* of November 21, 1952.
3. Ibid., Commission III, Paper no. 14; A ÚML, resolutions about the Slánský trial.
4. *Proces s vedením protistátního spikleneckého centra v čele s Rudolfem Slánským* (Proceedings of the Slánský Trial), Prague 1953, pp. 525, 540–44.
5. A CC KSČ, collection 02/2, vol. 102, doc. no. 118; ibid., collection 01, vol. 2, p. 10 (meeting of April 1–5, 1968, A. Novotný); Kaplan, "Conversations" (Antonín Novotný).
6. A CC KSČ, Political Trials, Commission III, Viliam Široký's written deposition of July 3, 1968; A CC KSČ, collection 01, vol. 2, p. 10 (meeting of April 1–5, 1968, A. Novotný).
7. Ibid., Commission I/II, doc. no. 381/a.
8. Last letters of the condemned.
9. A CC KSČ, Political Trials, Commission I/II, doc. no. 391.
10. Hájek.
11. A CC KSČ, collection 02/5, meetings of February 17 and April 7, 1952.
12. Archive of the Government Presidium, Prague (A GP), Protocols of Government Meetings, August 27, 1947.
13. A CC KSČ, Political Trials, Commission III, Paper no. 39; Written remarks of V.K. concerning political and military aspects of Czechoslovak-Israeli relations, 1947–1949; Brod, P., *Die Antizionismus und Israelpolitik der UdSSR,* 1980; *Rudé právo,* May 21 and July 27, 1948, p. 1, March 21, 1950, p. 5.
14. Hájek.
15. A CC KSČ, Political Trials, Commission I/I, doc. no. 28.
16. Ibid.
17. Ibid., Commission I/II, doc. no. 608.
18. Ibid., Commission III, Paper no. 23.
19. Ibid., Commission I/II, vol. 16, doc. no. 404.
20. Ibid., Commission I/I, doc. no. 28; Commission II, Urválek's statement of November 21, 1962.
21. Ibid., Commission I/II, doc. no. 41.
22. Ibid., Commission I/I, Doubek; collection 02/2, meeting of April 23, 1956.
23. Ibid., Commission I/II, doc. no. 56.

SELECTED BIBLIOGRAPHY

SOURCES IN CZECH AND SLOVAK

"A každý podezíral každého" (They All Mistrusted Each Other), an interview with Ladislav Kopřiva in *Reportér*, no. 25, 1968, supplement (pp. i–ix).

Antl, František. "Zpověď prokurátora" (A Prosecutor's Confession). *Rovnost* (Brno), nos. 71, 73–77, 79, 80, 1968.

Celostátní konference KSČ (The National KSČ Conference). Prague: CC KSČ, 1953.

Hájek, Bedřich. "Moje vzpomínky na padesátá léta a jejich dozvuky" (My Recollections of the 'Fifties and Their Aftermath). Unpub. ms., 1968.

Husák, Gustáv. "O nacionalistickej úchylke ve strane" (The Nationalist Deviation in the Party). *Nová mysl* (Prague), no. 5–6, 1950, pp. 516–525.

Kaplan, Karel. "Moje rozhovory" (My Conversations). Unpub. ms.

―――. "Zamyšlení nad politickými procesy" (Reflections about Political Trials). *Nová mysl* (Prague), vol. 21 (1968).

Kořalková, K. *Vytváření systému dvoustranných spojeneckých smluv mezi evropskými socialistickými zeměmi* (Formation of the System of Bilateral Treaties of Alliance Among European Socialist Nations). Prague: Academia, 1966.

Kratochvíl, Antonín. *Žaluji* (I Accuse), vols. 1–3. Haarlem: CCC; Rome: Křesťanská akademie, 1973–1977.

Löbl, Evžen. *Svedectvo o procese* (Testimony about the Trial). Bratislava: Vydavatelstvo politickej literatúry, 1968.

Porada Informačního byra komunistických stran v Maďarsku 1949 (The 1949 Cominform Meeting in Hungary). Prague: Rudé právo, 1952.

Proces proti titovským špionům a rozvratníkům v Československu (Proceedings in the Case of Titoist Spies and Subversives in Czechoslovakia). Prague: Ministry of Justice, 1950.

Proces s vedením protistátního spikleneckého centra v čele s Rudolfem Slánským (Proceedings in the Case of the Anti-State Conspiratorial Center Headed by Rudolf Slánský). Prague: Orbis, 1953.

Široký, Viliam. *Za šťastné Slovensko v socialistickém Československu* (For a Happy Slovakia in Socialist Czechoslovakia). Bratislava: Pravda, 1952.

312   SELECTED BIBLIOGRAPHY

SOURCES IN OTHER LANGUAGES

Brod, P. *Die Antizionismus und Israelpolitik der UdSSR*. Baden-Baden: Namos, 1980.

Hejzlar, Zdenek. *Reformkommunismus*. Cologne-Frankfurt: Europäische Verlagsanstalt, 1976.

Kaplan, Karel. *Dans les archives du Comité Central*. Paris: Albin Michel, 1978.

———. *Procès politiques à Prague*. Brussels: Complexe, 1980.

———. *Die politischen Prozesse in der Tschechoslowakei*. Munich: Oldenburg, 1986.

Kolman, Arnošt. *Die verirrte Generation*. Frankfurt: S. Fischer, 1979.

Krammer, Arnold. *The Forgotten Friendship: Israel and the Soviet Bloc, 1947–53*. Urbana: University of Illinois Press, 1974.

Lewis, Flora. *The Red Pawn: The Life of Noel Field*. Garden City, NY: Doubleday, 1965.

László Rajk and His Accomplices before the People's Court: A Transcript of the Rajk Trial. Budapest: Printing Press, 1949.

Loebl, Eugene. *Sentenced and Tried: The Stalinist Purges in Czechoslovakia*. London: Elek Books; Toronto: The Ryerson Press, 1969.

Löbl, Evžen. *Die Aussage*. Stuttgart, 1978.

London, Artur. *On Trial*. London: Macdonald; New York: Morrow, 1970.

Margolius Kovaly, Heda. *Under a Cruel Star: A Life in Prague 1941–1968*. Cambridge, MA: Plunkett Lake Press, 1986.

Massing, Hede. *This Deception*. New York: Duell, Sloan & Pearce, 1951.

Oren, Mordechai. *Prisonnier politique à Prague*. Paris: Julliard, 1960.

Pelikán, Jiří, ed. *Pervertierte Justiz*. Vienna: Europaverlag, 1972.

———. *The Czechoslovak Political Trials 1950–1954: The Suppressed Report of the Dubček Government's Commission of Inquiry, 1968*. Stanford: Stanford University Press, 1971.

Slánská, Josefa. *Report on My Husband*. London: Hutchinson, 1969.

Slingová, Marian. *Truth Will Prevail*. London: Merlin Press, 1968.

Steven, Stewart. *Operation Splinter Factor*. Philadelphia: Lippincott, 1974.

Ströbinger, Rudolf. *Der Mord am Generalsekretär*. Stuttgart-Bonn: Burg-Verlag, 1983.

INDEX OF NAMES